PUBLIC
ADMINISTRATION
in CANADA

SELECTED READINGS/FOURTH EDITION

Canadian Politics and Government
Books from Methuen

PUBLIC ADMINISTRATION in CANADA

SELECTED READINGS/FOURTH EDITION

Edited by KENNETH KERNAGHAN Brock University

ⁿ METHUEN

Toronto   New York   London   Sydney   Auckland

Canadian Cataloguing in Publication Data

Main entry under title:
Public administration in Canada

Texts of cases cited in this work may be found in
a companion volume, Canadian cases in public
administration, by W. D. K. Kernaghan.
Includes bibliographies.
ISBN 0-458-95250-8

1. Canada - Politics and government - Addresses,
essays, lectures.   I. Kernaghan, Kenneth, 1940–

JL108.P82 1982   354.71   C82-094263-4

Printed and bound in Canada

1 2 3 4 5   82   87 86 85 84 83

CONTENTS

PREFACE

The articles in this fourth edition have been selected and organized to provide a book for use either as a text or as a book of readings on public administration in Canada. This edition differs from the third edition in several important ways. Recent developments in the study and practice of public administration have required the inclusion of many new articles and the revision and updating of most of the others. New material has been included on crown agencies, intergovernmental administrative relations, bilingualism, decision making, financial administration, expenditure management, the merit system, ministerial responsibility, bureaucratic politics, representative bureaucracy, the ombudsman and freedom of information.

It is worth noting that a book of case studies, entitled *Canadian Cases in Public Administration*, has been published as a companion volume to this book of readings. The casebook contains twenty-four cases related to the essays in this book. At the end of each chapter of this book, preceding the bibliography, the cases most relevant to the essays in that chapter are listed. To assist teachers who wish to select a case related to a specific topic or problem, the casebook contains a subject index of the primary political-administrative issues covered by the cases. The use of the casebook in conjunction with the book of readings and formal lectures allows students to relate theoretical and descriptive material to actual administrative situations. Additional cases have been published in the *Case Program in Canadian Public Administration* by the Institute of Public Administration of Canada.

To make more space available for the actual articles, the introductory notes, which in previous editions have summarized briefly each part's contents, have been omitted from this edition. Bibliographies at the end of each part supply valuable references for further reading on particular subjects. For a comprehensive bibliography on Canadian public administration, students should consult W.E. Grasham and Germain Julien, *Canadian Public Administration Bibliography*, including supplements 1, 2 and 3.

The main purpose of this book is to provide a description and analysis of the institutions, processes and problems of Canadian public administration with a view to promoting better understanding and further study of the subject. It is hoped that students will come to understand the unique elements of administration in the public sector and to appreciate the challenges and opportunities of a career in Canadian government. The book is also intended to meet the needs of the increasing number of public officials engaged in training and development courses at all levels of Canadian government.

The choice of articles is based on an exhaustive review of the literature on public administration, and the articles are taken from a variety of sources. A broad selection of concepts, issues and developments in contemporary public administration has been provided. Although the articles relate primarily to the federal public service, much of the material is also relevant to the concerns of provincial and municipal public employees.

In Part I, an explanation of the meaning and development of public administration is based on a description of the evolution of organization theory.

This theoretical foundation prepares the reader for an inquiry into government organization and management functions which is provided in the next several chapters. Part II focuses on the unique environment and the complex political and administrative structures within which the Canadian public service operates.

Part III is concerned with the intimately related management issues of motivation, leadership, decision making and communications. Part IV centres primarily on the management of public funds. A discussion of the legal and institutional framework for the management of public money is followed by an explanation of the policy and expenditure management system. Part V contains an evaluation of the major aspects of public personnel administration and includes an analysis of the collective bargaining process for federal employees.

Parts VI and VII treat the critical issues of the politics and control of contemporary public services. Part VI explores the political milieu within which public administrators work and the close relationship between politics, policy and administration. Part VII examines the concept and practice of administrative responsibility and outlines existing and potential means of control and influence over the activities and decisions of public servants.

I wish to acknowledge my indebtedness to the authors and publishers who permitted their material to be printed in this volume. I am particularly grateful to the Institute of Public Administration of Canada for permission to reprint several articles from its learned journal, *Canadian Public Administration*, and to the authors who have written original essays for this book.

K.K.

Part I

PUBLIC ADMINISTRATION
and ORGANIZATION THEORY

1/Organization Theory
and the Nature of Man*

James L. Gibson

This essay seeks to add to the literature on the philosophy of organizations by emphasizing the value premises which underlie some of the major strands of thought.

The vehicle used to develop the literature is a classification system of three categories: the *mechanistic tradition*; the *humanistic challenge*; and the *realistic synthesis*. An essential feature of literature classified in the mechanistic tradition category is the view of man as a constant without peculiar features and malleable without incident into the organization structure; man is characterized as a machine—predictable, repairable and replaceable. The literature of the humanistic challenge is characterized by an awareness of man as a unique element in the organization structure; man is viewed as having a need structure and individual differences are tolerated. The literature of the realistic synthesis is not easily characterized, but its essential feature is to treat man as one of a number of variables in the organization, all of which are interdependent and interacting. Man is seen as being acted upon and as acting on the organization environment.

The Mechanistic Tradition

The writers of the mechanistic tradition focused on *two* aspects of organization theory.

At *one level*, Frederick W. Taylor and others analyzed the basic tasks of the individual members. The objective of Taylor and his followers was to reduce the contributions of each workman to the smallest, most

---

*Reprinted by permission from James L. Gibson, "Organization Theory and the Nature of Man," *Academy of Management Journal*, 9, no. 3 (September 1966): 233-245.

specialized unit of work possible and to eliminate any uncertainty about the expected outcome. Elementary to such analysis were (and are) work simplification studies which break down manual labour tasks into definite repetitive movements, and motion and time studies which establish time standards for the accomplishment of each movement. As Taylor himself said:

> Perhaps the most prominent single element in modern scientific management is the task idea. The work of every workman is fully planned out by the management at least one day in advance, and each man receives in most cases complete written instructions, describing in detail the task which he is to accomplish, as well as the means to be used in doing the work. And the work planned in advance in this way constitutes a task which is to be solved, as explained above, not by the workman alone, but in almost all cases by the joint effort of the workman and the management. This task specifies not only what is to be done but how it is to be done and the exact time allowed for doing it.[1]

To assure that each task is performed according to the plan, the worker is paid on an incentive basis which rewards him for meeting the expectations of the organization and punishes him if he does not. The application of scientism tended to reduce the skills of craftsmen to routine, procedural, predictable sequences of movement; workers were to be as interchangeable as the cogs in Eli Whitney's cotton gin.

Underlying the procedural prescriptions of scientific management were definite assumptions about the nature of man. Taylor said:

> A reward, if it is to be effective in stimulating men to do their best work, must come soon after the work has been done. But few men are able to look forward for more than a week or perhaps at most a month, and work hard for a reward which they are to receive at the end of this time.[2]

Later, in discussing the reasons for the failure of profit share schemes, he said: "Personal ambition always has been and will remain a more powerful incentive to exertion than a desire for the general welfare."[3] The view that man is motivated solely and predictably by economic considerations and is an isolated factor of production independent of social and group pressures guided the development of scientific management theories and practices.

The postulates of scientific management were quite appealing to those who were concerned with administrative aspects of organizations—the *second level* of analysis.

---

[1] Frederick W. Taylor, *Scientific Management* (New York: Harper and Brothers, 1911), p. 39.
[2] *Ibid.*, p. 94.
[3] *Ibid.*, p. 95.

Wolin suggests that Saint-Simon[4] laid the foundations of organization theory "with the conscious intent of establishing a defense against political instability and social disorder" in the aftermath of the French Revolution.[5] However, it was one hundred years later before a theory of organization structuring was articulated.

The most prominent writers of what is often called "Classical Organization Theory" were Luther Gulick,[6] Henri Fayol,[7] James D. Mooney and A.C. Reiley,[8] and L. Urwick[9] all of whom wrote from the perspective of business or military organizations. These writers owe an intellectual debt to Max Weber who provided the "ideal type" of administrative organization which he called a bureaucracy.[10] Even though Weber's model is based primarily on the European methods of organizing civil servants (chiefly the Prussian experience), the characteristics of his "ideal type" are illustrative of the main features of classical organization theory.

According to Weber, the essential characteristics of the "ideal type" are as follows:[11]

1. All tasks necessary for the accomplishment of the goals are broken down into the smallest possible unit; the division of labour is carried out to the extent that specialized experts are responsible for the successful performance of specified duties.
2. Each task is performed according to a "consistent system of abstract rules"[12] to assure uniformity and coordination of different tasks. This uncertainty in the performance of tasks due to individual differences is theoretically eliminated.

---

[4]See Henri de Saint-Simon, *Social Organization, The Science of Man, and other Writings*, edited and translated by Felix Markham (New York: Harper and Row, 1965).

[5]Sheldon S. Wolin, *Politics and Vision* (Boston: Little, Brown, and Co., 1960), p. 376.

[6]Luther Gulick and L. Urwick (eds.), *Papers on the Science of Administration* (New York: Institute of Public Administration, 1937).

[7]Henri Fayol, *General and Industrial Management* (London: Sir Isaac Pitman and Sons, 1949).

[8]J.D. Mooney and A.C. Reiley, *Principles of Organization* (New York: Harper and Brothers, 1939).

[9]L. Urwick, *The Elements of Administration* (New York: Harper and Brothers, 1943).

[10]Max Weber, *The Theory of Social and Economic Organization*, translated by A.M. Henderson and Talcott Parsons (New York: Oxford University Press, 1947). Michel Crozier in *The Bureaucratic Phenomenon* (Chicago: University of Chicago Press, 1964), a study of the French experience in organization of the civil service, points out three usages of the term bureaucracy: (1) The "traditional usage" is the political science concept of government by bureaus but without participation by the governed; (2) the Weberian usage is the sociological concept of rationalization of collective activities; and (3) the vulgar usage is the laymen's concept which implies the dysfunctional nature of "bureaucratic" organizations, i.e., red tape, procedural delays, frustrations of agents and clients, p. 3.

[11]Weber, *ibid.*, pp. 329-340. For more reflective analyses of the "ideal type" see Peter M. Blau, *Bureaucracy in Modern Society* (Chicago: University of Chicago Press, 1956), pp. 27-56 and Victor A. Thompson, *op. cit.*, pp. 12-21.

[12]Weber, *ibid.*, p. 330.

3. Each member or office of an organization is accountable to a superior for his or its decisions as well as for his or its subordinates. The authority is based on expert knowledge and is sanctioned and made legitimate by the ultimate source of authority—the chief official at the top of the hierarchical pyramid.
4. Each official in the organization conducts the business of his office in an impersonal, formalistic manner. He maintains a social distance between himself and his subordinates and between himself and the clients of the organization. The purpose of this impersonal detachment is to assure that personalities do not interfere with the efficient accomplishment of the mission.
5. "Employment in the bureaucratic organization is based on technical qualifications and is protected against arbitrary dismissal."[13] Promotions are based on seniority and achievement. Because employment is considered a career and the vagaries of making a living are eliminated, a high degree of loyalty for the organization is engendered in the members.

The inherent logic of the bureaucratic structure led Weber to believe that the bureaucratic form of administration is "superior to any other form in precision, in stability, in the stringency of its discipline, and in its reliability. It thus makes possible a particularly high degree of calculability of results for the heads of the organization and for those acting in relation to it."[14] Thus Weber presented the case for bureaucratic administration on precisely the same grounds that the Taylorites presented the case for Scientific Management. In fact Weber himself drew the analogy: "The fully developed bureaucratic mechanism compares with other organizations exactly as does the machine with nonmechanical modes of production."[15]

The bureaucratic form of organization was (and is) prominent in business practice. The proponents of its use in this context formulated "principles" which are obviously in the Weberian tradition. Haynes and Massie have codified these principles as follows:[16]

1. The Unity of Command principle: No member of an organization should report to more than one superior.

---

[13]Blau, *op. cit.*, p. 30.
[14]Weber, *op. cit.*, p. 334.
[15]*From Max Weber: Essays in Sociology*, translated by H.H. Gerth and C. Wright Mills (New York: Oxford University Press, 1946), p. 214 and quoted in Blau, *op. cit.*, p. 31.
[16]W. Warren Haynes and Joseph L. Massie, *Management* (Englewood Cliffs, N.J.: Prentice-Hall, Inc., 1961), pp. 39-43. Other writers, notably L. Urwick, *op. cit.*, pp. 119-129 have lengthened the list, but the four here seem to be primary. Herbert A. Simon refers to such principles as "proverbs" in *Administrative Behavior* (New York: The MacMillan Co., 1945), pp. 20-36 because they have neither empirical verification nor universality of application.

2. The Span of Control principle: No superior should have responsibility for the activities of more than five to eight subordinates.
3. The Exception principle: A superior should delegate responsibility for routine matters to subordinates.
4. The Scalar principle: Every organization should have a well defined hierarchical structure.

One is struck by the prescriptive nature of these principles, by their similarity to the characteristics of Weber's ideal type, and by their concern for order and certainty in carrying on the activities of the organization.

The evidence supplied in the foregoing discussion suggests the assumptions regarding the nature of man underlying scientific management and classical organization theory. March and Simon observe that two "views" of organization members are pervasive: "First, in general there is a tendency to view the employee as an inert instrument performing the tasks assigned to him. Second, there is a tendency to view personnel as a given rather than a variable in the system."[17] Mason Haire has been less polite: "These are the implicit assumptions about man on which classical organization theory seems to me to be based: He is lazy, shortsighted, selfish, liable to make mistakes, has poor judgment, and may even be a little dishonest."[18]

From another perspective, William F. Whyte argues that there are three assumptions underlying the theory: First, it is assumed that "man is a rational animal concerned with maximizing his economic gains," second, "each individual responds to economic incentives as an isolated individual," and third, "men, like machines, can be treated in a standardized fashion."[19]

The Humanistic Challenge

It was only in the 1930s that these assumptions and their implications for organization theory and practice were seriously challenged. The body of concepts that developed during the initial thrust of the industrial revolution and which I have characterized as mechanistic was soon confronted with evidence that seriously challenged its validity. This challenge (which I call the humanistic challenge) came from two sources:

1. There were those who questioned the basic assumptions of the scien-

[17]James G. March and Herbert A. Simon, *Organizations* (New York: John Wiley and Sons, 1958), p. 29.
[18]George B. Strother (ed.), *Social Science Approaches to Business Behavior* (Homewood, Illinois: The Dorsey Press, Inc., 1962), p. 175.
[19]William F. Whyte, *Money and Motivation* (New York: Harper and Brothers, 1955), pp. 2-3.

tific management approach regarding the motivation of men; and,
2. There were those who questioned the efficiency of the bureaucratic form of organization.

Although the two sources of challenge were seemingly unrelated, the emphasis of both was the same, namely: the participants of organizations are not constants and cannot be regarded as givens; and a large mass of empirical evidence was soon available to show that participants adjust the environment to meet their individual and group needs. And part of this adjustment process is related to motivations, as some industrial engineers were to discover.

In 1924, engineers at the Hawthorne Works, a division of the Western Electric Company in Chicago, began a series of tests to determine the relationship between certain variables and the rate of production.[20] A number of frustrating experiments caused the scientists to reject their original hypothesis (that a high and positive correlation exists between working conditions and the rate of output) and they formulated alternative hypotheses. The major sources of data for testing the revised hypotheses were the voluminous recordings of interpersonal conversations that the experimenters had accumulated. These conversations between workers and the scientists revealed that the workers were members of closely knit work groups and that these work groups had established acceptable patterns of behaviour for the members. These patterns of behaviour, in turn, were based on the sentiments of the members of the group, but these sentiments were easily disguised and difficult to isolate. Nevertheless, the scientists discarded their statistical techniques and "denuded of their elaborate logical equipment"[21] they went into the shop to learn the things that were important to the workers.

The findings of the Hawthorne studies challenged the basic assumptions of earlier organization theory, namely the social isolation of the worker and the primacy of economic incentives. For these two assumptions, the human relations school substituted the view that man desires "first, a method of living in social relationship with other people, and, second, as part of this economic function for and value to the group."[22] Thus man (according to Mayo and his followers) "is a uniquely social

[20]The Hawthorne Studies are reported in T.N. Whitehead, *The Industrial Worker*, 2 volumes (Cambridge, Massachusetts: Harvard University Press, 1938); Fritz J. Roethlisberger and William J. Dickson, *Management and the Worker* (Cambridge, Massachusetts: Harvard University Press, 1947); Fritz J. Roethlisberger, *Management and Morale* (Cambridge, Massachusetts: Harvard University Press, 1941); and Elton Mayo, *The Human Problems of an Industrial Civilization* (New York: The Macmillan Co., 1933).
[21]F.J. Roethlisberger, *ibid.*, p. 16.
[22]Mayo, *op. cit.*, p. 18.

animal who can achieve complete 'freedom' only by fully submerging himself in the group."[23] Based on the notion of man as a gregarious animal, the human relations school included in their ideology a view of a society in which man could best achieve his freedom. But the industrial society is not such a society and in fact the process of industrialization destroys the cultural traditions of former times which had enhanced social solidarity. The results of industrialization are social disorganization and unhappy individuals.

According to Mayo, the responsibility for restoring the bases for social stability belongs to administrators of large industrial firms. With leadership that is human-oriented rather than production-oriented the prospects for social stability and its concomitant, a meaningful life for the individual, are enhanced. In fact, Mayo has said: "If our social skills (that is, our ability to secure cooperation between people) had advanced step by step with our technical skill, there would not have been another European war."[24] Thus the ideology of the founders of the "human relations" approach consisted of three parts: (1) a view of man as a social animal; (2) a view of industrial society as incompatible with the basic nature of man; and (3) a view of the solution to man's dilemma as resting with industrial leaders.

The findings of the Hawthorne experiments were exceedingly important to those members of society primarily concerned with rational industrial supervision.[25] It had long been a mystery why workers would restrict output and produce far below standards established by exacting analyses. The Hawthorne studies provided both diagnosis and prescription. The practical application of human relations theory required careful consideration of the informal organization, work teams and symbols that evoke worker response. Unions were viewed in a new dimension and were seen as making a contribution to effective organization rather than as the consequence of malfunctions in the organization.[26] Participative management, employee education, junior executive boards, group decisions and industrial counselling became important means for improving the performance of workers in the organization. Industrial leaders were spurred on by researchers whose findings indicated that "every human being earnestly seeks a secure, friendly, and supportive relationship and one that gives him a sense of personal worth in the face-to-face groups

---

[23]Clark Kerr, *Labor and Management in Industrial Society* (Garden City, New York: Doubleday and Co., Inc., 1964), p. 54.
[24]Elton Mayo, *The Social Problems of an Industrial Civilization* (Boston: Division of Research, Graduate School of Business Administration, Harvard University, 1947), p. 33.
[25]Burleigh B. Gardner, *Human Relations in Industry* (Chicago: Richard D. Irwin, Inc., 1945) is a "classic" of this tradition.
[26]See William F. Whyte, *Pattern for Industrial Peace* (New York: Harper and Brothers, 1951).

most important to him."[27] Thus, in practice, the "herd hypothesis" replaced the "rabble hypothesis."

The research methodology, the ideology and the practice of human relations have been attacked on several points. The methodology of the supporting research is criticized for dealing with only immediate variables and for ignoring the external environment; the work is viewed as static and subject to little change over time. The findings of single case studies do not provide sufficient data for the construction of a rigorous theory of man and his organizations. But at a more fundamental level the ideological view of man is attacked. "They (the human relations advocates) begin by saying that man dislikes isolation and end by consigning him to the care of the managerial elite for his own salvation."[28] Thus by losing his identity man becomes free, or so assert the Mayo-ites.[29]

Critics of the practice of human relations have pointed to a number of defects. Most vehemently criticized has been the use of human relations techniques as a means of manipulating workers to accept the superior's view of reality. Indeed, one has said: "I am totally unable to associate the *conscious practice of human relations skill* (in the sense of making people happy in spite of themselves or getting them to do something they don't think they want to do) with the *dignity of an individual person created in God's Image.*"[30]

This tendency toward manipulation is, at least in part, due to a misunderstanding of the purpose of the social sciences, "to the belief that the function of the social sciences is the same as that of the physical sciences, namely, to gain control of something outside."[31]

A second misunderstanding, and one springing directly from the ideology of human relations, is the belief that the business firm is a total institution which provides for all the needs of its members and that such an institution has the "right" to demand total loyalty. The attempt to gain total loyalty underlies much of personnel and human relations work; administrators frequently use the tags "loyal service" and "loyal employee" to describe the record of a retiring organization member. On this point Peter Drucker has said: "It is not only not compatible with the

---

[27]Rensis Likert, *Motivation: The Core of Management* (New York: American Management Association, 1953). Reprinted in Harry Knudson, *Human Elements of Administration* (New York: Holt, Rinehart, and Winston, 1963), p. 81.

[28]Kerr, *op. cit.*, p. 57.

[29]It is not quite fair to say that Mayo "asserts" in this connection. In *Human Problems of an Industrial Civilization, op. cit.*, he analyzes various traditional cultures and presents as evidence of the social nature of man the many practices designed to achieve social integration, e.g., ritual custom, codes, family and tribal instincts.

[30]Malcolm P. McNair, "Thinking Ahead: What Price Human Relations?" *Harvard Business Review* (March-April, 1957): 15-23. Reprinted in Harold Koontz and Cyril O'Donnell, *Readings in Management* (New York: McGraw-Hill Book Co., Inc., 1959), p. 279.

[31]Peter Drucker, "Human Relations: Where Do We Stand Today?" in Knudson, *op. cit.*, p. 364. The purpose of the social sciences is to gain understanding of one's self, as Drucker explains.

dignity of man, but it is not permissible to believe that the dignity of man can or should be realized totally in a partial institution."[32] The present state of human relations theory might be expressed as follows: "Let's treat people like people, but let's not make a big production of it."[33]

The findings of post-Weber studies of bureaucratic behaviour are similar to the findings of the Hawthorne studies—the reaction of individuals to organizational factors is not always predictable.[34] Merton,[35] Selznick,[36] and Gouldner[37] suggest that treating people as machines not only leads to unforeseen consequences but can actually reinforce the use of the "machine model." Each researcher studied some form of procedure designed to control the activities of the members of the organization.

Merton analyzed the organizational need for control and the consequent concern for reliability of members' behaviour. In order to get the desired results, the organization implements standard rules and procedures. Control is achieved by assuring that the members are following the rules. Merton points out three consequences that result from concern for reliability of behaviour: (1) officials react to individuals as representative of positions having certain specified rights and privileges; (2) rules assume a positive value as ends rather than as means to ends; and (3) decision making becomes routine application of tried and proven approaches and little attention is given to alternatives not previously experienced.[38] The organization becomes committed to activities that insure the status quo at the expense of greater success in achieving organization objectives.

Selznick studied the consequences of a second technique for achieving control and reliability—the delegation of authority. As intended, the specialized competence required to carry out the delegate tasks has the positive effect of achieving organization goals, but there are unintended consequences. Delegation of authority "results in departmentalization and an increase in the *bifurcation of interests* among the subunits in the organization."[39] Members of the organization become increasingly dependent upon the maintenance of subunits and there is a growing disparity between the goals of the subunit and the goals of the organization. The content of decisions is increasingly concerned with subunit objectives and decreasingly concerned with organization goals, except

---

[32]*Ibid.*, p. 364.

[33]McNair, *op. cit.*, p. 285.

[34]This discussion is based on March and Simon, *op. cit.*, pp. 36-47.

[35]Robert K. Merton, "Bureaucratic Structure and Personality," *Social Forces*, 18, (1940): 560-568.

[36]Philip Selznick, *TVA and the Grass Roots* (Berkeley: The University of California Press, 1949).

[37]Alvin W. Gouldner, *Patterns of Industrial Bureaucracy* (New York: The Free Press of Glencoe, 1954).

[38]March and Simon, *op. cit.*, pp. 38-39.

[39]*Ibid.*, p. 41.

that there must not be too great a disparity between the two. Subunit officials seek to make legitimate their activities by squaring their decisions with precedent. Again there seems to be an inherent tendency in the bureaucratic structure toward conservatism and the maintenance of the status quo.[40]

Gouldner gives additional support to the thesis that organization techniques designed to implement control often entail unanticipated results. In his study of industrial organization he found, among other things, that the improvisation of rules to assure control results in the knowledge of *minimum acceptable levels of behaviour* and that members of organizations gear their activities to these minimum levels of behaviour if there is a high level of bifurcation of interest. As officials perceive this low performance, they react by increasing the closeness of supervision and by enacting additional rules and procedures. Again, the unintended consequences are increasing tension among members, increasing non-acceptance of organization goals, and increasing the use of rules to correct matters.[41]

To summarize, the essence of the humanistic challenge is that man in organizations is socially oriented and directed. He has multiple needs which affect and are affected by the work environment; he reacts unpredictably, yet predictably, to stimuli encountered in the organization. The "unintended consequences" of bureaucratic methods imply that man may be incompatible with organization needs. The scene is set, then, for contemporary organization theorists to devise a synthesis of the two polar positions.

The Realistic Synthesis[42]

An important feature of modern organization theory[43] is the systems approach which treats organizations as complex sets of mutually

[40]Such is the thesis of Robert Michels, *Political Parties* (Glencoe, Illinois: The Free Press, 1949), whose concept of the "iron law of oligarchy" is a classic description of the tendency of organization to become conservative as the demands for more specialized competence intensify.

[41]March and Simon, *op. cit.*, p. 45. Those studies are classics in the development of our knowledge of organizational behaviour. It is obvious that many of Downs' hypotheses are suggested by this literature, particularly the hypotheses that organizations value status quo solutions and consensus and that the content of decisions is limited to precedents.

[42]Some third dimension as a basis for synthesis and the criteria for its selection are a concern to many students of organization theory. The work of Warren B. Bennis and many others could be cited. The focus of this paper, however, is on *values* more than the whole panorama.

[43]Some presentations of modern organization theory are March and Simon, *op. cit.*; Mason Haire (ed.), *Modern Organization Theory* (New York: John Wiley and Sons, 1959); Albert H. Rubenstein and Chadwick J. Haberstroh, *Some Theories of Organization* (Homewood, Illinois: The Dorsey Press, Inc., 1960); Joseph A. Litterer, *The Analysis of Organizations* (New York: John Wiley and Sons, 1965); and Theodore Caplow, *Principles of Organizations* (New York: Harcourt, Brace and World, Inc., 1964).

dependent and interacting variables. In this framework the participants are one set of variables which act on all other variables. Because this paper is concerned only with the place of man in organization theory, I will outline the features of the systems approach (which I term the realistic synthesis) and then return to the discussion of man as a variable in the system.

The systems approach to organization theory presents the opportunity to view the organization as a totality. The emphasis is on the parts of the system, the nature of interaction among the parts, the processes which link the parts, and the goals of the system.[44] The key parts are the individual and his unique personality, the formal structure of jobs, the informal groups, the status and role patterns within the groups and the physical environment. Relating these parts are complex patterns of interactions which modify the behaviour and expectations of each. The basic parts are linked together by certain organizational processes including structured roles, channels of communication and decision making. These processes provide means for overcoming the centrifugal tendency of the parts[45] and for directing the parts toward the ultimate goals of the organization—growth, stability and social interaction.[46]

The systems approach is a realistic synthesis because it views the individual as only one of many parts, because it allows for modification of the parts, because it views conflict within the organization as a natural by-product of group endeavour, and because it anticipates dynamic rather than static patterns of interaction.

The realistic view of man in the organization acknowledges the contributions of the Hawthorne experiments, but it has added certain ideas that go beyond "human relations." The basic premise seems to be that man's needs and the organization's needs are inconsistent.[47] Man's behaviour is seen to be motivated by a hierarchy of needs and once the most basic needs are satisfied, the individual turns to the ultimate source of satisfaction—self-actualization. But to achieve self-actualization requires that the healthy individual be "independent, creative . . . exercise autonomy and discretion, and . . . develop and express . . . unique personality with freedom."[48] The organization, however, presents barriers to

[44]William G. Scott, "Organization Theory: An Overview and an Appraisal," *Academy of Management Journal* (April 1961): 7-26. Reprinted in *Organizations: Structure and Behavior*, ed. Joseph A. Litterer (New York: John Wiley and Sons, 1963), p. 19.

[45]John M. Pfiffner and Frank P. Sherwood, *Administrative Organization* (Englewood Cliffs, N.J.: Prentice-Hall, Inc., 1960), pp. 116-117.

[46]Scott, *op. cit.*, p. 22.

[47]This view is developed by Chris Argyris in *Personality and Organization* (New York: Harper and Brothers, 1957), and more recently in *Integrating the Individual and the Organization* (New York: John Wiley and Sons, 1964).

[48]George Strauss, "Some Notes on Power-Equalization" in *The Social Science of Organization*, ed. Harold J. Leavitt (Englewood Cliffs, N.J.: Prentice-Hall, Inc., 1963), p. 46.

this development of self-actualization and requires that the individual be dependent upon others for goal setting and direction and conform to norms far below the level of his ability or expectations. The results of this conflict are immature behaviour and frustration-oriented activities, the overt expression being determined by the unique personality of the individual. Argyris's studies indicate that an organization member experiencing frustration and conflict may behave in any one of the following ways.

(a) He may leave the organization.
(b) He may work hard and become president.
(c) He may adapt through the use of defence mechanisms.
(d) He may adapt by lowering his work standards and by becoming apathetic.[49]

Other students of organizational behaviour also perceive basic conflicts between the organization and the individual. Presthus argues that the reactions of members can be characterized by three bureaucratic types: the upward-mobiles; the indifferents; and the ambivalents. The upward-mobiles are those who react positively to the organizational requirements and by adopting the sanctioned behavioural patterns succeed in it.[50] The indifferents are the great majority who view their jobs as means to secure off-work satisfactions and who neither seek nor expect on-job satisfaction.[51] The ambivalents are a small minority who are unable to play the organizationally defined role which would enable them to realize their ambitions.[52] The similarity between these three patterns of behaviour and the adaptive responses which Argyris lists is evident.

Thus the contemporary view of the nature of man in organizations recognizes the essential conflict that exists. Whereas the mechanistic tradition considered conflict to be dysfunctional to organization purposes and felt that it could be neutralized by monetary payments and the humanist challenge viewed conflict as dysfunctional but believed that human relations techniques could control it, the realistic synthesis assumes that conflict is a normal aspect of organization life.

The problem posed, then, is how to harness the energies of conflict such that both organizational and individual needs are realized. Given the problem, we can accept at the outset that neither will be met perfectly—this being the essence of the conflict.[53] And whether conflict or

---

[49]Argyris, op. cit., pp. 78-79.
[50]Robert Presthus, The Organizational Society (New York: Alfred A. Knopf, 1962), pp. 164-204.
[51]Ibid., pp. 205-256.
[52]Ibid., pp. 257-285.
[53]Conflict and struggle for power in organizations lead to patterns of behaviour that are political in nature. Melville Dalton in Men Who Manage (New York: John Wiley and Sons, 1959) analyzes organizational politics.

cooperation is the *essential* nature of man does not seem to be relevant,[54] since research indicates that many organization members are *in fact in conflict* with the requirements of the organization.

I offer no final conclusions as to where recent efforts in organization theory and organization structuring will lead us; all the evidence is not in and final arguments have not been heard.[55] However, it is not difficult to concur with Haire's statement:

> Whenever we try to plan what an organization should be like, it is necessarily based on an implicit concept of man. If we look . . . at the outline of a "classical" organization theory and some more modern alternatives, we begin to see the change in the concept of man.[56]

2/The Intellectual Development of Public Administration*
Nicholas Henry

The study and practice of public bureaucracy is called public administration. Phrased more specifically, public administration is a broad-ranging and amorphous combination of theory and practice designed to promote a superior understanding of government and its relationship with the society it governs, as well as to encourage public policies more responsive to social needs and institute managerial practices on the part of the public bureaucracies that are substantially attuned to effectiveness, efficiency and, increasingly, the deeper human requisites of the citizenry. Admittedly, the preceding sentence is itself rather broad-ranging and amorphous, but for the purposes of this essay it will suffice. There are, however, additional characteristics of public administration.

As Stephen K. Bailey has noted, public administration is (or should be) concerned with the development of four kinds of theories:

---

[54]Nor is there a final answer since some men (e.g., Thomas Hobbes) have viewed the essence of man to be conflict, while others (e.g., John Locke) have viewed man as essentially cooperative. Realization of the individual through the group is not characteristic of Rousseau.
[55]See William W. Cooper, Harold J. Leavitt, and Maynard W. Shelly, *New Perspectives in Organization Research* (New York: John Wiley and Sons, Inc., 1964), for some indications.
[56]Strother, *op. cit.*, pp. 170-171.

---

*Reprinted by permission from Nicholas Henry, *Public Administration and Public Affairs* (Englewood Cliffs, N.J.: Prentice-Hall, Inc., 1975), pp. 4-18, 22.

1. "descriptive theory," or descriptions of hierarchical structures and relationships with their sundry task environments;
2. "normative theory," or the "value goals" of the field, that is, what public administrators (the practitioners) ought to do, given their realm of decision alternatives, and what public administrationists (the scholars) ought to study and recommend to the practitioners in terms of policy;
3. "assumptive theory," or a rigorous understanding of the reality of administrative man, one that assumes neither angelic nor satanic models of the public bureaucrat;
4. "instrumental theory," or the increasingly refined managerial techniques for the efficient and effective attainment of public objectives.

Taken together, Bailey's quartet of "theories" form three defining pillars of public administration: organizational behaviour and the behaviour of people in public organizations; the technology of management; and the public interest as it relates to individual ethical choice and public affairs.

In this essay we review the successive definitional crises of public administration—that is, how the field has "seen itself" in the past. These paradigms of public administration are worth knowing about because, first, one must know where the field has been in order to comprehend it. It is contended that public administration is unique, a field significantly different from both political science (public administration's "mother discipline") and administrative science (public administration's traditional alter ego) in terms of developing certain facets of organization theory and techniques of management. Public administration differs from political science in its emphasis on bureaucratic structure and behaviour and in its methodologies. Public administration differs from administrative science in that the evaluative techniques used by non-profit public organizations are not the same as those used by for-profit private organizations, and because profit-seeking organizations are considerably less constrained in considering the public interest in their decision-making structures and the behaviour of their administrators.

The Intellectual Development of Public Administration

In terms of public administration's development as an academic field, there has been a succession of five overlapping paradigms. As Robert T. Golembiewski has noted in a perceptive essay on the development of the field, each phase may be characterized according to whether it has "locus" or "focus." *Locus* is the institutional "where" of the field. A recurring locus of public administration is the government bureaucracy, but this has not always been the case and often this traditional locus has been blurred. *Focus* is the specialized "what" of the field. One focus of public administration has been the study of certain "principles of administration," but, again, the foci of the discipline have altered with the changing paradigms of public administration. As Golembiewski observes, the paradigms of public administration may be understood in terms of locus or focus; when one has been relatively sharply defined, the other has been conceptually ignored in academic circles and vice versa. We shall use the notion of loci and foci in reviewing the intellectual development of public administration.

The Beginning

Woodrow Wilson largely set the tone for the early study of public administration in an essay entitled "The Study of Administration," published in the *Political Science Quarterly* in 1887. In it, Wilson observed that it "is getting harder to *run* a constitution than to frame one," and called for the bringing to bear of more intellectual resources in the management of the state. Wilson's seminal article has been interpreted by later scholars in a number of differing ways. Some have insisted that Wilson was the originator of the "politics/administration dichotomy," or the naive distinction between "political" activity and "administrative" activity in public organizations that would plague the field for years to come. Other scholars have countered that Wilson was well aware that public administration was innately political in nature, and made this point clear in his article. The reality of the matter appears to be that Wilson himself was ambivalent about what public administration really was. As Richard J. Stillman II concluded in a thorough and timely reconsideration of "The Study of Administration," Wilson failed to amplify what the study of administration actually entails, what the proper relationship should be between the administrative and political realms, and whether or not administrative study could ever become an abstract science akin to the natural sciences. Nevertheless, Wilson unquestionably posited one unambiguous thesis in his article that has had a lasting impact on the field: Public administration was worth studying. Political scientists later on would create the first identifiable paradigm of public administration around Wilson's contention.

Paradigm 1: The politics/administration dichotomy, 1900–1926

Our benchmark date for the Paradigm 1 period corresponds to the publication of books written by Frank J. Goodnow and Leonard D. White; they are, as are the years chosen as marking the later periods of the field, only rough indicators. In *Politics and Administration* (1900), Goodnow contended that there were "two distinct functions of government," which he identified with the title of his book. Politics, said Goodnow, "has to do with policies or expressions of the state will," while administration "has to do with the execution of these policies." Separation of powers provided the basis of the distinction; the legislative branch, aided by the interpretive abilities of the judicial branch, expressed the will of the state and formed policy, while the executive branch administered those policies impartially and apolitically.

The emphasis of Paradigm 1 was on locus—where public administration should be. Clearly, in the view of Goodnow and his fellow public administrationists, public administration should centre in the government's bureaucracy. While, admittedly, the legislature and judiciary had their quanta of "administration," their primary responsibility and function remained the expression of the state will. The initial conceptual legitimation of this locus-centred definition of the field, and one that would wax increasingly problematic for academics and practitioners alike, became known as the politics/administration dichotomy.

The phrase that came to symbolize this distinction between politics and administration was, "there is no Republican way to build a road," the reasoning being that there could be only one "right" way to spread tarmac—the administrative engineer's way. What was ignored in this statement, however, was that there was indeed a Republican way to decide whether the road needed building, a Republican way to choose the location for the road, a Republican way to purchase the land, a Republican way to displace the people living in the road's way, and most certainly a Republican way to let contracts for the road. There was also, and is, a Democratic way, a Socialist way, a Liberal way, even an Anarchist way to make these "administrative" decisions as well. The point is that, in reality, the politics/administration dichotomy posited by Goodnow and his academic progeny was, at best, naive. But many years would pass before this would be fully realized within public administration's ranks.

Public administration received its first serious attention from scholars during this period largely as a result of the "public service movement" that was taking place in American universities in the early part of this century. Political science, as a report issued in 1914 by the Committee on Instruction in Government of the American Political Science Association stated, was concerned with training for citizenship, professional preparations such as law and journalism, training "experts and to prepare specialists for governmental positions," and educating for research work. Public administration, therefore, was a clear and significant subfield of political science. In 1912, a Committee on Practical Training for Public Service was established under the auspices of the American Political Science Association, and in 1914 its report recommended, with unusual foresight, that special "professional schools" were needed to train public administrators, and that new technical degrees might be necessary as well for this purpose. This committee formed the nucleus of the Society for the Promotion of Training for the Public Service, founded in 1914—the forerunner of the American Society for Public Administration, which was established in 1939 when public administration was at its most "separatist" stage of development in terms of political science.

Public administration began picking up academic legitimacy in the 1920s; notable in this regard was the publication of Leonard D. White's *Introduction to the Study of Public Administration* in 1926, the first textbook devoted in toto to the field. As Dwight Waldo has pointed out, White's text was quintessentially American Progressive in character and, in its quintessence, reflected the general thrust of the field: Politics should not intrude on administration; management lends itself to scientific study; public administration is capable of becoming a "value-free" science in its own right; the mission of administration is economy and efficiency, period.

The net result of Paradigm 1 was to strengthen the notion of a distinct politics/administration dichotomy by relating it to a corresponding value/fact dichotomy. Thus everything that public administrationists scrutinized in the executive branch was imbued with the colourings and legitimacy of being somehow "factual" and "scientific," while the study of public policy making and related matters was left to the political scientists. The carving up of analytical territory between public administrationists and political scientists during this locus-oriented stage can be seen today in political science departments: it is the public administrationists who teach organization theory, budgeting and personnel, while political scientists teach such subjects as American government, judicial behaviour, the presidency, state and local politics and legislative process, as well as such "non-American" fields as comparative politics and international relations. A secondary implication of this locus-centred phase was the isolation of public administration from other fields as well, such as business administration, which had unfortunate consequences later when these fields began their own fruitful explorations into the nature of organizations. Finally, largely because of the emphasis on "administration" and "facts" in public administration, and the substantial contributions by public administrationists to the emerging field of organization theory, a foundation was laid for the later "discovery" of certain scientific "principles" of administration.

Paradigm 2: The principles of administration, 1927–1937

In 1927, W.F. Willoughby's book, *Principles of Public Administration*, was published as the second full-fledged text in the field. While Willoughby's *Principles* was as fully American Progressive in tone as White's *Introduction*, its title alone indicated the new thrust of public administration: that certain scientific principles of administration were "there," that they could be discovered, and that administrators would be expert in their work if they learned how to apply these principles.

It was during the phase represented by Paradigm 2 that public administration reached its reputational zenith. Public administrationists were in high demand during the 1930s and early 1940s for their managerial knowledge, courted by industry and government alike. Thus the focus of the field—its essential expertise in the form of administrative principles—waxed, while no one thought too seriously about its locus. Indeed, the locus of public administration was everywhere, since principles were principles, and administration was administration, at least according to the perceptions of Paradigm 2. By the very fact that the principles of administration were indeed *principles*—that is, by definition, they "worked" in any administrative setting, regardless of culture, function, environment, mission or institutional framework and without exception—it therefore followed that they could be applied successfully anywhere. Furthermore, because public administrationists had contributed as much if not more to the formulation of "administrative principles" as had researchers in any other field of inquiry, it also followed that public administrationists should lead the academic pack in applying them to "real-world" organizations, public or otherwise.

Among the more significant works relevant to this phase were Mary Parker Follett's *Creative Experience* (1924), Henri Fayol's *Industrial and General Management* (1930), and James D. Mooney and Alan C. Reiley's *Principles of Organization* (1939), all of which delineated varying numbers of overarching administrative principles. Organization theorists often dub this school of thought "administrative management," since it focused on the upper hierarchical echelons of organizations. A related literature that preceded the work in administrative management somewhat in time, but which was under continuing development in business schools, focused on the assembly line. Often called "scientific management," researchers in this stream (notably Frederick W. Taylor's *Principles of Scientific Management* [1911] and various works by Frank and Lillian Gilbreth) developed "principles" of efficient physical movement for optimal assembly-line efficiency. While obviously related in concept, scientific management had little effect on public administration during its principles phase because it focused on lower-level personnel in the organization.

The "high noon of orthodoxy," as it often has been called, of public administration was marked by the publication in 1937 of Luther H. Gulick and Lyndall Urwick's *Papers on the Science of Administration*. This landmark study also marked the high noon of prestige for public administration. Gulick and Urwick were confidants of President Franklin D. Roosevelt and advised him on a variety of matters managerial; their *Papers* were a report to the President's Committee on Administrative Science.

Principles were important to Gulick and Urwick, but where those principles were applied was not; focus was favoured over locus, and no bones were made about it. As they said in the *Papers,*

> It is the general thesis of this paper that there are principles which can be arrived at inductively from the study of human organization which should govern arrangements for human association of any kind. These principles can be studied as a technical question, irrespective of the purpose of the enterprise, the personnel comprising it, or any constitutional, political or social theory underlying its creation.

Gulick and Urwick promoted seven principles of administration and, in so doing, gave students of public administration that snappy anagram, POSDCORB. POSDCORB was the final expression of administrative principles. It stood for:

P   lanning
O   rganizing
S   taffing
D   irecting
C
O }   ordinating
R   eporting
B   udgeting

That was public administration in 1937.

The Challenge, 1938-1947

In the following year, mainstream, top-of-the-heap public administration received its first real hint of conceptual challenge. In 1938, Chester I. Barnard's *The Functions of the Executive* appeared. Its impact on public administration was not overwhelming at the time, but it later had considerable influence on Herbert A. Simon when he was writing his devastating critique of the field, *Administrative Behavior.* The impact of Barnard's book may have been delayed because, as a former president of New Jersey Bell Telephone, he was not a certified member of the public administration community.

Dissent from mainstream public administration accelerated in the 1940s and took two, mutually reenforcing directions. One was the objection that politics and administration could never be separated in any remotely sensible fashion. The other was that the principles of administration were logically inconsistent.

Although inklings of dissent began in the 1930s, a book of readings in the field, *Elements of Public Administration*, edited in 1946 by Fritz von Morstein Marx, was one of the first major volumes which questioned the assumption that politics and administration could be separated. All the fourteen articles were written by practitioners and indicated a new awareness that what often appeared to be value-free "administration" actually was value-laden "politics." Was a "technical" decision on a budgetary emphasis or a personnel change really impersonal and apolitical, or was it actually highly personal, highly political and highly preferential? Was it ever possible really to discern the difference? Was it even worth attempting to discern the difference between politics and administration because, in reality, there was none? Was the underpinning politics/administration dichotomy of the field, at best, naive? Perhaps the frontal answer to these questions was published in 1950: John Gaus wrote in the *Public Administration Review* his oft-quoted dictum, "A theory of public administration means in our time a theory of politics also." The die was cast.

Arising simultaneously with the challenge to the traditional politics/administration dichotomy of the field was an even more basic contention: that there could be no such thing as a "principle" of administration. In 1946, Simon gave a foreshadowing of his *Administrative Behavior* in an article entitled, appropriately, "The Proverbs of Administration," published in *Public Administration Review*. The following year, Robert A. Dahl published a searching piece in the same journal, "The Science of Public Administration: Three Problems," in which he argued that the development of universal principles of administration was hindered by the obstructions of values contending for preeminence in organizations, differences in individual personalities, and social frameworks that varied from culture to culture. Waldo's work also reflected this theme. His *The Administrative State: A Study of the Political Theory of American Public Administration* (1948) attacked the notion of immutable principles of administration, the inconsistencies of the methodology used in determining them, and the narrowness of the "values" of economy and efficiency that dominated the field's thinking.

The most formidable dissection of the principles notion also appeared in 1947: Simon's *Administrative Behavior: A Study of Decision-Making Processes in Administrative Organization*. Simon showed that for every "principle" of administration there was a counter-principle, thus rendering the whole idea of principles moot. For example, the traditional administrative literature argued that bureaucracies must have a narrow "span of control" if orders were to be communicated and carried out effectively. Span of control meant that a manager could "control" properly only a limited number of subordinates; after a certain number was exceeded (authorities differed on just what the number was), communication of commands became increasingly garbled and control became increasingly ineffective and "loose." An organization that followed the principle of narrow span of control would have a "tall" organization chart (see Figure 1).

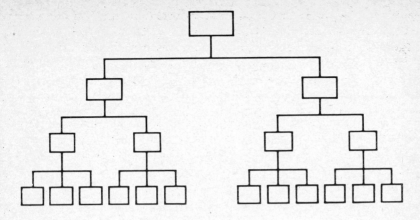

Figure 1
The "Principle" of Narrow Span of Control

Span of control made sense up to a point. Yet, as Simon observed, the literature on administration argued with equal vigour for another principle: that for organizations to maximize effective communications and to reduce distortion (thereby enhancing responsiveness and control), there should be as few hierarchical layers as possible; that is, a "flat" hierarchical structure. The logic behind this principle was that the fewer people who had to pass a message up or down the hierarchy, the more likely it would be that the message would arrive at its appointed destination relatively intact and undistorted. This, too, made sense up to a point. The "flat" hierarchy required to bring the bureaucracy in accord with this principle of administration would have an organization chart like that in Figure 2.

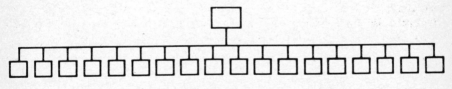

Figure 2
The "Principle" of Maximized Communications

Obviously, to Simon and now to us, the two "principles" were mutually contradictory and therefore could not be principles by definition. This dilemma encompassed the whole of the traditional public administration literature, but it was never more than suspected of being so stark a case until Simon published his book.

By mid-century, the two defining pillars of public administration—the politics/administration dichotomy and the principles of administration—had been abandoned by creative intellects in the field. This abandonment left public administration bereft of a distinct epistemological identity. Some would argue that an identity has yet to be found.

Reaction to the Challenge, 1947–1950

In the same year that Simon decimated the traditional foundations of public administration in *Administrative Behavior*, he offered an alternative to the old paradigms in an essay entitled "A Comment on 'The Science of Public Administration'" and published in the *Public Administration Review*. For Simon, a new paradigm for public administration meant that there ought to be two kinds of public administrationists working in harmony and reciprocal intellectual stimulation: those scholars concerned with developing "a pure science of administration" based on "a thorough grounding in social psychology," and a larger group concerned with "prescribing for public policy." This latter enterprise was far-ranging indeed. In Simon's view, prescribing for public policy "cannot stop when it has swallowed up the whole of political science; it must attempt to absorb economics and sociology, as well." Nevertheless, both a "pure science of administration" and "prescribing for public policy" would be mutually reenforcing components: "there does not appear to be any reason why these two developments in the field of public administration should not go on side by side, for they in no way conflict or contradict."

Despite a proposal that was both rigorous and normative in its emphasis, Simon's call for a "pure science" put off many scholars in public administration. For one thing, there already existed a growing irritation in the field with POSDCORB on the basis of its "pure science" claims; the challengers of the late 1940s had shown that the "principles of administration" were hardly the final expression of science, and consequently public administrationists were increasingly sceptical that the administrative phenomenon could be understood in wholly scientific terms. Second, Simon's urging that social psychology provided the basis for understanding administrative behaviour struck many public administrationists as foreign and discomforting; most of them had no training in social psychology. Third, since science was perceived as being "value-free," it followed that a "science of administration" logically would ban public administrationists from what many of them perceived as their richest sources of inquiry: normative political theory, the concept of the public interest, and the entire spectrum of human values. While this interpretation may well have rested on a widespread misinterpretation of Simon's thinking (understandable, perhaps, given the wake of *Adminis-*

trative Behavior), as Golembiewski contends, the reaction none the less was real.

The threat posed by Simon and his fellow challengers of the traditional paradigms was clear not only to most political scientists but to many public administrationists as well. For their part, the public administrationists had both a carrot and a stick as inducements not only to remain within political science but to strengthen the conceptual linkages between the fields. The carrot was the maintenance of the logical conceptual connection between public administration and political science: that is, the public policy-making process. Public administration considered the "internal" stages of that process: the formulation of public policies within public bureaucracies and their delivery to the polity. Political science was perceived as considering the "external" stages of the process: the pressures in the polity generating political and social change. There was a certain logic in retaining this linkage in terms of epistemological benefits to both fields. The stick, as we have noted, was the worrisome prospect of retooling only to become a technically oriented "pure science" that might lose touch with political and social realities in an effort to cultivate an engineering mentality for public administration.

Political scientists, for their part, had begun to resist the growing independence of public administrationists and to question the field's action orientation as early as the mid-1930s. Political scientists, rather than advocating a public service and executive preparatory program as they had in 1914, began calling for, in the words of Lynton K. Caldwell, "intellectualized understanding" of the executive branch, rather than "knowledgeable action" on the part of public administrators. In 1952, Roscoe Martin wrote an article appearing in the *American Political Science Review* calling for the continued "dominion of political science over public administration."

By the post-World War II era, political scientists were well under the gun, and could ill afford the breakaway of their most prestigious subfield. The discipline was in the throes of being shaken conceptually by the "behavioural revolution" that had occurred in other social sciences. The American Political Science Association was in some financially tight straits. Political scientists were aware that not only public administrationists had threatened secession in the past, now other subfields, such as international relations, were restive. And, in terms of science and social science both, it was increasingly evident that political science was held in low esteem by scholars in other fields. The formation of the National Science Foundation in 1950 brought the message to all who cared to listen that the chief federal science agency considered political science to be the distinctly junior member of the social sciences, and in 1953 David Easton confronted this lack of status directly in his influential book, *The Political System*.

Paradigm 3: Public administration as political science, 1950–1970

In any event, as a result of these concerns and icy conceptual critiques of the field, public administrationists leaped back with some alacrity into the mother discipline of political science. The result was a renewed definition of locus—the governmental bureaucracy—but a corresponding loss of focus. Should the mechanics of budgets and public personnel policies be studied exclusively? Or should public administrationists consider the grand philosophic schemata of the "administrative Platonists" (as one political scientist called them), such as Paul Appleby? Or should they explore quite new fields of inquiry, as urged by Simon, such as sociology, business administration and social psychology, as they related to the analysis of organizations and decision making? In brief, this third phase of definition was largely an exercise in reestablishing the conceptual linkages between public administration and political science. But the consequence of this exercise was to "define away" the field, at least in terms of its analytical focus, its essential "expertise." Thus writings on public administration in the 1950s spoke of the field as an "emphasis," an "area of interest" or even as a "synonym" of political science. Public administration, as an identifiable field of study, began a long, downhill spiral.

Things got relatively nasty by the end of the decade and, for that matter, well into the 1960s. In 1962, public administration was not included as a subfield of political science in the report of the Committee on Political Science as a discipline of the American Political Science Association. In 1964, Albert Somit and Joseph Tanenhaus's major survey of political scientists indicated a decline in faculty interest in public administration generally. In 1967, public administration disappeared as an organizing category in the program of the annual meeting of the American Political Science Association. Waldo wrote in 1968 that "many political scientists not identified with Public Administration are indifferent or even hostile; they would sooner be free of it," and added that the public administrationist has an "uncomfortable" and "second-class citizenship." Between 1960 and 1970, only four per cent of all the articles published in the five major political science journals dealt with public administration. In the 1960s, "P.A. types," as they often were called in political science faculties, pretty much shuffled through political science departments.

Paradigm 4: Public administration as administrative science, 1956–1970

Partly because of their second-class citizenship status in a number of political science departments, some public administrationists began searching for an alternative. Although Paradigm 4 occurred roughly concurrently with Paradigm 3 in time, it never has received the broadly based favour that political science has garnered from public administrationists as a paradigm (although its appeal is growing). None the less, the administrative science option is a viable alternative for a significant number of scholars in public administration. But in both the political science and administrative science paradigms, the essential thrust was one of public administration losing its identity and its uniqueness within the confines of some "larger" concept.

"Administrative science" is used here as a catchall phrase for studies in organization theory and management science. Organization theory draws primarily on the works of social psychologists, business administrationists, and sociologists, as well as public administrationists to better understand organizational behaviour, while management science relies chiefly on the research of statisticians, systems analysts, computer scientists and economists, as well as public administrationists, in order to measure program effectiveness more precisely and increase managerial efficiency. As a paradigm, administrative science provides a focus but not a locus. It offers techniques, often highly sophisticated techniques, that require expertise and specialization, but in what institutional setting that expertise should be applied is undefined. As in Paradigm 2, administration is administration wherever it is found; focus is favoured over locus.

A number of developments, often stemming from the country's business schools, fostered the alternative paradigm of administrative science. In 1956, the important journal *Administrative Science Quarterly* was founded by a public administrationist on the premise that public, business and institutional administration were false distinctions, that administration was administration. Public administrationist Keith M. Henderson, among others, argued in the mid-1960s that organization theory was, or should be, the overarching focus of public administration. And it cannot be denied that such works as James G. March and Simon's *Organizations* (1958), Richard Cyert and March's *A Behavioral Theory of the Firm* (1963), March's *Handbook of Organizations* (1965) and James D. Thompson's *Organizations in Action* (1967) gave solid theoretical reasons for choosing administrative science as the paradigm of public administration.

In the early 1960s, "organization development" began its rapid rise as a specialty of administrative science. As a focus, organization development represented a particularly tempting alternative to political science for many public administrationists. Organization development as a field is grounded in social psychology and values the "democratization" of bureaucracies, whether public or private, and the "self-actualization" of individual members of organizations. Because of these values, organization development was seen by many younger public administrationists as offering a very compatible area of research within the framework of administrative science: democratic values could be considered, normative concerns could be broached, and intellectual rigour and scientific methodologies could be employed. Yale University became a major promoter of the organization development idea in public administration; its graduates often emerged with Ph.D.'s in political science but with transcripts heavy with industrial management courses.

But there was a problem in the administrative science route, and a real one. If it were selected as the sole focus of public administration, could one continue to speak of *public* administration? After all, administrative science, while not advocating universal principles, nevertheless did and does contend that all organizations and managerial methodologies have certain characteristics, patterns and pathologies in common. If administrative science alone defined the field's paradigm, then public administration would exchange, at best, being an "emphasis" in political science departments for being, at best, a subfield in schools of administrative science. This often would mean in practice that schools of business administration would absorb the field of public administration. Whether profit-conscious "B-school types" could adequately appreciate the vital value of public interest as an aspect of administrative science was a question of genuine importance to public administrationists, and one for which the probable answers were less than comforting.

Part of this conceptual dilemma, but only part, lay in the traditional distinction between "public" and "private" spheres of American society. What is *public* administration, what is everything else (that is, "private" administration), and what is the dividing line between the two types has been a gnawing dilemma for a number of years.

"Real-world" phenomena are making the public/private distinction an increasingly difficult one to define empirically, irrespective of academic disputations. The research and development contract, the "military-industrial complex," the roles of the regulatory agencies and their relations with industry, and the growing expertise of government agencies in originating and developing advanced managerial techniques that influence the "private sector" in every aspect of American society, all conspired to make *public* administration an elusive entity in terms of determining its proper paradigm. This dilemma is not yet fully resolved. Consider the conceptual problems presented by the R & D contract alone, which is essentially a post-World War II phenomenon. Recently, each one of five "private" companies spent, as contractors, more than one billion dollars of federal funds in a year, a sum exceeding that expended by any one of five cabinet-level departments. In the same year, the one hundred corporations with the top-funded military contracts spent more federal moneys than all the civil agencies of the federal government combined, excluding interest on the national debt. Confusion about the *public* variety of the field of administration seems at least understandable; one scholar, in fact, has argued that we should begin talking about "publicadministration," since all kinds of managerial organizations increasingly find themselves relating to public, governmental and political concerns due to the growing interrelatedness of technological societies.

As a result of these factors, public administrationists recently have begun to appreciate that the "public" in public administration no longer can be conceived in simply institutional terms, which have been the terms traditionally favoured by the field. "Public" instead must be cast into philosophic, normative and ethical terms; "public," then, becomes that which affects the public interest. Thus, rather than concentrating on the Department of Defense as its proper "public" locus, and leaving, say, Lockheed Corporation to students of business administration, public administrationists now would examine the department's contractual and political relationships with Lockheed. Hence, the traditional definition of "public" (for example, the Department of Defense) is abandoned in favour of a more dynamic, normative definition (for example, the department *and* its relations with Lockheed). The field is beginning to call this new dimension of the public interest "public affairs."

The public/private, public interest/profit motive tensions represented by the administrative science paradigm do nothing to alleviate the problem of locus for public administration. Of these tensions, that of the public interest as it relates to public affairs is the most important. Without a sense of the public interest, administrative science can be used for *any* purpose, no matter how immoral. The concept of determining and implementing the public interest constitutes a defining pillar of public administration and a locus of the field that receives little if any attention within the context of administrative science, just as the focus of organization theory/management science garners scant support in political science. It would seem, therefore, that public administration should, and perhaps must, find a new paradigm that encourages both a focus and a locus for the field.

Paradigm 5: Public administration as public administration, 1970-?

Despite continuing intellectual turmoil, Simon's 1947 proposal for a duality of scholarship in public administration has been gaining a renewed validity. There is not yet a focus for the field in the form of a "pure science of administration," but at least organization theory primarily has concerned itself in the last two and a half decades with how and why organizations work, how and why people in them behave, and how and why decisions are made, rather than with how these things *should* happen. Additionally, considerable progress has been made in refining the applied techniques of management sciences, as well as developing new techniques, that often reflect what has been learned in the more theoretical realms of organizational analysis.

There has been less progress in delineating a locus for the field, or what the public interest, public affairs and "prescribing for public policy" should encompass in terms relevant to public administrationists. Never the less, the field does appear to be zeroing in on certain fundamental social factors unique to fully developed countries as its proper locus. The choice of these phenomena may be somewhat arbitrary on the part of public administrationists, but they do share commonalities in that they have engendered cross-disciplinary interest in universities, require synthesizing intellectual capacities, and lean toward themes that reflect urban life, administrative relations among "public" and "private" organizations, and the interface between technology and society. The traditional and rigid distinction of the field between the "public sphere" and the "private sphere" appears to be waning as public administration's new and flexibly defined locus waxes. Furthermore, public administrationists have been increasingly concerned with the inextricably related areas of policy science, political economy, the public policy-making process and its analysis, and the measurement of policy outputs. This latter aspect can be viewed, in some ways, as a linkage between public administration's evolving focus and locus.

Bibliography

Baker, R.S. *Administrative Theory and Public Administration*. London: Hutchinson, 1972.

Berkley, George E. *The Craft of Public Administration*. Boston: Allyn & Bacon, 1975.

Bernstein, Samuel J., and O'Hara, Patrick. *Public Administration*. New York: Harper & Row, 1979.

Brown, R.G.S. *The Administrative Process in Britain*. 2d ed. London: Methuen, 1979.

Caiden, Gerald E. *The Dynamics of Public Administration: Guidelines to Current Transformations in Theory and Practice*. New York: Holt, Rinehart & Winston, 1971.

Chapman, Brian. *The Profession of Government*. New York: Macmillan, 1959.

Dunsire, A. *Administration: The Word and the Science*. New York: John Wiley and Sons, 1973.

Gaus, John M. *Reflections on Public Administration*. University, Ala.: University of Alabama Press, 1947.

Heady, Ferrel. *Public Administration: A Comparative Perspective*. 2d ed. New York: Marcel Dekker, 1979.

Henry, Nicholas. *Public Administration and Public Affairs*. 2d ed. Englewood Cliffs, N.J.: Prentice-Hall, 1980.

Hodgson, J.S. *Public Administration*. Toronto: McGraw-Hill, 1969.

Kramer, Fred A. *Dynamics of Public Bureaucracy*. Cambridge, Mass.: Winthrop Publishers, 1977.

Marini, Frank, ed. *Toward a New Public Administration: The Minnowbrook Perspective*. Scranton, Pa.: Chandler, 1971.

McCurdy, Howard E. *Public Administration: A Synthesis*. Mento Park, Calif.: Cummings Publishing, 1977.

Miewald, Robert D. *Public Administration*. New York: McGraw-Hill, 1978.

Morstein, Marx F., ed. *Elements of Public Administration*. Englewood Cliffs, N.J.: Prentice-Hall, 1965.

Mosher, Frederick C. *Democracy and the Public Service*. New York: Oxford University Press, 1968.

Nigro, Felix A., and Nigro, Lloyd A. *Modern Public Administration*. 5th ed. New York: Harper & Row, 1980.

Ostrom, Vincent. *The Intellectual Crisis in American Public Administration.* University, Ala.: University of Alabama Press, 1973.

Presthus, R.V. *Public Administration.* 6th ed. New York: Ronald Press, 1975.

Rehfuss, John. *Public Administration as Political Process.* New York: Charles Scribner's Sons, 1973.

Richardson, Ivan L., and Baldwin, Sidney. *Public Administration.* Columbus, Ohio: Charles E. Merrill, 1976.

Self, Peter. *Administrative Theories and Politics.* 2d ed. London: George Allen & Unwin Ltd., 1977.

Sharkansky, Ira. *Public Administration.* 3rd ed. Chicago: Markham Publishing, 1975.

Simmons, Robert H., and Dvorin, Eugene P. *Public Administration.* Port Washington, N.Y.: Alfred Publishing, 1977.

Simon, Hebert A.; Smithburg, D.W.; and Thompson, V.A. *Public Administration.* New York: Alfred A. Knopf, 1950.

Starling, Grover. *Managing the Public Sector.* Homewood, Ill.: Dorsey Press, 1977.

Stein, Harold. *Public Administration and Policy Development: A Casebook.* New York: Harcourt, Brace, 1952.

Van Riper, Paul P. *History of the United States Civil Service.* Evanston and White Plains: Row, Peterson, 1958.

Waldo, Dwight, ed. *Public Administration in a Time of Turbulence.* Scranton, Pa.: Chandler, 1971.

Waldo, Dwight. *The Administrative State: A Study of the Political Theory of American Public Administration.* New York: Ronald Press, 1948.

Waldo, Dwight. *The Study of Public Administration.* New York: Macmillan, 1955.

White, L.D. *Introduction to the Study of Public Administration.* New York: Macmillan, 1955.

Willoughby, William F. *Principles of Public Administration.* Baltimore: Johns Hopkins Press, 1927.

Wilson, V. Seymour. *Canadian Public Policy and Administration.* Toronto: McGraw-Hill Ryerson, 1981.

Organization Theory

Albrow, Martin. *Bureaucracy.* London: Macmillan, 1970.

Argyris, Chris. *Integrating the Individual and the Organization.* New York: John Wiley & Sons, 1964.

Barnard, C.I. *The Functions of the Executive.* Cambridge, Mass.: Harvard University Press, 1938.

Bennis, Warren G. *Changing Organizations: Essays on the Development and Evolution of Human Organizations.* New York: McGraw-Hill, 1966.

Blau, P.M. *Bureaucracy in Modern Society.* New York: Random House, 1956.

Blau, P.M., and Scott, W.R. *Formal Organizations: A Comparative Approach.* San Francisco: Chandler Publishing, 1962.

Burns, Tom, and Stalker, G.M. *The Management of Innovation.* London: Tavistock Publications, 1961.

Crozier, Michel. *The Bureaucratic Phenomenon.* Chicago: University of Chicago Press, 1964.

Cyert, Richard M., and March, James G. *A Behavioural Theory of the Firm.* Englewood Cliffs, N.J.: Prentice-Hall, 1963.

Downs, Anthony. *Inside Bureaucracy.* Boston: Little, Brown, 1967.

Etzioni, Amitai. *A Comparative Analysis of Complex Organizations.* Glencoe, Ill.: Free Press, 1961.

Fayol, H. *General and Industrial Management.* London: Pitman, 1949.

Fesler, J.W. *Area and Administration.* University, Ala.: University of Alabama Press, 1949.

Follett, Mary Parker. *Dynamic Administration.* New York: Harper & Row, 1941.

George, Claude S., Jr. *The History of Management Thought.* Englewood Cliffs, N.J.: Prentice-Hall, 1968.

Gross, Bertram M. *The Managing of Organizations.* 2 vols. New York: Free Press, 1964.

Gulick, Luther, and Urwick, Lyndall, eds. *Papers on the Science of Administration.* New York: Institute of Public Administration, Columbia University, 1937.

Hummel, Ralph P. *The Bureaucratic Experience.* New York: St. Martin's Press, 1977.

Katz, Daniel, and Kahn, Robert L. *The Social Psychology of Organizations.* New York: John Wiley & Sons, 1966.

Lawrence, Paul, and Lorsch, Jay. *Organizations and Environments.* Cambridge, Mass.: Harvard University Press, 1967.

Likert, Rensis. *New Patterns of Management.* New York: McGraw-Hill, 1961.

Likert, Rensis. *The Human Organization: Its Management and Value.* New York: McGraw-Hill, 1967.

March, James G., ed. *Handbook of Organizations.* Chicago: Rand McNally, 1965.

March, James G., and Simon, Herbert A. *Organizations.* New York: John Wiley & Sons, 1958.

Mayo, Elton. *The Human Problems of an Industrial Civilization.* New York: The Viking Press, 1933.

Merrill, Harwood F. *Classics of Management.* New York: American Management Association, 1960.

Merton, Robert K., ed. *Reader in Bureaucracy.* New York: Free Press, 1953.

Millett, J.D. *Organization for the Public Service.* Princeton, N.J.: D. Van Nostrand Company, 1966.

Perrow, Charles. *Complex Organizations: A Critical Essay.* Glenview, Ill.: Foresman, 1972.

Presthus, Robert. *The Organizational Society: An Analysis and a Theory.* 2d ed. New York: St. Martin's Press, 1978.

Roethlisberger, F.J., and Dickson, William J. *Management and the Worker.* Cambridge, Mass.: Harvard University Press, 1939.

Scott, William G. *Organization Theory, A Behavioral Analysis for Management.* Homewood, Ill.: Richard D. Irwin, 1967.

Simon, Hebert A. *Administrative Behavior: A Study of Decision-Making Processes in Administrative Organization.* 3rd ed. New York: Free Press, 1976.

Taylor, Frederick W. *The Principles of Scientific Management,* 1911. Reprint. New York: Norton, 1967.

Thompson, James D. *Organizations in Action.* New York: McGraw-Hill, 1967.

Thompson, Victor A. *Modern Organization.* New York: Alfred A. Knopf, 1961.

Thompson, Victor A. *Without Sympathy or Enthusiasm: The Problem of Administrative Compassion.* University, Ala.: University of Alabama Press, 1975.

Weber, Max. *From Max Weber: Essays in Sociology.* Edited and translated by H.H. Gerth and C. Wright Mills. New York: Oxford University Press, 1946.

Weber, Max. *The Theory of Social and Economic Organization.* Translated by A.M. Henderson and Talcott Parsons. Fair Lawn, N.J.: Oxford University Press, 1947.

Woll, Peter. *American Bureaucracy.* 2d ed. New York: W.W. Norton, 1977.

Part II

CANADIAN PUBLIC ADMINISTRATION: ENVIRONMENT and FORMAL STRUCTURE

3/Challenge and Response: A Retrospective View of the Public Service of Canada*

J. E. Hodgetts

John Donne's statement that "no man is an island" applies with equal relevance to organizations created by man to serve his needs. Thus the central proposition I hope to demonstrate by this excursion into the past is that our public service has been shaped to the environment in which it has had to operate and that changes in the environment bring about alterations in the public service.

When the Founding Fathers met one hundred years ago they were seeking to grapple with the forces of change then confronting them. The result was a constitutional document that has proven surprisingly durable over the ensuing years. But constitutions are notably rigid, and it has been largely within the public services—local, provincial and federal—that we find the main evidences of adaptation to changing conditions and emergent social needs which have provided the necessary flexibility. I see no evidence for claiming that this administrative adaptation has followed any iron laws of administrative growth. We are here concerned with a most complex set of interacting forces in which the organization acted upon, that is, the public service, is far from passive. While the public service bears the marks of environmental factors that press upon it, society also bears the imprint of the activities and enhanced authority of public servants.

In considering the environmental pressures that have set the goals and moulded the shape of the public service over our first century, we find that some have remained relatively unchanged. These we may describe as the constants, or "the givens," with which the public service must live.

*Reprinted by permission from J.E. Hodgetts, "Challenge and Response: A Retrospective View of the Public Service of Canada," *Canadian Public Administration*, 7, no. 4 (December 1964): 409-421.

They include the pervasive impact of our geographical setting, the constitutional framework, the legal base of administration and the political system. The elements of the environment subject to the greatest change and requiring the greatest flexibility of response from the public service have been economic, technological, cultural and philosophical factors. I should like to show briefly how each of these has contributed to the public service we know today.

The powerful persuasion of geography has been noted by Sir Ernest Barker in his examination of the growth of public services elsewhere. The large Egyptian bureaucracy, for example, he attributed to the Nile and the costly irrigation works required to harness it. England's insular position, on the other hand, delayed the emergence of the large centralized bureaucracies which grew up on the Continent largely to service the needs of standing armies. In Canada, for the better part of its first half century, geography dictated the major goals which the public service was to pursue. The Department of the Interior, the giant amongst early federal departments, was described as late as 1936 as "the barometer of Western conditions." The so-called barometric departments were those concerned with opening up the West, encouraging its population and settlement and providing the water or rail transportation to serve as the linkage for these activities.

Not only did geography dictate the goals, it also imposed the conditions which governed the way in which the tasks of public servants had to be performed. If administrative apoplexy was to be avoided at the centre, public servants had to be widely dispersed: police and protective services, agents for immigration, for colonization and Indian affairs, fisheries overseers, customs collectors, surveyors and construction teams on railways and canals, spread often in isolated places across a continental domain.

New means of communication have alleviated the problems of communication and administration in remote outposts. But the harsh facts of our geography still exact a high price for preserving a union based on an artificial East-West axis against the counterpull of the geographically more natural North-South axis.

Thus, from the outset, geography forced Canada to adapt its services to dispersed operations. The subsequent expansion of welfare and regulatory activities necessitated the continuation of dispersed or area administration, governed now less by the limitations on our means of communications but more by the need to preserve a face-to-face relationship with individual citizens seeking benefits and services. Consequently a physical decentralization of the work force, which took root as a logical response to the challenge of administering across a continent, continues in being as a vital necessity to provide the flexible response to the contemporary state's positive welfare and regulatory functions. Decentralization is now as much dictated by the need to preserve democratic responsiveness of the administrative machine as it is a natural outcome of the original geographic challenge.

It is passing strange that this, perhaps the most obvious feature of our public service, has received so little formal analysis. It is one of a number of areas that warrant fuller discussion and study.

The second constant feature of the environment is the constitutional framework which was evolved one hundred years ago. It is no reflection on the Founding Fathers to claim that a division of labour between provinces and dominion made one hundred years ago is bound to become outmoded. Formal constitutional amendment has been infrequent and judicial interpretation has not always been in conformity with rapid changes in social philosophy, new needs or revolutionary transformations in technology. Flexibility has been provided by the development of what the Rowell-Sirois Commission called "administrative expedients." These have ranged from the sporadic assembling of a diplomatic conference between dominion and provincial leaders, ministerial or official conferences for more limited purposes—often in conjunction with national interest groups (as happened, for example, in the case of labour and agriculture)—formal agreements rather like treaties, joint advisory committees, the use of federal officers to perform provincial tasks (and vice versa), and the employment of federal funds to finance provincial programs.

At the outset, most of these expedients were not developed because potential conflict was restrained by the limited undertakings of public organizations at all levels. Beginning with fisheries and then moving into labour and industrial relations, on to health and welfare and the regulation of interprovincial trade, the respective jurisdictions began to touch, then overlap; inevitably friction was generated. The limitations on and unevenness of provincial revenues required action on a broader front. Thus, throughout the years, one can see the administrative response of the federal public service gathering momentum in distinct stages. First, it began to act as a centralized data-collecting source; from statistics it went on to research; research results required dissemination and so we move to extensive publication (and some would say public relations); next came conditional grants that required "policing" by federal officials; ultimately certain programs came to be operated by the federal government.

Two factors contribute to the perpetuation and even the continued expansion of the federal public service in such areas. First, there is the natural reluctance to dismantle an organization by giving up these programs. The historic rationale has been that the provincial services were less than adequate for the task involved—an estimate that today bears hard critical examination. The other factor has been the inability of the tax-poor provinces to carry the burden of these new services. Once again, I would offer this entire area as a rewarding subject for fresh examination: we need full-scale studies of provincial public services to begin with and of the administrative interrelations that have developed between provincial and federal public departments. Here, we must content ourselves with noting that the cumulative results of these developments have induced the federal government to assume fact-gathering, research, promotional and grant-dispensing responsibilities that are quite different in kind from the more directly program-oriented, operational jobs undertaken by the provinces. At the same time, these activities have introduced in unprecedented numbers new types of professional, scientific and technical personnel into the public service whose problems of adaptation to the traditional hierarchical organization have received far less study than they deserve.

The third fixed element of the environment is the legal foundation for public administration. At Confederation, the tension between executive and legislature built up during the previous period of colonial rule inclined the Canadian Parliament to adopt a more assertive attitude than the British Parliament towards the public service. The British North America Act bears signs of this attitude in the oft-invoked phrase tied to the few sections concerning the disposition of the public service "until the Parliament of Canada [or the provincial legislature] otherwise provides." The fact is that the Parliament of Canada has "otherwise provided" in much more detail than has ever been the case in the United Kingdom, the most outstanding testimonial being the Civil Service Act of 1868, which had its precursors in pre-Confederation times and continues to this day with its counterpart in every province. No such act, significantly, has ever been passed in Britain.

This is not the place to thread my way through a most complex maze. That it *is* a maze, I know, for in a personal effort to explore the legal foundations of public administration I found to my surprise that there were few available guides in this lonely enterprise. I do not propose to inflict the details of my explorations on you but I can at least state the problem and its implications for the public service.

The essential difficulty derives from the union of executive and legislative functions which we have inherited from Britain. That union creates what I might call a legal ambivalence from which it is hard to say whether the public service is directed by sovereign parliament or by the executive. Put in another way, the question is: are public servants employees of Parliament or employees of the executive, standing in the place of the Crown?

That this is not an academic question can be readily demonstrated by indicating the problem of identifying the centres of authority for handling the organization and management of the public service. Parliament clearly must authorize the creation of a department, but the executive determines when the department shall begin to function. Moreover, since a new department involves a money bill and only the executive can initiate such a bill, one must assume that even the major organizational units are dictated by the executive, with rather automatic ratification by Parliament. For more detailed reorganization, Parliament has in effect devolved authority on the executive through the Public Services Rearrangement and Transfer of Duties Act. A glance at the organic acts for each department shows that Parliament has made no effort to bind the executive's hands by stipulating a detailed organizational breakdown. Equally, the day-to-day organization-and-methods work has been left by Parliament entirely to the discretion of departments or to other management bodies.

In the field of management, the dichotomy is much more evident and perplexing. First, there is the question, previously noted, of the apparently dual allegiance of the public servant. For all practical purposes, including appointment, classification, promotion, pay scales and tenure, the civil servant appears to be a servant of the executive (which in practical terms might be logically extended to read a servant of the party in power). In the performance of his functions, he is responsible through the hierarchy to his minister. Yet many members of Parliament, stressing the term "public" in public servant, claim to occupy the role of employer. When at the same time they claim the Public Service Commission as their specially selected agency to perform this function on their behalf, further problems arise. Indeed the Public Service Commission is perhaps the chief victim of this legal dualism, on the one hand being regarded as the peculiar instrument of Parliament in its role of employer but on the other often sharing management functions with executive agencies, such as Treasury Board, which Parliament in its indecision has divided between them.

This commentary on the legal basis of administration could be prolonged but I have perhaps said enough to support the conclusion that because the legal ambivalence of our system has not been confronted head on we have grown into a confused system of divided management responsibilities that is cumbersome to work and difficult to live with.

The fourth and final fixed feature of the environment is our political system or, more accurately, the conventions that have grown up around that system. The three elements of this system that have left the deepest imprints on the public service are the conventions surrounding Cabinet making, the doctrine of ministerial responsibility and, that handmaiden of the party system, patronage.

The well-known convention that cabinets must be so constructed as to represent significant regional, provincial, religious and ethnic groupings in a pluralistic community needs no elaboration. Its implications for the public service, though obvious, have scarcely ever been noted. Even in 1867 a Cabinet of fourteen members was needed to meet all the claims for weighted representation. Critics at the time asked how it was that in the United States as compared to Canada "forty million instead of four were ably governed by an administration of seven members instead of fourteen." But the necessity of securing a representative Cabinet overrode any objections. On the other hand, if the American model did not commend itself, neither did the British system of making a distinction between the Cabinet and the much larger ministry. The Canadian convention, in short, was and continues to be that all ministers should be in the Cabinet.

The rejection of both the American and British models had these consequences: (1) for nearly half a century we were overstocked with departments and the slow accretion of government duties could readily be absorbed within a relatively static group of portfolios; (2) but, when the duties of the state began to mount at an accelerated pace, we were left little room to manoeuvre. If more departments were created to embrace the new tasks and if all ministerial heads by convention had to be in the Cabinet, that body would soon reach an unmanageable size. The alternative was to create a variety of nondepartmental entities to undertake the newer tasks. The generous provision of departmental portfolios and their extremely elastic bounds enabled us to absorb a great deal of this expansion and necessitated surprisingly few additions to the original departmental roster. But it has meant that some departments have come to embrace a variety of ill-assorted functions simply as a means of housing what otherwise might become administrative orphans. The consequent problems of coordination through the Cabinet and other centralized agencies have been acute.

The practical restrictions on the number of departmental portfolios also account in part for the profusion and variety of nondepartmental entities. The effort to seat them comfortably within the traditional framework of ministerial responsibility has led to an incoherent "second" public service that represents a piecemeal, haphazard response to the growing burden of state activities, even as it confuses the legislator and general citizen.

Indeed, the doctrine of ministerial responsibility is the second feature of the political setting whose implications for the public service need brief elaboration. The principle not only establishes a bridge across which most of the traffic between Parliament and the public service is routed but, applied collectively to the Cabinet, it ensures a unity of purpose and a coordination of direction at the top. Parliament benefits by being able to home in on one identifiable target; the public servant benefits because he does not have to debate publicly any challenge of his political overlords. His anonymity preserves the constitutional fiction of his political noncommitment and thus ensures his permanency in office whenever there is a change in the governing political party.

The benefits of the doctrine are obvious and desirable but a literal application in today's enlarged public service poses an impossible burden on the minister. This was recognized on the administrative side at the very beginning by giving the minister a permanent deputy and on the legislative side, but much more recently, by giving him a parliamentary secretary. But the fact remains that there have been constant pressures that force the minister into a "managing" rather than a "directing" role, thereby compelling ministers in both their individual and collective capacities, to concern themselves with too much detail, at the expense of general coordinating and policy-making functions. The convention that the Cabinet provides regional representation makes sense only if most matters are brought before Cabinet. Thus, in contrast to England where statutes generally confer authority on individual ministers, in Canada they more commonly confer powers on the governor-in-council, that is, ministers in their collective capacity. If to this we add the historic reliance on patronage, we can see why ministers have been unable to extricate themselves from direct involvement in the details of management. Sir George Murray's succinct epitaph (written in 1912) accurately described a predicament that certainly existed until 1939. "Ministers," he concluded, "both have too much to do and try to do too much."

The significance of patronage, the third element of the political system to be examined here, is that the measures taken to eradicate it have left an enduring mark on the public service. A formal self-denying ordinance is necessary, at some time or another, if patronage is to be eliminated. In Britain, this was done by executive decree but in Canada, as has been noted, by statute, authorizing a Civil Service Commission to institute a rigorous regimen of controls. Over time the desired result was achieved of preventing the unfit from gaining admission to the public service; but for many years this negative approach dominated to the exclusion of more positive measures required to attract the best candidates available. The Civil Service Commission was given additional and comprehensive authority over most of the personnel management field. Thus the orientation toward control, generated by its primary function as patronage eliminator, tended (so to speak) to rub off on to the other management responsibilities that demanded a more positive, service-minded approach.

A somewhat parallel development occurred in the field of expenditure control in an effort to prevent speculation and patronage. When the Glassco Commission came to examine this situation, it found that departmental managers' had been caught in the pincers of centralized agencies and have had to operate in that atmosphere of distrust which had been responsible in the first place for the imposition of such controls. It was the thesis of the Glassco Commission that, while the system had been a legitimate and logical response to the evils of patronage and dishonesty, the departments were, in the vernacular, "big boys now" and should be put more on their own mettle. The readjustments required to meet this thesis will make heavier calls on the initiative and ability of departmental managers and will require centralized agencies to think less in terms of negative control and more in positive terms of guidance, service and setting standards for the departments.

I may remind you at this stage that I distinguished at the beginning between the constant and variable elements of the environment that have helped mould our public service. Having touched on the constants, let me now turn to the variables, beginning with the economic setting.

Economic historians have familiarized us with the importance of staple products to Canada's economic growth and well-being. The characteristic features of staples such as fish, fur, timber, minerals, wheat and pulpwood is that they are all extractive enterprises, based on the exploitation of a great wealth in natural resources requiring bulk transportation and access to markets abroad. Neither the exploitation, transportation or marketing of these staples has taken place within an Adam Smith type of economy. Government has been heavily committed from the outset to mapping out and making inventory of these resources; it has been deeply engaged as regulator, constructor and operator of transport systems by water, rail and air; it moved early into promotional activities—the first trade commissioner dates back to the 1880s as does the first agricultural research station—and only slightly later do we find such services as forecasting facilities. Governments have engineered the formation of economic interest groups such as the livestock producers and the pulpwood producers—presumably the better to deal with them. Today the major concern of at least one-third of our federal departments is still with problems associated with the production, conservation, and transportation of, and the trade in, our main staple products.

This clear-cut identification of the departments with staple products is only one example—though a most persistent one—of how the unique features of the Canadian economy have shaped the public service. As government has more and more been drawn into an operating and regulatory role, we find that the new responsibilities have largely devolved on nondepartmental agencies. A point has now been reached where the number of people employed in these sectors of the public service is nearly as large as the number employed in the departmental system proper. It is not surprising that, in devising nondepartmental forms, governments have looked to the private industrial or commercial concerns for their models. We are still struggling to find a solution to the problems of grafting the consequent collection of heterogeneous administrative entities onto the conventional departmental system with its tradition of ministerial responsibility. We are also still seeking for ways to bridge the gap between the personnel in the public service proper and in the other portion excluded from it, to the end that there may be truly *one* public service. In short, the mixed economy, with its avoidance of outright governmental monopoly and its favouring of a system of economic parallelism in transport, communication and finance, has produced a corresponding organizational "mix" in the public service itself.

Nor does the impact of the world of private economic organization end here. It finds expression in a pervasive assumption that only a "businessman's approach" to the public service can produce efficiency. We find early expression of this philosophy in the attempt to levy appropriate charges for the services that governments provide specific groups of beneficiaries. And, in the report of the Glassco Commission, dozens of such services have been identified, accompanied by evidence that some pay their way, others are given free, some make a profit, others lose money. The royal commission's reminder that we need to set this part of our administrative house in order is merely a reiteration of the old plea to inject sound business principles into public administration. The commission's recommendation that many of these services might well be contracted out to private concerns is not so much a free enterpriser's special pleading but a legitimate concern to help public organizations keep their attention focused on their main job, subject to as few peripheral distractions as possible.

The major impact of the businessman's approach is to be found in the contemporary reliance on private management consultant firms that are refinements on the early school of efficiency experts nourished at the beginning of this century by Taylor and his followers. We owe to this school the detailed classification plans which were inaugurated after World War I in the civil service. The modern consultant is in the main an offshoot of the accountant, though his advice now ranges from financial and accounting practices through paperwork and systems analyses to feasibility studies on computers. His main customer is government and one of his most lasting marks will be found in the reports of the Glassco Commission. We find here the accountant's concern for identifying "real" costs; the businessman's concern for relating revenues from services to the costs of providing them; the need to import the new techniques of systems analysis that have proven effective in private business. In brief, there is the assumption that the differences between private and public organization are not so substantial that practices proven successful in the private realm cannot be applied with equal effectiveness to the public organization. This is an assumption that in my view must constantly be tempered by the other environmental factors I have been discussing and to which private organizations need pay much less attention.

Turning from the economic setting to the impact of changing technology on the public service, we find a two-edged situation. In the broadest sense, changing techniques affect the substance of administrative activity—they alter the things that have to be done by administrators, by inducing the state either itself to sponsor the development of the techniques or else to grapple with the social and other problems posed by their widespread adoption. In the narrower sense, new techniques influence administrative procedures. We live in an age of gadgetry and public servants are no more immune to the charm of applying gadgets to their daily labours than are others in private organizations.

The Canadian public service has grown up during a century in which there have been more technological innovations than in all of man's past history. It was born in the steamboat and railway age, witnessed the emergence of telegraph and telephone, saw the origin and full onslaught of the internal combustion engine and, while still adjusting to these developments, has had to make its peace with the air age, the electronics revolution, the atom, and now outer space.

The incredible fertility of man, the innovating engineer and scientist, has left man, the social scientist, staggering for breath. The steamboat and railway brought the state into the centre of activity as owner, maintenance man and operator or regulator. The automobile age has left its most indelible imprint on provincial and local public services, as they have had to grapple with highway construction, traffic regulations and all the social and economic problems of urban concentration that have sprung up in the wake of the automobile.

Jurisdiction over the air for transportation and communication purposes was settled in favour of the federal government in 1932 and the stage was set for a fresh crop of agencies and further adaptation of the public service to meet the challenges. From virtual monopolies of national services, designed to pioneer in these new fields, the state has gradually permitted the private sector to emerge as a full partner. Similarly, in responding to the nuclear revolution, the state has harnessed the conventional component by regulatory action but has assumed, itself, nearly the full burden of research and development. With the largest research resources and establishments in the country, the federal government's relationship with universities and the increasing importance of science in government now raise problems that we are only beginning to assess, let alone solve.

One should also observe that many technological changes have affected the means of communication and transportation. These have required such substantial capital investment that the state has had to become an active participant as developer and owner. The consequent fostering of an interdependent economy brought new regulatory problems, most of which had to be met on a national front. Worldwide application of these techniques has shrunk the world and produced further problems of international trade and communication that also fall naturally on the shoulders of the federal government.

Apart from these broad repercussions of technological change, there are also the products which derive from the new technology and affect the procedures of the public service. One of the most important consequences of the age of gadgets is the ease with which paper can now be created and the resulting problems of record keeping, storage, filing and so on. Historically, the mechanics of paper management were characterized unflatteringly but accurately as the "donkey work" in the civil service. (There is more than a shadow of home truth in the classification of the first females in the British public service as "female typewriters.") Yet, as the Glassco Commission has emphasized, the new gadgets and procedures necessitate an upgrading of those concerned with the management of paper if the government is not, like the sorcerer's apprentice, to be drowned in a flood of its own creation. At this point we can confidently coin a neo-Parkinsonian Law: *the quantity of paper will rise to meet the capacity of the machines available for processing it.* It is still difficult to know how the electronics revolution will affect an organization where there is so much routine repetitive work that lends itself to automation. At the least, its wide-scale application will necessitate major retraining programs.

The high costs of the more versatile automatic data-processing equipment imply that the new technology may force a reversal of the traditional pattern of dispersed and decentralized operations as work gets concentrated in a few large electronic machine shops. On the other hand, it may well be that centralized processing is quite compatible with—indeed, a genuine encouragement to—more effective decentralization, because the new machines can improve reporting and control techniques. It would be pure speculation to carry this line of inquiry further, but now we are in the throes of numbering the nation, it may not be too unrealistic to visualize our master cards going into the computer and slipping us anything from a birth certificate to an old age pension, a request for payment of back taxes to a passport. At the best we should see improved, though depersonalized, service to the public and the collation of new masses of data from which our social planners in the future should be able to make more confident and accurate predictions.

From this Orwellian world that is less fantastic than it seemed less than a decade ago, let us turn to the cultural setting. Canada is a middle power both in the figurative and literal sense, geographically positioned next door to the United States and still bound by tradition and sentiment to England. At good neighbour rallies, we extol the virtues of our undefended frontier, which on closer inspection is seen to bristle with defences, most of them of the Canadian government's own making. Tariffs and the all-Canadian railway were but the precursors of a host of other expressions of the do-it-yourself philosophy inspired by national pride and a reluctance to be beholden to our more powerful neighbour. The airplane and radio brought government monopolies as chosen instruments of national policy. The Canada Council was a far too modest answer to the American foundations; the proposal to redirect the Canadian advertisers' dollars to Canadian publications and the BBG's prescription of a fifty-five per cent quota of "Canadian content" for broadcasting are all evidences of the same spirit.

If a number of the federal government's most important cultural activities have evolved in response to our defensive posture toward United States cultural penetration, it is equally true that the organization of the public service itself bears marks of our constant borrowing. Here, however, we have tended to gyrate between American practice and British tradition. Our Public Service Employment Act and the Public Service Commission are more American than British in conception, intent and in the powers conferred; so, too, is our classification system. Our attempts to create a cadre of senior administrative officers and the abortive reports of such royal commissions as the Murray and Gordon Commissions show much clearer traces of the British pattern. The most recent reports from the Glassco Commission are an interesting amalgam of American management practices and British institutional devices, both adapted to the Canadian setting.

Apart from the significant and continuing pressure from these external cultural influences, the Canadian public service has to face a unique indigenous cultural factor—the principle of bilingualism enshrined in the B.N.A. Act. The hyphenated premierships, the double-barrelled ministries and, more particularly, the rotating capitals that characterized the pre-Confederation public service reveal that the bicultural nature of the earlier union gave much blunter expression than we have since given to the concept. For nearly a century the federal public service has shown at times even a deliberate disregard of this cultural fact of life and is now an obvious target for the moderate nationalist as well as the extremist in French-speaking Canada. The problem goes deeper than a mere recognition of two official languages, for it extends to the whole cultural context and will not be easily ameliorated by well-intended gestures on the part of English-speaking groups. The situation is probably most acute at headquarters, particularly at the senior officer level. Working within an essentially unilingual communication system, bilingualism becomes a one-way street where the only person who needs to be bilingual is the French-speaking officer. That he is called upon to make his home in an alien cultural environment only adds to the difficulties. With the rapid industrialization and bureaucratization of the Province of Quebec, the opportunities for advancement in executive ranks are so enhanced that it will probably be increasingly difficult to make the Ottawa service attractive to French-speaking recruits. On the other hand, Canada, as an officially bilingual country, has a potentially important contribution to make in fulfilling obligations to the international community. This fact by itself should be additional incentive to mount a more effective campaign to bring the federal public service into line with the realities of its long and much neglected bicultural tradition.

I close with a brief reference to what might be called the philosophical pressures that have shaped the public service. I am referring here to the familiar transition from a laissez-faire to a collectivist philosophy which is a worldwide phenomenon. The repercussions on the public service have been obvious. The new expectations and demands for broader and better services have led to an enormous growth in the number of public servants and an increasing complexity and variety of administrative organizations. It is an expansion shared by all levels of government and by no means confined to the federal public service. The vast expansion in the scale of operations means that more and more attention must be devoted to the auxiliary or housekeeping services that exist simply to look after the "care and feeding" of the public bureaucracy. Problems of internal management, as the Glassco Commission reveals, assume much more significant proportions and older techniques of centralized control prove incapable of coping with the new situations or else, in trying to cope, bring irritation and frustration in their wake. Public services geared to a slower, steadier breathing rhythm find that each day now brings what appears to be a new crisis, until the realization dawns that these are not crises, but part of the speeded-up rhythm of our lives. No organization, let alone any public official, can cope for long with crisis administration unless interested in abnormal psychology and ready to become a patient of the psychiatrist. Current preoccupation with planning evidences an effort to meet the new problems of administrative change not on a crisis basis but as part of normal administrative life.

The collectivist philosophy has changed the scale, the pace, the very tone of administration. These are problems of which the working civil servant is aware. The general public probably goes on believing in its old stereotype of the public servant who, like the fountains in Trafalgar Square, "plays from ten until four." And it is the response of the general public that brings me to my final point. The shift from laissez-faire to collectivism has been accompanied by an unprecedented shift in the balance of real power, discretion and initiative—away from courts, legislatures and even cabinets to public servants. The shift is inescapable and necessary but the public cannot be blamed for suspecting that the "faceless" men, the establishment, the mandarins or what you will are up to no good, that their rights are being invaded even as they are ostensibly being served by public employees. It is from this sense of unease that the proposals for an ombudsman, a public defender, emanate.

I have, perforce, had to use the technique of the quick-sketch artist to present this hasty, episodic perspective on our developing public services. I trust that if you stand far enough back the likeness is reasonably accurate in its general outlines and focus, even if many of the details need much more amplification, qualification or clarification.

4/The Executive and the Departmental Structure*
A. M. Willms

The Executive

Cabinet ministers in Canada bear extremely heavy responsibilities both as members of Parliament and as the top executives of government departments. Although the legislative and executive roles of ministers overlap, attention will be focused here on their executive functions as members of the Cabinet and heads of administrative departments.

The executive tasks of ministers have been well stated by the Glassco Commission:

> . . . ministers need not be administrative experts; on the contrary, it is desirable save in the stress of emergencies, that they do not become deeply involved in the administrative process. As members of the Cabinet, their principal obligation is to reflect and give effect to the collective point of view—drawing together the public interests, attitudes and aspirations that find expression in the political process, and, by reconciling these, providing the basis for an essential unity of government in policy and action. As heads of departments, it is the task of ministers to define the ends to be pursued, and to instill their own sense of purpose and of urgency in the permanent officials.[1]

For each government department there is a Cabinet minister who takes full responsibility for its actions and who is credited with its achievements. Each minister is responsible to Parliament for the operation of his department and by convention the act of every public servant in the department is regarded as the act of the minister. The extent to which a minister can in fact be held accountable for the maladministration of his departmental subordinates is not clear. In practice, a minister's

---

*For other articles on the executive in this book, see William A. Matheson, "The Cabinet and the Canadian Bureaucracy," and Privy Council Office, "The Policy and Expenditure Management System."

[1]*Royal Commission on Government Organization*, vol. 5 (Ottawa: Queen's Printer, 1963), p. 33.

survival in such circumstances depends largely on his influence within his party and whether the party feels it can face criticism of its administration without being defeated in Parliament or at the next election.

The Canadian Cabinet tends to be excessively large in membership because the prime minister traditionally appoints ministers to meet the demands for representation of provinces and regions and of ethnic, linguistic and religious groups. Clearly, the prime minister must take account of such a crucial political consideration despite possible adverse effects on the fulfillment of administrative needs. Canada now has twenty-five federal departments and about four times as many agencies. The number and diversity of these administrative units creates a span of control that is far too wide for a Cabinet which has onerous political and constitutional responsibilities. The Glassco Commission, however, recognized the primacy of political factors over administrative interests in organizing the executive structure of government.

> Above all, the organization of government, no less than the policies it pursues, must reflect the order of importance, in the minds of the public, of the problems requiring attention. Unless there is, in rough form, this correlation between the content of ministerial posts and the degree of public concern, government policy and action will almost certainly fail to respond adequately to public wants.[2]

Indeed, new departments or agencies may have to be established to emphasize or point up a new government policy. It may not be sufficient merely to enunciate new functions and allot these to an existing department or agency. To give these government activities prominence in the public mind another administrative unit may have to be created. The establishment of Central Mortgage and Housing Corporation immediately after the war and of the Department of Consumer and Corporate Affairs in 1967 are striking examples of this need. Since it is very difficult to dissolve a governmental unit once it has been set up, the number of units tends to increase.

A good case can be made on administrative-managerial grounds for fewer, more uniform, and necessarily larger administrative units. The following comments pertain specifically to departments although they are generally applicable to government agencies also. The overhead cost for adequate departmental services in small units may be disproportionately large, and the provision of such services as organization and methods or research and development may not be warranted. In addition, the existence of larger departments permits much more coherent government planning. Central control agencies such as the Treasury Board and the Public Service Commission can more readily stay out of

---

[2]*Royal Commission on Government Organization*, pp. 41-42.

planning when the allocation of scarce resources can be thrashed out in a few large departments. For example, if all the labour functions, including unemployment insurance, were centred in one department, the Treasury Board would be less concerned with the proportion of funds that should go to each of the various governmental units in the labour field. Larger departments also provide a wider field of training, development and advancement for capable junior and intermediate staff. The advantages of specialization can best be realized in larger departments, whether in the line functions, the staff functions or the departmental services. A substantial measure of decentralization is almost inevitable in larger departments and with fewer, but more comprehensive field offices, the government can expect greater effectiveness with smaller overhead costs. Moreover, in a federal state many government activities require consultation and coordination between provincial and federal administrators; fewer and larger departments would make such cooperation easier.

There are, however, persuasive arguments for a large number of smaller departments. Individual ministers and deputy ministers can handle a small department more effectively than a large department. This is not so much a factor of size in manpower or budget as of political sensitivity and diversity of functions. The more sensitive the departmental functions in the political-social-economic atmosphere of the day, the more care must be given to policy decisions and the more skill must be employed in representing the department to the Cabinet, Parliament and the public. The more diverse the functions, the more overall policies must be coordinated by the man who must answer to Parliament for their implementation.

Instead of decreasing the size of any department, perhaps the functions of government could be redistributed so that similar functions would come under one responsibility and the diversity of some of the larger departments would be decreased. Such a reallocation could actually reduce the number of departments.

Departmental Structure

In general, the structure of departments resembles the normal scalar pyramid of private or corporate enterprise. At the top is the deputy minister who is the administrative head of the department and at the bottom are the numerous employees who actually carry out most of the functions of the department. In between are the various levels of supervision, management and specialization which make up the pyramidal structure. There is some uniformity in the terminology used to describe departmental organization at or near the pyramid's peak. The deputy minister or deputy head is at the pinnacle; below him there are assistant deputy ministers or, in a few instances, associate deputy ministers. Below the assistant deputy minister in the departmental pyramid are the branch heads who are usually called directors or directors-general. The branches are often further subdivided into divisions with directors or chiefs in charge. The divisions are subdivided in turn into what may be called sections, units, groups, services, staff, offices or detachments, and the head of each may carry any one of a great variety of titles.

The deputy minister often has a staff to assist him in his management of the department and he may also retain direct control of one or several of the branches or of the administrative services. Sometimes the deputy minister has a government agency reporting to him. Thus the deputy minister of agriculture has the Agricultural Stabilization Board and the Board of Grain Commissioners reporting to him. The span of control of a deputy minister may cover anywhere from two or three to twelve or more subordinates. Most departments have only four or five assistant deputy ministers. As the size of the departments increases, this number tends to grow.

The planning and organization of an individual department's internal structure requires a different approach from that which is taken in dividing up the functions of government between departments and agencies. The different approaches reflect the different objectives involved. In the division of the total functions of government among administrative units, the primary aim is to allot functions to a structure that satisfies political and public needs. Although the aim of the internal organization of a department or agency is to carry out the assigned functions as efficiently and effectively as possible, the minister's political and constitutional role remains an important determinant of the final structure. An organization plan should:

1. Recognize the division of powers between the federal and provincial governments; in sensitive areas of jurisdiction even the appearance of federal overlapping into provincial fields must be avoided unless government policy on the subject is clear.
2. Recognize that the government exists to serve the people; recommendations that are administratively sound must also be acceptable to the segment of the population the agency has been set up to serve. In field organizations, in particular, it is sometimes necessary to modify organization principles to meet such a situation and to provide for local requirements.
3. Recognize that the minister concerned is one member of the Cabinet and that the functions of the agency, including the funds necessary for carrying them out, are often subject to balancing mechanisms within the Cabinet which supersede purely administrative considerations. Recommendations which propose the extension of an agency's functions into areas where other

agencies have an interest, for instance, should be made only after the most careful exploration with the agencies concerned.[3]

In planning the department's structure, an initial decision must be made as to whether the parts of the department will be organized according to the criteria of purpose, process, clientele or area. In the past, the factor of purpose (or function) has probably been given too much prominence in the building of branches, divisions and sections of departments. It is unwise to assume that if purpose is used to allocate the job to the department that it can also be used consistently in designing the whole departmental structure. It is often quite undesirable to emphasize the purpose factor within the department because:

1. Design of departmental branches or divisions by purpose often results in too much emphasis in each branch or division on a small part of the department's overall functions; there may be too much concern for the parts and not enough for the final product.

2. Subdivision by purpose leaves little scope for competition between units which is an effective form of setting work standards and motivating units and employees.

3. Specialization by purpose can lead to overspecialization with attendant difficulties in effective employee development.

There probably isn't a department or an agency that does not use all four organization factors in one way or another. It is the manager's responsibility to choose the factor or factors applicable and to decide to what extent each is necessary. In this decision consistency appears to have little virtue and the manager may combine the use of several or all of the factors as circumstances dictate.

---

[3]Civil Service Commission, *The Analysis of Organization in the Government of Canada* (Ottawa: Queen's Printer, 1964), pp. 13-14.

5/Central Agencies in Canada*

Colin Campbell, S.J.

In Canada one often hears criticisms of efforts to upgrade machinery and staffs performing central public service coordination and control functions.[1] Some observers fear that upgrading central agencies simply concentrates power in the hands of the prime minister so as to jeopardize individual ministerial responsibility for what goes on in departments and collective responsibility for what is decided by Cabinet.[2]

This essay maintains that many such concerns overlook a more profound phenomenon which has shown itself in several liberal democracies. Specifically, political executives require elaborate machinery and large staffs devoted to coordination and control just to get on with the job of governing. Yet development of machinery and staffs to handle the workload fuels fears among other players in the political system, be they career bureaucrats in operational departments, legislators or members of the attentive public, that too much power is gravitating to a few political and bureaucratic officials. Canadians, for instance, often accuse Pierre Elliott Trudeau of "presidentializing" the federal government. Many of the changes he has introduced, however, have their origins in the statutory and conventional authority of the Canadian prime ministership.[3] Further, they follow in many respects the principles of modern management sciences.[4] Thus the first basis for Trudeau's heightening prime ministerial power relates to the Canadian constitutional tradition. The second relates to modern decision technology which, although

---

*This essay is based in part on a more extensive essay entitled "Political Leadership in Canada: Pierre Elliott Trudeau and the Ottawa Model," in *Presidents and Prime Ministers*, ed. Richard Rose and Ezra N. Suleiman (Washington, D.C.: Enterprise Institute, 1980), pp. 50-93.

[1]See Thomas A. Hockin, ed., *Apex of Power: The Prime Minister and Political Leadership in Canada*, 2d ed. (Toronto: Prentice-Hall, 1977), esp. pp. 308-343. Hugh Heclo and Aaron Wildavsky, *The Private Government of Public Money: Community and Policy Inside British Politics* (Berkeley: University of California Press, 1974), discusses the pitfalls involved in viewing the prime ministership as presidential. See pp. 367-368.

[2]For a very helpful treatment of ministerial responsibility as applied to officials see Kenneth Kernaghan, "Power, Parliament and Public Servants in Canada: Ministerial Responsibility Re-examined," in *Parliament, Policy and Representation*, ed. Harold D. Clarke *et al.* (Toronto: Methuen, 1980), pp. 124-144.

[3]Colin Campbell, S.J., "Political Leadership in Canada: Pierre Elliott Trudeau and the Ottawa Model," in *Presidents and Prime Ministers*, ed. Richard Rose and Ezra Suleiman (Washington: American Enterprise Institute, 1980), pp. 50-93.

[4]George J. Szablowski, "The Optimal Policy-Making System: Implications for the Canadian Political Process," and Laurent Dobuzinskis, "Rational Policy-Making: Policy, Politics, and Political Science," in Hockin, pp. 197-210 and pp. 211-228, respectively; and Richard D. French, *How Ottawa Decides: Planning and Industrial Policy-Making 1968-1980* (Toronto: Lorimer, 1980).

highly developed in the United States, has origins and applications which transcend national boundaries. Thus it appears that use of the term *presidentialization* reflects in part a tendency among Canadians to label as "American" aspects of modern society that they do not like.

It is notable also that Canadian observers tend to exaggerate the resources available to presidents while understating the machinery and staffs available to prime ministers. In fact, the Canadian Cabinet decides all important matters through a hierarchical process of committee review. Here the prime minister always stands at the apex by virtue of his chairmanship of the crucial committees and of Cabinet itself. In interviews, central agency officials often assert that "we run a very lean shop here, certainly nothing like what is available in Washington." Such statements reflect profound distortions of the reality. In 1981, Canada's central agencies, which in this essay include the Privy Council Office, the Federal-Provincial Relations Office, the Ministries of State for Economic Development and Social Development, the Treasury Board Secretariat, the Office of the Comptroller General and the Department of Finance, together house close to 2300 officials, including over 200 senior executives receiving salaries between $43 300 and $93 600.

A detailed look at the resources of comparable central agencies in Canada and the United States refutes claims of lean resources in Canada. Canada's Privy Council Office (which includes, for accounting purposes, the Prime Minister's Office, the Privy Council Office and the Federal-Provincial Relations Office) and the Ministries of State for Economic Development and Social Development perform functions comparable to the United States White House Office, Special Assistance [of the Vice-President] to the President, the Council of Economic Advisers, the Policy Development Office, the National Security Council Staff and the Office of Administration (the latter simply provides some staffing and services to the others). The Treasury Board Secretariat and the Office of Comptroller General cover essentially the same matters as the Office of Management and Budget. The Department of Finance handles the same area as the Office of the Secretary in the Treasury Department. Canadian central agencies operating in each of these three functional areas tap dollar resources somewhat more than half those available to their United States counterparts. The United States agencies in general maintain larger complements of senior executives but, taken together, the Treasury Board Secretariat (TBS) and the Office of the Comptroller General (OCG) enjoy considerably more staff than does the Office of Management and Budget (OMB). Moreover, top career public servants in the United States earned a maximum in 1981 of $50 112 (U.S.). Thus the relatively high salary range for top officials in Canada suggests that, in dollar terms, the two countries devote comparable resources to central agency senior executives. Obviously, Canadian central agency resources far exceed the one-tenth of the United States figures which we might expect on the basis of the population of the two countries and, for that matter, on the basis of their annual expenditure budgets. We shall now examine the organization and functions of Canada's central agencies.

Serving the Prime Minister

As a result of the many functions the prime minister performs, he receives countless letters, documents, requests for appointments, telephone calls and invitations which add to the pressures on his time. He needs a large staff to assist in "squeezing forty-eight hours out of the P.M.'s average day"[5] and to assure that he is adequately briefed at all times. For this he calls primarily on *the Prime Minister's Office* (PMO), *the Privy Council Office* (PCO) and *the Federal-Provincial Relations Office* (FPRO).

Under Trudeau, *the Prime Minister's Office* houses a staff of close to a hundred, only thirty of whom are professionals. Many of the members, and certainly most of the professionals, are exempt staff—that is, political appointees who do not belong to the permanent public service. At the best of times, PMO is a loosely differentiated cluster of functions rather than a hierarchical organization. The principal secretary, who heads PMO and reports exclusively to the prime minister, is always a trusted partisan figure. The agency has employed policy advisers other than the principal secretary, and they, too, have reported directly to the prime minister. Among these, Ivan Head, who served as international relations adviser from 1970 to 1978, is the only such official who gained prominence in the Ottawa policy arena over a long period. During his tenure, Head usually exerted more influence on Canadian foreign policy than the incumbent secretary of state for external affairs.

On the domestic side, the policy unit set up in 1974 achieved the greatest power. The unit attempted to give organized and comprehensive advice to the prime minister on all major issues. This task proved too vast for the small staff of four professionals with relatively little experience on the Ottawa scene, and the unit disbanded in 1976 to be replaced by four assistant principal secretaries technically responsible for policy advice. In practice, the four officials focused on "desk work," that is, prodding ministers' activities on behalf of the party in various regions, monitoring the general political situation in these areas, and handling interest group consultations. Since Trudeau's return to office in 1980, only one senior policy adviser has operated out of PMO.

Officials in PMO also manage Trudeau's schedule. The executive assistant controls commitments of the prime minister's time, including those made to the PMO staff. A large Nominations Division handles the

[5]Colin Campbell and George J. Szablowski, *The Superbureaucrats: Structure and Behaviour in Central Agencies* (Toronto: Macmillan, 1979), p. 60.

hundreds of recommendations for political appointments which each year come to the prime minister. It also advises on the political implications of appointments to the higher echelons of the career public service. A special adviser on communications, assisted by a press secretary and several more professionals, attempts to manage the prime minister's media image and relations. Finally, the largest unit in PMO is directed by a correspondence coordinator and is responsible for answering the voluminous mail addressed to the prime minister.

Trudeau, in fact, receives most of his policy advice from career public servants in *the Privy Council Office* (PCO) and *the Federal-Provincial Relations Office* (FPRO). The head of PCO, whose formal title is clerk of the Privy Council and secretary to the Cabinet, occupies the most vital post in the public service. Strictly speaking, PCO is a Cabinet secretariat. In addition, it houses substantial advisory units with special responsibilities for briefing the prime minister. Technically, these units report to the clerk of the Privy Council or to one of his deputies, but actually their briefing material is channelled in written form through the clerk of the Privy Council or the associate secretary to the prime minister, or is presented personally.

The advisory units, or secretariats, are of four types. The first is fashioned as part of the clerk of the Privy Council's staff and includes Security and Intelligence, Emergency Planning, and Labour Relations. Security and Intelligence has attained notoriety. As part of its daily routine, the secretariat, which by PCO standards is extremely well manned (nine professionals), processes and analyzes centrally reports from all other government intelligence units. In the later 1970s, the suspicion developed that the unit has served as a Canadian counterpart, albeit in-house, of Richard M. Nixon's "Committee to Reelect the President" of Watergate fame. Testimony before the Commission of Inquiry Concerning Certain Activities of the Royal Canadian Mounted Police had implicated the secretariat as a conduit for illegally gathered intelligence from the RCMP to the Cabinet.

A second type of PCO secretariat reports formally to the deputy secretary of the Cabinet (operations). The assistant secretaries in this division, along with four to six other professionals who report to each assistant secretary, serve Cabinet committees covering "envelopes"[6] of government programs. Here assistant secretaries have two sets of staff responsibilities: those related to the operations of their committee, and those involving briefing the deputy secretary, the associate secretary, the clerk of the Privy Council and the prime minister on committee issues. The latter responsibility hinges on an important procedural fact: the

---

[6]See Privy Council Office, "The Policy and Expenditure Management System," in this book at p. 177.

deputy secretary (operations) serves as the clerk of the Privy Council's principal lieutenant in providing policy advice to the prime minister on issues currently before subject-matter Cabinet committees, and determining which items among those that must be settled by the entire Cabinet will get on the agenda for a given week. Under both Trudeau and Clark, the deputy secretary has become so integral to the day-to-day management of government affairs that he joins the clerk of the Privy Council, the associate secretary and top PMO staff each morning at 9:30 to brief the prime minister personally on matters requiring immediate attention and those on the Cabinet agenda. By virtue of the deputy secretary's role in the inner circle, assistant secretaries frequently gain access to the prime minister for further background briefing. Sufficient privileged intimacy of this type can lead to an assistant secretary's gaining direct access to the prime minister, thereby enhancing his opportunities for advancement.

A third type of PCO secretariat reports formally to the deputy secretary of the Cabinet (plans). Five units fall within this category. Two serve the prime minister in his capacity as chairman of the Priorities and Planning Committee (called the Inner Cabinet under Clark) and three serve the president of the Privy Council (a Cabinet minister) in his capacity as chairman of the Legislation and House Planning Committee. The Priorities and Planning unit, headed by an assistant secretary, works through the deputy secretary (plans) to the prime minister. Between 1976 and 1979, this unit, along with the now defunct Planning Projects unit, turned its attention to issues that had to be settled within a relatively short term for the government to regain credibility. The fact that the Planning Projects unit commissioned an exhaustive study of trends in public opinion about a host of policy issues reflects both the survival orientation of the last three years of the 1974-1979 Trudeau government and a much greater politicization of a career public service unit than even the most attentive watchers of PCO suspected at the time.

The three units working through the deputy secretary (plans) to the president of the Privy Council—that is, Legislation and House Planning, Orders-in-Council and the Office of the Legal Adviser—advise largely on procedural and tactical matters. These include guiding government bills through Parliament, processing orders-in-council, and assuring that government bills are consistent both with the original policy intentions of the Cabinet and with existing statutes. The first of these units is the only one likely to merit the direct involvement of the prime minister. A great stir arose in 1980 when a memo from this unit outlining tactics for the forthcoming parliamentary session, including passage of the joint resolution on patriating of the B.N.A. Act, leaked to the press.

Finally, three units comprise the fourth type of secretariat. These units serve the prime minister as the chief executive authority for machinery of government, senior personnel and communications. Their location in PCO reflects the importance Trudeau ascribes to major reorganizational and jurisdictional issues in the public service, the development and selection of senior career officials, and the need to monitor the release of government documents. Two units, under the director for machinery of government and the assistant secretary for communications, report directly to the associate secretary to the Cabinet in his capacity as the principal adviser of the prime minister on these matters.

The Federal-Provincial Relations Office (FPRO) evolved in 1975 from a secretariat of PCO. After the November 15, 1976 separatist victory in Quebec, the Cabinet Committee on Federal-Provincial Relations, which was originally served by FPRO, merged with the Priorities and Planning Committee, thereby adding to the seemingly contrived distinction between PCO and FPRO. Whether or not this distinction was contrived, the organizational differentiation of PCO and FPRO provided a framework for the further proliferation of units headed by officials at the assistant deputy minister level or higher with personal briefing responsibilities to the prime minister. Under the current Trudeau government, FPRO, headed by the secretary to the Cabinet for federal-provincial relations, has been streamlined into four units covering strategic planning, liaison, social policy and programs, and economic policy and programs. These units vary in size from four to thirteen professionals and each unit is headed by an assistant secretary.

This bird's eye view of the staff at the disposal of the prime minister perhaps drives home one point. Although Trudeau lacks a sufficient number of partisan policy advisers, he draws considerable policy advice from a highly differentiated and well-staffed constellation of secretariats which serves him in his capacity as chief executive in charge of Cabinet decision making.

Supporting Cabinet

Two types of secretariats work in support of the Cabinet and its committees:[7] those in the Privy Council Office and the Federal-Provincial Relations Office, and those established as separate central agencies serving Cabinet committees. PCO and FPRO are concerned essentially with briefing the prime minister, usually through the office hierarchy but often personally, on the timing and development of major issues before Cabinet and its committees. Officials within these secretariats also serve Cabinet committees in general and the chairmen in particular.

---

[7]For a description and depiction of the Cabinet committee system, see Privy Council Office, "The Policy and Expenditure Management System" in this book at p. 177.

The key secretariats of this type are those under the deputy secretary (operations) in PCO. The assistant secretaries for the four subject-matter committees staffed by PCO shoulder special responsibilities for briefing the chairman and for organizing the business of the committee. As a result, they play numerous bargaining and advocacy roles within the bureaucratic politics behind each major initiative. These include:

• Advising officials from operational departments on the best way to proceed on issues and, if the matter calls for an interdepartmental panel, which departments should be invited to join.
• Monitoring development of the new policy in the department or the interdepartmental panel.
• Deciding when the proposal is ready for initial discussion in the Cabinet committee.
• Ensuring that any conflicts, which emerged in the committee, especially those with the Department of Finance, the Treasury Board Secretariat and the Ministries of State for Economic Development and Social Development, are ironed out before final consideration by the Cabinet committee.
• Transmitting committee recommendations to the prime minister and the Cabinet.
• Communicating Cabinet decisions to all concerned parties.
• Ensuring that the decisions are actually implemented.[8]

This list of responsibilities is quite a tall order for assistant secretaries. Throughout the formation of policy, they must strive to channel their energies in productive areas. Much of their work will be routine, but they will have to come to the rescue if a department is floundering on an issue especially important to the prime minister or to the committee. In such circumstances departments which have played ball procedurally will likely get more sympathy and forbearance than those which have stepped on the toes of other departments or of PCO. During the implementation of policy the assistant secretary has to watch for foot dragging in departments less than enthusiastic about a particular decision. He/she might ultimately call for artillery: "If a minister and his officials are dragging their feet on something that is dear to the P.M.'s heart, we might try to get a letter out of him to the minister saying in effect, 'get off your ass.'"[9]

In the final months of Trudeau's 1974-1979 government, three secretariats operating as autonomous agencies served specific Cabinet committees and their chairmen. Two of these, *the Treasury Board Secretariat* (TBS) and *the Office of the Comptroller General* (OCG), reported

---

[8]Campbell and Szablowski, pp. 69-83.
[9]*Ibid.*, p. 81.

directly to the president of the Treasury Board (a Cabinet minister); the third—the secretariat for the Board of Economic Development Ministers, established in December 1978—reported to the president of that board (also a Cabinet minister). Joe Clark changed the name of the latter board to the Economic Development Committee. He also set up a fourth autonomous secretariat for a Cabinet committee named Social and Native Affairs. These latter two secretariats have been retained by the new Trudeau government to serve the Economic Development and Social Development Committees of Cabinet.

TBS and OCG, which together house several hundred professionals, advise the Treasury Board in the exercise of statutory authority given to it by Section 5 of the Financial Administration Act:

- The review of annual and longer-term expenditure plans and programs of the departments of government and the determination of budgetary priorities.
- General administrative policy in the public service.
- The organization of the public service.
- Personnel management in the public service, including the terms and conditions of employment.
- Financial management, including estimates, expenditures, financial commitments, accounts, fees or charges for the provision of services or the use of facilities, rentals, licences, leases, revenues from the disposition of property and procedures by which departments manage, record and account for revenues received or receivable from any service.[10]

Three *Treasury Board Secretariat* branches (Program, Administrative Policy and Personnel Policy) perform functions related respectively to expenditure budgeting, administrative policy and the financial management of materials and services provided to all government offices, and personnel management. A fourth branch, Official Languages, monitors implementation throughout the public service of the 1969 Official Languages Act and a 1973 resolution of Parliament, both of which mandate the expanded use of French in the federal government.

The Program Branch coordinates budgetary review, but within the priority guidelines provided by the Privy Council Office and the fiscal framework set by the Department of Finance. Clark transferred authority for substantive budgetary review in the fields of economic and social development to the new secretariats noted above. Trudeau has followed this practice and has also provided that the Foreign and Defence Policy Secretariat of PCO advise the Cabinet committee by the same name on expenditure matters. The cumulative effect of these reforms limits TBS's immediate jurisdiction over expenditure reviews to government opera-

---

[10]Revised Statutes of Canada, 1970, chap. F-10.

tions, a grab bag category concerned more with maintenance of infrastructure than delivery of programs.

The Office of the Comptroller General (OCG) evolved from two branches of TBS as a result of a chain of events that raised serious questions about the adequacy of financial administration in government. OCG focuses on one aspect of financial administration: program-oriented accounting. In addition to assuring that resources are actually expended on the programs for which they were allocated, OCG assesses whether they were used efficiently and whether the programs they supported were effective.

The Ministry of State for Economic Development (MSED) contains forty professionals and about sixty support staff. The secretariat was originally supposed to serve the Board of Economic Development Ministers, which was directed to:

- Define integrated economic development policy by industrial sector and region, review and concert submissions to the Treasury Board and the Cabinet in light of these, and improve program delivery.
- Advise the Treasury Board on the allocation of government resources to economic development programs.
- Lead and coordinate consultation on economic development with the provinces, business, labour and other public and private organizations.
- Conduct its own research and policy development.[11]

Thus the Trudeau government has taken economic development, previously a subsidiary concern of the Economic Policy Committee of the Cabinet, and dignified it with a minister of state and a secretariat with sweeping mandates. The Finance Department retains the lead in the formation of macroeconomic policy and the preparation of the budget—both the fiscal framework (expenditures) and taxation (revenues). However, the Ministry of State for Economic Development is the committee's principal source of advice on expenditure budgets under its control.

The Ministry of State for Social Development (MSSD) plays a similar role to that of the MSED with reference to the Social Development Committee of Cabinet. As well, it has played a key role in advising Cabinet on reforms of fiscal arrangements between the federal and provincial governments which will affect social programs. It maintains a complement of sixty-five, including support staff.

Finance: A Department Unlike the Others
The Department of Finance dominates the prime minister's and Cabinet's view of macroeconomic policy, including the fiscal framework. From time

---

[11]P.M. Pitfield, Privy Council, 1978-3803, pp. 2-3.

to time, other departments have encroached upon the department's advisory role. None, however, has sustained for long challenges to Finance's primacy in these crucial fields. Why has the department had so much success in protecting its prerogatives? The simple fact remains that Canada's highly structured machinery for interdepartmental decision making gives Finance preferential access to nearly every major deliberative body in town. First, the minister of finance belongs to nine of thirteen standing Cabinet committees. Key among these is Priorities and Planning. Within the field of economic policy, Priorities and Planning reviews the five-year fiscal framework proposed by the Department of Finance. On the basis of the agreed framework, the committee arrives at five-year expenditure guidelines and allocates resources to policy sectors. Meanwhile, the deputy minister of finance approximates the strategic position of his minister by virtue of his membership of official bodies parallelling Cabinet committees.

Together, the minister of finance and his deputy concentrate their efforts on Priorities and Planning and its officials' shadow committee, Senior Coordination. In the area of microeconomic policy, they only become directly involved in major matters. Under the Canadian Cabinet committee system, officials accompany ministers to meetings. The accompanying officials need not be the deputy ministers. Many times the director most immediately concerned goes to committee with the minister. Here a director assumes that he has been brought along to whisper in the minister's ear to assure adherence to the departmental line, to answer questions directed to him from other ministers, and— granting he has accumulated some experience with these forums—to participate when appropriate in the give and take of discussion. The deputy minister and subordinate colleagues often fill in for the minister on Cabinet committees he cannot attend. Likewise, Finance officials often sit in for the deputy minister on his committees. Thus the flexible attitude toward committee participation found in Canada contributes to the near-omnipresence of Finance in decisions not directly related to macroeconomic policy.

Conclusion

Obviously, Canadian central agencies have developed greatly, both in size and complexity, since Pierre Elliott Trudeau first became prime minister in 1968. In their attempts to explain the origins of central agency expansion, many observers have ascribed very great importance to Trudeau's leadership style. Such analyses err, however, if they argue that Trudeau "presidentialized" the Canadian system. Keeping in mind the fact that our country is about one-tenth the size of the United States, central agencies in Ottawa provide, proportionately, much greater resources for the prime minister and Cabinet than comparable organizations in Washington do for the president and Cabinet. Thus this essay suggested a much more fruitful line of inquiry. It stressed the degree to which Trudeau has viewed central agencies simply as instruments for enhancing coordination and control of government departments. In this respect, Trudeau has indulged his long-standing fascination with the rational basis of policy decisions. Highly developed central agencies, he believes, provide political executives with the necessary advisory mechanisms for rational decision making.

6/Federal Crown Corporations in Canada*
D. P. Gracey

The primary purpose of this essay is to review some of the attempts of the last decade to introduce a new approach to the control, direction and accountability of federal Crown corporations.[1] As background to this analysis, the essay reviews the rationale for creating Crown corporations, some of the elements of the present system of control, direction and accountability, and the present three-fold classification of the corporations falling under the *Financial Administration Act* (FAA).

The Crown corporation provides a valuable alternative to the traditional government department as an instrument for the achievement of public policy objectives. A Crown corporation can manage a given function with a higher degree of autonomy from the political process than the departmental form allows. It can also remove the management function from bureaucratic controls and allow for the use of personnel, budgetary and accounting practices generally associated with the private sector or at least different from those of departments.

Furthermore, the Crown corporation setup permits businessmen to be appointed to the boards of directors, thereby bringing their business expertise to the management of commercial or quasi-commercial activi-

---

*This is a revised and updated version of the essay which appeared in the third edition of this book.

[1]This article uses the definition of "Crown corporation" proposed in the Crown Corporations Bill (C-27) tabled in the House of Commons, November 26, 1979: any corporation wholly owned, whether directly or indirectly, by the government of Canada, rather than the definition found in Section 66 of the *Financial Administration Act*: any corporation ultimately accountable to Parliament (through a minister) for the conduct of its affairs.

ties on behalf of the government. The Crown corporation can also be an effective tool when gaps in the economy cannot be filled by the private sector because it is either inappropriate or impossible for the private sector to become involved. This may be the result of the strategic importance of the industry (that is, nuclear energy development) or of the industry's lack of attraction to private investors, possibly due to the high risk associated with the venture.

Finally, the Crown corporation structure establishes an institution that can contract, sue and be sued in its own name as well as borrow and acquire, hold, manage and dispose of property in a less cumbersome manner than a government department.

The first recognizable ancestor of the Crown corporation form is the Board of Works established by Lord Sydenham in 1841 in the United Provinces to construct a canal system. It is notable that because the board's relationship with government was unclear it was soon shorn of its corporate status. The Board of Works was, however, a precursor of a number of corporations established by the Dominion government in the immediate post-Confederation period to undertake public works projects, in particular the development and administration of harbours.

Canada's first major venture into public enterprise occurred in 1919 when Canadian National Railways (CNR) was established. The decision by the Canadian government to nationalize the financially troubled, but strategically vital, transcontinental railways under one government-owned corporate entity was based neither on ideology nor any kind of "national vision." Rather, it was a pragmatic step that the government took, somewhat unwillingly, to protect its own investment, that of private shareholders and Canada's credit in foreign capital markets.

It seems that neither the government nor the public was particularly enamoured of the CNR experiment, because the next venture into public enterprise did not occur until 1935 when R.B. Bennett's Conservative government created the company that eventually became the Canadian Broadcasting Corporation (CBC).

However, within the fifteen-year interval following the creation of the CBC, there were thirty-three government-owned corporations in existence. In that interval two significant events occurred: during World War II the federal government, in managing the war effort, decided to employ extensively management structures other than the traditional departmental form; and C.D. Howe, a Cabinet minister who felt comfortable with business organizations and uncomfortable with government bureaucracy, left behind a long list of government-owned corporations as he moved through various wartime and postwar ministerial portfolios.

By the midpoint of the century, therefore, the government-owned corporation seemed to have achieved a fairly high level of legitimacy. The problem was that in their haste to establish such corporations, governments had not developed a standard model for creating them; nor had they developed systems by which they could exert effective control, direction and accountability over them.[2]

In 1950, the Cabinet proposed a bill to Parliament, part of which was designed to provide a uniform method of financial control for Crown corporations and to provide for their annual reporting to Parliament via the tabling of annual reports and capital budgets through the appropriate minister.[3] In general terms the bill, which was approved by Parliament as the Financial Administration Act (FAA),[4] was intended to lay a foundation for a more uniform and systematic relationship between the executive and Parliament on the one hand and the Crown corporations on the other. Until the promulgation of the FAA, Crown corporations were not necessarily accountable to Parliament in the way they are now. As long as Crown corporations were able to conduct their affairs so as not to require Parliamentary appropriations or loans, they could avoid Parliamentary scrutiny indefinitely.

The FAA provided the foundation for the financial administration of the Government of Canada. Part VIII of the act is entirely devoted to the financial control of Crown corporations. And in Section 66, the term *Crown corporation* is defined as a corporation that is ultimately accountable to Parliament (through a minister) for the conduct of its affairs. Section 66 also establishes the threefold classification of Crown corporations.

The first classification includes what the FAA refers to as "departmental" Crown corporations (for example, National Museums of Canada, National Research Council). These corporations are always agents of Her Majesty[5] and, theoretically, are responsible for "administrative, supervisory or regulatory services of a government nature." Departmental corporations were to be in essence departments of government over which the Cabinet or appropriate minister would exert more or less

---

[2]For a more detailed description of the evolution and history of Crown corporations and other nondepartmental bodies see the Privy Council Office submission to the Lambert Commission (the Royal Commission on Financial Management and Accountability) *Responsibility in the Constitution*, Part II, "Non-Departmental Bodies" (Ottawa: 1978).

[3]The general relationships of the federal ministry to Crown corporations and the ways in which the ministry may exercise control over the corporations vary from one corporation to another.

[4]Revised Statutes of Canada, 1970, chap. F-10.

[5]Agent of Her Majesty status explicitly provides to a corporation, or implies, a range of legal privileges and immunities, including immunity from provincial or municipal taxation, and immunity from the execution of court judgements. Corporations with such status invariably fall under federal jurisdiction (i.e., the *Canada Labour Code*) for purposes of labour relations and are usually granted "sovereign status" when borrowing in the capital markets. Sovereign status means that their cost of money is identical to that of their principal—the government of Canada.

continuous control and direction in much the same way as it would over a department of government. Although the rationale does not hold true for all departmental corporations, it appears that a corporate personality for such organizations was deemed necessary to facilitate the acquisition, holding, management and disposal of property as well as to allow the corporations to sue and be sued in their own names. In a number of cases the departmental Crown corporations are now integrated within a department, their only distinguishing characteristic being their legal status as corporate entities.

The second group of corporations defined by the FAA are the "agency" Crown corporations (for example, National Capital Commission, Royal Canadian Mint). These corporations are always agents of Her Majesty and, theoretically, are "responsible for the management of trading or service operations on a quasi-commercial basis, or for the management of procurement, construction or disposal activities . . ."

The final classification includes those corporations known as "proprietary" Crown corporations. These are the companies which are sometimes referred to as "the commanding heights" of our public enterprise, such as Air Canada, Canadian National Railways and Petro-Canada. According to the FAA, proprietary Crown corporations are responsible for the "management of lending or financial operations" or commercial and industrial operations "including the production of or dealing in goods and supplying of services to the public." Proprietary Crown corporations are also expected to be financially self-sustaining, like private sector corporations, and are therefore "ordinarily required to conduct . . . operations without (Parliamentary) appropriations."

The corporations operating under the FAA are listed in an annex to the FAA known as the Schedules. The Schedules contain four groupings known as A, B, C and D. Schedule A includes all those organizations which are departments of government, are not incorporated, and are not Crown corporations. Schedules B, C and D include all the Crown corporations to which Part VIII applies. Schedule B includes all departmental corporations, Schedule C all agency corporations, and Schedule D all proprietary corporations.

Certain other corporations not included in the Schedules of the FAA have been described as "unclassified" Crown corporations. Indeed, in the past two decades the practice has developed of not adding newly created corporations to the Schedules of the FAA. Of the 178 Crown corporations identified in a joint Privy Council Office-Treasury Board Secretariat survey in 1977/78, only 54 appear in the Schedules and are, therefore, subject to the requirements imposed by the FAA.

Having established the definition and threefold classification of Crown corporations, the FAA went on to establish the pattern of financial control which the government would exert over them. Departmental corporations were to be subject to the general provisions of the FAA found in parts other than Part VIII. In other words, in their financial relationship to the government, departmental corporations were to be treated as ordinary departments of government, unless provisions in their special acts provided otherwise. The focus of Part VIII, therefore, is on the agency and proprietary corporations and the two groups are treated uniformly under Part VIII with two significant exceptions. Agency Crown corporations are required to submit annual capital and operating budgets.[6] (Capital budgets are approved by the Cabinet on the recommendation of the appropriate minister, the minister of finance and the president of the Treasury Board.) Proprietary Crown corporations are required to submit only annual capital budgets for approval by the Cabinet on the recommendation of the three ministers. After approval by the Cabinet, capital budgets are tabled in Parliament. Agency corporations also are enjoined to undertake their contractual commitments subject to regulations which may be promulgated by the Cabinet.

The rationale for requiring agency corporations to submit both operating and capital budgets to the executive for approval and to be subject to regulations respecting contracts was that they were to have much less independence from government than proprietary corporations. It was envisaged that proprietary corporations were to have as much independence from government as private sector corporations have from the shareholder. Proprietary corporations were to be managed by individuals from the private sector and their management of the corporations was not to be subject to the detailed supervision of the government. On the other hand, agency corporations were to be subject to both operational and policy supervision through annual operating and capital budgets and through control over contracts.

Given the fact that the FAA was promulgated nearly three decades ago, how relevant is Part VIII to today's political and administrative climate? Part VIII at the time of its presentation was seen to be a "new and experimental section which was very difficult to work out."[7] It is not difficult to understand, therefore, why serious deficiencies in the FAA have appeared, particularly in the last decade. The major problems have been highlighted in the 1976 *Report of the Auditor General*,[8] the Air Canada Inquiry Report,[9] the serious difficulties encountered by Atomic Energy of Canada Limited resulting in its reorganization in 1977, and, the

---

[6]FAA, *op. cit.*, Section 70 (1).
[7]Minutes of the House of Commons Standing Committee on the Public Accounts, 1951, p. 99.
[8]*Report of the Auditor General to the House of Commons* (for the Fiscal Year Ended March 31, 1976), (Minister of Supply and Services Canada: 1976), pp. 227-302.
[9]Honourable Willard Z. Estey, *Air Canada Inquiry Report* (Ottawa: Information Canada, October 1975).

charges of questionable payments and discounting practices levelled at PISA, the Swiss subsidiary of Polysar.

The major deficiencies of the FAA can be categorized as follows:

1. The schedules are seriously outdated. Aside from the fact that they now contain less than a third of the Crown corporations in existence, the Schedules have developed other serious flaws. For example, Crown corporations such as the St. Lawrence Seaway Authority have accumulated massive deficits and rely on government appropriations to continue their operations at current levels. Yet they continue to be listed in Schedule D to the FAA—the Schedule nominally reserved for those corporations "ordinarily required to conduct their operations without appropriations."

2. The FAA is silent on the manner in which Crown corporations or their subsidiaries should be established and the extent of government control over or even knowledge of their establishment. There has been since the early 1970s a proliferation of Crown corporations most of which have been incorporated under federal or provincial companies legislation rather than by special act of Parliament. One result has been a bewildering array of Crown corporations established with a multiplicity of purposes, structures and relationships with the government. Another result was the charge levied by the auditor general in 1976 that no one in the government appeared to be able to provide or even hazard an intelligent estimate of the number of Crown corporations in existence or in operation.[10]

3. The FAA requires approval of the governor-in-council for capital budgets submitted by Crown corporations, but does not indicate what the effect of approval is. As a consequence, many organizations treated budget submissions as nothing more than an information-sharing exercise. Once a budget was approved by the governor-in-council, these corporations did not hesitate to make significant amendments to it without even informing their minister or the government. As a consequence, the government's control and direction of Crown corporations through capital budgets was seriously diluted.

4. Particularly in the case of capital budget approvals, but also in other aspects of corporate operations, the FAA requires the involvement of up to three ministers and the governor-in-council. This in turn leads to the involvement of officials in the departments advising those ministers. This has resulted in a "bureaucratization" of the affairs of Crown corporations manifested by dilatory procedures, Crown corporations having to provide roughly similar information to several

---

[10]Auditor General's Report, *op. cit.*, p. 231.

departments, blurred accountability as to who is responsible for decisions, and a great deal of frustration on all sides.

5. Possibly the most serious deficiency of the FAA is that it was designed with the objectives of financial control and accountability in mind. It is silent on the issue of policy control and direction. This deficiency was highlighted in the early 1970s when ministers began to worry about what they saw as the "unresponsiveness" of certain Crown corporations to government policy initiatives. This issue more than any other focused attention on the question of the proper relationship between the government and individual ministers on the one hand and Crown corporations and their managements on the other.

Cabinet directed the Privy Council Office to undertake a general study of the policy responsiveness of Crown corporations. That study began in earnest in the summer of 1974. In 1976, partly in response to the auditor general, the study became a joint Privy Council Office-Treasury Board Secretariat exercise and was widened to include matters relating to the financial management and control of Crown corporations. On August 18, 1977 the government issued a Green Paper entitled *Crown Corporations—Direction, Control and Accountability*. This publication, which soon became known as the Blue Book (from the colour of its cover), elicited reactions from many Crown corporations, private sector firms, associations and individuals, chartered accountants and financial institutions. The Public Accounts Committee made the paper the subject of several hearings in early 1978.[11]

Soon thereafter, an "interdepartmental Crown corporations task force" was created under the chairmanship of the Privy Council Office. The objective of the task force was to consider the responses made to the Blue Book as well as the lessons learned from Air Canada, Atomic Energy of Canada Limited, Polysar and others, and to prepare recommendations for ministers' consideration.

What began in the summer of 1974 culminated on November 26, 1979 with the tabling of Bill C-27, the omnibus Crown Corporations Bill, by Perrin Beatty, minister of state (Treasury Board). In this case the term *omnibus* was an apt description. The bill was in several respects exceedingly complex. It and the Schedules covered ninety-seven pages and referred to virtually every aspect of the government's relationship with Crown corporations from the appointment of auditors to the incorporation or acquisition of subsidiaries.[12]

The overall purpose of the bill was to provide the government with a more effective means by which to ensure appropriate policy and financial

---

[11]See the Report of the Standing Committee on Public Accounts to the House of Commons, April 11, 1978 (the "Crown Corporations Report").

[12]Some wags also pointed out that in French *un omnibus* was a slow train.

control and direction; to provide increased accountability to the government and Parliament; and to leave to the managements of Crown corporations the flexibility and independence required to conduct their operations. As a result of these several aims, the bill contained several inherent conflicts. While the bill tried valiantly to resolve these conflicts it did not succeed on all fronts and much was left to administrative arrangements to resolve.

The principal measures of the bill included:

- Reorganized schedules, including four new categories.
- A requirement that the acquisition or incorporation of a Crown corporation (including subsidiaries) would need both explicit statutory authority and approval of the governor-in-council.
- A provision whereby Crown corporations could be issued legally binding directives by the governor-in-council to undertake activities "in the national interest." All directives would be made public within fifteen days of issuance and any Crown corporation that sustained verifiable losses or incremental costs as a result of implementing a directive could, if approved by Parliament, receive compensation from the government.[13]
- A series of provisions designed to strengthen boards of directors of Crown corporations and specifying a range of directors' and officers' duties, responsibilities and liabilities.
- A refined system of government controls over financial expenditures and commitments, including five-year "rolling" corporate plans and capital budgets, a definition of capital budget approval as being the authority by which Crown corporations could enter into capital expenditures and commitments, and changes to the government's control over debt financing by Crown corporations.
- Clarification of the meaning of "agent of Her Majesty" status, one effect of which would be a new approach to the recording of the liabilities of Crown corporations in the public accounts.
- A range of provisions designed to update and improve the financial management and control of Crown corporations in response to the auditor general's observations and recommendations in his 1976 and 1977 reports to Parliament.
- A provision by which the FAA's formula of application was reversed. C-27 would apply in the event of any conflict or inconsistency with the provisions of an individual corporation's special act or memorandum of incorporation.

---

[13]The directive power in its scope and effect was identical to the so-called "unanimous shareholder agreement" provided to shareholders under the Canada Business Corporations Act (CBCA).

The overall concept of the bill was to move the legal framework for the government's relationship with Crown corporations closer to the private sector model epitomized by the *Canada Business Corporations Act*. This concept not only preserved, but also strengthened the traditional arms'-length relationship between government and individual ministers on the one hand and Crown corporations on the other, as well as placing Crown corporations on a par with some of the latest developments in Canadian company law.

The bill did not completely eradicate the major deficiency of the FAA. C-27 would still not apply to all Crown corporations. Because of its special mandate, the Bank of Canada would not be brought within the purview of the legislation and, at least for the time being, the six "cultural" corporations would be exempted. In spite of almost heroic attempts, several anomalies also persisted in the Schedules.

C-27 lapsed on the order paper with the demise of the Clark government. At this point, neither the bill nor an amended version of it has been brought forward by the Trudeau government since its return to power in February 1980. The Crown corporations task force has been resuscitated under the chairmanship of the Treasury Board Secretariat. The president of the Treasury Board has announced that once certain "deficiencies" in C-27 are corrected, an improved bill will be introduced, probably in late 1981.

Several of the provisions of C-27 persist as administrative arrangements, however. In 1977, the president of the Treasury Board asked Crown corporations to make substantial adjustments to the form and content of annual capital and operating budgets, including the submission of corporate plans. In May 1979, the clerk of the Privy Council asked Crown corporations to seek government approval for the incorporation or acquisition of subsidiaries and of the terms, conditions and timing of long-term borrowings. He also asked that Crown corporations seek government approval for any significant departures from capital budgets approved by the governor-in-council.

C-27 did not address itself to all of the issues relating to Crown corporations that had surfaced in the last decade. One such issue is the role of public servants on the boards of directors of Crown corporations.

Appointment of senior public servants to the boards of Crown corporations comes about in one of two possible ways. In some cases, the special act incorporating the Crown corporation requires that public servants holding certain positions in the bureaucracy (for example, deputy minister of finance) serve ex officio on the board. In the majority of cases, the governor-in-council or the responsible minister exercises the discretion vested in him and appoints one or more public servants. In some cases, such as the Northern Transportation Company Ltd. (NTCL), a public servant will also be appointed as chairman of the board. Rarely will public servants appointed in this fashion be appointed as chief executive officers.

Although a policy has never been enunciated, there seem to be three reasons for the appointment of public servants to the boards of Crown corporations: to bring a special expertise to the deliberations of the boards; to act as a link between the boards and ministers (not necessarily the responsible minister); and, finally, to bring a particular departmental or ministerial interest before the board.

One can be reasonably certain that the practice has not been dictated by a desire to economize or by a lack of competent individuals from the private sector to be members of the boards. Indeed, one could be forgiven for thinking that governments were suspicious of their own actions in setting up certain Crown corporations and have circumscribed their independence by appointing public servants to the boards. In an extreme case, a board composed of public servants can appear and operate as any bureaucratic interdepartmental committee.

The present situation generally seems to be that a senior public servant "wears two hats" when serving on the board of a Crown corporation. One hat represents the department in which he is employed; the other his directorship. When serving as a director, does the senior public servant act in the best interests of the corporation or of his department? Is he to be a watchdog for the department and the government over the affairs of the Crown corporation? Is corporate information made available to him as a director to be made available to other officials of the department? To whom is he loyal? Obviously, when the public servant reports to a minister other than the minister to whom the corporation which he serves reports, the ambiguity can have serious implications.[14]

If the public servant sometimes finds his position ambiguous, the chairman of the board, who maintains the corporation's connection with the responsible minister, can be in a position of even greater ambiguity. The chairman may face a board consisting of one or more senior public servants from the department of the minister to whom he reports on behalf of the corporation. The appointment of public servants to the boards of Crown corporations involved in the management of activities on a commercial or quasi-commercial basis seems also to contradict one of the basic, though admittedly not the sole, raisons d'être of the Crown corporation form (that is, to separate the management of an activity from

---

[14]Common law and company law, in particular the CBCA, leave no doubt that a director must operate in the best interests of the corporation. It was partly for this reason that C-27 (Section 8) defined the "national interest" as being "the primary of the best interests of each Crown corporation." This was intended to offset the common law where the best interest is usually interpreted as maximizing the profitability of a corporation.

bureaucratic management and to bring individuals experienced in business to the management of such activities).

Many officers and private sector directors of Crown corporations feel that public servants are a valuable addition to their boards. Many do not, however, and some point to the relatively poor attendance record of some public servants at board meetings. In a very few Crown corporations, there is considerable irritation between the public servant director and the corporate officer and public sector director. One or two Crown corporations have gone to the extreme of requiring all their directors— but notably those from the public service—to sign oaths of "fidelity and secrecy" to the corporation in an attempt to define beyond all doubt where the directors' loyalty lies.

Public servants are sometimes allowed to assume preeminent positions on boards of directors because of the relative weakness or ineffectiveness of their private sector colleagues. Although examples abound of strong, experienced and diligent private sector individuals being appointed to boards of Crown corporations, governments sometimes sacrifice the long-term interests of Crown corporations for purposes of short-term political expediency and appoint private sector directors who do not meet a high standard of competence.

C-27 was also silent on another important issue. The Canadian Parliament to date has never had a single committee of the Senate or House of Commons to oversee, in even a cursory fashion, the operations of all Crown corporations. The United Kingdom has the Select Committee on Nationalized Industries (SCNI); Australia has the Senate Standing Committee on Finance and Government Operations; and the Province of British Columbia has its Crown Corporations Committee. Each of these committees has performed a valuable role.

As it is, parliamentary supervision of Crown corporations is shared among the Public Accounts Committee, the Miscellaneous Estimates Committee and a plethora of Senate and House of Commons committees. Aside from the study of Crown corporations undertaken by the Public Accounts Committee in 1978 (instigated by and focusing on the auditor general's 1976 and 1977 reports), none of these committees has attempted a general analysis of the operations, role or performance of Crown corporations.

The omnibus Crown Corporations Bill made no move to reorganize the method by which Parliament reviews and oversees Crown corporations. What it did require, however, was much more information of a higher standard of quality and integrity to be provided to Parliament by Crown corporations and the government. Many of these provisions originated from the auditor general's recommendations and observations in his 1976 to 1979 annual reports. If there were any movement to establish a Crown Corporations Committee, the Crown Corporations Bill would have provided a fund of information on which such a committee could have operated.

Finally, contrary to its intention, the Crown Corporations Bill did little to reduce the "bureaucratization" of Crown corporations. In fact, some Crown corporations argued that "bureaucratization" would have increased. If the arms'-length principle is to persist in Canada, departments will have to withdraw, to a degree, from their involvement with Crown corporations. Another alternative, of course, is to follow the Saskatchewan example and establish a single "holding company" for Crown corporations, thereby bringing them more within the government's direct control.

7/Regulatory Agencies and the Canadian Political System

Richard Schultz

"The question of delegation to an independent regulatory authority," according to one commentator, "is a settled one in Canada. It has not excited the passions of Canadian political scientists and politicians to the extent that it has in the United States."[1] If this is an accurate assessment, it can be argued that the question is "settled" not because of extensive analysis and appraisal but because of inertia and neglect. This is unfortunate because regulatory authorities are not at the "fringe" of the public sector in Canada but are primary instruments of social, economic and political control.[2] Moreover, they constitute a major institutional innovation in the Canadian parliamentary system inasmuch as they involve a transfer of power from elected representatives to appointed officials. In an era of government by discretion, it is no longer acceptable that the role of regulatory authorities in the political system be settled by default.[3]

---

[1] Ronald G. Penney, "Telecommunications Policy and Ministerial Control," *Canadian Communications Law Review*, 1970, p. 14.

[2] The "fringe," according to Desmond Keeling, is "Whitehall jargon" to describe regulatory and other "quasi-governmental agencies" in Britain. See Desmond Keeling, "Beyond Ministerial Departments: Mapping the Administrative Terrain," *Public Administration* (London): 54 (1976): 161.

[3] The Law Reform Commission of Canada recently estimated that there were some 15 000 discretionary powers that have been conferred on public authorities by federal statutes. See Philip Anisman, *A Catalogue of Discretionary Powers in the Revised Statutes of Canada 1970* (Ottawa: Information Canada, 1975).

This essay, which admittedly is an introductory overview, attempts to encourage greater attention to such bodies.

A recent survey suggested that there were over one hundred federal regulatory agencies[4] and much work needs to be done to establish a useful classification of them.[5] This essay will not attempt such a task but will limit itself to a discussion of some of the central problems of what may be called economic regulatory agencies from the perspective of public administration. The scope of this essay, then, is limited to the six federal regulatory agencies which, because of the nature of their functions, may be described as the most important of our regulatory bodies. The agencies in question are the Anti-Inflation Board (AIB), the Atomic Energy Control Board (AECB), the Canadian Radio-Television and Telecommunications Commission (CRTC), the Canadian Transport Commission (CTC), the Foreign Investment Review Agency (FIRA) and the National Energy Board (NEB). These agencies all share one common characteristic: they are entities that exist outside traditional departmental structures. Three of them, CRTC, CTC and NEB, also share another and more important attribute: they are, in varying degrees, independent. The nature of this independence, which is the central concern of this essay, will be discussed below.

Although these agencies account for a small proportion of government employees and government expenditures, they perform some of the most important functions of government—functions that are critical to individual welfare and social and economic development. The Canadian Transport Commission, for example, can have a tremendous impact on the transportation system in view of its power to "co-ordinate and harmonize" the operations of all federally regulated modes of transportation.[6] In the communications field, the impact of the Canadian Radio-Television and Telecommunications Commission has been widely felt because of its broad interpretation of its responsibilities to "supervise and regulate all aspects of the Canadian broadcasting system."[7]

Given their importance as instruments of governing, regulatory agencies—especially those that are independent—should interest the student of Canadian public administration because these agencies have a special degree of delegated power in the political system. Moreover, this delegation is unique because it transforms the traditional lines of responsibility governing the relations between politically accountable authorities

---

[4]Canadian Consumer Council, "Inventory of Provincial and Federal Regulatory Agencies," Ottawa: 1971.
[5]For two useful starting points, see André Gelinas, *Les organismes autonomes et centraux* (Montreal: Les Presses de l'Université du Québec, 1975) and D.C. Hague *et al.*, *Public Policy and Private Interests: The Institutions of Compromise* (London: Macmillan, 1975), esp. Appendix III.
[6]National Transportation Act, (NTA), *Revised Statutes of Canada*, Section 21, Chapter N-17.
[7]Broadcasting Act, *Revised Statutes of Canada*, Section 15, Chapter B-11.

and the bureaucracy. The Canadian parliamentary system is governed by the principles of ministerial responsibility, both individual and collective, to Parliament.[8] Ministers, however, are only partially, and in some cases not at all, responsible to Parliament for the actions of independent regulatory agencies. The student of public administration must determine the justification for the existence of agencies, the reasons for the independence of some of them, the nature of their powers and the consequences of transferring political power.

Origins of Regulatory Agencies

Regulatory agencies are, in Hodgetts's phrase, "structural heretics" in the Canadian political system because of their nondepartmental form.[9] Given, as Hodgetts also states, that such departures from the departmental norm to varying extents do "violence to the constituted system of ministerial responsibility,"[10] one needs to determine why such agencies have been created. Moreover, the question is not simply one of historical curiosity, because a host of regulatory activities in areas such as food and drug protection, health and safety standards and working conditions are performed by the traditional departments. This argues that there must be exceptional circumstances to justify the creation of "structural heretics."

The exceptional circumstances are to be found in the nature of the function common to all the agencies considered in this essay: the function of economic regulation. By economic regulation we mean government intervention by regulatory instruments into those areas traditionally reserved in a market economy for private economic decision makers—the owners and managers of firms and industries. More specifically, economic regulation entails a government role in the setting of prices, the controlling of entry into particular sectors of economic activity and the establishment of standards of service. Economic regulation by government is a "halfway house" between an unfettered market and public ownership in an economy based primarily on private enterprise. In general, regulation is intended to be a surrogate for the competitive forces of the market place when competition is deemed either not possible or not practicable.[11] Moreover, regulation traditionally has been the means by which Canadian governments have imposed public social

---

[8]J.E. Hodgetts, *The Canadian Public Service* (Toronto: University of Toronto Press, 1973), pp. 48-51.
[9]*Ibid.*, Chapter 7.
[10]*Ibid.*, p. 141.
[11]On the functions of economic regulation, see Roger Noll, *Reforming Regulation* (Washington: Brookings Institution, 1971); Clair Wilcox, *Public Policies towards Business*, 4th ed. (Homewood, Ill.: Irwin-Dorsey, 1971), and Michael J. Trebilcock, "Winners and Losers in the Modern Regulatory State" (Paper read at the 1975 Meeting of the Institute of Public Administration of Canada), esp. pp. 14-15.

objectives on sectors of the economy such as transportation and com-munications to supplement the economic objectives of private decision makers.

The nature of economic regulation, it is argued, provides the reasons for establishing agencies outside the traditional departmental structures. It is important to emphasize, however, that the creation of regulatory agencies, notwithstanding the reasons to follow, has not been the result of a coherent, well-defined philosophy. In general, there are three basic reasons cited in defence of the creation of separate agencies. In the first place, economic regulation is a highly complex responsibility and requires a type of expertise not usually found in government bureaucracies. Secondly, traditional structures cannot provide the flexibility or con-tinuity of policy necessary for the experimental and innovative needs of economic regulation.

Before turning to the third reason, it should be noted that the reasons already cited were far more compelling in an earlier era of governmental activity in Canada—when the civil service was based primarily on patronage rather than on merit and was far less dependent on specialized knowledge than it is today. The fact that the majority of members of the recently created Anti-Inflation Board, for example, were seconded from other government departments would suggest that the argument regarding specialized knowledge is no longer convincing.

The third traditional argument—and the only one that remains convincing today—is that a separate agency is required to insulate the function of economic regulation from political pressures. Inasmuch as regulation involves either public interference in the exercise of tradi-tional private proprietary rights (as in the transportation and energy sectors) or competing private applications for control of sections of the public domain (as in radio and television licences), impartiality must be exercised to ensure that there is no partisan interference in the regulatory process. This has been a particularly telling argument in Canada and the United States. In Britain, however, regulation traditionally has been performed within government departments and there has been less concern with political interference.[12]

The Concept of Regulatory Independence
The concern for impartiality also explains the independence of some regulatory agencies. A nondepartmental identity was not deemed suffi-cient in Canada to ensure that economic regulation would be "taken out

---

[12]On the British experience in air transport regulation, see Sir Ronald Edwards, Chairman, *British Air Transport in the Seventies*, Report of the Committee of Inquiry into Civil Air Transport (London, HMSO: 1969).

of politics." To reinforce an impartial nature, some agencies were made independent. It is important to note that independence was not extended to all regulatory agencies despite the similarity of their functions. The appointed regulators were granted a quasi-judicial status: they serve, not like deputy ministers or the heads of Crown corporations, "at pleasure" but on condition of "good behaviour" and can be removed only for "cause."

Notwithstanding this general statement of the rationale for agency independence, the concept of independence requires substantial clarification. It is unclear, for example, why some regulators are independent and others are not. Why are the members and administrator of the AIB or the Commissioner of the FIRA not independent while members of the CTC or CRTC are? The administrator, for example, may make binding orders similar to those made by the CTC or CRTC, yet he serves at pleasure.

The second aspect of regulatory independence that requires clarification is the fact that the independence of some regulators does not necessarily mean that the whole of the regulatory process must be impartial. It may only mean that the regulators' role in the decision-making process is governed by the principles and requirements of impartiality. The position of the NEB best illustrates the significance of this comment. The members of the NEB are so independent that they cannot be removed before the end of their terms except by a joint address of the House of Commons and the Senate. Yet the overwhelming majority of NEB decisions require Cabinet approval. Cabinet, in making its decision on a particular application, is not governed by any requirement that it act impartially because it is permitted to exercise its discretion and make its decision on any grounds it sees fit. It is important to realize, therefore, that it is the appointed regulators who must act impartially and it is they who are granted a special degree of independence but the ultimate decisions need not be impartially determined. The significance of this distinction will become clearer if we turn to a discussion of the nature of the powers of regulatory agencies.

The Powers of Regulatory Agencies

The independent status of regulators can be viewed as a shield enabling them to ward off interference, partisan or otherwise, in exercising their impartial discretion. As such, the quasi-judicial status of regulators is concerned with the question, "independence from what?" It is equally important to ask "independence for what?" because, unless we assess the significance of the functions of regulatory agencies, the independence that is granted to regulators may not be of much significance. This section is concerned, therefore, with the nature and scope of independent regulatory decision making. Again, it is important to remind the reader of the difficulties in making general statements of equal validity for all agencies because of the variety among agencies. Indeed, it should be remembered that some regulatory agencies, although outside the departmental norm, do not possess an independent decision-making capacity. The AIB and the FIRA, for example, are not decision makers but are primarily negotiating and advisory agencies.

The powers of decision-making agencies can be divided into two general categories, adjudicative and legislative. The former is the power to decide on individual applications for licences, routes, tariffs, standards of service, etc. The latter is the power to make policy principally by means of a regulation-making power. In some instances there are problems in distinguishing between legislative and judicial functions because the distinction between the two activities is not always clear. Yet the statement that one cannot draw the line between them has generally gained credence through repetition rather than sufficient examination. The problems, in fact, appear to have been overstated.

In this paper we need not attempt to resolve the issue. It is precisely because policy can emerge from both adjudicative and legislative decisions that attention to the political control of such functions is needed. An analysis of independent policy making by regulatory agencies is appropriate for an appreciation of the extent to which such bodies do "violence to the constituted system of ministerial responsibility." What emerges from such an analysis is the ironic fact that, despite the rationale of impartial decision making invoked to justify the creation of such bodies, independent exercise of the adjudicative function appears to be subject to greater control than independent exercise of the legislative function. This varies, as will be shown, with the individual agency.

The political controls on adjudicative decision making can be assessed from two viewpoints. They can be positive or negative, active or passive. Positive-negative refers to whether politically accountable authorities can substitute their own decisions for regulatory decisions or whether they are limited to rejecting such decisions. Active-passive refers to political power to initiate a review of regulatory decisions. This power is an active one if politically accountable authorities can review at their own discretion; it is passive if the review is dependent on an appeal from an interested party.

There is no uniform system of political control of regulatory decisions. Cabinet exercises active control over NEB decisions, for example, in that all major decisions on certificates and licences require Cabinet approval before they are valid. Yet this control is also negative in that Cabinet cannot substitute or vary a decision made by the NEB but can only reject it. With respect to the CTC the situation is somewhat confused in that Cabinet has both active and positive power over CTC decisions[13]

---

[13]NTA, Section 64.

while the minister of transport, who exercises control on his own, has positive but passive control over CTC licensing decisions.[14] The CRTC, on the other hand, appears to have the most discretion in terms of independent decision making because Cabinet exercises only negative and passive control over CRTC decisions.[15]

One need not attempt to explain the haphazard nature of political control of regulatory adjudicative decisions. What is significant, at least in formal terms, is the extent to which such decisions are subject to political control. As suggested earlier, this is somewhat unusual in that the primary rationale for an independent regulatory agency was the need for an impartial decision-making body. The Canadian situation is fundamentally at odds with the American in this regard because for comparable agencies in the United States, there is no process of appeal to political authorities nor do such authorities have the right to veto or substitute adjudicative decisions.[16] The only existing appeal with respect to American independent regulatory agencies is to the courts. The extent to which the political controls are exercised is, of course, far more significant than their existence in the statutes. This is an area where a great deal of research is required to assess the utility and practice of such controls.

There is another aspect of political control of adjudicative decisions that merits comment. Regulatory agencies are created in principle to implement government policy in particular sectors of the economy. The quality of the statutory policy statements as guides for regulatory decision makers is therefore an important consideration in any assessment of regulatory policy making. From this perspective we find that, in general, the potential of regulatory policy making is great because of the vague and general nature of statutory policy statements. Some regulators have little more to guide them than the requirement that applications be assessed in terms of "present and future public convenience and necessity."[17] For others, such as the CRTC, the statements of policy are so widely and vaguely drawn that anything can be read into them.[18] In the case of the CTC, the difficulties are compounded because of the nature of the statement of "national transportation policy" which calls for an "economic, efficient and adequate transportation system."[19]

The lack of definitive statements of statutory policy to guide regulators has major consequences for independent agency policy

---

[14]*Ibid.*, Section 25.

[15]Broadcasting Act, Section 23.

[16]Noll, *op. cit.*, p. 5.

[17]See, for example, the Aeronautics Act, *Revised Statutes of Canada*, 1970, Section 16 (3), Chapter A-3.

[18]Broadcasting Act, Section 3.

[19]NTA, Section 3. On this point see Hudson Janisch, *The Regulatory Process of the Canadian Transport Commission* (Ottawa: Law Reform Commission of Canada, 1978).

making. The inevitable consequence, to paraphrase Lowi, is that such "broad discretion makes a politician out of a regulator."[20] Regulatory agencies are not restricted to what Currie, in the case of the Board of Transport Commissioners, suggested they do best, namely regulating "in fields where parliamentary direction is reasonably precise."[21] Rather, they become intimately involved in the resolution of political issues that cannot possibly be resolved solely—or even primarily—on technical, impartial grounds. From our perspective the issue lies in the transference of the political process from Parliament, to which ministers are accountable, to independent agencies, which have often proven themselves singularly incapable or unwilling to manage that process. The more important problem is that the normal principles of accountability no longer apply because the resolution of highly political issues is entrusted to nonaccountable authorities.

Given the lack of specificity in policy statements, one must question the ability of politically accountable authorities to clarify any policy confusion or fill any policy vacuum that may develop. Once again there is no uniform set of political controls that exist. Under the Atomic Energy Control Act, the designated minister may issue directions to the AECB with respect to the carrying out of the purposes of the Act and the Board is required to comply with such directions.[22] Under the Broadcasting Act, there is a provision for such directions on three specific matters.[23] There are no comparable controls with respect to the CTC or the NEB. As a consequence, short of rejecting individual regulatory decisions of these bodies or legislative amendments, there is no opportunity for elected officials to develop or clarify the policy that regulators are mandated to implement. Furthermore, even if individual decisions are rejected on policy grounds, there is no guarantee that the policy considerations will set precedents with regulators for future decisions.[24]

Policy making by regulatory agencies, it has been argued, is an "inevitable concomitant of judicial power,"[25] although the scope for such activity is dependent on the degree of specificity of the agency mandate and the opportunity for binding supplementary political policy directives. It is important, therefore, to recognize that policy may emerge from adjudication and to provide for adequate safeguards on the exercise of

---

[20]Theodore Lowi, *The End of Liberalism* (New York: W.W. Norton & Company, 1969), pp. 300-301.

[21]A.W. Currie, "The Board of Transport Commissioners as an Administrative Body," in *Canadian Public Administration*, ed. J.E. Hodgetts and D.C. Corbett (Toronto: Macmillan, 1960), p. 239.

[22]Atomic Energy Control Act, *Revised Statutes of Canada*, 1970, Section 7, Chapter A-19.

[23]Broadcasting Act, Section 22.

[24]Janisch, *op. cit.*

[25]Louis L. Jaffe, "The Independent Agency—A New Scapegoat," *Yale Law Journal*, 65 (1955-56), p. 1070.

such power. It is unlikely, however, that an independent legislative function will be delegated to regulatory agencies.

Not all agencies possess legislative power and this, in itself, is an interesting comment on those agencies that do. The governor-in-council must approve all policy regulations—as opposed to "house by-laws"—of the AIB, the AECB, the FIRA and the NEB before such regulations can take effect. There is no similar control over CTC or CRTC regulations.

Why should an independent regulatory agency possess an independent legislative power? Professor Hodgetts suggests the reason may be that regulatory agencies are expected to perform "functions which called for both adjudicative and law-making operations which were substantially different from those traditionally associated with conventional departments."[26] Yet excluding the AIB and FIRA, which are not independent, this does not explain why the CRTC and CTC can make regulations independently while a comparable body, the NEB, cannot. Moreover, such law making may cover technical matters which in other cases are the responsibility of the departments. The CTC, for example, is responsible for railway safety regulations while the minister of transport is responsible for aircraft safety. What is particularly ironic in this situation is that, unlike the CTC, the minister requires the approval of Cabinet for his regulations.

There is obviously no logical explanation for the fact that some agencies have an independent legislative function while others do not. However, more is involved than a question of abstract institutional logic. Regulation making is an important power in the arsenal of regulatory authorities because agency regulations are not necessarily limited to technical matters. The CRTC regulation on the deletion of American commercials on cable television is a major policy issue and has involved Canada in a serious international dispute with the United States. Similarly, the CTC has brought about a major intergovernmental dispute involving Alberta's purchase of Pacific Western Airlines. This dispute was specifically a result of a CTC regulation that extended the scope of a section of the National Transportation Act.[27] There can be no argument, furthermore, that the drafting of regulations, as opposed to their individual application, should be done impartially. This follows from the conclusion of Chief Justice Laskin of the Supreme Court in the Marshall Crowe case: while the NEB's quasi-judicial function must be discharged "in accordance with the rules of natural justice . . . to a degree that would

---

[26]Hodgetts, *The Canadian Public Service*, p. 144.
[27]On this aspect of the regulatory process, see Richard Schultz, "The Regulatory Process and Federal-Provincial Relations," in G. Bruce Doern, ed., *The Regulatory Process in Canada* (Toronto: Macmillan, 1977).

reflect integrity of its proceedings and impartiality in the conduct of those proceedings," this was not "a prescription that would govern an inquiry" under the relevant sections of the NEB Act.[28] By inference, impartiality would not govern regulation-making sections. It is only the adjudicative function that must be performed impartially. There is no justification, therefore, for granting a direct legislative function to an independent regulatory agency. Yet the existence of a power to make public policies not subject to political controls constitutes a fundamental breach of the principles of political accountability and responsibility in the Canadian political system.

Summary and Conclusions

In this essay it has been impossible to deal with all the major aspects of regulatory agencies in the Canadian political system. Consequently many important issues have been ignored. Attention has been concentrated on the questions of regulatory independence and political control and accountability.

Although regulatory agencies are not the only "structural heretics" in the bureaucratic system, they may be the most important. They are a major institutional innovation in that they are granted a policy-making responsibility over which there may be minimal or nonexistent political controls.

An analysis of the nature of regulatory independence reveals that an appropriate degree of independence must be granted without conflicting with the traditional principles of political accountability. There is a need to ensure impartiality and objectivity, in so far as the regulatory adjudicative functions are involved, and there can be no serious challenge to this position. The problem is that the adjudicative function may give regulatory bodies a powerful defence against political intervention in the regulatory process not only where such intervention is unacceptable but also where it is desirable and necessary. Independence, then, must be balanced with responsiveness and accountability.

The basic thesis of this essay is that regulatory agencies "should not have more independence from the political process and more opportunity to apply expertise to non-technical decisions than is consistent with effective, democratic government."[29] Existing political controls over some regulatory agencies suggest that such agencies in fact do have a degree of independence that is inconsistent with the principles of democratic government. Politically accountable authorities should be

---

[28]Majority Reasons for Decision, *The Committee for Justice and Liberty v. The National Energy Board*, Supreme Court of Canada, p. 16.
[29]Lloyd N. Cutler and David R. Johnson, "Regulation and the Political Process," *Yale Law Journal* B4 (1975): 1406.

able to issue binding policy directives to all, and not just some, regulatory agencies. Granting such a power to elected officials is based on the recognition that there cannot be, nor should there be, "a detailed, once-for-all list of . . . objectives crystallized in statute."[30] Consequently, political authorities must possess the necessary power to provide amplification and interpretation of statutory objectives and the means to implement them, in order to keep regulatory policy in accordance with current political needs. Similarly, there should be a consistent set of controls over independent policy making by regulation of regulatory agencies. An independent legislative function is not a necessary attribute for effective impartial regulation.

There is no logic in a regulatory system where some agencies are subject to extensive and effective political controls while other similar agencies are not. The issue involves not only logic, however, but also a fundamental principle—ministerial responsibility in the parliamentary system. As Hodgetts has stated, "the Canadian system of parliamentary government can only impose responsibility on Ministers of the Crown."[31] When ministerial responsibility is diluted or nonexistent, effective democratic control over the instruments of governing is lessened. The "question of delegation to an independent regulatory authority" must no longer be considered "settled."

8/Intergovernmental Administrative Relations in Canada
Kenneth Kernaghan

Intergovernmental relations are critically important in the Canadian political system and intergovernmental officials are central participants in the conduct of these relations. This essay examines the role of these intergovernmental officials. The first part of the essay describes the striking growth since the early 1960s in the machinery for intergovernmental liaison. The second part utilizes three models of intergovernmental relations to explain the functions of intergovernmental officials. The third part focuses on the political role of these officials and the fourth part assesses the extent to which intergovernmental officials are

---

[30]Sir Ronald Edwards, op. cit., p. 13.
[31]J.E. Hodgetts, "The Public Corporation in Canada," in Government Enterprise: A Comparative Study, ed. W. Friedmann and J.F. Garner (London: Stevens & Sons, 1970), p. 226.

held responsible for the power they exercise in the political system. The primary emphasis of the essay is on federal-provincial administrative liaison but many of the observations made here are directly relevant to the activities of officials involved in provincial-municipal and inter-provincial relations.

It is difficult to distinguish precisely between *intergovernmental officials* and other public servants. The term is normally used to refer only to so-called intergovernmental affairs specialists. These are senior administrative officials who are engaged solely or primarily in inter-governmental business. They are usually housed in separate departments or other administrative units (for example, central agencies) responsible for the coordination of intergovernmental matters both within their own government and with other governments. But, in varying degrees, many other officials are involved in intergovernmental relations. Thus the term intergovernmental officials also refers to those officials whose formally designated responsibilities require them to spend the majority of their working hours on intergovernmental matters but who are not usually described as intergovernmental affairs specialists. The most prominent among these officials are senior public servants in operating departments who look after intergovernmental issues affecting their department. In addition, there are officials, notably in senior positions, who devote relatively little time to intergovernmental issues but whose occasional involvement has a major influence on the outcome of inter-governmental negotiations. It is evident that a large number of public servants are engaged in intergovernmental activities. The major focus of this essay, however, is on the intergovernmental affairs specialists.

Machinery for Intergovernmental Relations

In the field of intergovernmental relations, an impressive array of administrative structures has been developed and these structures have been regularly upgraded. The network of intergovernmental structures includes separate departments or other administrative units within government, administrative units within individual departments and agencies, intergovernmental secretariats and a large number of liaison bodies. The creation of these structures has both resulted from and stimulated the proliferation of intergovernmental conferences and meetings. The major reasons for the development of this complicated web of intergovernmental contacts, especially between federal and provincial governments, are the expansion of the activities of all governments, the increased interdependence of federal and provincial responsibilities, and the consequent need to design and operate machinery to manage these contacts.

As early as 1972, there were 482 federal-provincial liaison bodies, ranging in scope and importance from the First Ministers' Conference to such specialized federal-provincial committees as that on meteorites. Gérard Veilleux has observed that if each of these bodies had met once during 1972, one federal-provincial meeting would have been held for every four working hours in Canada.[1] But some federal-provincial bodies meet more than once and some do not meet at all during a particular year. In 1975, a total of 782 federal-provincial meetings were held. They involved first ministers (6 meetings), ministers (167 meetings) and officials (609 meetings) and they took the form of 490 bilateral, 45 regional and 247 multilateral meetings.[2] During the same year, a single province (Alberta) participated in 337 federal-provincial meetings and 60 interprovincial meetings—an increase from 182 and 54 meetings respectively in 1974.[3] And by 1977, 30 interprovincial liaison bodies had been established of which 17 were at the ministerial level.[4]

The number of officials attending intergovernmental meetings varies greatly from one meeting to another, but it is notable that one of the largest gatherings, namely the First Ministers' Conference, attracted 57 Cabinet ministers and 130 officials in January 1974.[5] The number of intergovernmental officials attending such meetings does not, however, take account of the large number of officials who do not attend the meetings but who are actively engaged in preparation for the participation of ministers and other officials.

The critical importance of intergovernmental relations in the Canadian political system can be seen in the financial and human resources devoted to the conduct of these relations. The expansion since the 1960s in intergovernmental machinery and the number and quality of the officials operating this machinery are striking. The development of administrative structures geared specifically to the management of intergovernmental relations was a response to the large and growing number of meetings and the desire of governments to coordinate and rationalize the efforts of individual departments in various policy fields. There is virtually no policy field in which federal and provincial governments are not engaged in consultation and negotiation.[6]

In 1961, the Province of Quebec established a Department of

---

[1]Gerard Veilleux, "L'évolution des mécanismes de liaison intergovernmentale," in *Confrontation and Collaboration: Intergovernmental Relations in Canada Today*, ed. Richard Simeon (Toronto: Institute of Public Administration of Canada, 1979), pp. 44-45.
[2]See "Federal-Provincial Administrative Liaison in Canada," in *Public Administration in Canada*, 3rd ed., ed. Kenneth Kernaghan (Toronto: Methuen, 1977), pp. 80-81.
[3]R.D. Olling, "Canadian Conference Activity 1975: Alberta Participation," in *Canadian Federalism: Myth or Reality*, 3rd ed., ed. J. Peter Meekison (Toronto: Methuen, 1977), p. 237.
[4]Veilleux, p. 39.
[5]D.V. Smiley, *Canada in Question: Federalism in the Seventies*, 2d ed. (Toronto: McGraw-Hill Ryerson, 1976), p. 61.
[6]Table I in Kernaghan, "Federal Administrative Liaison in Canada," p. 80, shows federal-provincial activity in 17 specific policy areas and in a miscellaneous category.

Federal-Provincial Relations[7] and gradually the federal government and other provincial governments have developed increasingly sophisticated mechanisms for handling intergovernmental business. At the federal level, the Federal-Provincial Relations Office is headed by the secretary to the Cabinet for federal-provincial relations. In addition, ten federal departments, including External Affairs, have formal federal-provincial units. The provinces have adopted a variety of arrangements, but the trend is clearly in the direction of separate departments or agencies of intergovernmental relations. The governments of Alberta, Newfoundland, Ontario and Saskatchewan have joined Quebec by establishing separate departments.

Intergovernmental secretariats have also been established to provide support services for the meetings of the many liaison bodies. The major secretariat is the Canadian Intergovernmental Conference Secretariat which was set up in 1973 to serve the conferences of first ministers and all other intergovernmental bodies requesting its assistance.[8] Some federal-provincial bodies (for example, the Council of Ministers of Education and the Canadian Council of Resource and Environment Ministers) have established their own secretariat.

The institutionalization of intergovernmental relations has naturally been accompanied by a considerable expansion in the number of officials involved in these relations. Among these officials, the influence of the intergovernmental affairs specialists is especially notable. These specialists play a central role in government both in the organizational sense and in the development and implementation of policy. They must be adept in intragovernmental as well as intergovernmental bargaining. Their influence is based to a large extent on their ability to wend their way skilfully through the labyrinth of intergovernmental affairs in search of agreement with officials in their own government and in other governments. An important element of their expertise is in the *process* of intergovernmental relations. They must also be more knowledgeable in a general way about the *substance* of a broad range of policy fields than senior officials in operating departments. Richard Schultz notes, however, that "central agencies are staffed by individuals who, while they may be specialists in the 'machinery of government' or in intergovernmental relations, are essentially amateurs and generalists when specific policy issues are discussed."[9]

---

[7]In 1967 this department was renamed the Department of Intergovernmental Affairs. It is notable that for a brief period in 1961, at the end of the Frost era, Ontario had a Department of Economics and Intergovernmental Relations.
[8]This organization is the successor to the Constitutional Conference Secretariat established in 1968.
[9]Richard Schultz, "Prime Ministerial Government, Central Agencies, and Operating Departments: Towards a More Realistic Analysis," 2d. ed., in *Apex of Power*, ed. Thomas A. Hockin (Scarborough: Prentice-Hall, 1977), p. 232.

One of the primary aims of the intergovernmental affairs specialist in a central agency vis-à-vis officials within his own government, "is to ensure that operating agencies will not by collaborative intergovernmental interactions weaken the power of federal or provincial jurisdiction as such."[10] The extent to which these specialists perform primarily either a controlling or an advisory function to achieve this end varies from one government to another. There is a risk that serious intragovernmental conflict between the specialists and officials in operating departments will result from "over-coordination" of intergovernmental relations within a single government. Officials in some intergovernmental units are more inclined than those in others to intervene in the intergovernmental activities of the various government departments. The mandate, organization, resources and operation of these units merit further study.

A critical element in the intergovernmental policy process is the multitude of informal contacts, especially by telephone, which supplement the formal meetings of officials. The respect and trust among officials developed during formal contacts pave the way for frank and productive discussions outside of and between formal meetings. During these discussions, officials exchange a great deal of information about their government's position on matters of continuing concern and negotiation. An essential attribute of intergovernmental officials is their ability to obtain current information on the perceptions and positions of other governments. This information is a crucial input in determining the officials' advice to their political and administrative superiors. The ability of officials to gather such information enables them to exercise influence in the policy process apart from that which flows from their hierarchical position.

In the 1950s and early 1960s, the undeveloped state of formal machinery for intergovernmental liaison meant that informal contacts among officials were essential to the effective conduct of federal-provincial relations. Despite the sophisticated infrastructure that has been built since that time, the increased magnitude and complexity of intergovernmental relations has meant that informal communications are still important to the smooth operation of the formal machinery. Indeed, this informal interaction has increased substantially since the mid-1960s.[11]

It is clear that the participation of officials in formal intergovernmental meetings is only the tip of a sizeable iceberg. Below the waterline is a complex network of formal and informal interactions which affect significantly the outcome of intergovernmental negotiations. This net-

---

[10]Donald V. Smiley, "An Outsider's Observations of Federal-Provincial Relations Among Consenting Adults," in Simeon, *Confrontation and Collaboration*, p. 110.
[11]Veilleux, p. 36.

work includes interaction between officials and other political actors, among officials in a single department or agency, between officials in different departments and agencies, and among officials in different orders of government.

Models of Intergovernmental Relations

Three distinct but complementary models can be used to explain the role and the power of officials in the process and outcomes of intergovernmental relations in Canada. I have labelled these the *cooperation, bargaining* and *bureaucratic politics* models.

The *cooperation* model refers to intergovernmental relations involving to a very large extent program specialists from each order of government. Harmonious and productive interaction is facilitated because these program specialists share a body of knowledge and skills and possess a common set of professional attitudes and values relating to their particular policy fields (for example, welfare officials, foresters).[12] In this model, program specialists are permitted to exercise a large measure of autonomy from control by political and administrative superiors, especially those in intergovernmental relations units, treasury boards and finance departments. The value of this model for explaining policy development and implementation in certain federal-provincial relations has been demonstrated well in respect to the Canada Assistance Plan.[13]

The type of interaction depicted in this model was more prevalent in the postwar period up to the early 1960s than it is now. Gradually during the 1960s and increasingly during the 1970s, the influence of program specialists suffered a relative decline as a result of the growing ascendancy in intergovernmental relations of central agency officials who pursued broader public policy goals than officials from program departments. Donald Smiley anticipated that these central agencies would not develop "the kind of allegiance to common procedures and values which so much facilitates intergovernmental relations among program specialists" because "the concerns of the former relate to fundamental political choices about which consensus is more difficult to establish than in respect to more technical matters."[14]

The reduction in the importance of horizontal relations among

---

[12]This model is elaborated in Donald V. Smiley, "Public Administration and Canadian Federalism," *Canadian Public Administration* 7 (September 1964): 371-88 and *Constitutional Adaptation and Canadian Federalism Since 1945* (Ottawa: Information Canada, 1970), chap. 7.
[13]Rand Dyck, "The Canada Assistance Plan: the Ultimate in Cooperative Federalism," *Canadian Public Administration* 19 (Winter 1976): 587-602. Professor Dyck acknowledges some limited relevance for the bargaining model but notes that "the policy development involved in the Canada Assistance Plan can best be understood in terms of Smiley's discussion of shared norms among program administrators" (p. 598).
[14]Smiley, "Public Administration and Canadian Federalism," p. 387.

program specialists resulting from the increased influence of central agencies was accompanied by the creation and growth of new structures and arrangements for the coordination of intergovernmental relations within each government. As a consequence of the institutional central- ization of intergovernmental relations, fewer matters were handled at the lower levels of the governmental pyramid; rather, intergovernmen- tal conflicts gravitated towards the political and senior administrative levels. Since ministers and senior administrators tended not to share values, attitudes and skills to the same extent that program specialists did, the level of intergovernmental conflict increased. Indeed, during the 1960s and especially during the 1970s, much of the intergovernmental activity in Canada has been pervaded by conflict between the federal and provincial governments.[15] In this milieu, the bargaining model explains the process and outcomes of intergovernmental relations better than the cooperation model.[16]

The bargaining model refers to intergovernmental relations involv- ing primarily ministers and senior administrators from each order of government. Interaction takes the form of a bargaining process in which these ministers and officials present and defend their government's position on specific public policy issues. The focus of attention is on the political resources, strategies and tactics used by participants in the process. Richard Simeon, on the basis of his study of federal-provincial negotiation over three broad policy issues, concluded that the participants in federal-provincial relations "are not scattered throughout the system in the form of federal cabinet members, members of Parliament, bureau- crats and party leaders; rather they are concentrated and limited largely to provincial premiers, senior cabinet members, and senior officials on the one hand, and their federal counterparts on the other."[17]

A third model, which complements both the cooperation and bargaining models, is the *bureaucratic politics* model. This model, which has been applied most frequently to the study of foreign policy, especially in the United States,[18] has also been applied recently to the study of inter- governmental relations in Canada.[19] In its application to foreign policy,

---

[15]For a discussion of the several factors in intergovernmental relations that lead to conflict rather than consensus, see D.V. Smiley, *Canada in Question*, pp. 70-79.
[16]For an explanation and application of what I call the bargaining model, see Richard Simeon, *Federal-Provincial Diplomacy: the Making of Recent Policy in Canada* (Toronto: University of Toronto Press, 1962), especially chaps. 2 and 13.
[17]*Ibid.*.
[18]Graham T. Allison, *The Essence of Decision* (Boston: Little, Brown, 1971), and Graham T. Allison and Morton H. Halperin, "Bureaucratic Politics: A Paradigm and Some Policy Implications," *World Politics* 24 (Supplement, Spring 1972): 40-79.
[19]See Richard Schultz, *Federalism, Bureaucracy and Public Policy* (Montreal: McGill-Queen's University Press, 1980); Simon McInnes, "Federal-Provincial Negotiation: Family Allow- ances 1970-1976," (Ph.D. thesis, Carleton University, April 1978); and Kim Richard Nossal, "Bureaucratic Politics in Canadian Government," in this volume at p. 266.

Allison and Halperin note that the bureaucratic politics model focuses "primarily on the individuals within a government, and the interaction among them, as determinants of the actions of a government...."[20] Similarly, in its application to intergovernmental relations, this model refers to bargaining over intergovernmental matters among ministers and officials in departments and agencies *within* each order of government. The bureaucratic politics model involves *intra*governmental bargaining rather than *inter*governmental cooperation and bargaining. Despite the use of the term *bureaucratic politics*, the model is concerned with interaction among both ministers and officials.

Richard Schultz and Simon McInnes, in their case studies of federal-provincial negotiations, focus on the impact of *intra*governmental bargaining on *inter*governmental bargaining. Schultz contends that

> the bureaucratic politics model . . . attempts to answer questions such as why the negotiators adopted the objectives, strategies and tactics they did. . . . Interactions between governments may not . . . explain, by themselves, the outcomes of intergovernmental negotiations. From the bureaucratic politics perspective, the complex intergovernmental process cannot be separated from the direct relations between governments.[21]

Schultz also offers the bureaucratic politics model as a complement to what he describes as Simeon's "government-as-unitary-actor" model. Simeon states that the "perceptions, attitudes and behaviour" of political leaders and officials are his main concern but that in his book "Canada's eleven governments are the actors" and that "for most purposes each will be considered as a single unit."[22] Schultz notes Simeon's emphasis on the federal and provincial *governments* as the major actors.

In the field of intergovernmental relations, governments are often treated as single actors because they normally present a united front in negotiations with other governments. This united front may, however, be a mask that conceals conflict among ministers and officials *within* governments. Neither departments and agencies nor whole governments are homogeneous entities. The process of intragovernmental bargaining which is intertwined with that of intergovernmental bargaining has been ignored or unduly minimized by many students of Canadian federalism. Intragovernmental bargaining over intergovernmental matters involves both elected and appointed officials but much of this bargaining takes the form of internal administrative politics. Intragovernmental bargaining occurs not only over the substance of intergovernmental policy but also over the distribution of resources between intergovernmental affairs

---

[20]Allison and Halperin, p. 43.
[21]Schultz, *Federalism, Bureaucracy and Public Policy*, pp. 434-35.
[22]Simeon, *Federal-Provincial Diplomacy*, p. 13.

and other government activities. Thus officials who are not significantly engaged in intergovernmental relations indirectly affect the success of these relations by influencing the resources devoted to intergovernmental activities both in the government as a whole and in individual departments and agencies.

The Politicization of Intergovernmental Officials

Politicization refers here to the process by which officials become increasingly involved in politics either in the partisan sense or in the broader sense of the authoritative allocation of values for society. Officials in general have become more politicized as a result of departures in recent years from some aspects of the traditional doctrine of political neutrality. I have argued elsewhere that

  a) public servants are more active participants in the political process than the traditional doctrine of political neutrality suggests;
  b) this participation accounts in large part for the nature and extent of the power which public servants exercise in contemporary Canadian government."[23]

It is useful in this essay to consider whether intergovernmental officials have become more politicized and, if so, whether this politicization has taken different forms and emphases from that of other officials.

The overriding objective of intergovernmental relations is the determination of policy. It is clear from earlier discussion in this essay that officials are centrally involved in the intergovernmental policy process. Like other public servants, intergovernmental officials use their knowledge, experience and discretionary authority to exercise power in the formation and administration of public policy; they engage in consultation and bargaining with other political actors; and their ministers rely heavily on them for advice on the technical, administrative and political aspects of complex issues. Thus, in the intergovernmental field, as in other areas of government, the line between the policy contributions of ministers and officials is blurred.

However, the role of intergovernmental officials in the policy process may be distinguished from that of other officials in two significant ways. First, neither political leaders nor officials exercise control, in the sense of authority, over their counterparts in other governments; they cannot direct and command officials in other jurisdictions. Rather, they must exercise influence through a process of bargaining. Of course, officials throughout government engage in bargaining, most notably with representatives of interest groups. But the interaction of officials

---

[23]Kenneth Kernaghan, "Changing Concepts of Power and Responsibility in the Canadian Public Service," *Canadian Public Administration* 21 (Fall 1978): 389-406.

with interest group representatives is usually from a position of greater strength than with intergovernmental officials in another government. Interest groups strive to influence official decisions and recommendations, but officials, with the explicit or tacit approval of their minister, retain the ultimate power to decide or recommend. Thus much of official interaction with interest groups takes the form of consultation rather than negotiation.

A second important feature of the role of intergovernmental officials, especially of those who actually participate in formal meetings, is that they enjoy more discretionary power in the bargaining process than most other officials. They are, therefore, more involved in politics in the broad sense than many of their colleagues. The major reason for this situation is the nature of the intergovernmental policy process. Usually several governments, and often all eleven governments, are involved in a complicated bargaining process. The outcome of negotiations is frequently a tentative agreement representing a delicate balancing and accommodation of numerous and diverse interests. The federal and provincial cabinets and individual ministers are sometimes reluctant to force a renewal of these intricate negotiations unless their objection to the agreement worked out by their officials is substantial.

Donald Smiley has stated that the federal-provincial relations specialist, "in his stance toward other governments . . . has a single-minded devotion to the power of his jurisdiction. And because his counterparts in other governments have the same motivations, conflict is inevitable."[24] But the extent of concern over jurisdiction varies from government to government and from official to official. Some governments, such as Quebec, and some individuals (for example, Claude Morin when he was deputy minister of intergovernmental affairs) have been primarily disposed toward protection of jurisdiction. Other governments and other officials have sought to minimize future intergovernmental conflict by seeking to rationalize the distribution of powers through disentanglement and the clarification of accountability. Resistance to such rationalization, in so far as it involves the movement of a power to another order of government, has often come from the department currently exercising that power rather than from intergovernmental affairs specialists.

As noted earlier, senior public servants in general have become more politicized. However, both scholars and practitioners of intergovernmental relations have perceived a tendency among intergovernmental officials to become somewhat more politicized than other bureaucrats. A

---

[24]Smiley, "An Outsider's Observations," p. 110. See also Veilleux, "L'évolution," p. 45, and Roy E. Lloyd, "The Effects of the Changing Nature of Federal-Provincial Relations on the Role of the Bureaucracy" (Paper presented to the Annual Conference of the Institute of Public Administration of Canada, Victoria, September 1977), p. 9.

distinguishing feature of the traditional doctrine of political neutrality is that public servants are confined to the explanation of policy and that its defence is the responsibility of ministers. But in the course of intergovernmental negotiations, the line between explanation and defence of policy becomes clouded. As a result, intergovernmental officials tend to be more involved in "politics" in the broad sense of that term.

Moreover, some intergovernmental officials occasionally develop an especially intense commitment to the objectives of their own government or their own minister that goes somewhat beyond the loyalty expected from public servants. This strong sense of loyalty appears primarily among senior intergovernmental specialists whose working environment is often highly political in the partisan sense and whose duties require the management of conflict with other governments. They may be motivated both by pressure "not to let the minister down" and by personal commitment to government policies. It is natural for such loyalty and commitment to result from the obligation continually to explain and defend those policies. Vigorous defence by intergovernmental officials of the policies of the government of the day is not usually prompted by partisan support for the governing party, but it does on occasion have that appearance.

The Responsibility of Intergovernmental Officials
The decision-making process in government is often so lengthy and complex that it is difficult for legislatures and the public to pinpoint those who are actually, rather than formally, responsible for certain decisions. This problem is exacerbated in the sphere of intergovernmental relations since an important locus of decision making is an intergovernmental body of ministers or officials. All officials are subject to a broad range of controls and influences from within and from outside government, including Cabinet members, legislators, journalists, pressure group officials, individual citizens, and administrative superiors, peers and subordinates. There is not space here to examine the interaction of all these political actors with intergovernmental officials. Attention will, therefore, focus on relations between intergovernmental officials in different jurisdictions and between these officials on the one hand and Cabinet members and legislators on the other.

We have already described the elaborate network of formal and informal contacts between intergovernmental officials in different governments. One of the most striking changes in the nature of these contacts during the past decade has been the greatly increased influence of provincial officials in relation to their federal counterparts. In federal-provincial meetings, provincial governments are treated as equal in status to the federal government. Indeed, the term *levels of government* with its connotation of differences in rank is now used less frequently; the term *orders of government* is increasingly used.

The power of provincial officials in intergovernmental relations rests on a broad range of factors, including the constitutional distribution of responsibilities, the wealth of the province, the electoral success of its political leaders, and the administrative and technical skills of its officials. The relative importance of these factors varies over time and depends to a large extent on the issue under consideration. It is generally acknowledged, however, that a major reason for the growth of provincial power has been the influence of provincial officials resulting from their increased expertise. The expertise of federal officials, which explained to a large extent the federal government's dominant influence in intergovernmental relations during the 1950s and early 1960s, is now more closely matched by the expertise of provincial officials.

In the intergovernmental policy process, officials exercise significant power, in the sense of influence, over Cabinet members and legislators. Gordon Robertson, former secretary to the Cabinet for federal-provincial relations, has asserted that "intergovernmental business in Canada . . . is conducted by Cabinet members, notably by First Ministers. . . . Interministerial conferences are thus an adjunct to executive power, a demonstration of where power actually resides, and the centrepiece of what Donald Smiley has called 'executive federalism.'"[25] This assertion does not take adequate account of the fact that executive federalism involves relations between both ministers *and officials* and that officials exercise significant influence over policy development before, during and after interministerial conferences. Moreover, as noted earlier, officials exert much policy influence in connection with the very large number of intergovernmental meetings below the ministerial level. The influence of intergovernmental officials arises not only from their expertise but from the formal and informal bargaining, often on a multilateral basis, in which they engage on behalf of their ministers.

But the influence of intergovernmental officials in relation to ministers should not be exaggerated. Cabinet members, either individually or collectively, possess ultimate control over the government's stance on all intergovernmental matters. Officials must be highly sensitive to the desires of the Cabinet as a whole and of individual ministers in regard to both the substance and strategy of negotiations. Moreover, Cabinet members are the central actors in taking decisions on major and politically sensitive intergovernmental issues and in much of the negotiation leading to those decisions.

Compared to Cabinet members, legislators have little control or influence over intergovernmental activities. Indeed, legislators do not exercise much power over the executive in general or officials in particular

---

[25]Gordon Robertson, "The Role of Interministerial Conferences in the Decision-Making Process," in Simeon, *Confrontation and Collaboration*, p. 80.

in any area of government activity.[26] There is general agreement with the observation that intergovernmental business in Canada "is conducted by governments . . . not by legislatures" and that "this works because a Cabinet in our parliamentary system can normally 'deliver' legislative support on virtually any matter, save possibly in minority situations."[27]

According to the constitutional convention of collective ministerial responsibility, the Cabinet is responsible to the sovereign legislature. Yet there is normally much more discussion of intergovernmental matters in conferences than in the federal Parliament or provincial legislatures. There are few opportunities for legislators to examine intergovernmental policy issues before legislation incorporating agreements reached at conferences is presented to the legislature. Since this legislation is often the outcome of complicated and protracted negotiations among governments, ministers are understandably reluctant to make changes at the legislative stage with which other governments may disagree.[28] It is notable also that the federal Parliament and the provincial legislatures have not developed intergovernmental machinery, for example, standing committees, to parallel the sophisticated mechanisms established by the executive.

Despite the claims of some journalists and politicians to the contrary, informed observers of the Canadian federal system deny that federal-provincial conferences constitute a third order of government. There are differences of opinion, however, about the effect of intergovernmental meetings on the accountability of governments to Parliament and the legislatures. Gordon Robertson has stated that "federal-provincial conferences do not in fact reduce the accountability as such of governments to Parliament and to legislatures. Parliament is the locus of responsibility and accountability for our national government but, because of the nature of our system, it is not the public and apparent locus of regional argument and compromise."[29] In a formal sense, this statement is

---

[26]See Kenneth Kernaghan, "Power, Parliament and Public Servants: Ministerial Responsibility Reexamined," *Canadian Public Policy* 5 (Summer 1979): 383-96.

[27]Robertson, p. 80.

[28]Robert Stanfield, former leader of the federal Progressive Conservative party, has noted that "the frustrations of Members of Parliament are increased by federal-provincial deals, agreements and resulting legislation which confront Parliament as *faits accomplis*." "The Present State of the Legislative Process in Canada: Myths and Realities," *The Legislative Process in Canada: the Need for Reform*, ed. W.A.W. Neilson and J.C. MacPherson (Institute for Research on Public Policy; distributed by Butterworth (Canada) Ltd., Toronto; 1978), p. 44. In a comment on Mr. Stanfield's paper, Gordon Gibson, former leader of the Liberal party in British Columbia, said that "federal-provincial agreements are so cast in stone from the time of the agreement that even if the opposition were able to convince the government that amendments should be made it would be too late to change things in any significant respect," p. 52.

[29]Robertson, p. 83.

accurate, but the weight of opinion supports Donald Smiley's contention that "to the extent that the actual locus of decision-making in respect to an increasing number of public matters has shifted from individual governments to intergovernmental groupings, the effective accountability of executives both to their respective legislatures and to those whom they govern is weakened."[30]

The accountability of intergovernmental officials is a serious concern, but accountability is only one of several values associated with the broad concept of administrative responsibility. Responsible intergovernmental officials must also be concerned with such values as responsiveness and effectiveness. It is important to determine not only whether these officials are accountable to ministers and legislators but whether they are sensitive to the needs and desires of other political actors and whether they are successful in achieving their government's objectives. Thus, in addition to intergovernmental and intragovernmental conflicts, officials face personal value conflicts (for example, accountability versus responsiveness or responsiveness versus effectiveness).

It is evident that intergovernmental management involves to a very large extent the management of conflict and complexity. Alan Cairns has observed that "contemporary intergovernmental coordination is not a simple matter of agreement between a handful of political leaders and their staff advisers. It requires . . . the containment of ineradicable tendencies to conflict between the federal vision of a society and economy, and ten competing provincial visions. . . ."[31] The key role of intergovernmental officials in seeking to harmonize these diverse perspectives ensures that the management of intergovernmental relations will remain a dominant concern of students and practitioners of Canadian public administration.

---

[30]"An Outsider's Observations," p. 107.
[31]Alan Cairns, "The Governments and Societies of Canadian Federalism," *Canadian Journal of Political Science* 10 (December 1977): 722.

9/Bilingualism in the
Public Service of Canada*

Kenneth Kernaghan

The story of the underrepresentation of French-speaking persons in the Canadian public service is well documented.[1] Barriers to equal opportunity to participate in the service have existed both in the government and in the francophone community for most of this century.[2]

During the post-Confederation period before the 1918 Civil Service Act, francophones were numerically well represented in the public service. They were not, however, as well represented as anglophones at the senior levels. Moreover, many of the francophone appointments rested on patronage and the 1918 Act emphasized merit and efficiency. This emphasis reflected the movements at this time for the abolition of patronage and for scientific management. The public service, especially after 1918, was pervaded by an anglophone linguistic and cultural bias. Merit and efficiency were linked to formal education and technical qualifications. French-language or bilingual competence was not considered a component of merit or likely to enhance efficiency. Furthermore, written examinations and interviews for recruitment and promotion reflected anglophone values and the anglophone educational system to the disadvantage of francophones. Finally, the view was widely held that the Quebec educational system was a significant barrier to francophone representation because it emphasized education for such occupations as law, medicine and the priesthood and did not therefore provide its graduates with the technical, scientific and commercial skills required for appointment to the public service.

All these factors combined to reduce the motivation of francophones to seek or retain positions in the federal administration. The result was a decline in the proportion of francophones in the public service from 21.58 per cent in 1918 to 12.25 per cent in 1946 and a decline at the deputy minister level during the same period from 14.28 per cent to zero.[3]

During the early 1960s, the so-called Quiet Revolution focused national attention on francophone grievances about their inadequate

---

*Reprinted and updated by permission from Kenneth Kernaghan, "Representative Bureaucracy—the Canadian Perspective," *Canadian Public Administration*, vol. 21 (Winter 1978), pp. 489-512.
[1]See *Royal Commission on Bilingualism and Biculturalism* (Ottawa: Queen's Printer, 1969), Book 3, Part 3, pp. 98-112; Harvey Rich, "The Canadian Case for a Representative Bureaucracy," *Political Science*, 27 (July-December, 1975): 103-108; and V. Seymour Wilson and Willard A. Mullins, "Representative Bureaucracy: Linguistic/Ethnic Aspects in Canadian Public Policy," *Canadian Public Administration*, vol. 21 (Winter 1978), pp. 513-538.
[2]See Kenneth Kernaghan, "Representative Bureaucracy," in this volume at p. 321.
[3]Wilson and Mullins, p. 520.

participation in the public service. And the Glassco Commission reported in 1963 that francophones were badly under-represented in the service. The commissioners noted that public confidence in the public service will depend on "how representative it is of the public it serves" and to achieve representativeness "a career at the centre of government should be as attractive and congenial to French-speaking as to English-speaking Canadians."[4]

Then, in 1966, Prime Minister Pearson made his landmark statement on bilingualism in the public service in which he promised, inter alia, that "the linguistic and cultural values of the English-speaking and French-speaking Canadians will be reflected through civil service recruitment and training."[5] The report of the Royal Commission on Bilingualism and Biculturalism, which was appointed by Mr. Pearson, gave enormous impetus to the realization of this goal. Prime Minister Trudeau, in accepting in principle the broad objectives proposed for the public service in the *Report*, stated that "the atmosphere of the public service should represent the linguistic and cultural reality of Canadian society, and that Canadians whose mother tongue is French should be adequately represented in the public service—*both in terms of numbers and in levels of responsibility*."[6]

In a concerted effort to increase francophone representation in the public service, the major strategies adopted by the Liberal government have included more active recruitment of francophones, the designation of language requirements for public service positions, the establishment of French-language units in the public service, and the development of an extensive language training system.

These strategies have complemented one another in helping to create a public service milieu to which francophones would be attracted and in which the French culture could flourish. The effort of the Public Service Commission to bring more francophones into the service through more vigorous recruitment has not been a sufficient strategy in itself. The designation of a large number of positions as requiring either bilingual or French-language competence assured that francophones would be attracted to these positions and that they would be appointed to them. Similarly, the creation of administrative units working in French guaranteed the appointment of francophones to these positions. Finally, the sophisticated and costly language-training programs were aimed at bringing about an environment in which francophones and anglophones could communicate with each other and with the public in their mother tongues.

---

[4]*Royal Commission on Government Organization* (Ottawa: Queen's Printer, 1963), vol. 1., pp. 27-29.
[5]House of Commons, *Debates*, April 6, 1966, p. 3915.
[6]*Ibid.*, June 23, 1970, p. 8487. Emphasis added.

Individual public servants and public service unions have severely attacked these measures to increase francophone representation on the grounds that the measures violate the merit principle and amount to "reverse discrimination" against anglophones. The government's response to this merit versus representation issue is that bilingual competence is an element of merit and that by increasing the number of positions requiring bilingual competence the government "will increase the opportunities for qualified francophones and thus at one and the same time preserve the merit principle and achieve the goal of a more representative Public Service."[7]

The government's strategies have helped to reduce institutional barriers in the government to francophone representation. Attitudinal change is more difficult to measure but there appears to be less overt resistance to government programs in this area and the public service milieu is now a much more bilingual one. In addition, a significant perceived barrier in the francophone community has been largely overcome. Since 1945, the Quebec educational system has produced increasing numbers of university and college graduates with the requisite qualifications for public service appointments.

The general impact of the government's efforts is that there are now more incentives for francophones to seek employment in the federal government. A mutually reinforcing circle of influences has been developed: the designation of bilingual and French positions has resulted in the appointment of more francophones; therefore, the French language is spoken more frequently; the working environment has thus become more attractive to francophones; more francophones have presented themselves for appointment to the public service; more francophones can be appointed because of the bilingual and French positions; and so on.

The most tangible indicator of progress is the fact that francophones are now represented in the public service in almost exact proportion to their numbers in the total population—an increase from 12.25 per cent of the service in 1946 to 26.8 per cent in 1980. Perhaps of even greater significance in view of the important policy role of senior public servants is the fact that 23 per cent of the senior executive category is now composed of francophones. It is notable that these increases have been achieved without using the strategy of a quota system.

Despite this apparent progress, some academic scholars have questioned the contribution to national unity of increased francophone representation. Posgate and McRoberts stated in 1976 that the representation of Quebec francophones in the executive ranks of the public service has

---

[7]C.M. Drury, *Minutes of Proceedings and Evidence of the Standing Committee on Miscellaneous Estimates*, March 9, 1971, issue no. 11:8.

not increased substantially.[8] However, this assertion is based on the 1966-1971 period rather than on the subsequent years during which the expansion of francophone representation at the senior levels was more rapid. They then cite statements by Léon Dion in the September 22, 1975 issue of *Le Devoir* as evidence that "among Francophones who were recruited to the civil service, Québécois were vastly underrepresented."[9] Dion did not provide the source of his information. Officials of the Public Service Commission informed this author that data on the geographical origin of francophone recruits have not been collected by the federal government. Nevertheless, in 1978, Hubert Guindon, relying on the statements by Posgate, McRoberts and Dion, concluded that since most of the increase in francophone representation "is recruited from French Canadians outside Quebec who are, therefore, already bilingual, its political irrelevance for Quebec"[10] is clear. This conclusion is based on information which is either badly dated or unsupported but the federal government is unable to provide hard evidence on this matter.

In any event, the percentage of Quebec francophones at the senior levels of the public service is an inadequate measure of their potential influence in the service. It is essential to know in what departments and agencies they are employed. Quebec francophones can clearly exercise more influence in the policy process if they hold senior positions in such administrative units as the Privy Council Office, Treasury Board and the Department of Finance rather than in less central and less significant departments and agencies.

Moreover, in regard to the total number of francophones in the public service, whether they are from Quebec or other parts of Canada, the Public Service Commission has drawn attention to some problems. In 1977, only 14.1 per cent of public servants said that French is the language they use most frequently in their work; many of the francophones at the officer levels hold positions in language-related programs which will probably be reduced in size in the coming years; francophones are employed largely in service departments and compose only a small percentage of employees in the scientific and technical areas; a sufficient number of francophone graduates of universities, colleges and CGEPs has not been attracted to the public service in recent years; and francophones have been leaving the public service at a faster rate than anglophones.[11]

---

[8]Dale Posgate and Kenneth McRoberts, *Quebec: Social Change and Political Crisis* (Toronto: McClelland and Stewart, 1976), p. 141.
[9]*Ibid.*, p. 142.
[10]Hubert Guindon, "The Modernization of Quebec and the Legitimacy of the Canadian State" in *Modernization and the Canadian State*, ed. D. Glenday, H. Guindon and A. Turowetz (Toronto: Macmillan, 1978), p. 221.
[11]Public Service Commission, *Annual Report 1977* (Ottawa: Minister of Supply and Services, 1978), p. 27.

The Public Service Commissioners concluded in 1977 that "the proportion of francophones in the federal Public Service has not yet reached that 'critical mass' that would allow the two language communities to survive, to be self-sustaining and to come into their own, yet this is one of the preconditions for efficient and high-quality service to all Canadians."[12] The evidence provided in subsequent annual reports of the commission reaffirms this conclusion.

Case References
Canadian Cases in Public Administration

Dr. Stockfield's Resignation
The Shared Authority
B and B or Not
Fear of Flying
This Hour Has Seven Days
The Foot and Mouth Disease Epidemic, 1952

Bibliography

Andrew, Caroline, and Pelletier, Réjean. "The Regulators." In *The Regulatory Process in Canada*, edited by G. Bruce Doern, pp. 147-64. Toronto: Macmillan, 1978.

Aucoin, Peter. "Portfolio Structures and Policy Coordination." In *Public Policy in Canada*, edited by G. Bruce Doern and Peter Aucoin, pp. 213-38. Toronto: Macmillan, 1979.

Aucoin, P., and French, R. *Knowledge, Power and Public Policy.* Science Council of Canada, Special Study no. 31. Ottawa: Information Canada, 1974.

Ashley, C.A., and Smails, R.G.H. *Canadian Crown Corporations.* Toronto: Macmillan, 1965.

Bowland, J.G. "Geographical Decentralization in the Canadian Federal Public Service." *Canadian Public Administration* 10 (September 1967): 323-61.

Brown-John, C. Lloyd. "Advisory Agencies in Canada: an Introduction." *Canadian Public Administration* 22 (Spring 1979): 72-91.

Bryce, R.F. "Reflections on the Lambert Report." *Canadian Public Administration* 22 (Winter 1979): 572-80.

Campbell, Colin, and Szablowski, George J. *The Superbureaucrats: Structure and Behaviour in Central Agencies.* Toronto: Macmillan, 1979.

Canada. Royal Commission on Bilingualism and Biculturalism. *Report.* vol. 3. Ottawa: Queen's Printer, 1967.

Canada. Royal Commission on Government Organization (Glassco Commission). *Report:* vol. 1, *Management of the Public Service*, reports 1-4; vol. 2, *Supporting Services for Government*, reports 5-11; vol. 3, *Supporting Services for Government*, reports 12-13; and *Services for the Public*, reports 14-18; vol. 4, *Special Areas of Administration*, reports 19-23; vol. 5, *The Organization of the Government of Canada.* Ottawa: Queen's Printer, 1962/63.

Cloutier, Sylvain. "Senior Public Service Officials in a Bicultural Society." *Canadian Public Administration* 11, no. 4 (Winter 1968): 395-406.

Cole, Taylor. *The Canadian Bureaucracy, 1939-1947.* Durham, N.C.: Duke University Press, 1949.

Cole, Taylor. *The Canadian Bureaucracy and Federalism: 1947-1965.* Denver, Colorado: University of Denver Press, 1966.

---

[12]*Ibid.*, pp. 27-28.

Dobell, W.M. "Interdepartmental Management in External Affairs." *Canadian Public Administration* 21, no. 1 (Spring 1978): 83-102.

Doern, G. Bruce. "Regulatory Processes and Regulatory Agencies." In *Public Policy in Canada*, edited by G. Bruce Doern and Peter Aucoin, pp. 158-89.

Doern, G. Bruce, "The Cabinet and Central Agencies." In *Public Policy in Canada*, pp. 27-61.

Doern, G. Bruce, ed. *The Regulatory Process in Canada*. Toronto: Macmillan, 1978.

Doern, G. Bruce et al. "The Structure and Behaviour of Canadian Regulatory Boards and Commissions: Multidisciplinary Perspectives." *Canadian Public Administration* 18, no. 2 (Summer 1975): 189-215.

Doern, G. Bruce. "The Teaching of Public Administration in Canadian Universities." In *Executive Manpower in the Public Service: Make or Buy*, edited by Kenneth Kernaghan, pp. 80-102. Toronto: Institute of Public Administration of Canada, 1975.

Doerr, Audrey D. *The Machinery of Government in Canada*. Toronto: Methuen, 1980.

Garant, Patrice. *La fonction publique: canadienne et québécoise*. Québec: Les Presses de l'Université Laval, 1973.

Gélinas, André. "Le cadre général des institutions administratives et la déconcentration territoriale." *Canadian Public Administration* 18, no. 2 (Summer 1975): 253-68.

Gélinas, André. "Le rapport Lambert: les organismes de la couronne." *Canadian Public Administration* 22, no. 4 (Winter 1979): 541-56.

Gélinas, André, ed. *Public Enterprise and the Public Interest*. Toronto: Institute of Public Administration, 1978.

Gow, James Iain, ed. *Administration publique québécoise*. Montreal: Librairie Beauchemin, 1970.

Hanson, A.H. *Public Enterprise: A Study of its Organization and Management*. Brussels: International Institute of Administrative Sciences, 1956.

Hicks, Michael. "The Treasury Board of Canada and its Clients: Five Years of Change and Administrative Reform, 1966-71." *Canadian Public Administration* 16, no. 2 (Summer 1973): 182-205.

Hill, Mary O. *Canada's Salesman to the World: The Department of Trade and Commerce, 1892-1939*. Montreal: McGill-Queen's University Press, 1977.

Hodgetts, J.C. "The Public Service: Its Past and the Challenge of its Future." *Canadian Public Administration* 17, no. 1 (Spring 1974): 17-25.

Hodgetts, J.E., and Corbett, D.C., eds. *Canadian Public Administration*. Toronto: Macmillan, 1960.

Hodgetts, J.E., and Dwivedi, O.P. *Provincial Governments as Employers: A Survey of Public Personnel Administration in Canada's Provinces*. Montreal: McGill-Queen's University Press, 1974.

Janisch, H.N. *The Regulatory Process of the Canadian Transport Commission*. The Law Reform Commission of Canada. Ottawa: Supply and Services, 1978.

Kernaghan, W.D.K. "An Overview of Public Administration in Canada Today." *Canadian Public Administration* 11, no. 3 (Fall 1968): 291-308.

Kernaghan, W.D.K., ed. *Bureaucracy in Canadian Government*. Toronto: Methuen, 1969.

Kuruvilla, P.K. "Administrative Culture in Canada: Some Perspectives." *Canadian Public Administration* 16, no. 2 (Summer 1973): 284-97.

Laframboise, H.L. "Portfolio Structure and a Ministry System: A Model for the Canadian Federal Service." *Optimum* 1, no. 1 (1970): 29-46.

Langford, John. "Crown Corporations as Instruments of Policy." In *Public Policy in Canada*, edited by G. Bruce Doern and Peter Aucoin, pp. 239-74.

Langford, John W. *Transport in Transition: The Reorganization of the Federal Transport Portfolio*. Montreal: McGill-Queen's University Press, 1976.

Lucas, A.R., and Bell, T. *The National Energy Board*. Law Reform Commission. Ottawa: Supply and Services, 1977.

Prince, Michael J., and Chenier, John. "The Rise and Fall of Policy Planning and Research Units: An Organizational Perspective." *Canadian Public Administration* 23, no. 4 (Winter 1980): 519-41.

Robertson, Gordon. "The Role of Interministerial Conferences in the Decision-Making Process." In *Confrontation and Collaboration—Intergovernmental Relations in Canada Today*, edited by Richard Simeon, pp. 78-88.

Roman, Andrew J. "Regulatory Law and Procedure." In *The Regulatory Process in Canada*, edited by G. Bruce Doern, pp. 68-93.

Savoie, Donald J. *Federal-Provincial Collaboration.* Montreal: McGill-Queen's University Press, 1981.

Schultz, Richard. "Prime Ministerial Government, Central Agencies and Operating Departments: Towards a More Realistic Analysis." 2d ed. In *Apex of Power,* edited by Thomas A. Hockin. Toronto: Prentice-Hall, 1977.

Schultz, Richard. "The Regulatory Process and Federal-Provincial Relations." In *The Regulatory Process in Canada,* edited by G. Bruce Doern, pp. 128-46.

Schultz, Richard J. *Federalism, Bureaucracy and Public Policy.* Montreal: McGill-Queen's University Press, 1980.

Schultz, Richard J. *Federalism and the Regulatory Process.* Montreal: Institute for Research on Public Policy, 1979.

Simeon, Richard, ed. *Confrontation and Collaboration—Intergovernmental Relations in Canada Today.* Toronto: Institute of Public Administration, 1979.

Smiley, Donald V. "An Outsider's Observations of Federal-Provincial Relations Among Consenting Adults." In *Confrontation and Collaboration—Intergovernmental Relations in Canada Today,* edited by Richard Simeon, pp. 105-13.

Smiley, Donald V. "The Structural Problem of Canadian Federalism." *Canadian Public Administration* 14, no. 3 (Fall 1971): 326-43.

Stevenson, Donald. "The Role of Intergovernmental Conferences in the Decision-Making Process." In *Confrontation and Collaboration—Intergovernmental Relations in Canada Today,* edited by Richard Simeon, pp. 89-98.

Tupper, Allan. "The State in Business." *Canadian Public Administration* 22, no. 1 (Spring 1979): 124-50.

Veilleux, Gérard. "Intergovernmental Canada: Government by Conference? A Fiscal and Economic Perspective." *Canadian Public Administration* 23, no. 1 (Spring 1980): 33-53.

Veilleux, Gérard. "L'évolution des méchanismes de liaison intergouvernementale." In *Confrontation and Collaboration—Intergovernmental Relations in Canada Today,* edited by Richard Simeon, pp. 35-77.

Wilson, V. Seymour. "Federal-Provincial Relations and Federal-Policy Processes." In *Public Policy in Canada,* edited by G. Bruce Doern and Peter Aucoin, pp. 190-214.

Yeomans, D.R. "Decentralization of Authority." *Canadian Public Administration* 12, no. 1 (Spring 1969): 9-25.

Part III

PROBLEMS OF MANAGEMENT

10/Motivating Environment*
Paul Hersey and Kenneth H. Blanchard

In 1924 efficiency experts at the Hawthorne, Illinois, plant of the Western Electric Company designed a research program to study the effects of illumination on productivity. At first, nothing about this program seemed exceptional enough to arouse any unusual interest. After all, efficiency experts had long been trying to find the ideal mix of physical conditions, working hours and working methods which stimulate workers to produce at maximum capacity. Yet by the time these studies were completed (over a decade later), there was little doubt that the work at Hawthorne would stand the test of time as one of the most exciting and important research projects ever done in an industrial setting. For it was at Western Electric's Hawthorne plant that the Human Relations Movement began to gather momentum, and one of its early advocates, Elton Mayo of the Harvard Graduate School of Business Administration, gained recognition.[1]

Elton Mayo's Hawthorne Studies
In the initial study at Hawthorne, efficiency experts assumed that increases in illumination would result in higher output. Two groups of employees were selected: an *experimental* or *test group* which worked under varying degrees of light, and a *control group* which worked under normal illumination conditions in the plant. As lighting power was increased, the output of the test group went up as anticipated. Unexpectedly, however, the output of the control group went up also—without any increase in light.

Determined to explain these and other surprising test results, the

---

*Reprinted by permission from Paul Hersey and Kenneth H. Blanchard, *Management of Organizational Behaviour*, 2nd ed. (Englewood Cliffs, N.J.: Prentice-Hall, 1972), pp. 43-66.
[1]For detailed descriptions of this research see F.J. Roethlisberger and W.J. Dickson, *Management and the Worker* (Cambridge: Harvard University Press, 1939); T.N. Whitehead, *The Industrial Worker*, 2 vols. (Cambridge: Harvard University Press, 1938); Elton Mayo, *The Human Problems of an Industrial Civilization* (New York: The Macmillan Company, 1933).

efficiency experts decided to expand their research at Hawthorne. They felt that in addition to technical and physical changes, some of the behavioural considerations should be explored, so Mayo and his associates were called in to help.

Mayo and his team started their experiments with a group of women who assembled telephone relays, and, like the efficiency experts, the Harvard men uncovered astonishing results. For over a year and a half during this experiment, Mayo's researchers improved the women's working conditions by implementing such innovations as scheduled rest periods, company lunches and shorter work weeks. Baffled by the results, the researchers suddenly decided to take everything away, returning the working conditions to the exact way they had been at the beginning of the experiment. This radical change was expected to have a tremendous negative psychological impact on the women and reduce their output. Instead, their output jumped to a new *all-time high*. Why?

The answers to this question were *not* found in the production aspects of the experiment (that is, changes in plant and physical working conditions), but in the *human* aspects. As a result of the attention lavished upon them by experimenters, the women were made to feel they were an important part of the company. They no longer viewed themselves as isolated individuals, working together only in the sense that they were physically close to each other. Instead, they had become participating members of a congenial, cohesive work group. The relationships that developed elicited feelings of affiliation, competence and achievement. These needs, which had long gone unsatisfied at work, were now being fulfilled. The women worked harder and more effectively than they had previously.

Realizing that they had uncovered an interesting phenomenon, the Harvard team extended their research by interviewing over twenty thousand employees from every department in the company. Interviews were designed to help researchers find out what the workers thought about their jobs, their working conditions, their supervisors, their company and anything that bothered them, and how these feelings might be related to their productivity. After several interview sessions, Mayo's group found that a structured question-and-answer-type interview was useless for eliciting the information they wanted. Instead, the workers wanted to talk freely about what *they* thought was important. So the predetermined questions were discarded, and the interviewer allowed the worker to ramble as he or she chose.

The interviews proved valuable in a number of ways. First of all, they were therapeutic; the workers got an opportunity to get a lot off their chests. Many felt this was the best thing the company had ever done. The result was a wholesale change in attitude. Since many of their sugges-tions were being implemented, the workers began to feel that management viewed them as important, both as individuals and as a group; they were now participating in the operation and future of the company and not just performing unchallenging, unappreciated tasks.

Second, the implications of the Hawthorne studies signalled the need for management to study and understand relationships among people. In these studies, as well as in the many that followed, the most significant factor affecting organizational productivity was found to be the interpersonal relationships that are developed on the job, not just pay and working conditions. Mayo found that when informal groups identified with management, as they did at Hawthorne through the interview program, productivity rose. The increased productivity seemed to reflect the workers' feelings of competence—a sense of mastery over the job and work environment. Mayo also discovered that when the group felt that their own goals were in opposition to those of management, as often happened in situations where the workers were closely supervised and had no significant control over their job or environment, productivity remained at low levels or was even lowered.

These findings were important because they helped answer many of the questions that had puzzled management about why some groups seemed to be high producers while others hovered at a minimal level of output. The findings also encouraged management to involve workers in planning, organizing and controlling their own work in an effort to secure their positive cooperation.

Mayo saw the development of informal groups as an indictment of an entire society which treated human beings as insensitive machines that were concerned only with economic self-interest. As a result, workers had been taught to look at work merely as an impersonal exchange of money for labour. Work in American industry meant humiliation—the performance of routine, tedious and oversimplified tasks in an environment over which one had no control. This environment denied satisfaction of esteem and self-actualization needs on the job. Instead only physiological and safety needs were satisfied. The lack of avenues for satisfying other needs led to tension, anxiety and frustration in workers. Such feelings of helplessness were called *anomie* by Mayo. This condition was characterized by workers feeling unimportant, confused and unattached—victims of their own environment.

While anomie was a creation of the total society, Mayo felt its most extreme application was found in industrial settings where management held certain negative assumptions about the nature of man. According to Mayo, too many managers assumed that society consisted of a horde or mob of unorganized individuals whose only concern was self-preservation or self-interest. It was assumed that people were primarily dominated by physiological and safety needs, wanting to make as much money as they could for as little work as possible. Thus management operated and organized work on the basic assumption that workers, on the whole, were a contemptible lot. Mayo called this assumption the "Rabble Hypothesis." He deplored the authoritarian, task-oriented management practices that it created.

Douglas McGregor's Theory X and Theory Y

The work of Mayo and particularly his exposure of the Rabble Hypothesis may have paved the way for the development of the now classic "Theory X—Theory Y" by Douglas McGregor.[2] According to McGregor, traditional organization with its centralized decision making, superior-subordinate pyramid, and external control of work is based upon assumptions about human nature and human motivation. These assumptions are very similar to the view of man defined by Mayo in the Rabble Hypothesis. Theory X assumes that most people prefer to be directed, are not interested in assuming responsibility, and want safety above all. Accompanying this philosophy is the belief that people are motivated by money, fringe benefits and the threat of punishment.

Managers who accept Theory X assumptions attempt to structure, control and closely supervise their employees. These managers feel that external control is clearly appropriate for dealing with unreliable, irresponsible and immature people.

After describing Theory X, McGregor questioned whether this view of man is correct and if management practices based upon it are appropriate in many situations today: Isn't man in a democratic society, with its increasing level of education and standard of living, capable of more mature behaviour? Drawing heavily on Maslow's hierarchy of needs, McGregor concluded that Theory X assumptions about the nature of man are generally inaccurate and that management approaches that develop from these assumptions will often fail to motivate individuals to work toward organizational goals. Management by direction and control may not succeed, according to McGregor, because it is a questionable method for motivating people whose physiological and safety needs are reasonably satisfied and whose social, esteem and self-actualization needs are becoming predominant.

McGregor felt that management needed practices based on a more accurate understanding of the nature of man and human motivation. As a result of his feeling, McGregor developed an alternate theory of human behaviour called Theory Y. This theory assumes that people are *not*, by nature, lazy and unreliable. It postulates that man can be basically self-directed and creative at work if properly motivated. Therefore, it should be an essential task of management to unleash this potential in man. The

---

[2]Douglas McGregor, *The Human Side of Enterprise* (New York: McGraw-Hill Book Company, 1960). See also McGregor, *Leadership and Motivation* (Boston: MIT Press, 1966).

properly motivated worker can achieve his own goals *best* by directing *his own* efforts toward accomplishing organizational goals.

Table 1
List of Assumptions About Nature of Man which
Underline McGregor's Theory X and Theory Y

Theory X	Theory Y
1. Work is inherently distasteful to most people.	1. Work is as natural as play, if the conditions are favourable.
2. Most people are not ambitious, have little desire for responsibility, and prefer to be directed.	2. Self-control is often indispensable in achieving organizational goals.
3. Most people have little capacity for creativity in solving organizational problems.	3. The capacity for creativity in solving organizational problems is widely distributed in the population.
4. Motivation occurs only at the physiological and safety levels.	4. Motivation occurs at the social, esteem and self-actualization levels, as well as physiological and security levels.
5. Most people must be closely controlled and often coerced to achieve organizational objectives.	5. People can be self-directed and creative at work if properly motivated.

Managers who accept the Theory Y image of human nature do *not* usually structure, control or closely supervise the work environment for employees. Instead, they attempt to help their employees mature by exposing them to progressively less external control, allowing them to assume more and more self-control. Employees are able to achieve the satisfaction of social, esteem and self-actualization needs within this kind of environment, often neglected on the job. To the extent that the job does not provide need satisfaction at every level, today's employee will usually look elsewhere for significant need satisfaction. This helps explain some of the current problems management is facing in such areas as turnover and absenteeism. McGregor argues that this does not have to be the case.

Management is interested in work, and McGregor feels that work is as natural and can be as satisfying for people as play. After all, both work and play are physical and mental activities; consequently, there is no inherent difference between work and play. In reality, though, particularly under Theory X management, a distinct difference in need satisfaction is discernible. Whereas play is internally controlled by the individual (he decides what he wants to do), work is externally controlled by others (the worker has no control over his job). Thus management and its assumptions about the nature of man have built in a difference between work and play that seems unnatural. As a result, people are stifled at work and hence look for excuses to spend more and more time away from the job in order to satisfy their esteem and self-actualization needs (provided they have enough money to satisfy their physiological and safety needs). Because of their conditioning to Theory X types of management, most employees consider work a *necessary evil* rather than a source of personal challenge and satisfaction.

Does work really have to be a necessary evil? No—especially in organizations where cohesive work groups have developed and where the goals parallel organizational goals. In such organizations there is high productivity, and people come to work gladly because work is inherently satisfying.

George C. Homans's Human Group Theory

Management is often suspicious of strong informal work groups because of their potential power to control the behaviour of their members and, as a result, the level of productivity. Where do these groups get their power to control behaviour? George C. Homans has developed a model of social systems which may be useful to the practitioner trying to answer this question.[3]

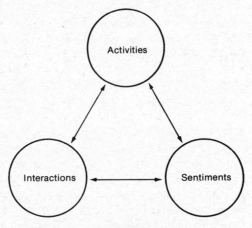

Figure 1
The Mutual Dependence of Activities,
Interactions and Sentiments

There are three elements in a social system. *Activities* are the tasks that people perform. *Interactions* are the behaviours that occur between people in performing these tasks. And *sentiments* are the attitudes that

---

[3]George C. Homans, *The Human Group* (New York: Harcourt, Brace & World, Inc., 1950).

develop between individuals and within groups. Homans argues that while these concepts are separate, they are closely related. In fact, as Figure 1 illustrates, they are mutually dependent upon each other.

A change in any of these three elements will produce some change in the other two.

In an organization certain activities, interactions and sentiments are essential, or required from its members, if it is to survive. In other words, jobs (activities) have to be done that require people to work together (interactions). These jobs must be sufficiently satisfying (sentiments) for people to continue doing them. As people interact on their jobs, they develop sentiments toward each other. As people increase interaction with each other, more positive sentiments will tend to develop toward each other. The more positive the sentiment, the more people will tend to interact with each other. It can become a spiralling process until some equilibrium is reached. As this spiralling process continues, there is a tendency for the group members to become more alike in their activities and sentiments—in what they do and how they feel about things. As this happens, the group tends to develop expectations or norms that specify how people in the group "might" tend to behave under specific circumstances. For example, a group of workers might have a norm that "you should not talk to the boss, or help him, any more than necessary." If the group is cohesive enough, that is, the group is attractive to its members and they are reluctant to leave it, then it will have little trouble in getting members to conform. People who deviate significantly from group norms usually incur sanctions from the group. "The group has at its disposal a variety of penalties, ranging from gentle kidding to harsh ostracism, for pressuring deviant members into line."[4] The group member may react in several ways. He may decide to go ahead and continue to deviate from group norms. If the resulting pressure from his peers becomes too great, he may leave the group.

The influence group pressures can have in achieving conformity in the perceptions and behaviour of people is well documented. For example, S.E. Asch conducted a classic experiment in which groups of eight college men were each asked to match the length of a line with one of three unequal lines.[5] Seven members of each group were privately told to give the same incorrect answer. The uninstructed member was the last one asked to give his answer and was thus confronted with the dilemma

---

[4]Anthony G. Athos and Robert E. Coffey, *Behavior in Organizations: A Multi-dimensional View* (Englewood Cliffs, N.J.: Prentice-Hall, Inc., 1968), p. 101.
[5]S.E. Asch, "Effects of Group Pressure upon the Modification and Distortion of Judgments," in *Groups, Leadership and Men*, ed. Harold Guetzkow (New York: Russell and Russell Publishers, 1963), pp. 177-90. Also in Dorwin Cartwright and Alvin Zander, *Group Dynamics*, 2nd ed. (Evanston, Ill.: Row, Peterson & Company, 1960), pp. 189-200.

of either reporting what he saw as being correct or reporting what all the others had said in order to be congruent with the group. Asch reported that "one-third of all the estimates were errors identical with or in the direction of the distorted estimates of the majority."[6] If pressure can cause distorted behaviour in this kind of exercise, imagine what peer group pressure can induce with more subjective judgments.

It should be reiterated that strong informal work groups do not have to be a detriment to organizations. In fact, as Mayo discovered at Hawthorne, these groups can become powerful driving forces in accomplishing organizational goals if they see their own goals as being satisfied by working for organizational goals.

Chris Argyris's Immaturity-Maturity Theory

Even though management based on the assumptions of Theory X is perhaps no longer appropriate in the opinion of McGregor and others, it is still widely practised. Consequently, a large majority of people today are treated as immature human beings in their working environments. It is this fact that has produced many of our current organizational problems. Chris Argyris, while at Yale University, examined industrial organizations to determine what effect management practices have had on individual behaviour and personal growth within the work environment.[7]

According to Argyris, seven changes should take place in the personality of an individual if he is to develop into a mature person over the years.

First, an individual moves from a passive state as an infant to a state of increasing activity as an adult. Second, an individual develops from a state of dependency upon others as an infant to a state of relative independence as an adult. Third, an individual behaves in only a few ways as an infant, but as an adult, he is capable of behaving in many ways. Fourth, an individual has erratic, casual and shallow interests as an infant but develops deeper and stronger interests as an adult. Fifth, a child's time perspective is very short, involving only the present, but as he matures, his time perspective increases to include the past and the future. Sixth, an individual as an infant is subordinate to everyone, but he moves to equal or superior position with others as an adult. Seventh, as a child, an individual lacks an awareness of a "self," but as an adult, he is not only aware of, but he is able to control "self." Argyris postulates that these

---

[6]*Ibid.*
[7]Chris Argyris, *Personality and Organization* (New York: Harper & Row, Publishers, 1957); *Interpersonal Competence and Organizational Effectiveness* (Homewood, Ill.: Dorsey Press, 1962); and *Integrating the Individual and the Organization* (New York: John Wiley & Sons, Inc., 1964).

changes reside on a continuum and that the "healthy" personality develops along the continuum from "immaturity" to "maturity."

These changes are only general tendencies, but they give some light to the matter of maturity. Norms of the individual's culture and personality inhibit and limit maximum expression and growth of the adult, yet the tendency is to move toward the "maturity" end of the continuum with age. Argyris would be the first to admit that few, if any, develop to full maturity.

Table 2
Immaturity-Maturity Continuum

Immaturity	Maturity
Passive	Active
Dependence	Independence
Behave in a few ways	Capable of behaving in many ways
Erratic shallow interests	Deeper and stronger interests
Short time perspective	Long time perspective (past and future)
Subordinate position	Equal or superordinate position
Lack of awareness of self	Awareness and control over self

In examining the widespread worker apathy and lack of effort in industry, Argyris questions whether these problems are simply the result of individual laziness. He suggests that this is *not* the case. Argyris contends that, in many cases, when people join the work force, they are kept from maturing by the management practices utilized in their organizations. In these organizations, they are given minimal control over their environment and are encouraged to be passive, dependent and subordinate; therefore, they behave immaturely. The worker in many organizations is expected to act in immature ways rather than as a mature adult.

According to Argyris, keeping people immature is built into the very nature of the formal organization. He argues that because organizations are usually created to achieve goals or objectives that can best be met collectively, the formal organization is often the architect's conception of how these objectives may be achieved. In this sense the individual is fitted to the job. The design comes first. This design is based upon four concepts of scientific management: task specialization, chain of command, unity of direction and span of control. Management tries to increase and enhance organizational and administrative efficiency and productivity by making workers "interchangeable parts."

Basic to these concepts is that power and authority should rest in the hands of a few at the top of the organization, and thus those at the lower end of the chain of command are strictly controlled by their superiors or the system itself. Task specialization often results in the oversimplification of the job so that it becomes repetitive, routine and unchallenging. This implies directive, task-oriented leadership where decisions about the work are made by the superior, with the workers only carrying out those decisions. This type of leadership evokes managerial controls such as budgets, some incentive systems, time and motion studies and standard operating procedures which can restrict the initiative and creativity of workers.

Argyris feels that these concepts of formal organization lead to assumptions about human nature that are incompatible with the proper development of maturity in human personality. He sees a definite incongruity between the needs of a mature personality and the formal organizations as they now exist. Since he implies that the classical theory of management (based on Theory X assumptions) usually prevails, management creates childlike roles for workers that frustrate natural development.

An example of how work is often designed at this extremely low level was dramatically illustrated by the successful use of mentally retarded workers in such jobs. Argyris cites two instances, one in a knitting mill and the other in a radio manufacturing corporation, in which mentally retarded people were successfully employed on unskilled jobs. In both cases, the managers praised these workers for their excellent performance. In fact, a manager in the radio corporation reported:

> The girls proved to be exceptionally well-behaved, particularly obedient and strictly honest and trustworthy. They carried out work required of them to such a degree of efficiency that *we were surprised they were classed as subnormals for their age.* Their attendance was good, and their behavior was, if anything, certainly better than that of any other employee of the same age.[8]

Disturbed by what he finds in many organizations, Argyris, as did McGregor, challenges management to provide a work climate in which everyone has a chance to grow and mature as an individual, as a member of a group by satisfying his own needs, while working for the success of the organization. Implicit here is the belief that man can be basically self-directed and creative at work if properly motivated, and, therefore, management based on the assumption of Theory Y will be more profitable for the individual and the organization.

More and more companies are starting to listen to the challenge that Argyris is directing at management. For example, the president of a large company asked Argyris to show him how to motivate his workers better. Together they went into one of his production plants where a product similar to a radio was being assembled. There were twelve women

---

[8]N. Breman. *The Making of a Moron* (New York: Sheed & Ward, 1953).

involved in assembling the product, each doing a small segment of the job as designed by an industrial engineer. The group also had a foreman, an inspector and a packer.

Argyris proposed a one-year experiment during which each of the women would assemble the total product in a manner of her own choice. At the same time they would inspect, sign their name to the product, pack it, and handle any correspondence involving complaints about it. The women were assured that they would receive no cut in pay if production dropped but would receive more pay if production increased.

Once the experiment began, production dropped 70 per cent during the first month. By the end of six weeks it was even worse. The women were upset, morale was down. This continued until the eighth week, when production started to rise. By the end of the fifteenth week production was higher than it had ever been before. And this was without an inspector, a packer or an industrial engineer. More important than increased productivity, costs due to errors and waste decreased 94 per cent; letters of complaint dropped 96 per cent.

Experiments like this are being duplicated in numerous other situations.[9] It is being found over and over again that broadening individual responsibility is beneficial to both the workers and the company. Giving people the opportunity to grow and mature on the job helps them satisfy more than just physiological and safety needs, which, in turn, motivates them and allows them to use more of their potential in accomplishing organizational goals. While all workers do *not* want to accept more responsibility or deal with the added problems responsibility inevitably brings, Argyris contends that the number of employees whose motivation can be improved by increasing and upgrading their responsibility is much larger than most managers would suspect.

Frederick Herzberg's Motivation-Hygiene Theory

As people mature, we have noted that needs such as esteem and self-actualization seem to become more important. One of the most interesting series of studies that concentrates heavily on these areas was directed by Frederick Herzberg of Case-Western Reserve University.[10] Out of these studies has developed a theory of work motivation which has broad implications for management and its efforts toward effective utilization of human resources.

---

[9]For other examples of successful interventions, see Argyris, *Intervention Theory and Method: A Behavioral Science View* (Reading, Mass.: Addison-Wesley Publishing Company, 1970).
[10]Frederick Herzberg, Bernard Mausner, and Barbara Snyderman, *The Motivation to Work* (New York: John Wiley & Sons, Inc., 1959); and Herzberg, *Work and the Nature of Man* (New York: World Publishing Co., 1966).

Herzberg, in developing his motivation-hygiene theory, seemed to sense that scholars like McGregor and Argyris were touching on something important. Knowledge about the nature of man, his motives and needs, could be invaluable to organizations and individuals.

> To industry, the payoff for a study of job attitudes would be increased productivity, decreased absenteeism, and smoother working relations. To the individual, an understanding of the forces that lead to improved morale would bring greater happiness and greater self-realization.[11]

Herzberg set out to collect data on job attitudes from which assumptions about human behaviour could be made. The motivation-hygiene theory resulted from the analysis of an initial study by Herzberg and his colleagues at the Psychological Service of Pittsburgh. This study involved extensive interviews with some two hundred engineers and accountants from eleven industries in the Pittsburgh area. In the interviews, they were asked what kinds of things on their job made them unhappy or dissatisfied and what things made them happy or satisfied.

In analyzing the data from these interviews, Herzberg concluded that man has two different categories of needs which are essentially independent of each other and affect behaviour in different ways. He found that when people felt dissatisfied with their jobs, they were concerned about the environment in which they were working. On the other hand, when people felt good about their jobs, this had to do with the work itself. Herzberg called the first category of needs *hygiene factors* because they describe man's environment and serve the primary function of preventing job dissatisfaction. He called the second category of needs *motivators* since they seemed to be effective in motivating people to superior performance.

Hygiene Factors
Company policies and administration, supervision, working conditions, interpersonal relations, money, status and security may be thought of as hygiene factors. These are not an intrinsic part of a job, but they are related to the conditions under which a job is performed. Herzberg relates his use of the word *hygiene* to its medical meaning (preventative and environmental). Hygiene factors produce no growth in worker output capacity; they only prevent losses in worker performance due to work restriction.

Motivators
Satisfying factors that involve feelings of achievement, professional growth and recognition that one can experience in a job that offers

---

[11]Herzberg, Mausner, and Snyderman, *The Motivation to Work*, p. ix.

challenge and scope are referred to as motivators. Herzberg used this term because these factors seem capable of having a positive effect on job satisfaction often resulting in an increase in one's total output capacity.

In recent years motivation-hygiene research has been extended well beyond scientists and accountants to include every level of an organization from top management all the way down to hourly employees. For example, in an extensive study of Texas Instruments, Scott Meyers concluded that Herzberg's motivation-hygiene theory "is easily translatable to supervisory action at all levels of responsibility. It is a framework on which supervisors can evaluate and put into perspective the constant barrage of 'helpful hints' to which they are subjected, and hence serves to increase their feelings of competence, self-confidence, and autonomy."[12]

Table 3
Motivation and Hygiene Factors

Hygiene Factors Environment	Motivators The Job Itself
Policies and administration	Achievement
Supervision	Recognition for accomplishment
Working conditions	Challenging work
Interpersonal relations	Increased responsibility
Money, status, security	Growth and development

Herzberg's framework seems compatible with Maslow's hierarchy of needs. Maslow refers to needs or motives, while Herzberg seems to deal with the goals or incentives that tend to satisfy these needs. Examples can be cited. Money and benefits tend to satisfy needs at the physiological and security levels; interpersonal relations and supervision are examples of hygiene factors that tend to satisfy social needs, while increased responsibility, challenging work and growth and development are motivators that tend to satisfy needs at the esteem and self-actualization levels.

Figure 2 shows the relationship between these two frameworks.

We feel that the physiological, safety, social and part of the esteem needs are all hygiene factors. The esteem needs are divided because there are some distinct differences between status per se and recognition. Status tends to be a function of the position one occupies. One may have gained this position through family ties or social pressures, and thus this position is not a reflection of personal achievement or earned recogni-

---

[12]Scott M. Meyers, "Who Are Your Motivated Workers?" in David R. Hampton, *Behavioral Concepts in Management* (Belmont, Calif.: Dickenson Publishing Co., Inc., 1968), p. 64. Originally published in *Harvard Business Review*, January-February 1964, pp. 73-88.

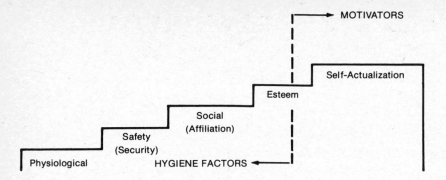

Figure 2
The Relationships Between the Motivation-Hygiene
Theory and Maslow's Hierarchy of Needs

tion. Recognition is gained through competence and achievement. It is earned and granted by others. Consequently, status is classified with physiological, safety and social needs as a hygiene factor, while recognition is classified with self-actualization as a motivator.

Perhaps an example will further differentiate between hygiene factors and motivators. This might help explain the reason for classifying needs as Herzberg has done as well as in a hierarchical arrangement.

Let us assume that a man is highly motivated and is working at 90 per cent of capacity. He has a good working relationship with his supervisor, is well satisfied with his pay and working conditions, and is part of a congenial work group. Suppose his supervisor is suddenly transferred and replaced by a person he is unable to work with, or he finds out that someone whose work he feels is inferior to his own is receiving more pay. How do these factors affect a man's behaviour? Since we know performance or productivity depends on both ability and motivation, these unsatisfied hygiene needs (supervision and money) may lead to restriction of output. In some cases this is intentional, while in others the individual may not be consciously aware that he is holding back. In either case, though, productivity will be lowered as illustrated in Figure 3.

In this illustration, even if his former supervisor returns and his salary is readjusted well above his expectations, his productivity will probably increase only to its original level.

Conversely, let us take the same person and assume that dissatisfaction has not occurred; he is working at 90 per cent capacity. Suppose he is given an opportunity to mature and satisfy his motivational needs in an environment where he is free to exercise some initiative and creativity, to make decisions, to handle problems, and to take responsibility. What effect will this situation have on this individual? If he is able to fulfil

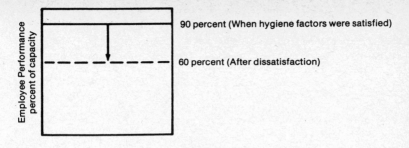

Figure 3
Effect of Dissatisfying Hygienes

successfully his supervisor's expectations in performing these new responsibilities, he may still work at 90 per cent capacity, but as a person he may have matured and grown in his ability and may be capable now of more productivity, as illustrated in Figure 4.

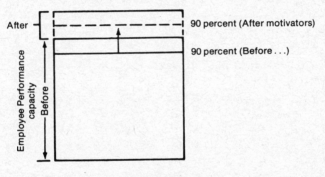

Figure 4
Effect of Satisfying Motivators

Hygiene needs, when satisfied, tend to eliminate dissatisfaction and work restriction but do little to motivate an individual to superior performance or increased capacity. Satisfaction of the motivators, however, will permit an individual to grow and develop in a mature way, often implementing an increase in ability. Herzberg encourages management to design into the work environment an opportunity to satisfy the motivators.

Prior to Herzberg's work, many other behavioural scientists were concerned with worker motivation. For several years there was an emphasis on what was termed "job enlargement." This was purported to be an answer to the overspecialization that had characterized many industrial organizations. The assumption was that a worker could gain more satisfaction at work if his job was enlarged, that is, if the number of operations in which he engaged was increased.

Herzberg makes some astute observations about this trend. He claims that doing a snippet of this and a snippet of that does not necessarily result in motivation. Washing dishes, then silverware, and then pots and pans does no more to satisfy and provide an opportunity to grow than washing only dishes. What we really need to do with work, Herzberg suggests, is to *enrich* the job. By job enrichment is meant the deliberate upgrading of responsibility, scope, and challenge in work.

Rensis Likert's Management Systems

Most managers, if asked what they would do if they suddenly lost half of their plant, equipment or capital resources, are quick to answer. Insurance or borrowing are often avenues open to refurbish plant, equipment or capital. Yet when these same managers are asked what they would do if they suddenly lost half of their human resources—managers, supervisors and hourly employees—they are at a loss for words. There is no insurance against outflows of human resources. Recruiting, training and developing large numbers of new personnel into a working team take years. In a competitive environment this is almost an impossible task. Organizations are only beginning to realize that their most important assets are human resources and that the managing of these resources is one of their most crucial tasks.

Rensis Likert and his colleagues of the Institute for Social Research at the University of Michigan emphasized the need to consider both human resources and capital resources as assets requiring proper management.[13] As a result of behavioural research studies of numerous organizations, Likert implemented organizational change programs in various industrial settings. It appears these programs were intended to help organizations move from Theory X to Theory Y assumptions, from fostering immature behaviour to encouraging and developing mature behaviour, from emphasizing only hygiene factors to recognizing and helping workers to satisfy the motivators.

Likert in his studies found that the prevailing management styles of organization can be depicted on a continuum from System 1 through System 4. These systems might be described as follows.

System 1
Management is seen as having no confidence or trust in subordinates, since they are seldom involved in any aspect of the decision-making

---

[13]Rensis Likert, *The Human Organization* (New York: McGraw-Hill Book Company 1967); see also Likert, *New Patterns of Management* (New York: McGraw-Hill Book Company, 1961).

process. The bulk of the decisions and the goal setting of the organization are made at the top and issued down the chain of command. Subordinates are forced to work with fear, threats, punishment and occasional rewards and need satisfaction at the physiological and safety levels. The little superior-subordinate interaction that does take place is usually with fear and mistrust. While the control process is highly concentrated in top management, an informal organization generally develops which opposes the goals of the formal organization.

System 2

Management is seen as having condescending confidence and trust in subordinates, such as master has toward servant. While the bulk of the decisions and goal setting of the organization are made at the top, many decisions are made within a prescribed framework at lower levels. Rewards and some actual or potential punishment are used to motivate workers. Any superior-subordinate interaction takes place with some condescension by superiors and fear and caution by subordinates. While the control process is still concentrated in top management, some is delegated to middle and lower levels. An informal organization usually develops, but it does not always resist formal organizational goals.

System 3

Management is seen as having substantial but not complete confidence and trust in subordinates. While broad policy and general decisions are kept at the top, subordinates are permitted to make more specific decisions at lower levels. Communication flows both up and down the hierarchy. Rewards, occasional punishment and some involvement are used to motivate workers. There is a moderate amount of superior-subordinate interaction, often with a fair amount of confidence and trust. Significant aspects of the control process are delegated downward with a feeling of responsibility at both higher and lower levels. An informal organization may develop, but it may either support or partially resist goals of the organization.

System 4

Management is seen as having complete confidence and trust in subordinates. Decision making is widely dispersed throughout the organization, although well integrated. Communication flows not only up and down the hierarchy but among peers. Workers are motivated by participation and involvement in developing economic rewards, setting goals, improving methods and appraising progress toward goals. There is extensive, friendly superior-subordinate interaction with a high degree of confidence and trust. There is widespread responsibility for the control process, with the lower units fully involved. The informal and formal organizations are often one and the same. Thus, all social forces support efforts to achieve stated organizational goals.[14]

In summary, System 1 is a task-oriented, highly structured, authoritarian management style, while System 4 is a relationships-oriented management style based on teamwork, mutual trust and confidence. Systems 2 and 3 are intermediate stages between two extremes which approximate closely Theory X and Theory Y assumptions.

To expedite the analysis of a company's present behaviour, Likert's group developed an instrument which enables members to rate their organization in terms of its management system. This instrument is designed to gather data about a number of operating characteristics of an organization. These characteristics include leadership, motivation, communication, decision making, interaction and influence, goal setting and the control process used by the organization.

In testing this instrument, Likert asked hundreds of managers from many different organizations to indicate where the *most* productive department, division or organization they have known would fall between System 1 and System 4. Then these same managers were asked to repeat this process and indicate the position of the *least* productive department, division or organization they have known. While the ratings of the most and the least productive departments varied among managers, almost without exception each manager rated the high-producing unit closer to System 4 than the low-producing department. In summary, Likert has found that the closer the management style of an organization approaches System 4, the more likely it is to have a continuous record of high productivity. Similarly, the closer this style reflects System 1, the more likely it is to have a sustained record of low productivity.

Likert has also used this instrument not only to measure what an individual believes are the present characteristics of his organization but also to find out what he would like these characteristics to be. Data generated from this use of the instrument with managers of well-known companies have indicated a large discrepancy between the management system they feel their company is now using and the management system they feel would be most appropriate. System 4 is seen as being most appropriate, but few see their companies at present utilizing this approach. These implications have led to attempts by some organizations to adapt their management system to approximate more closely System 4. Changes of this kind are not easy. They involve a massive reeducation of all concerned from the top management to the hourly workers.

---

[14]Descriptions adapted from Likert, *The Human Organization*, pp. 4-10.

Summary and Conclusions

We have tried through the material presented to examine what is known today about understanding and motivating employees. The attempt has been to review theoretical literature, empirical research and case examples with the intention of integrating these sources into frameworks which may be useful to managers for analyzing and understanding behaviour. Analyzing and understanding are necessary, but the real value of the application of the behavioural sciences will be their usefulness in directing, changing and controlling behaviour.

11/Leadership*
Felix A. Nigro

Frequently the complaint is heard that an organization "lacks leadership." What is meant is that action of some sort should have been taken, but no one assumed the initiative in trying to get others to see the need for action, and thus nothing was accomplished. In other cases, the criticism is that the organization does not have "good leadership." Decisions are made and action taken, but those responsible for persuading others to accept their ideas led them in the wrong direction. These statements reveal both the *nature* and the importance of leadership. The essence of leadership is influencing the actions of others. Where the attempt to exercise such influence is not even made, there is a default of leadership. Where the attempt is made and others are persuaded to agree to certain action but the anticipated results do not materialize, the consequences may be serious for the organization.

Approaches to Leadership

The Trait Approach

Not too long ago even learned, as distinguished from popular, discussions of leadership had a certain mystic quality. The leader was conceived of as someone blessed with certain qualities which made it relatively easy for him to bend others to his will. Nobody was really sure of the exact complement of leader personality traits, but it was generally assumed that many of these characteristics were inherited. Today most social

---

*Reprinted by permission from F.A. Nigro, *Modern Public Administration* (New York: Harper & Row, 1965), pp. 252-280.

scientists are convinced that the trait approach to leadership is fallacious, because those conducting research on the qualities of leaders have been unable to agree on what those qualities are. In 1940, one scholar compiled a long list of traits which were identified in one or more studies as distinguishing characteristics of leaders as opposed to nonleaders. Only about 5 per cent of these traits, however, were common to four or more of the studies. Such a low percentage of agreement could hardly substantiate the claim that leaders basically have the same personality characteristics. Examination of the research conducted since 1940 has shown the same lack of consistency in the findings on leadership qualities.[1] Cartwright and Zander summarize the present state of knowledge as follows:

> On the whole, investigators in this field are coming to the conclusion that, while certain minimal abilities are required of all leaders, these are also widely distributed among non-leaders as well. Furthermore, the traits of the leader which are necessary and effective in one group or situation may be quite different from those of another leader in a different setting. This conclusion, if adequately substantiated, would imply that the selection of leaders must consider a man's suitability for the type of functions he is to perform in a given situation and it would raise questions about the desirability of formal arrangements which maintain the responsibilities of leadership in the same person regardless of the changing task of the group and the changing requirements upon leaders.[2]

The Situation Approach

Accordingly, most writers now support this situational approach, although actually it is not new. Long before the term *situational approach* came into usage, Mary Parker Follett was calling attention to the emergence in American life of "leadership by function." In the late 1920s, this wise lady, whose writings are classics in management literature, gave several lectures on leadership.[3] In these lectures, she noted that in scientifically managed organizations three types of leadership could be distinguished: the leadership of position, of personality and of function. There was nothing new about the first two, because they represented the

---

[1]Dorwin Cartwright and Alvin Zander (eds.), *Group Dynamics, Research and Theory*, 2nd ed. (New York: Harper & Row, 1960), p. 490.

[2]*Ibid.*, p. 491. See also Robert G. Wall and Hugh Hawkins, "Requisites of Effective Leadership," *Personnel* 39, no. 3 (May-June 1962): 21-28.

[3]See Mary Parker Follett, "Some Discrepancies in Leadership Theory and Practice," in *Dynamic Administration*, ed. Henry C. Metcalfe and L. Urwick (New York: Harper & Row, 1940), pp. 270-294. See also in this same collection of her papers the essay, "Leader and Expert," pp. 247-269.

accepted views on leadership. The man holding a position which gave him formal authority over others obviously could make himself a leader. If he had a forceful personality, he could do this much more easily. This kind of individual combined the leadership of position with that of personality.

Something was absent, however, in such a conception of leadership. It failed to take into account the possibility that some persons, in fact quite a few in modern specialized organizations, exercised leadership because of their expert knowledge. The organization depended on them to give sound technical advice to their superiors. In many situations these experts actually did the "leading," because others were influenced by their judgments. Miss Follett stressed that "we have people giving what are practically orders to those of higher rank. The balance of stores clerk, as he is called in some places, will tell the man in charge of purchasing when to act. The dispatch clerk can give 'orders' even to the superintendent. The leadership of function is inherent in the job and as such is respected by the president of the plant." She noted that "the man possessing the knowledge demanded by a certain situation tends in the best managed businesses, and other things being equal, to become the leader at that moment."[4]

A distinction must be made between *formal* and *effective* authority. Formal authority is the basis for what Miss Follett called leadership of position. Sometimes someone in a position of formal authority is unable to persuade others to accept his ideas. He lacks effective authority. The explanation for this may very well be that he does not possess "the knowledge demanded by the situation." In any event, not all effective authority is concentrated in the hands of a few persons at the top of the organization. Subordinates frequently exercise effective authority because they "know best" about a particular operation.

It should be made clear that Miss Follett did not consider that the leadership of function and the leadership of personality could not be combined in the same person. Nor did she deny that personality played a very large part in leadership. She did believe, however, that leadership of function was becoming more important than leadership of personality. She felt that the success of an organization depended a good deal on its being "sufficiently flexible to allow the leadership of function to operate fully—to allow the men with the knowledge and the technique to control the situation."[5] Miss Follett makes an interesting point about Joan of Arc. This great woman possessed leadership of personality because of the "ardor of her conviction and power to make others share that convic-

---

[4] *Ibid.*, p. 277.
[5] *Ibid.*, p. 278.

tion." Yet it is also related that "no trained artillery captain could excel Joan of Arc in the placement of guns."[6]

What are some of the other factors which affect the requirements for leadership, apart from expertise in a particular subject matter field? A change in the nature of the situation which confronts the group may call for a different kind of leader. The pilot in a bomber crew may be an excellent leader while the plane is in flight, but prove a very poor one if it crashes "and the crew is faced with the task of surviving or finding its way to safety."[7] The qualities needed to keep the crew working together efficiently in the air are not necessarily the same as those required when the men are afoot in a desperate situation for which advance planning was not possible. Similarly, the kind of activity influences the leadership requirements. The competent head of a public agency might be unsuited for a leadership role in a church group, yet a minor employee in the same public agency might be admirably equipped to lead the church group. Within the church, one person might be excellent for work with preschool children, another for youth activities, and so on. Thus the characteristics of the followers obviously constitute an important variable in the situation. It takes one kind of person to lead a labour gang, another to direct professional activities. Within the professional ranks, supervisors lacking certain formal qualifications deemed essential by the subordinates will prove ineffectual; a dean without the Ph.D. will not command the respect of many of the university professors. If the leadership assignment requires conciliation of various groups, the individual's personal background can eliminate him from consideration, as in an international agency, where the person's nationality might make him unacceptable to one or more parties to a dispute. These are only a few of the ways in which the situation can vary, thus altering the requirements for leadership. Readers of this essay will probably be able to supply other examples.

Leadership Style

Usually three types of leadership styles or patterns are identified: authoritarian, democratic and laissez-faire. Because democracy is so important a value to Americans, it will disturb some people that democracy may not be feasible with some work groups and in some work situations. Therefore, it is advisable to make clear at once in any discussion of leadership style that, as Golembiewski states, "the research literature does not consistently support any one leadership style."[8] On

---

[6]*Ibid.*, p. 172.
[7]Cartwright and Zander, *op. cit.*, p. 495.
[8]Robert T. Golembiewski, "Three Styles of Leadership and Their Uses," *Personnel* 38, no. 4 (July-August 1961): 35. See also Erwin S. Stanton, "Which Approach to Management—Democratic, Authoritarian or ...?," *Personnel Administration* 25, no. 2 (March-April 1962): 44-47.

the other hand, while Pfiffner and Sherwood also recognize this to be so, their analysis is that "most of the research has seemed to support the desirability of moving toward the democratic type."[9] At this point, it seems wise to refer to some of these research studies.

Research Findings on Leadership

One of the most famous of these experiments was conducted with a group of ten-year-old boys at the University of Iowa in the late 1930s.[10] Four adult leaders were "trained to proficiency" in the three different leadership styles, authoritarian, democratic and laissez-faire. The specific leadership behaviour under each style is shown in Table 1. Each of these adult leaders was assigned to direct the activities of a boys' club consisting of five boys who met after school to engage in hobby activities. The boys in each of the four groups were roughly similar in terms of social and economic background and mental, physical and personality characteristics. The adult leaders were shifted every six weeks from one club to another, and every time they switched to a new group they changed to a different leadership style. All the boys' clubs met in the same places and carried out the same activities under the same conditions. During these meetings, observers were present to study the boys' behaviour in detail. The boys themselves were later interviewed to determine their reaction to each leadership style. Home visits were also made to the parents to discover what the impact of each leadership pattern had been on the boys' conduct at home.

The basic findings were as follows:

1. Under laissez-faire supervision, the boys proved less efficient. Furthermore, they did not like the club activities as much as when they were treated democratically. They did less work and poorer work than when under democratic supervision. The complete freedom they had under laissez-faire conditions led them to play more than when under either democratic or authoritarian supervision.

2. If efficiency is evaluated both in terms of work production and social satisfactions, democracy was clearly superior to both laissez-faire and autocracy. The boys worked as efficiently under authoritarian as they did under democratic supervision, but they enjoyed themselves more under democracy.

3. There was a significant difference in the boys' behaviour when a

---

[9]John M. Pfiffner and Frank P. Sherwood, *Administrative Organization* (Englewood Cliffs, N.J.: Prentice-Hall, 1960), p. 364.

[10]The description of these experiments which follows is from Ralph White and Ronald Lippitt, "Leader Behavior and Member Reaction in Three 'Social Climates'" in Cartwright and Zander, *op. cit.*, pp. 527-553.

Table 1
Characteristics of the Three Treatment Variables[11]

Authoritarian	Democratic	Laissez-faire
1. All determination of policy by the leader	1. All policies a matter of group discussion and decision, encouraged and assisted by the leader	1. Complete freedom for group or individual decision, with a minimum of leader participation
2. Techniques and activity steps directed by the authority, one at a time, so that future steps were always uncertain to a large degree	2. Activity perspective gained during discussion period. General steps to group goal sketched, and when technical advice was needed two or more alternative procedures from which choice could be made	2. Various materials supplied by the leader, who made it clear that he would supply information when asked. He took no other part in work discussion
3. The leader usually dictated the particular work task and work companion of each member	3. The members were free to work with whomever they chose, and the division of tasks was left up to the group	3. Complete nonparticipation of the leader
4. The dominator tended to be "personal" in his praise and criticism of the work of each member; remained aloof from active group participation except when demonstrating	4. The leader was "objective" or "fact-minded" in his praise and criticism, and tried to be a regular group member in spirit without doing too much of the work	4. Infrequent spontaneous comments on member activities unless questioned, and no attempt to appraise or regulate the course of events

democratic, as contrasted with a dictatorial, adult leader temporarily left the room. The boys in democracy kept right on working, but those under iron rule "stopped working as if glad to be relieved of a task which they 'had' to do." Work production went down precipitously during leader-out periods under autocracy, whereas the decline was only slight under democracy.

4. The boys showed more originality and creative thinking under democracy than under either laissez-faire or autocracy, for "there was a larger amount of creative thinking about the work in progress than in

---

[11]From Ralph White and Ronald Lippitt, "Leader Behaviour and Member Reaction in Three 'Social Climates'" in *Group Dynamics, Research and Theory*, ed. D. Cartwright and A. Zander (New York: Harper & Row, 1960), p. 528.

autocracy, and it was more sustained and practical than in laissez-faire."[12]

5. Autocracy can create much hostility and aggression, including aggression against scapegoats. "Dominating ascendance," meaning imperious treatment of one boy by another, illustrated by such language as "shut up," took place much more often in the autocratically managed groups. Real hostility between the boys and aggressive demands for attention were also more characteristic of the autocratic groups. Destruction of work materials and property was not unusual when the meetings of the autocratic groups ended, but it did not take place at all in the democratic groups.

As to scapegoat behaviour, it was evidenced in the autocratic, but not in the democratic groups. Held down by the adult leader when he was playing the authoritarian role, the boys vented their spleen on some innocent member of the group. They took out on him their accumulated resentments against the adult leader. They could not openly defy the leader, so they directed their "aggressions" against other club members who had done nothing to them.

Upon return to democratic or laissez-faire treatment after autocracy, the boys sometimes released their "bottled-up tensions." The change to relative freedom after repressive control resulted in their breaking loose and engaging in much aggressive behaviour, with the democratic adult leader now the scapegoat. The boys appeared to say to themselves, "Aha! *Now* I can do what I've been wanting to do in this club.[13] After a couple of days, however, the "thrill of new-found freedom" wore off and the boys again exhibited the "spontaneous interest" characteristic of democracy.

6. There was more group-mindedness and friendliness in democracy. The pronoun "we" was used much more often in the democratic than in the autocratic groups. The kinds of remarks made by the boys in the democratic groups indicated the existence of greater group cohesion than under autocracy. "Friendly playfulness" was more pronounced, and there was a greater readiness to share group property.

A number of studies made with adult workers have also shown that democratic supervision produces better results. Frequently cited are those of the Institute for Social Research of the University of Michigan. The major finding was that work output was directly correlated with the amount of freedom the supervisor gave the worker. A comparison was made between the production achieved by groups of clerical workers functioning under "close" or "general" supervision. Close supervision meant that the supervisor "watched" the subordinates and checked constantly on how they were carrying out their tasks. Under general

---

[12]*Ibid.*, p. 541.
[13]*Ibid.*, p. 545.

supervision, the supervisor put the workers on their own and employed an honour system. It was found that production was highest in work units headed by supervisors who practised general supervision. Furthermore, the high supervisors, in terms of production, in most cases themselves received general, rather than close, direction from their own superiors. Finally, the high supervisors were generally content to leave the detailed performance of the work to their subordinates, and to concentrate on their supervisory responsibilities. In this respect, they were "people-oriented." The low supervisors tended to neglect their supervisory responsibilities and to spend too much time actually trying to do a share of the production job themselves. Accordingly, they were considered to be "work-oriented."[14]

Later studies at Michigan and elsewhere, however, showed that employee-centred behaviour by the supervisor did not necessarily result in increased production. They showed that "all kinds of combinations may occur—high morale and low production, low morale and low production, high morale and high production—which indicates the lack of any fixed and clear-cut relationship."[15] For this reason, Golembiewski argues that it is a mistake to try to answer the question, "Which kind of leadership should we use?" The really pertinent question he feels is, "Which kind of leadership *when?*"[16]

Selecting the Appropriate Leadership Style

Robert Tannenbaum and Warren H. Schmidt take up this problem in a most stimulating essay.[17] Their analysis is particularly valuable because they organize it around the central question of decision making. Figure 1 reproduces a continuum which they have prepared showing the range of possible leadership behaviour available to the manager. They explain each of the "behaviour points" shown on the bottom line of the continuum.

1. **The manager makes the decision and announces it.** Here the executive gives his subordinates no opportunity to participate directly in the decision-making process. He decides what the problem is, determines the possible courses of action, selects one of them, and then tells the subordinates to carry it out. In making his decision, he

---

[14]Daniel Katz, Nathan Maccoby, and Nancy C. Morse, *Productivity, Supervision, and Morale in an Office Situation*, (Ann Arbor, Mich.: Survey Research Center, Insitute for Social Research, 1950).

[15]Pfiffner and Sherwood, *op. cit.*, p. 415.

[16]Golembiewski, *op. cit.*, p. 35.

[17]Robert Tannenbaum and Warren H. Schmidt, "How to Choose a Leadership Pattern," *Harvard Business Review*, Vol. 36, No. 2, March-April, 1958, pp. 95-101.

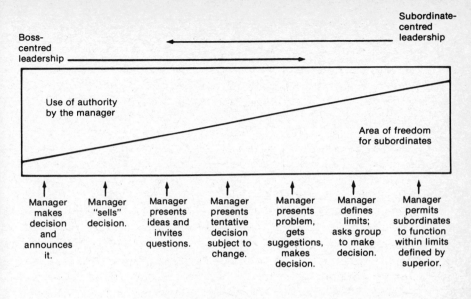

Figure 1
Continuum of Leadership Behaviour.[18]

may or may not take into account how the employees will react to it.
He may or may not use coercion in getting them to do as he says.

2. **The manager "sells" his decision.** There is no difference between this
   and 1, except that the manager does try to persuade the subordinates
   to accept the decision. He recognizes that some employees may not
   like the decision and may try to resist it, so he is careful to make clear
   what they will gain by accepting it. Note that the area of authority
   exercised by the manager remains large.

3. **The manager presents his ideas and invites questions.** The difference
   between this and 2 is that the manager gives the subordinates the
   opportunity to explore with him the implications of the decision.
   Instead of simply explaining why they should accept it, he invites them
   to ask questions, and he takes the time to go into some detail about
   "his thinking and his intentions." At this point on the continuum, the
   "area of freedom for subordinates" begins to look significant.

4. **The manager presents a tentative decision subject to change.** Here for
   the first time, the subordinates are allowed to have some influence on
   the decision. The executive retains responsibility for identifying the
   problem and developing a proposed solution, but only on a tentative

---

[18]From Robert Tannenbaum and Warren H. Schmidt, "How to Choose a Leadership
Pattern," *Harvard Business Review*, Vol. 36, No. 2, March-April 1958, p. 96.

basis. Before making a final decision, he asks the subordinates to give their frank reactions, but he also makes clear that he is retaining the right to decide the question as he sees fit.

5. **The manager presents the problem, gets suggestions, and then makes his decision.** In 1 through 4 above, the manager in every case makes the decision himself, although in 4 it is a tentative one. In 5, he asks the subordinates for their opinions before he makes any decision, final or tentative. He respects their knowledge of operating problems and knows that they may be able to suggest solutions that would not occur to him. After evaluating their ideas, as well as his own, he "selects the solution that he regards as most promising."

6. **The manager defines the limits and requests the group to make a decision.** Here the manager delegates to the subordinates the authority to make a certain decision. He states exactly what the problem is and makes clear the restriction on what the employees can decide. As a hypothetical example, the manager tells the subordinates that a new parking lot will be built for the use of the employees. A ceiling figure of $100000 for the construction costs has been fixed. So long as this figure is not exceeded, the group can decide to build whatever kind of lot it wants, an underground one or a surface one with multilevel facilities. The management may not like the employees' decision but will accept it within the financial limit.

7. **The manager permits the group to make decisions within prescribed limits.** The difference between 6 and 7 is that in 7 a general grant of decision-making power is made, not limited to any one problem. The example given is of teams of managers or engineers whose responsibility is not only to identify problems but also to decide what to do about them. The only limits on what the group can do are those specified by the official to whom the team leader reports. This leader may or may not himself participate in the making of the decision. If he does, he has no more authority than any other team member. He commits himself in advance to support whatever decision the group makes.[19]

Under 6 and 7, the subordinates' "area of freedom" widens greatly. The question remains, however, as to which of the leadership behaviours shown on the continuum is appropriate at a particular time. Tannenbaum and Schmidt identify three sets of factors which bear upon this question:

Forces in the manager.

Forces in the subordinates.

Forces in the situation.[20]

---

[19]*Ibid.*, p. 97.
[20]*Ibid.*, p. 98.

Forces in the Manager

By "forces in the manager" Tannenbaum and Schmidt mean his own preferences, based on his past history and experiences. Is he the type who strongly believes that people should participate in decisions which affect them as individuals? Or is he someone who has long been convinced that the supervisor must stoically assume the burden of making the decisions himself because he is paid to do so? How much confidence does he have in other people in general and in his present subordinates in particular? Some managers are so constituted that they become uneasy if there appears to be an element of risk and uncertainty in the operations they supervise. This kind of executive is better off if he frankly acknowledges to himself that he is not the person to make delegations of authority as broad as those shown on behaviour points 6 and 7 of the continuum.

Forces in the Subordinates

"Forces in the subordinates" refers to the expectations of the employees as to how the supervisor should behave in his relations with them. It also means the personality requirements of each individual in the group as these bear upon the question of the kind of direction he responds to best. The executive can allow greater freedom to subordinates under the following conditions:

1. The subordinates have relatively high needs for independence.
2. They *want* to assume responsibility, rather than to avoid it.
3. They have a "relatively high tolerance for ambiguity," meaning they would rather receive broad instructions than be tied down by clear-cut instructions.
4. They are interested in the problem and believe that it is important.
5. They understand the goals of the organization and identify with them.
6. They have the necessary knowledge and experience to be able to deal with the problem.
7. They are accustomed to sharing in decision making. This is what they expect and are prepared for, rather than being denied such a role.[21]

If these conditions do not exist, there may be no alternative to running "a one-man show." Depending on his assessment of these factors, the executive may on one occasion decide to make the decisions himself, on another to let the subordinates participate. If the manager has the respect of the subordinates, they will understand why in the one case he brings them in and in the other he does not.

---

[21]*Ibid.*, p. 99.

Forces in the Situation

"Forces in the situation" refers to the "critical environmental pressures" which surround the manager, stemming from "the organization, the work group, the nature of the problem, and the pressures of time."[22]

As to the organization, it has values and traditions which condition the manager's behaviour. Someone newly appointed from the outside "quickly discovers that certain kinds of behaviour are approved while others are not." There is a great compulsion for him to select that kind of behaviour on the continuum which conforms to his superiors' concepts of how he should conduct himself. Sometimes this is referred to as the "management climate" in the agency; in other words, the lower-ranking executives tend to imitate the behaviour of the higher ones. The latter are a very important part of the "situation."

Other organizational factors influencing the extent of employee participation are: the size of the organization units; their geographical distribution; and whether or not information about work plans must be kept confidential. In a very large and dispersed organization, it may be impossible to have as much employee participation as the management would like. If the activity is one involving the national security, work plans and other information obviously cannot be communicated as freely to the employees.

"Group effectiveness" is another consideration. Before he gives a problem to the work group to solve, the manager must be convinced that it is equal to the task. Has the group functioned effectively in the past? Does it seem confident of its ability to cope with this kind of assignment?

The "nature of the problem" also sets limits on the extent to which the manager can safely delegate. Perhaps the problem is one with which the work group is not familiar, so he must handle it himself. There is no virtue in asking any one subordinate or a group of workers to take on responsibilities they are not ready to assume. Yet the executive wants to be sure that he is making full use of the special knowledge and abilities of his staff. Tannenbaum and Schmidt suggest that the manager should ask himself, "Have I heard the ideas of everyone who has the necessary knowledge to make a significant contribution to the solution of this problem?" If he asks this question and answers it honestly, he is more likely to select the most appropriate leadership pattern.

"Pressure of time," meaning the need to act quickly, may force the manager to make the decision himself, without consulting with his subordinates. Leisurely consideration of every problem is not possible in the swift-moving environment of government. The manager does not by any means have full control of his time schedule; his own supervisors set

---

[22]*Ibid.*, p. 100.

deadlines for him. Unforeseen situations arise which make it necessary for him to make the best decision possible in a very short period of time. In such circumstances, all he can do is consult with as many subordinates as possible, assuming that he even has time to do this.

The great value of the preceding analysis is that it makes clear the different considerations which should influence the decision as to leadership style. If the "boss-centred" type is used on occasion, this does not mean that the managers in question must be tyrants at heart. Of course, some may have such tendencies, evidenced by their use of "boss-centred" leadership even when it is not necessary. The point is that the manager should use the leadership pattern which is called for by the particular situation.

12/Decision Making*
Ivan L. Richardson and Sidney Baldwin

Decision making , simply stated, is the process of choosing one course of action from among the choices available. Individuals make many decisions every day that affect their lives in a variety of ways. Administrative organizations also have to make decisions to establish goals, priorities, procedures and programs, and to mount responses to problem situations.

Individual decision making, however, is different from decisions made within the setting of a complex organization. Most basic organizational decisions are collective decisions, "collective" in the sense that there are many actors, from both inside and outside the organization, involved in the process. Who are the actors in the process? The actors include any individual or groups that would be affected by the decision—individual employees, supervisors, administrative decision makers, elected legislators and chief executives, political parties, pressure groups, unions and competing administrative units, to name a few. Because all of these actors make inputs into decision making, it is a terribly complex process which normally involves numerous meetings, consultations, trade-offs and compromises. To be effective, decisions have to be acceptable to the actors, or at least within limits of what they will tolerate. It is a slow,

*Reprinted and slightly abridged by permission from Ivan L. Richardson and Sidney Baldwin, *Public Administration: Government in Action* (Columbus, Ohio: Charles E. Merrill, 1976), pp. 133-45.

time-consuming, tedious process which involves a lot of "selling" of ideas, bargaining and brokerage among competing alternatives and groups.

Decision making is central to administration. It is what administration is all about. Administrative and organizational theories, communications, supervision and all other aspects are meaningless without decisions, which are the mechanism for triggering a product from organizations. As Herbert Simon said, "the task of 'deciding' pervades the entire administrative organization quite as much as does the task of 'doing'—indeed, it is integrally tied up with the latter."[1] The same author, in discussing the present society where most organizations now produce services rather than tangible products, believes that the major organizational problem "is not how to organize to produce efficiently (although this will always remain an important consideration), but how to organize to make decisions—that is, to process information."[2]

The Decision Makers
The formal organization chart theoretically indicates the hierarchy of decision making and decision makers. But, since it presents only the formal side of an organization, it does not present a true picture. In practice, decisions are also made by those who do not occupy any formally prescribed supervisory position. Actually, decisions are made throughout an organization from the lowest paid nonprofessional to the top administrator.

Formal Decision Makers
The formal decision makers are those who occupy supervisory positions in the hierarchy. With the position comes the authority or legitimate right to make decisions which can be expected to influence the behaviour of subordinates. The subordinates, on the other hand, expect such behaviour from the superior and are conditioned to respond to directives. It is actually a system of expected behaviour—supervisors expect to have the right to make decisions and have them executed and subordinates expect to receive directives and to obey them.

Few decision makers, even though they may have the right to do so, make decisions unilaterally and simply issue orders. They understand that ordering something to happen is no guarantee that it will occur. If there has been no prior consultation or advance preparation, the direc-

---

[1]Herbert A. Simon, *Administrative Behavior: A Study of Decision-Making Processes in Administrative Organization*, 2d ed. (New York: Free Press, 1957), p. 1.
[2]Herbert A. Simon, "Applying Information Technology to Organization Design," *Public Administration Review* 33, no. 3 (May-June 1973): 269-70.

tive may be in conflict with the expectations of the informal organization, in which case the order may be followed for fear of sanctions, but it may be executed with less than enthusiasm and to the minimal degree possible.

Informal Decision Makers

A considerable number of organizational decisions are made by those who are not in the formal decision hierarchy and with no decision authority. Specialists in functional fields, administrative assistants, secretaries and a variety of other employees either make or influence decisions.

Types of Decisions

Decisions, both individual and organizational, are not of the same complexity. Simon has classified decisions into two general categories— programmed and unprogrammed. Programmed decisions are those triggered by stimuli which are recurring, known and familiar. There are standardized operating procedures and programs which have been developed for meeting similar situations in the past. These programs may be recalled, modified if necessary, and applied to the problem. This does not imply that alternatives are not considered, but it requires no extensive gathering of new data or much conscious deliberation. Many decisions fall in this category.

Unprogrammed decisions are of a different order. The situation is either totally new, involves conditions that recur infrequently, or consists of conditions that have changed drastically. In such situations, there is no routine, automatic response or existing program which may be used and the decision process becomes much more complex. There is uncertainty about the scope of the problem, possible alternative solutions, the consequences of alternatives and the methodology in general. Such issues may be value-laden, involve controversial areas, and have a variety of political implications.

Decision Models

How do administrators make nonprogrammed decisions? Administrative theorists have developed a variety of decision-making models which have generated considerable debate. The models come in essentially two variations—"normative" and "descriptive." The "normative" model attempts to show the decision maker how he or she should make the decision. The "descriptive model," on the other hand, describes or simulates the behaviour followed by decision makers. Of course, no one model is acceptable to all. We will look at some of the models and comment on their utility for the practitioner.

Rational Comprehensive Model

Rationality has been a historic theme, not only in decision making, but in the whole area of administrative theory.[3] In fact, most democratic political theory as well as economic theory is based on the concept of the rationality of man.

When faced with a nonprogrammed decision, the rational comprehensive model assumes that a decision maker would:

1. Identify the problem.
2. Clarify his goals, and then rank them in their order of importance.
3. List all possible means—or policies—for achieving each of these goals.
4. Assess all the costs of the policies and the benefits that would seem to follow from each of the alternatives.
5. Select the package of goals and associated policies that would bring the greatest relative benefits or the least relative disadvantages.[4]

If such a model is followed, a completely rational choice which produces an "optimal" or best possible choice from all possible alternatives should result. However, for the day-to-day decision maker the model is of little use due to inherent problems.

Problems with Rationality

All administrators take pride in the fact that their decisions are rational. But administrators, functioning under the daily pressures of the real world, operate in an environment quite different from that of the purely rational model. In addition to their own preferences, administrators receive a mass of conflicting inputs from inside—which Sharkansky calls "withinputs"—and from outside the organization.[5] These conditions create problems in utilizing the rational model. The major obstacles include individual differences, organizational barriers, the outside environment, time constraints, the civil service and the securing and processing of information.

---

[3]The rationality theme is discussed in the writings of Chester Barnard, Herbert Simon, James March, March and Simon, Cyert and March, Charles Lindblom and Chris Argyris, to name a few. Some current controversy is reflected in Chris Argyris, "Some Limits of Rational Man Organizational Theory," *Public Administration Review* 33, no. 3 (May-June 1973): 253-67. In this article, he critiqued some of the work done by others, including Simon. For the response, see Herbert Simon, "Organizational Man: Rational or Self-Actualizing," *Public Administration Review*, 33, no. 4 (July-August 1973): 346-353. Argyris responds in pages 354-57 of no. 4.

[4]Charles E. Lindblom, *The Policy Making Process* (Englewood Cliffs, N.J.: Prentice-Hall, 1968), p. 13.

[5]Ira Sharkansky, *Public Administration: Policy Making in Government Agencies* (Chicago: Markham, 1970), p. 35.

Individual Differences

The setting of goals and decision making in general is complicated by the goals, preferences and vested interests of the individuals that make up the organization. These complications arise from three sources. First, all employees have their own values, need system and set of goals for their own personal improvement and well-being. "Therefore, the goals of every bureau member are different to at least some degree from those of every other member."[6]

Second, the operating style of each administrator is shaped by his or her own value system, experience, personality and preferences. "Bureaucratic officials in general have a complex set of goals including power, income, prestige, security, convenience, loyalty (to an idea, an institution, or the nation), pride in excellent work, and desire to serve the public interest. But, each is significantly motivated by his own self-interest even when acting in a purely official capacity."[7] The third factor, which is essentially a product of the first two, is the matter of bias. There is not only disagreement on goals among members, but also a divergence between the stated goals of the organization and those of its members. These conflicts introduce a variety of biases that enter into decision making.[8]

Organizational Barriers

The structure and processes of most bureaucratic organizations inhibit the use of a rational decision-making model. The inhibiting characteristics include size, geography, structure, specialization and established procedures.

The size of an organization plays an important part in determining the decision process. The process in a small organization is quite different from that of a large complex one. A small organization permits more face-to-face contact, and closer interpersonal relations, as well as decreasing the problems of communication and consultation.

Geography is also important. If an organization is geographically dispersed, with field units in various locations, the decision process is complicated by obstacles to the flow of data, information and directives. In addition, the loyalties and goals of the field personnel may be different from those in the central office.

The structure of an organization has an impact. The traditional, layered, hierarchical organization imposes a variety of obstacles, such as

---

[6]Anthony Downs, *Inside Bureaucracy* (Boston: Little, Brown, 1967), p. 76. Used by permission.
[7]Downs, *Inside Bureaucracy*, p. 2.
[8]For a discussion of these ideas as well as five types of bureaucratic officials and their behaviour patterns, see Downs, chapter VII.

competition among the subunits, differing priorities, different client and support groups, filtering of communications, distance between top decision makers and the level of policy execution, and alienation of personnel. On the other hand, if the organization is set up on the newer concept of transient task forces or as a more horizontal, flatter structure, the decision process could be more direct and participative.

The fragmentation of organizations into specialized units can also create an important obstacle. These units, staffed by personnel with a particular expertise or profession, have their own language, codes of conduct, expectations and behavioural patterns, which may or may not coincide with those of the organization. Such units, whose staff naturally think their function is vital, will struggle to establish organizational goals which emphasize their role. The potential for conflict between the administrators of specialized functions and the administrator with the overall responsibility is always present and is usually a given in practice.

Administrative procedures and the accompanying "red tape" are impediments to decision making. Any large organization develops procedures—usually contained in operating manuals—covering almost all phases of the administrative process. This has the advantage of standardizing and making procedures predictable, but it also creates red tape and a resistance to change. The manuals and directives become the "bible," cited as the basis for legitimizing all actions. This documentation often becomes a type of "security blanket" and, hence, a major obstacle to innovative decision making and change. Since established procedures define lines of authority, document routing, roles and other characteristics, employees become comfortable with them and resist decisions that would alter the status quo.

Inputs from Outside the Organization

Each administrative unit has transactions with others outside its own immediate environment—political parties, legislature, chief executive, pressure groups, citizens and other administrative units. These outside forces expect to have some influence in making the decisions that will affect them. In a pluralistic society, their attitudes, demands and expectations must be considered. However, they are not interested in following all of the steps prescribed by the rational decision model. Their inputs are designed to influence decisions in such a manner as to protect or enhance their positions, which to them is a rational process.

Time Frame

The time element is an important obstacle. In the first place, problems requiring decisions always come with a time frame attached. Some decisions have to be made quickly while others may be more leisurely, but none exist without some time concept. Secondly, time is always in short supply. Time must be allocated among decision making and the myriad of other administrative functions. Because of these two pressures, the time needed to follow all of the steps prescribed by the rational decision-making model is not available to the practising administrator.

The Civil Service
The merit system can be an obstacle to decision making. The system makes it difficult to remove or impose other sanctions against employees and thus complicates the decision process. Since subordinates see no great risk, they feel comparatively free to oppose the apparent desires of the top administrator and to be less than enthusiastic in executing a policy with which they do not agree. Unless these actions are so visible or violent that they constitute gross insubordination or some other sanctionable action, the administrator has little control. But even if administrators believe there are sufficient grounds for disciplinary action, they may decide that the potential gain is not worth the time and trauma of going through all of the procedures prescribed by the civil service rules.

Securing and Processing Information
The rational model assumes that all information is available to the decision maker. This is usually not possible. Anthony Downs indicates the major obstacles as follows:

1. Information is costly because it takes time, effort and sometimes money to obtain data and comprehend their meaning.
2. Decision makers have only limited capabilities regarding the amount of time they can spend making decisions, the number of issues they can consider simultaneously, and the amount of data they can absorb regarding any one problem.
3. Although some uncertainty can be eliminated by acquiring information, an important degree of ineradicable uncertainty is usually involved in making decisions.[9]

Even if every piece of information could be accumulated and processed, decisions would still be affected by two additional constraints. First, it is impossible to think of all the possible alternative solutions to a problem. As Herbert Simon says, "imagination falls down also in conceiving all the possible patterns of behavior that the individual might take."[10] Second, decisions would still be influenced by the forces inside and outside the organization.

Because of the problems involved here, most organizations do not attempt a total search. The extent depends upon the inclination of the

[9]Downs, *Inside Bureaucracy*, p. 3.
[10]Simon, *Administrative Behavior*, p. 84.

decision maker, time, availability of resources, intensity of the internal and external interest in the issue, and the level of organizational tolerance for uncertainty and ambiguity.

Impact of the Rational Model

From the above problems, it is evident that the rational model is impractical. Most decisions are not "optimal" but represent compromise solutions to problems. As Simon says, "the alternative that is finally selected never permits a complete or perfect achievement of objectives, but is merely the best solution that is available under the circumstances. The environmental situation invariably limits the alternatives that are available."[11]

This does not mean that decisions are not based on data, analysis, consultation and consideration of alternatives—in short, totally irrational. But administrators look for a satisfactory solution, which is the next model.

Satisficing Model

In the rational model, the decision maker follows the prescribed procedures and reaches an optimal decision—the alternative that provides the greatest benefit at the least cost. In contrast, the "satisficing" model allows the decision maker to select a satisfactory decision based on the information and alternatives available. As Herbert Simon says, ". . . administrative man satisfices—looks for a course of action that is satisfactory or good enough."[12] Such decisions not only meet the needs of the organization but also are acceptable to the competing forces active in the decision process. March and Simon believe that "most human decision making, whether individual or organizational, is concerned with the discovery and selection of satisfactory alternatives: only in exceptional cases is it concerned with the discovery and selection of optimal alternatives."[13]

Heuristic Model

William J. Gore also argues that the rational choice model is not appropriate for all occasions. When that which rationality dictates is too far removed from what can practically be done, employees seek solutions that are within their concepts and understanding of the situation. Substituting these choices for the purely rational is called the "heuristic" process. He feels that the "concept of an organization as a rational system

---

[11]*Ibid.*, p. 6.
[12]*Ibid.*, p. xxv. For other discussion of the concept see James March and Herbert Simon, *Organizations* (New York: John Wiley, 1958); Sharkansky, *Public Administration*, chapter 3.
[13]March and Simon, *Organizations*, pp. 141-42.

of action will coexist with a conception of organization as a social system or as a collective, heuristic strategy."[14] In such a social system, human emotions, desires, personalities, and irrationality enter into decision making.

Incremental Decision Making
As a substitute model, Charles Lindblom proposed a "muddling through" model of incremental decision making.[15] In this model there is no attempt to be comprehensive and analyze all possible alternatives. Relying on past organizational decisions and policies, the decision maker: (1) attacks only the issues that differ from existing policies or norms, (2) reevaluates problems on a case-by-case basis, (3) approaches each problem in a piecemeal, incremental fashion, and (4) proceeds through a succession of limited comparisons among only a few selected alternatives. Such a procedure is a process of compromise and accommodation because it is less threatening and therefore can secure the support needed to implement the decision.

This model was praised by some and criticized by others. Dror attacked it on a variety of bases including its emphasis on past experience as a guide and its conservatism, both of which provide "reinforcement of the pro-inertia and anti-innovative forces prevalent in all human organizations."[16] He said that acceptance of the model "reflects the widespread disposition of administrators and students of public administration to accept the present as a guide to the future, and to regard contemporary practice as a norm for the future."[17] As a suggestion, Dror proposed what he called a "normative optimum" model which was a compromise between the rational model and the incremental model.

Mixed Scanning
Amitai Etzioni, after discussing the defects of the rational-comprehensive and disjointed incremental models, proposed a "mixed scanning" model

---

[14]William J. Gore, *Administrative Decision Making: A Heuristic Model* (New York: John Wiley, 1964), p. 17.
[15]Charles Lindblom, "The Science of Muddling Through," *Public Administration Review* 19 (Spring 1959): 78-88. He later changed the title from "incremental decision making" to "disjointed incrementalism" in David Braybrooke and Charles E. Lindblom, *A Strategy of Decision* (New York: The Free Press of Glencoe, 1963). See also Charles E. Lindblom, *The Intelligence of Democracy* (New York: Free Press, 1965), and John J. Bailey and Robert J. O'Connor, "Operationalizing Incrementalism: Measuring the Muddles," *Public Administration Review* 35, no. 1 (January-February 1975): 60-66.
[16]Yehezkel Dror, "Muddling Through—'Science' or Inertia?" *Public Administration Review* 24, no. 3 (September 1964): 155. Lindblom's reply to the Dror article is contained in the same issue.
[17]*Ibid.*, p. 156.

as a substitute. In this model, decisions are divided into two categories—fundamental and incremental—and each requires a different technique for scanning or searching for information and alternatives. The fundamental decisions, which establish policy, require a detailed (rationalistic) search for information, while a truncated search is adequate for incremental decisions. He says that "fundamental decisions are made by exploring the main alternatives the actor seeks in view of his conception of his goals, but—unlike what rationalism would indicate—details and specifications are omitted so that an overview is feasible. Incremental decisions are made but within the contexts set by fundamental decisions (and fundamental reviews). Thus, each of the two elements in mixed scanning helps to reduce the effects of the particular shortcomings of the other; incrementalism reduces the unrealistic aspects of rationalism by limiting the details required for decisions, and contextuating rationalism helps to overcome the conservative slant of incrementalism by exploring longer-run alternatives."[18]

Impact of Models on Practical Decision Making

Models serve some very valuable functions in administration. By focusing on the complexities and defects of decision making, they serve as "think" pieces to induce administrators to look at and evaluate their techniques. But most administrators do not adopt a prescribed model and follow it in their daily routine. This is not to say that decision makers do not follow logical procedures. But since the environment of decision making will vary with the type, size, and location of administrative units, most administrators develop a more or less personalized decision model which will incorporate elements from the various models as well as what has worked in their past experience. Administrators must also rely on a particular brand of acquired sensitivity similar to radar: they have to be able to receive and translate the signals received from within the organization, from politicians, from pressure groups and other power groups, into decisions that generate the support necessary to insure implementation of the policy, or possibly survival, of the organization. This support can come in the form of budgets, clientele support and/or acceptability to the employees.

The model and techniques developed will vary with the administrator and the conditions under which he or she operates. The ability to read and evaluate what these environmental factors are is crucial to the success of an administrator. As an illustration, a highly successful city manager moves to another city, uses the models that had been productive,

---

[18]Amitai Etzioni, "Mixed Scanning: A Third Approach to Decision Making," *Public Administration Review* 27, no. 5 (December 1967): 389-90.

and soon becomes unacceptable to the new city council. As one administrator said, there is little evidence "that decision making by following a
difficult model is an inescapable requirement for success in the life of a
public administrator."[19] He concluded by saying that administrators "will
continue to be skeptical of prescribed methodology as a road to administrative salvation."[20]

Future Decision Making

Decisions will always have to be made by someone, but what will the
future decision-making process look like? The possible changes which
have been suggested span a wide range of options. It seems clear that
there will be some changes. The more important ones will probably
include the following:

1. The process will become more complex. The rapidity of change in all
   areas of society will undoubtedly continue. Changes will occur not
   only in the technical areas, but in the areas of values and expectations
   as well. Such change intensifies existing problems, creates new
   concerns, creates a closer interdependence among the segments of
   society, and affects more people which will increase the interest and
   expectations of more people and groups and make solutions even
   more critical.
2. There will be an increasing demand for more participation by the
   affected groups. This pressure will come from inside and outside the
   organizations. The inside demands which already exist will be intensi-
   fied as the educational level and professionalization of the public
   servant increases. The professionals, accustomed to being consulted
   on professional matters as a team member, expect the same role in
   administrative decisions which affect them. This, combined with
   increasing unionization of the white-collar labour force, will force
   more participation by employees.

   The outside pressures for participation will increase. The demands
   of an ever growing number of groups and interests—women, minorities, the aging, conservationists and a host of other groups—will be
   heard. As Kaufman says, organizations "will routinely be obliged to
   take explicit account of groups of people and types of demands
   hitherto neglected by or excluded from the processes of decision in
   many social institutions."[21]

---

[19]Roger W. Jones, "The Model as a Decision Maker's Dilemma," *Public Administration Review*
24, no. 3 (September 1964): 159.
[20]*Ibid.*, p. 160.
[21]Herbert Kaufman, "The Direction of Organizational Evolution," *Public Administration
Review* 33, no. 4 (July-August 1973): 302.

3. Structural changes will alter the decision process. If the organizational form shifts from the hierarchical pyramid toward the temporary, task force format, work groups will be smaller with more direct participation by the team members.
4. The computer will probably have an increasingly important impact. Humans will not be replaced, but decisions may be shared with machines. Simon points out that with computers there is a tremendous capacity for information storage, data collection, modelling, simulation and other techniques for decision making. The problem is not a lack of information but how administrators organize to select alternatives and find the time they need to process the information, assess alternatives and make decisions.[22]

Decision makers, then, will have to accommodate to these modifications. Some will welcome the changes and others will resist; but all will have to adjust to their new role in the decision process.

13/Communications*
Felix A. Nigro

Communications has been defined as "that process whereby one person makes his ideas and feelings known to another."[1] However, experience has shown time and time again that more is required than the desire to communicate. One must be able to adjust to situations and personalities. Any organization relies on at least a fair degree of harmonious interaction among its employees in order to achieve its objectives, and, wherever there is friction, there will be a block at that point in the communications network. Yet even when people enjoy good working relations, successful communication is not easy. Also needed is the ability to make one's thoughts entirely clear to the other person, and for this to be possible, the individual's own thinking must be absolutely clear. Vague instructions reflect cloudy thinking; "If an executive cannot shape up in his own mind

[22]See Simon, "Applying Information Technology," pp. 268-88.

*Slightly abridged by permission from Felix A. Nigro, *Modern Public Administration* (New York: Harper & Row, 1965), pp. 188-207.
[1]Lawrence A. Appley, *Management in Action* (New York: American Management Association, 1956), p. 182.

a clear concept of policies, objectives, programs, and organization struc-ture, and cannot produce a clear picture in the minds of others, he is seriously handicapped."[2]

Decisions must be explained properly to those who are to put them into effect. The individual may know exactly what he wants to say but is unable to express himself clearly. Yet if a sound decision is communicated poorly, the desired results will not be obtained. Decisions themselves are based on communications received from different sources, and subor-dinates present their recommendations, both written and oral. In written communications, the individual may use the wrong words or employ expressions that cloud his real meaning, and similar confusion results from lack of clarity in oral communications. Sometimes, too, a cause of the difficulty is failure on the part of one or both of the communicators to listen properly. All of these aspects are vital in the decision-making process discussed previously, and for this reason, it is frequently stated that communications and decision making are inseparable.

Further power in the organization is measured by the respect com-manded by an official's communications. Since communication is basically interaction, study of the communications pattern in an organization will reveal the role of each of the participants.

> Let us suppose that a man is foreman in a factory, and that we are watching him at work. What do we see and hear? We watch him, perhaps, overseeing a battery of punch presses, going from one man to another as they tend the machines, answering their questions and showing them, if they have made mistakes, where they have gone wrong. We see him also at his desk making out records. That is, we see that he has a certain kind of job, that he carries on certain activities. We see also that he deals with certain men in the plant and not with others. He goes to certain men and talks to them; others come to his desk and talk to him. He gets his orders from a boss and passes on the orders to members of his own department. That is, he communicates or, as we shall say . . . interacts with certain persons and not with others, and this communication from person to person often takes place in a certain order—for instance, from the boss to the foreman and then from the foreman to the workers—so that we can say . . . that the foreman occupies a position in a chain of communications.[3]

Types of Communications
From the standpoint of the direction in which communications flow, three types can be distinguished: (1) downward; (2) upward; and (3) lateral. Let us discuss each of these in turn.

---

[2]*Ibid.*, p. 186.
[3]George C. Homans, *The Human Group* (New York: Harcourt, Brace, and World, 1950), pp. 11-12.

Downward Communication

Downward communication refers to the directives and other messages which originate with the officials at the top of the organization and are transmitted down through the hierarchy—through the intervening levels of supervision—until they reach the lowest-ranking worker in the chain. The traditional approach to administration concentrated on this kind of communication and pretty much ignored the other two. It was assumed that the management was in a position to make decisions which were in the best interests of the workers. Once made, these decisions could be "dropped in the chute," so to speak, and be expected to slide smoothly down the hierarchy. If any hitch developed in the implementation of the decisions at any point in this downward chain, it was attributed to the shortcomings of the workers concerned. Furthermore, top management held the ultimate authority, so it could invoke means to force compliance with its instructions.

The Hawthorne experiments showed that downward communication was not so simple. Management could not make decisions which would be accepted at lower levels without first encouraging upward communication, that is, the transmission of information and opinions by the workers up the same hierarchy, in other words, travelling the reverse route. In large organizations, downward communication is difficult enough to begin with, because orders must descend through numerous intermediate levels before the point of execution is reached. Misunderstandings can easily occur when instructions pass through so many people. If little upward communication exists, the difficulties are multiplied, because the orders themselves are apt to be unrealistic and to meet with worker resistance.

Upward Communication

Many years have passed since the Hawthorne experiments, but few organizations have been able to develop really effective systems of upward communication—that is, messages that are passed from the lower levels of the hierarchy up to the management. Earl Planty and William Machaver identify a number of barriers to upward communication:

1. Physical distance or inaccessibility.
2. Dilution or distortion at each level.
3. The attitude of the supervisor.
4. The inferior status of the subordinate.
5. Tradition.[4]

---

[4]See Earl Planty and William Machaver, "Upward Communications: A Project in Executive Development," *Personnel* 28, no. 4 (January 1952): 304-317.

Workers separated by great distances from the source of authority at the top of the organization have difficulty in communicating upward. A field worker, for example, may have relatively infrequent contact with the head of the field office. The latter in turn may have only limited opportunity to see, and therefore to express his ideas fully to his superiors at headquarters. The same is true even when all the workers are located in the same area. The larger the organization, the greater the number of links in the supervisory chain, and the principle of "following channels" requires that no link in this chain be bypassed; everyone must deal through his immediate chief. It is not surprising, then, that few messages that are voluntarily initiated by the lowest worker ever travel upward until they finally reach the desk of the top executive. Reports required by the top management must traverse this route, but they do not have the spontaneity that really should characterize the system of upward communication.

As information is passed up the hierarchy, it is subject to a filtering process at each level. Some of this is deliberate; a good deal is unconscious. The picture of operations as described by a subordinate may not square with the superior's conception of the situation, particularly when the subordinate reports that some things are not going well at all. "Problems" are disturbing, and a typically human reaction is to refuse to believe that they exist or are as serious as they are painted to be. (Good news ascends the hierarchy much more easily than bad news.) The tendency is to "edit" the reports to present a brighter picture. An agency head can sometimes appear to be unbelievably blind as to what is really going on in his agency; yet based on the reports he gets everything *is* fine: these reports simply do not present him with all the facts. Consequently, the upwards reporting system is often of very limited value in locating trouble spots in the agency's operations.

The executive represents to the subordinate someone who wields power and could damage the subordinate's prospects for advancement. This creates a communications block, for the subordinate is wary even though the superior may urge him to be frank. Subordinates who, for one reason or another, feel secure in their positions tend to express themselves the most frankly to their superiors. The subordinate is handicapped at the outset of any upward communication, because he is not free to break in on the superior and intrude on his time. If the chief has something on his mind, he can, at any time, ask the subordinate to see him as soon as possible. In a sense, he controls their time; they in no sense control his. They must, rather, petition an audience with him. There are usually several who want to see the chief at the same time, and he is very busy, as it is, satisfying the other demands on his time.

Upward communication is in a very important sense "unnatural." It is like rowing upstream, against the current. Downward communication has the great force of tradition behind it. There is nothing at all unusual about communications originating at the top of the hierarchy and being routed downward. By contrast, upward communication is unconventional. In most organizations, it is not established procedure for the employees spontaneously to direct upward any large numbers of communications. The employee who attempts to do so may even take a risk. Further, the management that genuinely wants to encourage upward communication will have difficulty because the upward route will generally have been used so rarely in the past that the employees will remain reluctant to use it.

Management can embark on a program to stimulate upward communication. The management should not expect such communication to be spontaneous with the employees, nor is it enough simply to tell the workers that upward communication is desirable. Most of the employees will require clear evidence that the management really is interested in their opinions. Since an important change is being made in the worker's accustomed role, he understandably needs help and encouragement in making the shift from mere cog to full participant in the aims of the organization. Some workers may be so used to playing an insignificant role that they have become quite indifferent to the future of the organization. Thus the management must change the whole outlook of these workers if it is to succeed in getting them to participate in any system of upward communication.

Superior officers should follow a consistent policy of listening to their subordinates. This may involve adapting to a willingness to face bad news. The management should encourage its supervisors to do this, and the example set by the agency head in this respect will normally have a great influence on the other executives. If he encourages communications from below, and accepts even negative reports, his key assistants are likely to do the same with their subordinates.

The most unfriendly atmosphere for upward communication is one in which the management seems to isolate itself, keeping information to itself and considering many matters "confidential" and not to be revealed outside the inner circle. A management which practises such limited downward communication automatically inhibits upward communication and, in effect, builds a wall between itself and the rest of the organization. For subordinates to initiate upward communication in such an atmosphere would be almost tantamount to defiance. Fortunately, such an attitude by the management is now considered old-fashioned and tends to be the exception rather than the rule.

The supervisor should exercise care in selecting his "communicators"—that is, those who provide him with information—and make sure that these communicators are not merely "reflectors" of what he is predisposed to seeing. Some executives make a point of surrounding themselves with at least one or two "no" men in a conscious effort to avoid the "conspiracy of smoothness." For example, Attorney-General Robert Kennedy acted as a "communicator" in his brother's Cabinet. Some newspaper reports indicated that, as the president's brother, the attorney-general was able to be far more blunt with the chief executive than any other member of the administration, and this bluntness may explain why the late president depended so much on his younger brother.

The superior officer should also strive to correct those of his personal habits which prevent the subordinate from speaking to him freely. Again, the superior must first be aware of these mannerisms, and humans are typically blind when it comes to personal failings. Yet some self-prompting is possible once the supervisor has become aware of these tendencies and has really decided to encourage the subordinate. It should be pointed out here that superior officers frequently feel a compulsion to demonstrate their superiority to their subordinates. With some, this is a protective device; if they *appear* to know more than their subordinates, they can feel they are living up to their official roles in the organization. Other supervisors are vain and would in any case treat their subordinates with condescension. While the supervisor must never forget his responsibilities as a superior officer, his position hardly means that he is always better apprized of all the facts than is the subordinate. Once the supervisor recognizes that his subordinates are likely to possess information that he does not, he is much more apt to encourage subordinates to communicate with him freely.

Another common mistake is for the superior to state his own position before he listens to the subordinate, rather than inviting the subordinate to give his opinions on the particular problem. There may be no intention on the part of the superior to force his views on the subordinate, but the latter is quickly placed in a difficult position: he must agree with the boss. Few people will want to challenge the chief so openly. Encouraging one's subordinates to express their views holds another advantage. Some workers prefer to leave all decisions to someone else in order to avoid the responsibility. Such an attitude generally serves to impair the calibre of the individual's work, which ultimately reflects on the supervisor, and adds as well to his load of decision making. If, however, the supervisor encourages free expression of ideas from his subordinates, he is likely to lead this sort of individual to develop his capacity for greater responsibility. The supervisor will never succeed in this if he merely asks his subordinates for reactions to his own ideas.

Where it is indicated and feasible, the superior officer should *use* the information given to him by his subordinates. Nothing is more destructive of free expression—and of upward communication—than the chief's failure to act upon the ideas and problems reported to him. The subordinates are led to believe that they are wasting their time, and may even wish that the superior had not gone through the formality of listening. The purpose of communication is to achieve organizational objectives. Action at some point is essential if subordinates are to continue to feel motivated in contributing to these objectives by communicating significant information to their superiors.

Lateral Communication

Lateral communication is that which takes place among workers of the same level in the hierarchy, or among individuals of different levels who are not in a superior-subordinate relationship. Lateral relationships will frequently go from one agency to another, and are not restricted to intra-agency relationships. We use the term *lateral* instead of *horizontal* in order to be able to include *all* across-the-organization contacts.

Traditional organization theory is based on the organization chart and the system of *scalar* authority it depicts. The scalar principle means that the different positions of authority are shown in descending order of importance. The limitations of the chart give the clue to the inadequacies of traditional theory, as is so well revealed in the following statement:

> The relation between the scheme of activities and the scheme of interaction in an organization is usually represented by the familiar organization chart, which shows the organization divided into departments and subdepartments, the various officers and subofficers occupying boxes, connected by lines to show which persons are subordinates to what other ones. Every such chart is too neat; it tells what the channels of interaction ought to be but not always what they are. The pyramid-type chart is particularly misleading because it shows only the interaction between superiors and subordinates, the kind of interaction that we shall call, following Barnard, *scalar*. It does not show the interaction that goes on between two or more persons at about the same level of the organization, for instance, between two department heads. . . .
>
> This kind of interaction we shall call lateral interaction, though we must remember that there are borderline cases where the distinction between scalar and lateral interaction disappears. The conventional organization chart represents the scalar but not the lateral interaction. *If it were not for the unhappy association with predatory spiders, the facts would be much better represented by a web, the top leader at the center, spokes radiating from him, and concentric circles linking the spokes. Interaction takes place along the concentric circles as well as along the spokes.*[5]

Lateral communication is of great importance in assuring coordination of organizational objectives. The members of the organization should work together as a cohesive unit but, if they are to do so, they must communicate their plans and intentions to one another clearly. Tradi-

[5]Homans, *op. cit.*, pp. 104-105. Italics ours.

tional organization theory has emphasized coordination through command; that is, through the downward communications of the superior. As Thompson explains: "each person's behavior is considered to be determined by the commands of his superior. If every superior is able to give integrated, rationally consistent commands, the organization will automatically be a coordinated system of behavior."[6] The fallacy in this reasoning is that the superior officer is not in a position to give subordinates these "integrated, rationally consistent commands."[7] The subordinates are likely to know the details of operations in their bailiwicks better than he can be expected to know them. Thompson continues:

> Specialization has long outrun human ability to coordinate in this fashion. Not only is the person in the command position increasingly dependent upon subordinates for the interpretation of incoming data and the initiation of activities, but interdependencies far beyond command jurisdictions have developed. Consequently, most coordination is programmed, built into routines.[8]

The concept of coordination by command is basically authoritarian in nature: The way to get the subordinates to work together is to order them to do so; if they fail to obey, punitive corrective measures should be taken. Overlooked is the fact that there are serious limits to the coordination which can be imposed on the employees from above. Such coordination tends to be nominal, simply because it is forced on the worker and, at best, he only grudgingly complies. Real team play is characterized by spontaneity. The individual wants to cooperate because he derives *personal* satisfaction from functioning as a member of the team.

In modern organizations, decision making is not monopolized by just a few top people. Management depends on the specialized skills and knowledge of its subordinates and modern administrations recognize this. Today, they invite workers to participate in the decision-making process. Logically, this requires the encouragement of both upward and lateral communication. The wise superior finds it advantageous to encourage his subordinates, not only to express their ideas to him freely, but also to settle as many problems as possible among themselves. If they are to cooperate in this manner, they must obviously be in close contact with one another.

Obstacles
Just as in the case of upward communication, the lateral pattern of interaction presents its difficulties. In some respects, effective lateral

---

[6]Victor A. Thompson, *Modern Organization* (New York: Knopf, 1961), p. 181.
[7]*Ibid.*
[8]*Ibid.*, p. 183.

communication is even more difficult to achieve. In upward communication, the subordinate must adjust to only one person—his immediate supervisor. In lateral communication, workers must deal with several co-workers, and any one department head must try to work together harmoniously with all other department heads; he must also develop effective working relationships with department heads and other officials of outside agencies.

The very division of an organization into specialized parts creates barriers to lateral communication and coordination. Specialists typically develop strong loyalties, not to the organization as a whole, but to their own areas of interest. The tendency is for them to regard members of other specialized groups as threats to their own positions in the organization. The members of each specialized group think its function is the most important in the agency. Furthermore, specialized professions have their peculiar frames of reference and technical language. The members of each can communicate among themselves effectively, but they frequently have difficulty grasping the point of view of outsiders.

Horizontal cliques also provide the clue to much of the difficulty in lateral communications. Besides the frictions between specialists, there are rivalries and consequent tensions between the different organization units. Departments compete with other departments for bigger appropriations and more prominent roles in the total government program. Similarly, within any one department, the bureaus and other subdivisions fight for special status. The rival organization units eye one another with suspicion and sometimes with considerable hostility. Instead of freely exchanging information on operating plans, they may try to keep one another in the dark. Deviousness, instead of open discussion of mutual problems, may characterize the conversations between their respective personnel. The principal officials in each department may play their cards close to their chests, always afraid of being outmanoeuvred by the other party.

The very complexity of modern organization also creates difficulties, just as it does in the case of downward and upward communications. The more persons an official must consult, both within and outside the agency, the more complicated the process of lateral communication becomes. Often he is uncertain about whom he should consult, because the lines of responsibility within the agency are not that clearly defined. If he must check with another agency, his problem becomes even more difficult, for he may be unfamiliar with the work assignments of the officials in that agency. Valuable time is lost before he can identify the particular individual with whom he should deal. Furthermore, both in intra- and interagency contacts, physical separation may delay and impede communications, as is illustrated in communications between widely separated field offices. Merely looking at the organization chart of a large public agency will give some idea of the complexities of lateral communication. Although the interaction between the numerous departments, divisions and organization units is not shown on the chart, the very number of these horizontally placed units suggests the intricate pattern of interrelationships necessary for efficient operation. Naturally, the red tape increases as documents and other communications are directed laterally from points inside and outside the agency.

A further difficulty arises from the fact that the person initiating a lateral communication usually cannot exert the same pressure as can a supervisor on his own subordinates. In dealing with coequals, representatives of other agencies or even the subordinates of others, the official must usually rely on persuasion. This may mean far more delay in lateral than in downward communication, where the traditional flow of authority does give the communication at least some ring of urgency.

Improving Lateral Communication
The first step in developing efficient communications is to build a sound organization structure and to make clear everybody's responsibilities. As to achieving coordination, George F. Grant stresses what he calls "unity by agency objective."[9] By this he means that employees at all levels will work together better if the leaders of the agency clearly explain the importance of the agency program and of their own particular contributions to it. Many different techniques can be employed in this effort, but obviously a very superior quality of leadership is required if the employees throughout the agency are to be induced to work together as a team. Furthermore, there may be important limits to the degree to which any individual may be expected to identify with the organization with which he works. Thompson writes:

> Although some individuals undoubtedly give considerable loyalty to their bread-and-butter organization, it is only one loyalty among many. If the organization becomes the only object of one's loyalty, then the organization becomes a totalitarian state. Most people probably give their first or primary loyalty to their primary groups—the family, the informal work group, etc. The sharing of values and reality perceptions throughout the larger organization is, therefore, an illusion.[10]

One need not wholly agree with Thompson, but there must be some realization of the limitations to employees' identification with organizational goals. Yet professional ties improve communication in grant-in-aid and other intergovernmental programs. Individuals within the same

[9]George F. Grant, "Unity and Specialization in Administration," in *Public Administration, Readings and Documents*, ed. Felix A. Nigro (New York: Holt, Rinehart and Winston, 1951), pp. 126-35.
[10]Thompson, *op. cit.*, p. 185.

profession can get along well, despite the fact that they are of different governmental levels, due to their professional loyalties.

Apart from vocational specialization, there is another important way in which the members of modern organizations are specialized; they are "socially specialized," that is, they have become specialized in working with one another. In efforts to improve lateral communication, it must be recognized that it takes a good deal of time before individuals can become specialized in this way:

> We understand people easily through our experience with them, which teaches us their special use of words, the meaning of intonation and gestures, whether they are matter of fact or emotional, given to exaggeration or understatement, are reticent or voluble, and many other subtle characteristics of communication. Without the confidence that accompanies this kind of understanding, reticence, hesitation, indecision, delay, error, and panic ensue.
>
> "Know your people" is nearly as important as "know your language" in the communication upon which organized effort depends. The difficulty of communication on matters of concrete action between individuals who have not known each other is a matter of common experience, but its importance with respect to organization seems to be forgotten because the organizations we know have, in fact, developed usually through long periods. At a given time nearly everyone has habitual relations with most of those with whom he needs to communicate regularly.[11]

The agency head naturally wants his subordinates to cooperate and to pull together; yet it takes a real effort to get even the heads of organization units to work together properly. Above all, the agency head must be aware of the probable existence of at least some sensitive relationships between them. With this awareness, he is in a much better position to induce coordinated efforts. The staff conference is frequently mentioned as a valuable tool for achieving coordination, yet the experienced executive knows that some of his subordinates may come to these meetings determined to conceal their real thoughts and plans from the others. He will also be well aware that some of the positions taken may be reactions to certain individuals and their personalities, rather than to the objective situation. Subordinate A may react negatively to suggestions made by subordinate B simply because it is B who makes them. If C were to make them, his reaction might be different. Thus if the executive is to be successful in improving lateral communication, he must first be effective in improving the interpersonal relationships among his subordinates. Unless he understands his role in this way, the kinds of communications

---

[11]Chester I. Barnard, "Education for Executives," in *Human Relations in Administration*, ed. Robert Dubin (Englewood Cliffs, N.J.: Prentice-Hall, 1961), p. 20.

he evokes from them will likely consist of mere words unsupported by any real desire to cooperate. Surface appearances of harmony may be maintained during the conference—polite words may be exchanged—but as a coordinating device, the meeting will have been a failure. Obviously, there are limits to what the executive can do to promote better personal relationships between his subordinates. It is a certainty, however, that he will have very little success unless he is first able to interpret accurately the feelings behind the communications they initiate, both when in a staff conference or when conferring with him individually.[12]

Informal Communications

The formal communications network will always be supplemented by an informal one. If clearances are difficult to obtain through the formal channels, contact can be made informally with a friend who can expedite things. The "grapevine" can damage the organization by carrying ugly gossip and false information, but it can also play a constructive role. Valuable information that an individual will normally not be willing to communicate through the official channels is often transmitted to superior officers very rapidly through the grapevine. For instance, John Jones may be unhappy about a certain condition in his office, but he is not inclined to "jump" channels and complain to the management. He expresses himself freely to his friends, one or more of whom may have an "in" with the top officials in the agency. They informally communicate John Jones's dissatisfactions, whereupon management can look into a situation of which it had not been aware. Thus, the friendship ties characteristic of the informal organization remove some of the communication blocks in upward communication. They perform the same function in facilitating lateral and even downward communication: the superior officer may want to give a subordinate personal advice, but he feels that his official capacity does not permit it. He talks freely to another employee who is in a position to pass the advice on to the person concerned. Obviously, considerable skill must be developed in utilizing these informal channels if the desired results are to be obtained. The dangers are great, because information which is fed into the gossip mill can easily be distorted and do more harm than good.

Eugene Walton observes that the "organization's informal communications network begins to hum whenever the formal channels are silent or ambiguous on subjects of importance to its members."[13] This indicates

---

[12]An excellent treatment of this problem is Warren H. Schmidt and Robert Tannenbaum, "The Management of Differences," in *Leadership and Organization: A Behavioral Science Approach,* ed. Tannenbaum, Weschler, and Masarik (New York: McGraw-Hill, 1961), pp. 101-118.
[13]Eugene Walton, "How Efficient is the Grapevine?" *Personnel* 38, no. 2 (March-April 1961): 45.

that the management stands to profit from knowing what kind of information is being transmitted through the grapevine. Walton has investigated the means by which employees learn of significant organization developments. In cases where the employees have heard about these developments mostly through the grapevine, there is a clear indication that the official channels were not functioning as efficiently as they should have been. Of course, no matter how good the formal system of communications, the grapevine will still exist, but it should not have to do the job of advising employees of management policies. This is the responsibility of the formal organization.

In closing this chapter, the following words of Herbert A. Simon are very much to the point:

> No step in the administrative process is more generally ignored, or more poorly performed, than the task of communicating decisions. All too often, plans are "ordered" into effect without any consideration of the manner in which they can be brought to influence the behavior of the individual members of the group. Procedural manuals are promulgated without follow-up to determine whether the contents of the manuals are used by the individuals to guide their decisions. Organization plans are drawn on paper, although the members of the organization are ignorant of the plan that purports to describe their relationship.[14]

Case References

Canadian Cases in Public Administration

Dr. Stockfield's Resignation
The Shared Authority
Dr. Aphid's Accident
The Frustrated Purchasing Agent
The Vague Purchasing Assignment
The Successful Leader
This Hour Has Seven Days
The Foot and Mouth Disease Epidemic, 1952

Bibliography

Argyris, Chris. *Personality and Organization*. New York: Harper & Row, 1957.
Baker, Walter A. "Accountability, Responsiveness and Public Sector Productivity." *Canadian Public Administration* 23, no. 4 (Winter 1980): 542-57.
Blake, R.R., and Mouton, J.S. *The Managerial Grid*. Houston, Texas: Gulf Publishing Company, 1964.
Davis, Keith. *Human Relations At Work*. New York: McGraw-Hill, 1962.
Dubin, R., ed. *Human Relations in Administration*. Englewood Cliffs, N.J.: Prentice-Hall, 1961.

---

[14]Herbert A. Simon, *Administrative Behavior*, (New York: Macmillan, 1957), p. 108.

Dubin, R. et al. *Leadership and Productivity*. San Francisco: Chandler Publishing Company, 1965.

Gellerman, Saul W. *Management by Motivation*. New York: American Management Association, 1968.

Gellerman, Saul W. *The Management of Human Relations*. New York: Holt, Rinehart & Winston, 1966.

Gore, William J. *Administrative Decision-Making: A Heuristic Model*. New York: John Wiley, 1964.

Gore, William J., and Dyson, J.W., eds. *The Making of Decisions: A Reader in Administrative Behaviour*. New York: Free Press, 1964.

Harmon, Michael M. "Social Equity and Organizational Man: Motivation and Organizational Democracy." *Public Administration Review* 34, no. 1 (January-February 1974): 11-18.

Herzberg, Frederick; Mausner, B.; and Snyderman, B. *The Motivation to Work*. New York: John Wiley, 1959.

Kirkhart, Larry, and Gardner, Neely, eds. "Symposium: Organization Development." *Public Administration Review* 34, no. 2 (March-April 1974): 97-140.

Lindblom, Charles. "The Science of Muddling Through." *Public Administration Review* 19, no. 1 (1959): 79-88.

McGregor, D.M., *The Human Side of Enterprise*. New York: McGraw-Hill, 1960.

Redfield, Charles E. *Communication in Management*. Chicago: The University of Chicago Press, 1969.

Selznick, Philip. *Leadership in Administration: A Sociological Interpretation*. New York: Row, Peterson, 1957.

Tannenbaum, Robert et al. *Leadership and Organization*. New York: McGraw-Hill, 1961.

Wilson, H.T. "Rationality and Decision in Administrative Science." *Canadian Journal of Political Science* 6, no. 2 (June 1973): 271-94.

Part IV

FINANCIAL ADMINISTRATION
in CANADA

14/Financial Administration
in Canada*
Treasury Board

The financial structure of the federal government of Canada rests on a constitutional and statutory framework dating back to the British North America Act of 1867. That act gave constitutional foundation to the principles of financing government that are basic to responsible government, while other necessary financial administrative machinery and procedures were established by subsequent legislation, most notably the Financial Administration Act.

The Financial Administration Act provides the statutory basis not only for most of the financial practices followed by departments and agencies, but also for the assignment of responsibilities for financial administration. The act, in respect of financial administration, sets out the responsibilities for the Treasury Board, the minister of finance, the receiver general, the Department of Supply and Services and departments and agencies. In addition, a separate act provides the basis for the responsibilities of the auditor general.

Within the confines of the constitution, the authority of Parliament is supreme. Ultimate control of the public purse and the financial structure of the government rests with Parliament. This is reflected in the fundamental principles that no tax shall be imposed and no money shall be spent without the authority of Parliament, and that expenditures shall be made only for the purposes authorized by Parliament.

The principle of parliamentary control of public money is embodied in the concept that there shall be a single fund for receiving and recording all revenues and expenditures. This concept was firmly established in the British North America Act, which directs that all "duties and revenues" shall form one Consolidated Revenue Fund, and in a key provision of the

---

*Reprinted and abridged by permission from Treasury Board, *Guide to the Policy and Expenditure Management System* (Ottawa: Treasury Board, 1980).

Financial Administration Act which defines the fund as "the aggregate of all public moneys that are on deposit at the credit of the Receiver General." All public money shall be paid into the Consolidated Revenue Fund and all payments made from this fund shall be appropriated by Parliament.

The British North America Act provides that all federal bills that impose a tax or that appropriate public funds must originate in the House of Commons, that all requests for appropriations must come from the government through responsible ministers, and that the government is solely responsible for such requests. Ministers and their officials are responsible for using public money in accordance with the authority granted by Parliament.

The following sections describe the arrangements under which public money flows into the Consolidated Revenue Fund, is disbursed from the fund, controlled and accounted for, and finally audited on behalf of Parliament.

A. Sources of Public Money

The government has two major sources of money—revenues and borrowings. The main sources of federal revenue are the personal and corporate income tax, commodity taxes and customs duties. The other major source of money to finance government operations is borrowings. The minister of finance, within borrowing limits established by acts of Parliament, is authorized to borrow money by the issue and sale of securities at such rates of interest and subject to such terms and conditions as the governor-in-council may approve.

The minister of finance, under the Financial Administration Act, has the responsibility for the management of the Consolidated Revenue Fund and the supervision, control and direction of all matters relating to the financial affairs of the government not by law assigned to the Treasury Board or to any other minister. The receiver general is responsible for establishing accounts for the deposit of public money with such banks and fiscal agents as are designated by the minister of finance.

B. The Application of Public Money

Information on the government's planned revenues and expenditures is presented to Parliament primarily in two types of document—the budget speech delivered by the minister of finance at any time in the fiscal year, and the estimates of expenditure for the fiscal year that are tabled by the president of the Treasury Board in the House of Commons. The budget speech is the occasion on which the minister of finance brings under review the whole financial position of the government, present and prospective, and announces the government's plans and proposals. The information contained in the estimates outlines the Parliamentary authority, either existing or required, for expenditures.

The presentation of the expenditure plans to Parliament is based on two principles:

1. that estimated financial requirements of government should so far as possible be presented to Parliament for consideration at one time; and
2. that the responsibility for the preparation and submission of these plans rests with the government. Statutory recognition of this is given in the Financial Administration Act, which places on the Treasury Board, in its role as a committee of the Privy Council, responsibility for financial management, including estimates and the review of expenditure plans.

All expenditures require the approval of Parliament. Authorization by Parliament may be in the form of either annual appropriations or continuing appropriation authorities. The distinctions between these two types of authorities are outlined below.

Annual Appropriation Authorities
An annual appropriation is an authorization by Parliament in the form of an appropriation act in respect of a specific fiscal year for the expenditure of public money. For legislative purposes, every department's spending plans in the estimates are subdivided into "votes," each of which becomes the subject of Parliamentary authority and is detailed in the schedules to the appropriation act. Since annual appropriation acts cover only one fiscal year, any unused appropriation lapses at the end of the fiscal year.

Continuing Appropriation Authorities
Continuing appropriation authorities provide a nonlapsing spending authority to pay money out of the Consolidated Revenue Fund for specific purposes. Appropriations provided in separate acts of Parliament, commonly known as statutory payments, are by far the most significant. These payments, such as old age security payments, pension and annuity payments, confer a right and an obligation to make a payment whenever a claim qualifies within the provisions of the legislation. The basic conditions laid down in the acts governing expenditures made under statutory appropriations can be changed only by parliamentary amendment of the legislation.

Estimates
The main purpose of the estimates is to present to Parliament the spending proposals for the coming fiscal year. With the tabling of main estimates in February, Parliament begins its examination of the government's expenditure budget. The estimates include the proposed votes

(spending and authorities) that Parliament is being asked to approve through passage of an appropriation act, including budgetary appropriations (amounts that have an impact on budgetary surplus or deficit) and nonbudgetary appropriations (amounts required for the making of loans, investments and advances). In addition, the estimates include for the information of Parliament estimated budgetary and nonbudgetary expenditures under the authority of various statutes previously passed by Parliament.

Under current procedures, Parliamentary deliberations on the estimates do not conclude until the end of June. Parliament is therefore asked to vote interim supply at the end of March to make it possible for the government to finance its operations from the start of the fiscal year on April 1 to the end of June. Interim supply usually comprises three-twelfths of each vote in the estimates—one twelfth for each of the first three months—although it may be more in some specific instances where the expenditure pattern of a program requires it.

The estimates are referred to the appropriate standing committee of the House of Commons and to the Standing Committee on National Finance of the Senate for detailed consideration. The committees of the House are required to report to the House of Commons by May 31 of the fiscal year; the Senate Committee reports to the Senate at about the same time.

After the committees of the House of Commons and the Senate have reported on the estimates, an appropriation act is introduced in the House of Commons. It is only when this appropriation act is approved by the House of Commons and the Senate, and subsequently given royal assent and release of the appropriation through a warrant signed by the governor general, that all the expenditures proposed in the estimates may actually take place.

When the normal process of Parliamentary approval of appropriation acts based on estimates is unavoidably interrupted, for example, by dissolution of Parliament, the Financial Administration Act provides for authorization of expenditures "urgently required for the public good" through the issuance of special governor general's warrants.

It is not possible at the start of a fiscal year to identify all requirements for funds during the fiscal year. In every fiscal year there are certain to be unforeseen events which give rise to additional costs. Moreover, there may be circumstances during the course of the fiscal year in which the government sees fit to alter its expenditure plans as reflected in tabled estimates. The authority necessary to cover these types of adjustments to estimates is sought through supplementary estimates.

The first supplementary estimates are normally presented to Parliament in November, about nine months after the presentation of the main estimates; final supplementary estimates are normally tabled in March. Both are referred to the standing committees of the House of Commons and the Senate for review. These committees follow much the same procedure as that followed in the review of main estimates. After the reviews by the committees are completed and reported, an appropriation act is introduced. When the act is approved, the procedures for the release of supply are similar to those of the main estimates.

C. Control Of and Accounting For Public Money

Independent of the functions of planning and authorizing the amounts of money to be obtained or expended for particular items or in total, there must exist adequate means for the accounting for and control of public money.

In the Financial Administration Act, Parliament has laid the foundation for a system of administering all facets of the government's financial activities and has incorporated provision for the effective control and safeguarding of public money. This includes the power and responsibility of ministers for maintaining control over receipts and expenditures, thereby enabling them to present a strict accounting.

With respect to receipts, the cardinal rule in the act is that all public money must be deposited in the Consolidated Revenue Fund. The general management of the fund, the banking arrangements and borrowings, are in the hands of the minister of finance. The form of accounts and records to be maintained is the responsibility of the Treasury Board.

Apart from payments to provincial governments authorized by the British North America Act, the Financial Administration Act assigns to ministers responsibility for all expenditures, conferring on them individually and on the government collectively powers whereby they may maintain control. Each minister is responsible for the legality, the necessity and the advisability of all payments from public funds under his administration. The responsibility for overall control of public spending is conferred primarily on the Treasury Board.

The Financial Administration Act authorizes the Treasury Board to direct departments and agencies to submit to the board a division into allotments of each vote included in its estimates. Once approved by the Treasury Board, these allotments cannot be varied or amended without the approval of the board and expenditures charged to appropriations are limited to such allotments. To avoid overexpenditures within a fiscal year, commitments coming in course of payment within the year for which Parliament has provided or has been asked to provide appropriations are recorded and controlled by the departments concerned. In addition, departments must maintain records of commitments made under contract that will fall due in succeeding years.

The primary source of information on all actual financial transactions of the government is the Public Accounts of Canada, which are required by the Financial Administration Act to be tabled in Parliament. They include:

(a) a report on the financial transactions for the fiscal year;
(b) statements of the revenues and expenditures, and of the assets and liabilities, supported by detailed statements and information, by departments; and
(c) financial reports by the various Crown corporations.

The other chief accountability reports are the annual statements of budgetary and nonbudgetary financial transactions and of the government's cash and debt position, issued by the minister of finance and published in the *Canada Gazette.*

Parliament not only appropriates money for the government— "grants supply to the Crown"—it also legislates through the Financial Administration Act how ministers and their officials must account for the use of appropriation authorities. Under the act, the Treasury Board is authorized to regulate the manner and form in which departments and agencies keep their financial records. This includes the establishment of the rules of accounting and financial practices with respect to the control of public money; for financial reporting by departments and agencies; and for the establishment of standards for the internal management and control within departments.

The Public Accounts Committee of the House of Commons is constituted at the beginning of the first session of each Parliament by resolution of the House to examine and inquire into such matters as may be referred to it by the House. This reference invariably includes the annual Public Accounts and the report of the auditor general.

D. Audit

An integral step in Parliament's control of government spending is the independent examination of the government's accounts by the auditor general of Canada, who is an officer of Parliament.

The legislative responsibilities of the auditor general include the expression of opinions on financial statements and annual reporting on cases where, in the opinion of the auditor general, there has been insufficient accounting for or control of public resources, or where money has not been expended for purposes intended. In addition, the auditor general has authority to report cases where money has been expended without due regard for economy and efficiency and where in his opinion procedures established to measure and report effectiveness are unsatisfactory.

The House of Commons' Standing Committee on the Public Accounts reviews the Public Accounts of Canada and the annual reports of the auditor general; these documents form the basis of the committee's inquiries. The results of the committee's review are reported to the House of Commons.

15/The Evolution of the Expenditure Budget
David Siegel

The budget is one of the most important pieces of legislation with which a legislative body deals on an annual basis. There certainly are more significant items which legislatures discuss—declaring war, reinstating or abolishing capital punishment, a municipality's official land-use plan— but these are usually only contemplated at wide intervals.

> The budget is the single most important policy statement of any government. The expenditure side of the budget tells us "who gets what" in public funds, and the revenue side of the budget tells us "who pays the cost." There are few government activities or programs which do not require an expenditure of funds, and no public funds may be spent without budgetary authorization. Deciding what goes into the budget (the budgetary process) provides a mechanism for reviewing government programs, assessing their cost, relating them to financial resources, making choices among alternative expenditures, and determining the financial effort that a government will expend on these programs. Budgets determine what programs and policies are to be increased, decreased, lapsed, initiated, or renewed. The budget lies at the heart of public policy.[1]

This essay examines four styles of budgeting and the way in which each style relates to the major purposes of budgets. The four *styles*, which are discussed in the order of their historical development, are line-item budgeting, performance budgeting, planning-programming-budgeting and zero-base budgeting. The three primary *purposes* of budgets are "control, better management, and planning and policy choice."[2] The meaning of each of these three terms is explained in turn.

A central aspect of democratic government is political control of the appointed bureaucracy. "*Control* refers to the process of binding operat-

---

[1]Thomas Dye, *Understanding Public Policy* (Englewood Cliffs, N.J.: Prentice-Hall, 1972), p. 205.
[2]Donald Gow, *The Progress of Budgetary Reform in the Government of Canada* (Ottawa: Information Canada, 1973), p. 1.

ing officials to the policies and plans set by their superiors."[3] A satisfactory budgeting system must have some method of ensuring that managers do not overspend budgets and that they do not spend money on programs which have not been properly authorized.

A system of *better management* will go beyond simply ensuring that subordinates are following orders; it will also ensure that work is organized so as to achieve efficiency and effectiveness. Robert Anthony defines management as "the process by which managers assure that resources are obtained and used effectively and efficiently in the accomplishment of the organization's objectives."[4]

"*Planning* involves the determination of objectives, the evaluation of alternative courses of action and the authorization of select programs."[5] If planning is a part of the budgetary system then the system can be used to provide information about the future direction of programs and to assist in the selection of optimal programs. A budgetary system might have a feedback mechanism to make sure that planned results are being obtained and to compare these results to those attainable from alternative programs.

An ideal budgeting system would serve all three of these purposes. However, it has proven very difficult to develop a practical system which serves all three purposes adequately.

The Line-Item Budget

Chronologically, the first type of budgeting system developed—and the most rudimentary—is *the line-item budget*. In a line-item budget, detail is provided on the object of the expenditure, that is, the resource which will be purchased by the budgetary allocation, such as salaries, office rent, stationery, travel.

This kind of budgeting system is very useful for control purposes. It allows elected officials to specify clearly how they want money spent and then to compare the amounts spent with the amounts budgeted to ensure that no overexpenditure has occurred. The key person in this kind of system is the accountant whose job it is to maintain records carefully and to ensure that appropriation limits are not exceeded. The mark of a good manager is that he or she does not exceed the established budgetary limit.

The weakness of a line-item budgeting system is that it does not provide for either management or planning. In general, this is because it

---

[3]Allen Schick, "The Road to PPB: The Stages of Budget Reform," *Public Administration Review* 26 (December 1966): 244 (emphasis in original).
[4]Robert N. Anthony, *Planning, and Control Systems: A Framework for Analysis*, as quoted in Schick, "The Road to PPB," p. 244.
[5]*Ibid.*, p. 244 (emphasis in original).

does not provide for any measurement of the outputs achieved by programs. It measures resources consumed but it provides no information about the volume, quality or even nature of the services delivered. Thus the abilities of managers can be evaluated solely by whether they have overexpended their budget, rather than by what they have accomplished.

In the absence of information about the nature of the services provided, decision makers cannot easily make intelligent revisions in the amounts originally requested by operating departments. As a result, this type of budgeting is frequently referred to as "bottom-up" budgeting. A central feature of this budgetary process is the preparation by managers at the operating level of requests for funds needed to carry out their activities. It is very difficult for senior managers and elected officials to challenge budgetary estimates established by means of this bottom-up approach.

The problem is exacerbated by the fact that line-item budgeting systems are usually characterized by a weak or totally absent central evaluative mechanism. There will be some central body to coordinate preparation of the budget, but its emphasis will likely be on consolidating information provided by operating departments and, possibly, on reducing some of the largest increases requested. There will seldom be staff and expertise to perform any complex evaluations.

In terms of styles of decision making, line-item budgeting is most likely to be incremental. The absence of information about the outputs of particular programs means that the best guide to the appropriate expenditure for this year is simply last year's expenditure plus revisions for inflation and for changes in the population served. Elected officials tend to evaluate budgets in this manner as well. Programs involving requests for larger than average increases are singled out for special consideration, while programs requiring average increases are approved with few questions. Nobody is really able to discuss the quality of these programs because that information is simply not available. Line-item budgeting is still in use in some jurisdictions in Canada but, because of the flaws identified above, there has been a movement to other types of budgeting.

Performance Budgeting

The first major revision in budgeting systems constituted an effort to inject a management orientation in addition to the control orientation evident in line-item budgeting. The style of budgeting shifted to what has been called *performance budgeting*. This had its full flowering in the Hoover Commissions[6] in the United States, but there are several

---

[6]Commission on Organization of the Executive Branch of Government, *Budget and Accounting* (June 1955), pp. 11-15.

examples of its use in Canada. The idea of performance budgeting is to capture the unit cost of performing certain activities and to compare these actual costs with some standard cost or to use them to compare the performance of different managers. The value of this approach is the introduction of the principle that the good manager not only avoids evil by not overspending his or her budget but also, given a set budget, maximizes output. This consideration of outputs is an important breakthrough. It provides decision makers with more information than they had previously. They will now know both the amounts requested by the operating units and the quantity of service provided. Moreover, they will have at least a rough idea of the efficiency with which the service is provided. It has been suggested that this stage was largely skipped in Canada, but in fact there was limited use of performance budgeting in the Post Office and the Department of Veterans Affairs.[7] In sum, performance budgeting is a system which covers both the control and management functions mentioned earlier, but it still does not provide any forward-looking planning orientation.

Planning-Programming-Budgeting

Planning-programming-budgeting (PPB) was brought into the United States federal government in 1961 by Robert McNamara, the Secretary of Defense. His application of PPB in the Department of Defense is considered to mark the beginning of a new generation of budgetary techniques. When McNamara and his assistant secretary, Charles J. Hitch, first came to the Pentagon they were concerned that the secretary had little capacity for managing the entire department as an entity. Rather they found a situation where each service—army, navy and air force—had much planning and operational autonomy. McNamara and Hitch were also concerned that financial planning and strategic or operational planning were done independently by separate units. For this reason, the latter type of planning tended to be somewhat unrealistic. Finally, there were few quantitative techniques to aid the secretary in decision making, particularly in making trade-offs between the desires of the different services. McNamara and Hitch planned to solve these problems by introducing a budgetary system which combined planning, programming and budgeting.[8]

By the late 1960s this method had found its way to Canada. A 1969 federal government publication describes the concepts which are common to all PPB systems as:

---

[7]Gow, *op. cit.*, pp. 10 and 14.
[8]Charles J. Hitch, *Decision-Making for Defense* (Berkeley: University of California Press, 1965), pp. 21ff. Contrary to widely held belief, McNamara deserves credit only for implementing and popularizing PPB. Its roots have been traced back as far as 1907. Thomas D. Lynch, *Public Budgeting in America* (Englewood Cliffs, N.J.: Prentice-Hall, Inc., 1979), p. 30.

(a) the setting of specific objectives;
(b) the systematic analysis to clarify objectives and to assess alternative ways of meeting them;
(c) the framing of budgetary proposals in terms of programs directed toward the achievement of the objectives;
(d) the projection of the costs of these programs a number of years in the future;
(e) the formulation of plans of achievement year by year for each program; and
(f) an information system for each program to supply data for the monitoring of achievement of program goals and to supply data for the reassessment of the program objectives and the appropriateness of the program itself.[9]

There are a number of differences between PPB and its forerunners. The basic building block of a PPB system is the program, not the line item or the individual unit of service as had previously been the case. In general, PPB was an attempt to introduce various elements of a rational system of decision making into the budgetary process. The six steps described above contain many of the elements of rational decision making[10] which contains the following stages. First, certain goals and objectives are discussed and agreed upon. Secondly, a rational decision-making technique, such as cost-benefit analysis or cost-effectiveness analysis, is used to determine the optimum program to attain that goal. Thirdly, this program is simply implemented. Finally, there is—or should be—some feedback system to ensure that the program is actually delivering its expected results. Thus in the PPB system planning has been added to the control and management features of performance budgeting.

This means that there is substantially more information available to aid decision makers in arriving at appropriate budgetary allocations. The most significant factor is that PPB is output-oriented. When program managers approach decision makers for funds, the managers must come armed with information about the services provided. If a department wants a substantial increase in its budget in order to improve service, it must supply enough hard, quantified data to convince decision makers that this is a worthwhile use of funds—more worthwhile than any of the other myriad demands being made for funds. In the first place, decision makers are given adequate information about the service provided and about the consequences of their budgetary decisions on that service. Then a feedback mechanism is established to ensure that managers

---

[9]Honourable C.M. Drury, *Planning-Programming-Budgeting Guide* (Ottawa: Queen's Printer, 1969), p. 8.
[10]See, for example, Yehezkel Dror, *Public Policymaking Reexamined* (Scranton, Pa.: Chandler Publishing Company, 1968), chap. 14.

actually deliver the results promised. Managers can now be evaluated on their abilities to plan and manage the delivery of services; not just on whether they overspend their budget.

A major benefit of PPB is that it is a "top-down" form of budgeting. We saw above how top-level decision makers can frequently be trapped by bottom-up forms of budgeting such as line-item budgeting. If decision makers want to reduce expenditure but have little detail about the operation of various programs, then they must either make cuts blindly or refrain from making them altogether—a most difficult choice.

With top-down budgeting, the first thing that happens is that decision makers decide generally which broad functional areas will be emphasized (for a significant budget increase) and which will be de-emphasized (for a budget reduction). This allows top-level decision makers to signal their desires by shifting resources between functions and also allows those below them to make choices with regard to specific programs. The idea of the system is to put "politicians on top, experts on tap"—a situation which many feel was not the case prior to PPB.

Another desirable feature of PPB is that it involves multi-year planning. This permits decision makers to project the costs of today's decisions into the future. It also prevents the use of the strategy usually referred to as the "thin edge of the wedge." In this strategy, an operating department begins a new program with only minimal amounts of funding. Since the amounts are nominal, the central budget agency pays scant attention and readily grants its approval. Not until subsequent years does it become obvious that the program will need substantially more resources in the long run than it needed in its first year of operation. Of course, the entire program could always be terminated, but a shrewd manager will prevent this by developing a strong clientele early. PPB aims to prevent the "thin edge of the wedge" strategy by requiring that all requests for new programs be supported by estimates of their costs for a multi-year period. This is further evidence of the planning element of PPB.

The history of the use of PPB in the Canadian federal government is significant because it reveals a number of interesting innovations and adjustments over the years. PPB was first introduced in 1965. The initial consensus was that its success was somewhat mixed; still the Treasury Board continued to push for its use. In an effort to improve the success of PPB, the federal government experimented with two major innovations in management practices in the early 1970s—management by objectives (MBO) and operational performance management systems (OPMS).

Management by Objectives

Management by objectives is not a new innovation. Its inception is usually traced to Peter Drucker's book, *The Practice of Management,* written in 1954.[11] MBO is a participative style of management in which objectives are not *imposed* on subordinates by superiors, but rather objectives are established by the *mutual agreement* of superiors and subordinates. The process begins at the top two tiers of the hierarchy. Officials at these levels consult and agree about what are reasonable objectives for productive activity and for the upcoming year. When agreement on overall objectives is attained, the responsibility for attaining them is parcelled out among the various subordinates—always with their agreement that they will be able to accomplish their objectives. The process is then repeated at descending levels of the bureaucracy. The subordinates involved in the above process, in turn, consult with their subordinates about reasonable objectives. Thus there develops a series of "contracts" throughout the organization by which subordinates have agreed to meet a certain objective in the coming year. The final step is a senior management review to ensure the consistency of all objectives throughout the organization.

In the early 1970s, a number of departments took steps to implement MBO.[12] An objectives-oriented system such as this would merge easily with PPB. However, the criticism has been levelled that, in fact, the two innovations were developed separately by separate groups—PPB by financial officials and MBO by personnel officials—and were never really merged.[13] Whether it was for this or other reasons, MBO was never adopted successfully in a large number of departments.

Operational Performance Management Systems

At roughly the same time as MBO was being imported, Treasury Board was developing its own system to supplement PPB and MBO. The key to the operation of both these systems is good measurement of the performance, or outputs, achieved by programs. Operational performance measurement systems (OPMS) are the performance measurement aspects of PPB and MBO.[14]

The concept of OPMS began with the idea that the ultimate goal of all government programs is to foster "individual and collective well-being," as evidenced by such things as national integrity, social justice, national

---

[11]Peter Drucker, *The Practice of Management*, (New York: Harper and Row, 1954).

[12]J.S. Hodgson, "Management by Objectives—The Experience of a Federal Government Department," *Canadian Public Administration* 16 (Fall 1973): 422-31.

[13]H.L. Laframboise, "Administrative Reform in the Federal Public Service: Signs of a Saturation Psychosis," *Canadian Public Administration* 14 (Fall 1971): 312.

[14]Treasury Board, *Operational Performance Measurement*, vol. 1: A Managerial Overview; vol. 2: Technical Manual (Ottawa: Information Canada, 1974); D.G. Hartle, "Operational Performance Measurement in the Federal Government," *Optimum* 3 (1972): 5-18; Henning Frederiksen, "Is Operational Performance in Government Measurable?" *Optimum* 6 (1975): 23-41.

wealth and individual fulfilment. Of course, it is impossible to measure most of these things in a tangible way, and even if it were possible to measure overall changes, measuring the impact of a *particular* program on national integrity would be most contentious. Therefore OPMS called for a hierarchy of proxy measures. It is impossible to measure the effect of industrial incentives on social justice. However, if we posit a series of means/ends relationships through which industrial incentives cause certain things to occur which ultimately have an impact on social justice, then it is possible to measure some of these intermediate steps. For example, a certain amount of money (inputs, in OPMS terminology) is provided for industrial incentives; this is converted into a certain number of grants awarded to industries (operational outputs); these are converted into a certain number of new jobs (program outputs); and these, in turn, are converted into increased earned income (program effects) which results in improved social justice. We cannot measure that final step, but we can measure all of the proxies leading to it. OPMS also prescribes the calculation of a number of ratios between the various proxies, for example, a measure of operational efficiency would be determined by dividing operational outputs by program inputs. These ratios could be used to measure changes in a program over time or to compare programs.

Other Innovations in the PPB System

A few other notable innovations have been made in the basic PPB system. The federal government requires that departments prepare their budget requests in three packages. The "A" budget is the request for the continuation of existing programs with adjustments made for inflation and changes in the population served. The "B" budget is the request for the establishment of new programs and the "X" budget is a listing of the programs which a department would eliminate if it were forced to reduce its budget by a stated percentage.[15] In other words, "X" budget items are the lowest priority programs as ranked by the department. The idea is that "A" budget items would not be evaluated in depth because these programs were approved previously, but that there would be an in-depth review of the costs and benefits of new programs, the "B" budget items, before they were allowed to begin.

A number of municipalities have adopted another innovation. For each program, the manager is required to estimate the ramifications—in terms of levels of service—if the program were to operate with the same budget as last year (adjusted by inflation and population served) and at two other levels of funding, say, 80 per cent and 120 per cent of last year's

---

[15]A.W. Johnson, "The Treasury Board of Canada and the Machinery of Government of the 1970's," *Canadian Journal of Political Science* 4 (September 1971): 355.

funding. This provides decision makers with a significant amount of knowledge which they can use in deciding on funding levels.

A third innovation is the federal government's newly implemented policy and expenditure management system, or "envelope" system.[16] This involves a hierarchical form of decision making in which the Cabinet Committee on Priorities and Planning divides the total expenditure budget into ten functions, or envelopes. Each envelope then becomes the responsibility of a particular cabinet committee which subdivides the funds still further between individual departments. For example, the Cabinet Committee on Priorities and Planning allocates a particular level of funding to the economic development envelope. The Cabinet Committee on Economic Development then allocates these funds to the various departments represented on this committee by their ministers. The significance of this system is that it allows those most deeply involved in each policy area—the members of the committees—to make decisions about their own policy fields. This innovation, coupled with a second innovation, which involves giving some of these committees their own expert secretariats, seems to be a significant improvement on other forms of PPB.

Problems of the PPB System

PPB was clearly the major budgeting innovation of the 1960s and the early 1970s. Virtually every governmental unit of any size in North America experimented with some form of program budgeting. The success of those experiments was mixed. The Canadian federal government seems to be attaining a modicum of success with the envelope system after a long history of reform of the budgetary process. First, there was PPB which was supplemented by OPMS and experienced a failed marriage with MBO before finally becoming the envelope system. Other jurisdictions have been less successful. In the United States federal government, the death of PPB was reported as early as 1973.[17]

The reasons for the problems experienced with PPB are many and varied.[18] As noted above, it is an attempt to apply rational modes of decision making to the budget process. Therefore, many of the general criticisms of rationality are also applicable to PPB. The high cost in both

---

[16]Privy Council Office, *The Policy and Expenditure Management System* (March 1981); Rick Van Loon, "Stop the Music: The Current Policy and Expenditure Management System in Ottawa," *Canadian Public Administration* 24 (Summer 1981): 175-99.

[17]Allen Schick, "A Death in the Bureaucracy: The Demise of Federal PPB," *Public Administration Review* 33 (March-April 1973): 146-56.

[18]One of the most prolific and perceptive critics of PPB has been Aaron Wildavsky, "The Political Economy of Efficiency: Cost-Benefit Analysis, Systems Analysis, and Program Budgeting," *Public Administration Review* 26 (December 1966): 292-310, and "Rescuing Policy Analysis from PPB," *Public Administration Review* 29 (March-April 1969): 189-202.

dollars and time of implementing the system and the sheer complexity of some attempts were clearly problems. In some cases, the amount of time spent "getting ready to get ready" seriously weakened the credibility of those seeking to implement PPB. Also the attempt to impose one system of evaluation on diverse programs led to some difficulties. Schick argues that the success of PPB in the United States Department of Defense stems from the fact that it was home-grown there; its failure in other departments stems from its status as a foreign intruder unable to adapt to the local customs.[19]

There is one outstanding reason for the problems of PPB which is too often overlooked. Changes in budgeting systems are not mere minor technical adjustments in systems used by accountants. Certain changes in budgeting systems amount to vast shifts of power within organizations.[20] This was the case with PPB. PPB usually involved a shift from a decentralized form of budgeting to a highly centralized one. In a decentralized system, individual departments present budget requests, but little information, to politicians. The politicians, in turn, do not have a group of qualified experts from whom they can seek advice. All of this means that the head of the department has fairly broad scope to manage the department with minimum intrusion from any other department.

PPB introduces a new actor to the scene—the strong central budget agency. If detailed documentation is to be prepared, cost-benefit analysis performed and trade-offs made between various programs, there must be an organization to do these things. If the system is to function correctly, this organization must have the right to request significant amounts of information from departments and evaluate that information in order to make recommendations to politicians. This would allow the budget agency to have a clear "window" into the operation of departments and so provide the agency with the ability to exercise some degree of control over operating departments. Thus operating departments tend to oppose the introduction of PPB because they fear the increased exposure which this window provides.

Additional difficulties with a rational system of budgeting surround the related problems of specifying goals, measuring benefits achieved, and predicting future conditions.[21] Government programs usually serve multiple goals and many times people will disagree on the relative priority of those goals. Is the purpose of a youth employment program to have certain work activities carried out? To assist young people in

---

[19]Schick, "A Death in the Bureaucracy," p. 147.

[20]This shift in power is described very well in A. Clayton, "Brother Could You Spare a Dime?" *Optimum* 12 (1981): 7-19.

[21]Peter Self, *Econocrats and the the Policy Process: The Politics and Philosophy of Cost-Benefit Analysis* (London: Macmillan, 1975).

developing good work habits? To provide funds to young people to continue their schooling? The likely answer is that it is all three, but which one is seen as paramount will have an effect on how the program is designed and evaluated.

A related problem is the inability to measure in a rigorous, quantified fashion the benefits derived from government services. Everyone agrees that it is beneficial that the garbage is picked up, but how do we determine objectively the value of that benefit in dollars and cents so that we can compare its costs and benefits? It is arguable that we could measure *some* of the public health benefits, but what about the aesthetic, convenience and other benefits?

A final problem has to do with the difficulty of predicting the future. Many programs have a large initial cost, and a stream of benefits which flows far into the future. The value assigned to that stream of benefits depends on the number of people who will enjoy them. For example, the total benefit derived from the construction of a second airport in Toronto is highly sensitive to whether one assumes that the level of usage remains steady, increases slightly or increases significantly.[22] Yet no one is able to predict with sufficient precision which situation will occur.

For these and other reasons, many have suggested that PPB has failed. It might well be the case that PPB has not failed, but rather that some people expected (and others promised) more than PPB could ever deliver. Stated baldly, some felt that PPB was a rational device which would enable us to remove politics from the budgetary process. Programs would be selected using various economic techniques. Politicians and interest groups would be so swayed by the clear and unequivocal answers provided by these techniques and by the totally impartial rationality of the system that they would immediately confirm the results. In retrospect, the kindest thing one can say is that this sort of thinking was naive. "[O]ne might wonder how a paper tiger such as PPB could possibly wreck the entrenched values defended by the armies of interest groups which patrol the budget scene."[23]

Zero-Base Budgeting

In the 1970s, as the glamour of PPB waned, it began to be supplanted by the latest budgetary innovation—*zero-base budgeting*. Of course, PPB is still very widely used, but the glamorous new technique of the late 1970s and early 1980s is ZBB. Charles Beard, writing in 1917, provided a rationale

---

[22]Sandford F. Borins, *The Toronto Airport(s)*, Case Program in Canadian Public Administration (Toronto: Institute of Public Administration of Canada, 1977).
[23]Schick, "A Death in the Bureaucracy," p. 149.

for this shift: "Budget reform bears the imprint of the age in which it originated."[24] PPB was one of the casualties of the economic downturn of the mid-1970s. PPB is a budgetary system for a dynamic, expanding government. It evaluates new programs and allows us to determine which new programs we want to begin this year and which ones we must put off until next. It is more difficult to use in times of holding the line or cutting back. Enter zero-base budgeting.

Zero-base budgeting (ZBB) derives its name from the fact that managers are required to justify every dollar spent from zero up.[25] The implication is that if they cannot, their programs will be reduced or eliminated. The basic building block of ZBB is the decision package. This is similar, but not identical, to the program in PPB. A municipal recreation department might have decision packages for administration, outdoor rinks, outdoor pools, community programs, and so on. A manager must provide significant amounts of information in order to justify the contin-uation of programs. Systems vary between jurisdictions, but some of the usual components are:

- description of actions performed,
- achievements from actions (both a narrative and some quantitative measures might be required),
- consequences of not approving package,
- alternative methods of accomplishing the same objective.

This approach obviously provides decision makers with much valuable information in a comparable format across all departments.

After preparation of these documents for each decision package, the ranking begins. It starts at the lowest level at which a manager has more than one decision package under his or her control. This lowest-level manager will rank each of these decision packages in order of priority and pass this ranking along to his or her supervisor. This person will receive decision packages from a number of subordinates which he or she in turn ranks. This process continues up the hierarchy. In most governments using ZBB, as the process approaches the senior levels of the bureaucracy, committees are usually struck to do the ranking. This frequently cul-minates with a ranking done by the committee of politicians responsible for the functional area.

At the conclusion of this process, there exists a ranking of all decision packages from the most attractive to the least attractive. At the same time that the ranking process is taking place, a decision is made concern-ing the level of total expenditure for the year. The final step is simply to

---

[24]As quoted in Schick, "The Road to PPB," p. 247.
[25]The definitive work about ZBB has been written by the man who developed it. Peter A. Pyhrr, *Zero-Base Budgeting*, (Toronto: John Wiley, 1973).

start at the top of the list, add up proposed expenditures and accumulate until one arrives at the desired expenditure level. All programs above this line are accepted; all of those below are rejected.

Like PPB, zero-based budgeting is a rational budgeting system. However, it has two features which set it apart from the way most PPB systems have operated.[26] The first is that it allows new programs to compete on an equal basis with existing ones. The use of the "A" and "B" budget system by the federal government means that some "B" budget items might well be more desirable than some "A" items, but because of the accident of timing, the "A" item will be continued and the "B" item rejected. This would not happen with ZBB, where both established and new programs are ranked in the same manner. The second feature of ZBB is that it allows the revenue constraint to be set first and expenditure to be adjusted to revenue. This might be one reason why ZBB has been most attractive to local governments which are usually prohibited from budgeting for a deficit. ZBB has not made the same inroads into federal or provincial governments although its implementation is being studied by some provincial governments.

Many of the criticisms of PPB are applicable also to ZBB. Both systems are attempts to achieve rationality in expenditure management. This is both their strength and their weakness. An additional flaw of ZBB is the effect on the morale of employees of this annual review to determine whether some of their programs will continue to exist. Presumably organizations could be eliminated with great loss of jobs on the occasion of one of these reviews. If that is not really the case, then ZBB is not doing what it set out to do. This realization could well motivate managers to maximize their short-term successes with possible poor consequences on longer-term performance.

ZBB, like PPB, is a budget system for the time. PPB pointed the way to new programs; ZBB shows where to make cuts.

A discussion of the evolution of the expenditure budget process would not be complete without some comment on two related developments of the 1970s in the federal government—the increasing importance of program evaluation and the establishment of the Office of the Comptroller General.

---

[26]John Strick has argued rather persuasively that there is little which ZBB can accomplish which a well-designed PPB system cannot. John C. Strick, "Zero-Base Budgeting: An Innovation or a Rediscovery of Old Concepts?" *Canadian Tax Journal* 28 (January-February 1980): 43-52. The only reservation which I can register concerns the psychology of budgeting. If people perceive a particular development as new, different and better, it will likely alter their behaviour in some way whether it is actually new, different and better or not.

Program Evaluation

Jordan and Sutherland have defined program evaluation as "the assessment of the effectiveness, efficiency, and/or economy with which public funds produce the results for which they are appropriated."[27] Unlike PPB and ZBB which specify uniform methods of analysis for all programs, the new style of program evaluation can take any number of different forms. It is "the application of the best current empirical methods of investigation in the social sciences."[28] Economic programs might be the subject of rigorous econometric analysis. Social programs might be evaluated by means of questionnaires completed by clients. These kinds of evaluations tend to be rather lengthy, complex activities and so are not conducted annually as a part of the budget cycle, but rather are conducted on some recurring multi-year cycle or simply as requested by officials.

There have been some difficulties in establishing the general concept of program evaluation. Not the least of these revolves around the question of what ought to be evaluated—efficiency or effectiveness. Efficiency is a measure of how well inputs are used to achieve outputs, for example, a measure of the cost of processing a grant application. Effectiveness is a measure of how well a program is attaining its established goals, for example, whether the grant actually reduces unemployment. The former is relatively easy to measure, the latter considerably harder, largely because of the difficulty of articulating goals. Politicians tend to be either loath to state openly any goal for a program or effusive about huge numbers of goals to be accomplished by a program. It is likely that each actor in the process will have a different goal.

This presents the evaluator with a conundrum. One could evaluate and improve efficiency—but that is not likely where the real savings can be made. Of course, it would be better if family allowance cheques were prepared at a lower cost, but the real money spent on this program is the amount provided to recipients, not the marginal amounts involved in administration. The temptation, then, is to evaluate effectiveness, but how does one evaluate the level of attainment of a goal in the absence of a clear statement of what that goal is? Jordan and Sutherland are somewhat tentative in speculating about which type of evaluation will become predominant in the federal government, but they quote Comptroller General Harry Rogers as suggesting that efficiency evaluation might be

---

27J.M. Jordan and S.L. Sutherland, "Assessing the Results of Public Expenditure: Program Evaluation in the Canadian Federal Government," *Canadian Public Administration* 22 (Fall 1979): 598.

28Harry Rogers, "Program Evaluation in the Federal Government," in *The Public Evaluation of Government Spending*, ed. G. Bruce Doern and Allan M. Maslow (Montreal: Institute for Research in Public Policy, 1979), p. 81.

the best route along which to proceed.[29] On the other hand, the auditor general's recent thrust for comprehensive auditing seems to be an approach to effectiveness evaluation.

The Office of the Comptroller General

A related development was the creation of the Office of the Comptroller General in 1978. This was a government response to persistent recommendations by the auditor general that there should be a "chief financial officer" of the federal government. The comptroller general has described the duties of his office in this manner:

> It has broad authority and responsibility for financial management and related administrative practices and controls in the government of Canada. For instance, we establish the accounting principles and practices for the financial statements of the government of Canada and the structure of accounts to be used for the preparation of financial reports by government departments and agencies. We are also vitally concerned with the form and content of financial reports, so that we can improve their use by government departments and agencies in problem identification and decision making. We establish the internal *audit* ground rules on financial matters that are to be followed by departments and agencies. We conduct regular reviews of all these activities with departments to identify the extent of their compliance and the need for them to take corrective actions or make further progress. We play a significant role in the development of training programs for financial officers in government, and in the hiring standards and grades that are established for these positions. We also participate in the selection processes of senior financial officers. We share this role with the hiring departments, the Public Service Commission and the Personnel Policy Branch of the Treasury Board Secretariat.
>
> But the responsibilities of my Office of primary interest in the present context are the responsibilities we have for the development of government-wide procedures to ensure that the efficiency and effectiveness of government operations are measured by departments and agencies. These responsibilities are discharged through two major Treasury Board policies. The first applies to the routine measurement of the performance of government programs. The second has to do with procedures that departments and agencies use to carry out the periodic evaluation of all the programs under their jurisdiction.[30]

The creation of the Office of the Comptroller General closes the circle. Departments have been developing some capacity for program evaluation since the inception of PPB, and traditionally Treasury Board has had a mandate to oversee this evaluation exercise. However, with the

---

[29]Rogers, "Program Evaluation," p. 589.
[30]Rogers, *op. cit.*, p. 80. (Emphasis in original.)

creation of the Office of the Comptroller General, this oversight function has been institutionalized. Not only has the evaluation function developed rather well within a number of departments, but also a central agency has been created to evaluate the evaluations. The role of this new central agency is to ensure that departments are performing evaluations and to ensure that these evaluations are of the appropriate quality. This movement toward evaluation marks a definite move to add the planning element to the control and management elements and so develop a budget system which contains all three of these essential elements.

Summary

This paper began by suggesting that a good budgeting system would serve three purposes: "control, better management, and planning and policy choice." The evolution of the expenditure budget system has involved a movement from a relatively rudimentary system which provided only control—line-item budgeting—to some of the more recent developments which go a long way toward serving all three purposes. The clear shift over time has involved budgeting systems becoming more concerned with the measurement of outputs and the evaluation of efficiency and effectiveness. This should provide for better accountability, in that civil servants can now be held accountable not just for staying within the approved budget, but for actually providing the appropriate level of service.

16/The Policy and Expenditure Management System*
Privy Council Office

The New System

The fundamental purpose of the new system is to ensure greater ministerial control over the management of policies and expenditures. It seeks to do this by integrating the processes of policy making and fiscal and expenditure planning within the Cabinet committee system.

The policy and expenditure management system has taken into account criticisms directed at the management of expenditures, including

*Reprinted and abridged by permission from *The Policy and Expenditure Management System* (Ottawa: Privy Council Office, 1981).

the lack of incentives to review ongoing programs; the *ad seriatim* consideration of new proposals in isolation from clearly articulated objectives and expenditure limits; uncertainty created by seeking to constrain spending growth through the continued use of expenditure reductions (that is, "X" budgets) to keep within expenditure limits; and the effect of this on longer-term planning.

The objective is to ensure that policy and program decisions are taken in the context of and with a responsibility for costs and expenditure limits and that, in turn, expenditure decisions are taken with an understanding of and responsibility for the government's policies and priorities. Objectives and resources are inextricably related and the requisites of rational decision making require that they be considered together within the new system.

The ranking of priorities and objectives without consideration of resources is irrational. The question is not "What do you want?" as if there are no limits, but rather "What do you want compared to what others want?" A department with one billion dollars will not only do more than it would with a million, but might well do different things. Resource limits shape objectives, priorities, policies and programs.

Similarly, applying resources to policies and programs without consideration of priorities and objectives is irrational. The question is not "What can you spend?" as if there were no purpose, but rather, "How does it contribute to what you want?" A department with a particular set of objectives will require more or less resources than one with another set. Objectives and priorities affect how resources are applied.

In its essence, the new system involves two significant features:

1. The preparation of a long-term fiscal plan encompassing government revenues and expenditures over a five-year period, that is, setting out the overall financial constraints within which policy choices must be considered.
2. The establishment of specific expenditure limits (resource envelopes) for policy sectors, related to the government's priorities, and the assignment of the responsibility for managing a particular policy sector's resources to the appropriate policy committee of Cabinet.

The new policy and expenditure management system is an integral component of the current Cabinet committee system. (See Chart I: Cabinet Committee System.) Through the decentralization of decision-making authority to Cabinet committees, the structure captures the advantages of small group decision making while reinforcing the collective responsibility of Cabinet as a whole.

The Cabinet committee system is an extension of Cabinet. It

includes four policy committees—Economic Development, Social Development, Foreign and Defence Policy and Government Operations—each responsible for its respective policy sectors. Together with the Cabinet Committee on Priorities and Planning, they form the basis for the new system and are responsible for taking the policy and program decisions in their sectors within the context of their assigned resource envelopes.

There are four coordinating committees: Priorities and Planning, Treasury Board, Legislation and House Planning, and Communications. The Cabinet Committee on Priorities and Planning is central to the policy and expenditure management system with the responsibility for setting the overall direction for government policy, including the establishment of the fiscal plan and the determination of resource envelopes for each policy committee. Priorities and Planning also provides the forum for the consideration of federal-provincial issues as well as other areas of high priority.

In addition, the Special Committee of Council handles regulations and other proposed orders-in-council not requiring the attention of full Cabinet. Other special committees deal, as required, with matters relating to security and intelligence, labour relations, public service and Western affairs. From time to time, special problems assume importance requiring ad hoc committees until a satisfactory solution is reached.

The policy and expenditure management system and the Cabinet committee system are supported by a system of secretariats and committees. The two Ministries of State—for Economic Development and Social Development—provide the support secretariats for their respective Cabinet committees. These ministries focus on substantive sectoral strategy and priorities, cross-departmental coordination, resource allocation and management, and the analyses of program effectiveness. For the Cabinet Committees on Foreign Policy and Defence, and Government Operations, this support is provided by the Privy Council Office (in addition to the usual Cabinet secretariat functions it provides to all committees) with the assistance of other interdepartmental mechanisms and central agencies.

Supporting the collective decision making of ministers in these committees are deputy minister committees which provide a forum for testing the adequacy and timeliness of proposals and a mechanism for encouraging the resolution of issues not requiring referral to the Cabinet committees. The Coordinating Committee of Deputy Ministers, chaired by the secretary to the Cabinet, "mirrors" the Cabinet Committee on Priorities and Planning and handles significant cross-sectoral issues. It is not the purpose of these committees to determine the content or timing of proposals to Cabinet committees; that is the responsibility of ministers. Rather, these committees of deputy ministers are to ensure that the necessary coordination in the preparation of proposals has taken place and that the essential information is made available to the Cabinet committees.

The Privy Council Office provides the secretariat support to Cabinet and its committees and, in respect of the policy and expenditure management system, focuses on overall government and prime ministerial priorities, cross-sectoral problems and the integrity and functioning of the overall system.

The Treasury Board Secretariat supports both the Treasury Board and the policy committees by focusing on the expenditure framework, resource costing, management systems, envelope system accounting and the efficiency aspects of programs.

The Department of Finance supports the policy and expenditure management system through focusing on the prospects for the economy, the fiscal framework, tax expenditures and fiscal policy, federal-provincial issues relating to major programs and Crown corporations.

Longer-Term Plans

As the Lambert Commission[1] pointed out, sound management must be based on a planning process that establishes goals, seeks out the best ways of achieving these goals, identifies the required resources and measures the benefits arising from their attainment. The starting point must be the development of a fiscal plan encompassing the total spectrum of revenues and expenditures to provide a clear picture of the planned role of the government in the economy and setting out specific expenditure limits for each policy area.

Expenditures—overall and for each policy sector—are projected for a five-year period. This allows departments and agencies to plan over a reasonable period with a clear sense of what resource limits will be and requires continuing analysis of expenditure trends to detect problems in later years which might, in light of the legislative process and the financial interdependence between levels of government, require immediate action to effect later savings. Reviewing projections of expenditures provides a means of identifying particular budgetary pressures and selecting those areas where change is desirable in light of the government's longer-term objectives.

To develop this plan it is necessary first to set out where the government wishes to be at a particular point in the future and then to identify the key constraints on doing so, an approach essential for achieving government objectives. Sudden and arbitrary changes are difficult and often counterproductive, given federal/provincial arrangements and the need for Parliament to approve the government's proposals.

---

[1]Canada, Royal Commission on Financial Management and Accountability, *Final Report* (Ottawa: Supply and Services, 1979).

Finally, a long-term plan provides ministers with a context within which they can examine future costs of ongoing programs and new initiatives and take these costs into full account in considering current decisions.

The five-year expenditure projections include:

- the current fiscal year;
- the limits for the coming fiscal year; and
- the planning projections for the three subsequent fiscal years.

Each year, and as required by new circumstances, the planning projections are adjusted: the third-year projections, after necessary adjustment, become the fixed limit for the coming fiscal year and are replaced by a projection for an additional year ahead.

These targets could and will change, depending upon economic circumstances. They provide, none the less, an essential element of realistic planning—a clearly stated objective.

Resource Envelopes

The creation of resource envelopes and their integration into the decision-making process of the Cabinet committee structure are central to the new system. The envelope basically defines the resources that are available over time to a policy committee for a particular policy sector. Based on the budgetary requirements of departments, agencies and Crown corporations within the sector, the policy committee of Cabinet responsible for that particular sector provides direction on the use of the resources.

Total government expenditures have been divided into ten envelopes. Most of these envelopes provide opportunities for the reduction or elimination of expenditures on programs within the envelope in order to yield resources for the expansion of other programs or the development of new ones. While the envelope is defined in terms of an expenditure budget, decisions on the envelope are arrived at with reference to all the means available to achieve a particular objective over time: tax expenditures, loan guarantees, and the use of regulatory and legislative devices, as well as direct funding. This inhibits, for example, escaping the discipline of the envelope limit by expanding tax incentives.

The resource envelopes, together with information on the major policy areas, are intended to serve two basic purposes:

1. Review of Relationship Between Expenditures and Objectives

To display for ministers quickly and conveniently the relationship of particular programs within a particular policy sector, not only to other programs within that sector but to the objectives and expenditure goals of the government as a whole. As such, envelopes are expected to facilitate the identification of expenditure pressure areas, and the comparison of expenditure trends to the government's objectives.

2. Management of Policy Sectors

To provide policy committees with both the opportunity and the incentive to develop systems for reviewing programs within their policy sectors and for reallocating resources from less effective to more effective programs. This will become imperative given the requirement that the funding for new initiatives and activities be generated from savings on existing programs.

Following the broad functions of government programs and keeping in mind the Lambert recommendations, a set of policy areas and envelopes have been established. The program content of the envelopes has been designed to maximize policy trade-offs within each envelope while ensuring that ministers' responsibilities for their respective departments and agencies are not dispersed across several envelopes and committees.

As implementation of the system proceeds the government will wish to consider certain adjustments to envelopes to improve its effectiveness. The envelopes assigned to the Cabinet committees are as follows:

1. Cabinet Committee on Priorities and Planning

Fiscal Arrangements
Public Debt

2. Cabinet Committee on Social Development

Justice and Legal Affairs—consists of those government programs aimed at maintaining and enhancing justice and protection of the individual. Ninety per cent of the expenditures are allocated to the two major programs—RCMP and Correctional Services.

Social Affairs—consists of all social programs including major statutory programs that involve direct payments to individuals from the federal government (income maintenance), or payments to support essential social services through arrangements with the provinces (Established Programs Financing), as well as cultural programs.

3. Cabinet Committee on Economic Development

Economic Development—consists of those government programs that are directly related to the key economic sectors, including resources, manufacturing and tourism, as well as horizontal policy activities such as competition policy, regional development and transportation.

Energy—includes energy and energy-related programs including the government's planned new initiatives.

4. Cabinet Committee on Government Operations
Services to Government—includes those programs and activities of government whose primary purpose is to provide support and services to program departments or which are primarily service-oriented (for example, Post Office). It also includes executive functions (mainly central agencies) and agencies which report to Parliament but for which the government retains a financial and management responsibility.

Parliament—a separate envelope has been defined for those elements outside the direct control of the government.

5. Cabinet Committee on Foreign and Defence Policy
External Affairs and Aid—includes external affairs and assistance to developing countries.

Defence—both capital and operating expenses for the Department of National Defence.

Responsibility of Ministers
To achieve the integration of the priorities setting and resource allocation processes, the following aspects of the responsibility of the president of the Treasury Board, the minister of finance and the chairmen of the respective policy committees are of importance.

A. The Policy Committee Chairmen
Each chairman's primary responsibility is to develop, in concert with his policy committee, a policy and resource overview of the sector and to forge the individual actions and responsibility of ministers into a common government approach for that sector. On this basis, the chairman:

1. Leads the process of policy and program development in the policy sector and provides the linkage to the Cabinet Committee on Priorities and Planning to ensure coordination across sectors.
2. Is responsible for ensuring that the committee has the information necessary to give full consideration of trade-offs that must be made among departments in that sector, and to agree on broad allocations for departments and programs within the envelope assigned. This would include recommendations and decisions on cutting back expenditures and reallocating the savings to other programs.

B. Minister of Finance
On the basis of the minister's responsibilities for the government's economic policies and its financial position, including the management of the national debt and the borrowing requirements of Crown corporations, the Minister of Finance:

1. Sets the government's fiscal framework.
2. In consultation with the president of the Treasury Board, makes recommendations on the size of the envelopes.
3. Assesses and advises on the macroeconomic consequences of envelope decisions.
4. Assesses other means, including tax incentives, that may be more effective than expenditures in meeting the government's objectives.
5. Ensures that decisions on the allocation of resources are fully compatible with the government's economic and financial policies.

C. President of the Treasury Board

The president of the Treasury Board maintains an overview of the government's expenditure plans and the management of the envelopes. In particular, the president of the Treasury Board:

1. Based on an assessment of budgetary pressures and ongoing reviews of expenditures, advises, in consultation with the minister of finance, on the size of the envelopes.
2. Exercises overall responsibility for the accounting of expenditures, including the preparation and tabling of Main Estimates based on decisions of the Policy Committees.
3. Advises on the current state of commitments in each envelope and anticipated demands on each envelope. In particular, ensures that the chairman is aware when there is a danger that an envelope may be breached in a current or future year.
4. Advises on the cost implications of ongoing programs and any specific policy or program proposals before committees in light of the analytic work of the Treasury Board Secretariat and the comptroller general, with particular emphasis on efficiency criteria.

The Working of the System

In general terms the system works in the following way, with the annual cycle beginning each September, over a year and a half before the start of the fiscal year in April. (See Chart II: Policy and Expenditure Planning Cycle.)

1. Envelope Setting (Late Summer/Early Fall)

The dollar value for each envelope is decided upon each year by the Cabinet Committee on Priorities and Planning in the context of establishing the fiscal plan and the general directions for each policy sector on the basis of:

- a fiscal plan submitted by the minister of finance assessing the economic environment, projected revenues and expenditures, and the financial requirements of the government;

- a presentation from the minister of finance, in consultation with the president of the Treasury Board, on the overall expenditure level and the appropriate levels for each envelope; and
- policy sector reports from each committee chairman outlining the strategy for his sector.

2. Directions for Policy Sectors (Early Winter)

Each policy committee of Cabinet is assigned the responsibility for managing its envelopes. On the basis of its policy and program objectives, the committee provides the necessary direction to departments and agencies in preparing their strategic overviews. This includes the overall direction for the department and the identification of reviews and lower-priority programs within the sector as the means to generate funds for program expansion and new initiatives.

3. Strategic Overviews and Operational Plans (Spring/Early Summer)

On the basis of committee directions and planning guidelines, departments and agencies prepare and submit strategic overviews and operational plans to the policy committees and the Treasury Board for review. The Treasury Board carries out a review of the operational plans to determine the costs of carrying out those policies and programs which have to that point been approved by the committees. With this up-to-date costing, and within the context of the multi-year envelope ceilings, policy committees decide upon the policy proposals and program reviews to be undertaken.

4. Priorities and Planning (Late Summer/Early Fall)

The Cabinet Committee on Priorities and Planning considers any revisions to the fiscal plan in light of a revised economic outlook and considers committee strategic work plans, including policy proposals and program reviews.

5. Ongoing Process (Throughout the Year)

On the basis of the decisions by Priorities and Planning, policy committees revise their strategic work plans and, on this basis, departments and agencies prepare proposals (new initiatives and reviews) for consideration by the policy committees in the context of the policy sector priorities and envelope levels.

In order to assist policy committees in their planning, it is intended that the resource envelopes be established on a five-year basis and be updated annually in order to maintain a continuing five-year perspective.

Bearing in mind the likelihood that economic assumptions will change, the system is intended to allow progressively tighter planning for any particular fiscal year through a five-year period.

In 1981 the first limits were defined and established for fiscal year 1985/86 in light of the current economic assessment, the proposed tax structure, the anticipated fiscal stance of the government and other variables such as expenditure trends.

In 1982 the overall target for 1985/86 will be revised and refined in light of the latest assessments of economic prospects and other variables.

In 1983, after further updating of the targets for 1985/86 has been done, along with the preparation of strategic work plans for the policy sectors and the government as a whole, strategic decisions will be taken on programs to be undertaken and detailed work on these programs will begin.

In 1984 final planning decisions will be taken for 1985/86, again within the context of the latest assessments of the economy, expenditure trends, and so forth.

With the beginning of the 1985/86 fiscal year, program changes will be introduced and the government's overall program will be managed and evaluated. The information developed in this process will in turn feed into planning for future years. At this point, initial limits will be established for 1989/90.

Conclusion

Implementation of the new policy and expenditure management system is well advanced. It has already proved to be an important instrument for the government in assessing how individual policies mesh with others and with the government's overall priorities and objectives. It has permitted the government to consider systematically its strategic and long-term approach to specific policy sectors and to assign resources in accordance with these objectives. The integration of the policy and expenditure management system with the Cabinet committee system represents a significant improvement over the previous system.

It is recognized that as implementation proceeds, certain adjustments and changes will prove necessary. The creation of an energy envelope providing a visible focal point for the government's integrated energy program reflects one such adjustment. It is also recognized that, as with any significant change in the government's decision-making process, it may take some time for the full benefits of the system to become clear.

It is hoped that, with time, the new system will achieve the objective of ensuring that expenditures reflect priorities and broaden the opportunities for real choice by ministers in deciding upon objectives in relationship to resources and resource levels in relationship to objectives.

Case References

Canadian Cases in Public Administration

Mr. Smith's Expense Accounts
The Renfrew Group

Chart I
Cabinet Committee System

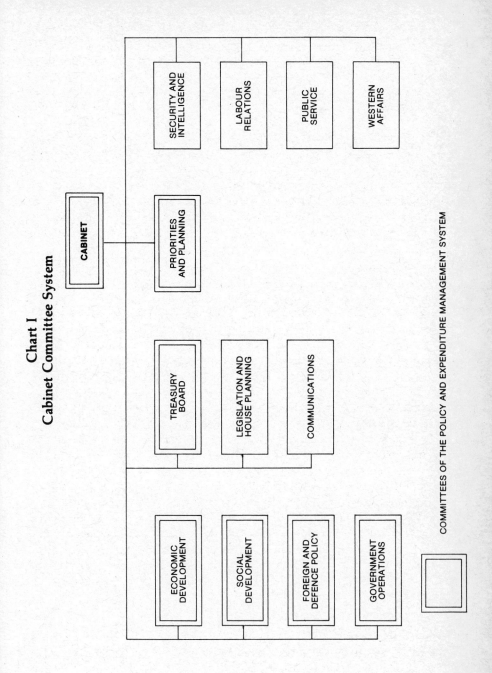

CABINET

PRIORITIES AND PLANNING

SECURITY AND INTELLIGENCE

LABOUR RELATIONS

PUBLIC SERVICE

WESTERN AFFAIRS

TREASURY BOARD

LEGISLATION AND HOUSE PLANNING

COMMUNICATIONS

ECONOMIC DEVELOPMENT

SOCIAL DEVELOPMENT

FOREIGN AND DEFENCE POLICY

GOVERNMENT OPERATIONS

COMMITTEES OF THE POLICY AND EXPENDITURE MANAGEMENT SYSTEM

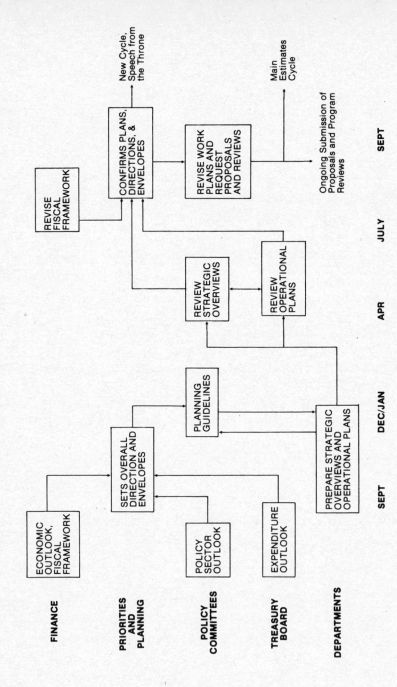

Chart II
Policy and Expenditure Planning Cycle

Bibliography

Baker, Walter. "Administrative Reform in the Federal Public Service: the First Faltering Steps." *Canadian Public Administration* 16, no. 3 (Fall 1973): 381-98.

Baker, Walter A. "Management by Objectives: A Philosophy and Style of Management for the Public Sector." *Canadian Public Administration* 12, no. 3 (Autumn 1969): 427-43.

Balls, Herbert R. "Common Services in Government." *Canadian Public Administration* 17, no. 2 (Summer 1974): 226-41.

Balls, Herbert R. "The Watchdog of Parliament: the Centenary of the Legislative Audit." *Canadian Public Administration* 21, no. 4 (Winter 1978): 584-617.

Bird, Richard M. *The Growth of Government Spending in Canada.* Toronto: Canadian Tax Foundation, 1970.

Canada. *Report of the Auditor General.* Ottawa: Supply and Services, annual.

Canada, Royal Commission on Financial Management and Accountability. *Final Report.* Ottawa: Supply and Services, March 1979.

Canada, Treasury Board. *Planning Programming Budgeting Guide.* Ottawa: Queen's Printer, 1969.

Denham, Ross A. "The Canadian Auditors General — What is their Role?" *Canadian Public Administration* 17, no. 2 (Summer 1974): 259-73.

Doern, G. Bruce. "The Budgetary Process and the Policy Role of the Federal Bureaucracy." In *Structures of Policy-Making in Canada,* edited by G. Bruce Doern and Peter Aucoin, pp. 39-78. Toronto: Macmillan, 1971.

Fenno, Richard F., Jr. *The Public Purse.* Boston: Little, Brown, 1966.

Golembiewski, R.T., ed. *Public Budgeting and Finance, Readings in Theory and Practice.* Itasca, Ill.: F.E. Peacock Publishers, 1968.

Hartle, D.G., "Techniques and Processes of Administration." *Canadian Public Administration* 19, no. 2 (Spring 1976): 21-33.

Hartle, Douglas. *The Expenditure Budget Process in the Government of Canada.* Toronto: Canadian Tax Foundation, 1978.

Hodgson, J.S. "Management by Objectives." *Canadian Public Administration* 16, no. 3 (Fall 1973): 422-31.

Jordan, J.M., and Sutherland, S.L. "Assessing the Results of Public Expenditure: Program Evaluation in the Canadian Federal Government." *Canadian Public Administration* 22, no. 4 (Winter 1979): 581-609.

Kroeker, H.V. *Accountability and Control: The Government Expenditure Process.* Montreal: C.D. Howe Institute, 1978.

Laframboise, H.L. "Administrative Reform in the Federal Public Service: Signs of a Saturation Psychosis." *Canadian Public Administration* 14, no. 3 (Fall 1971): 303-25.

Langford, John. "The Identification and Classification of Federal Public Corporations: A Preface to Regime Building." *Canadian Public Administration* 23, no. 1 (Spring 1980): 76-104.

Lyden, Fremont J., and Miller, E.G., eds. *Planning-Programming-Budgeting: A Systems Approach to Management.* 2d ed. Chicago: Markham Publishing, 1972.

McInnes, Simon. "Improving Legislative Surveillance of Provincial Public Expenditures: the Performance of the Public Accounts Committees and Auditors General." *Canadian Public Administration* 20, no. 1 (Spring 1977): 36-86.

Newland, Chester A., ed. "Forum on Management by Objectives in the Federal Government." *The Bureaucrat* 2, no. 4 (Winter 1973): 351-426.

Novick, D. ed. *Program Budgeting.* Cambridge, Mass.: Harvard University Press, 1965.

"Planning-Programming-Budgeting System Reexamined: Development, Analysis and Criticism: A Symposium." *Public Administration Review* 29, no. 2 (March-April 1969): 111-202.

Sutherland, S.L. "On the Audit Trail of the Auditor General: Parliament's Servant, 1973-1980." *Canadian Public Administration* 23, no. 4 (Winter 1980): 616-44.

Thomas, Paul G. "Parliament and the Purse Strings." In *Parliament, Policy and Representation,* edited by Harold D. Clarke et al., pp. 160-80. Toronto: Methuen, 1980.

Van Loon, R. "Stop the Music: the Current Policy and Expenditure Management System in Ottawa." *Canadian Public Administration* 24, no. 2 (Summer 1981): 175-99.

Ward, N. *The Public Purse: A Study in Canadian Democracy.* Toronto: University of Toronto Press, 1962.

Wildavsky, Aaron. *The Politics of the Budgetary Process.* Boston: Little, Brown, 1964.

Part V

PUBLIC PERSONNEL ADMINISTRATION in CANADA

17/Public Personnel Administration*

R.H. Dowdell

The Personnel Function in Management

The management of an organization is the body of executive and super-visory personnel responsible for defining its objectives, framing its policies and directing the activities of its work force. Management's resources include time, material and people (money may be considered either as a resource in itself or the ability to acquire resources). These resources must be efficiently and effectively employed if management is to achieve its objectives.

Because they behave according to the laws of physics and chemistry, management's material resources possess qualities which are either known or immediately discoverable and their behaviour is predictable. Such is not the case with people. Despite the recent discoveries in the behavioural sciences, much remains unknown about the qualities of Homo sapiens, and his behaviour cannot be so reliably predicted in the work situation or anywhere else. In a sense, the human resources of an organization are not "resources" at all, for all organized social activity is maintained to meet human needs and purposes, and the organization's employees are, in some measure, part of the reason for its existence.

A number of developments have made the task of "people manage-ment" in organizations progressively more complicated.

1. The business enterprise or government department of the nine-teenth century characteristically employed a few score or at most a few hundred people. The owner-manager, or the minister, hired many of his staff personally and knew a good deal about their backgrounds and personal idiosyncrasies. The predominant feature of modern organiza-tions is their large scale. Federal government departments are classed as small if they employ less than two thousand to three thousand people.

---

*Updated and abridged from the third edition of this book.

Thirty-six per cent of the civilian public service (exclusive of federally owned corporate enterprises) is employed in three departments: Post Office (59 000), National Defence (34 000) and National Revenue (23 000). Six other departments each employ in the ten to twenty thousand range and account for another 25 per cent. For most employees, whether in the private or public sector, personal relationships are limited to a small fragment of the enterprise. They are separated by many layers of hierarchy from top management, which comes to depend on rules and procedures instead of face-to-face contact in daily activity. The quality of large organizations that Weber described as *rationalism* results in decisions which are based on policies and regulations rather than on personal knowledge and the recognition of individual needs. There are now approximately 584 000 people at work in the federal government (including the armed forces). The total of their wages and salaries is about $3 billion annually. Less than half of these employees are under the jurisdiction of the Public Service Commission, which has exclusive authority under the Public Service Employment Act to make appointments to and within all departments and agencies which have not been granted staffing authority under a separate act. Every year the number and remuneration of federal employees increase, with a regularity that has become a major source of social and political concern. How can the public be certain that all of these people are really needed, and are working with optimum effectiveness? These questions derive from the large scale of government employment, and are addressed to some of the biggest problems in modern public personnel management.

2. In the last fifty years, scientists and managers have systematically studied people at work. Frederick W. Taylor and Frank B. Gilbreth—the founders of "scientific management"—proved that the attention given to improving the way a man works pays off handsomely in productivity. But their belief in piece-rate incentives was based on the wrong assumptions about why people work, and the kinds of satisfactions they derive from it. Motivating forces of a quite different sort came to light in the studies of group influence and communication techniques at the Hawthorne, Illinois, works of the Western Electric Company. The "Hawthorne studies" set the tone for the "human relations" school, pioneered by F.J. Roethlisberger and Elton Mayo. More recently, men like Rensis Likert, Douglas McGregor, Abram Maslow and Frederick Herzberg—to mention only a few—have done what the physical scientist did in connection with material resources: investigated the characteristics of people so that they can be employed more effectively and in a way that makes work a more meaningful human experience.

3. Knowledge in itself would do little to improve the management of people at work were it not for a change in the attitudes of the community at large. Since early in this century, society has expressed an increasing

concern for human welfare, including the treatment accorded by employers. The law gives employees powerful leverage in pursuit of their own interests by recognizing their right to form associations and by requiring management to negotiate wages and working conditions with them. A management that is harsh, neglectful or indifferent may eventually find itself in violation of other laws on safe working conditions, minimum wages and employment benefits. In addition, the community can apply economic or political sanctions to an employer who is considered to be guilty of unfair management practices.

4. The typical working man of the 1980s is more highly educated than his father was, and he has a more acute sense of social awareness. In addition to bargaining about wages and working conditions, he is beginning to demand, through his union, a voice in other aspects of management. Productive technology and plant location, for example, have widespread effects on the community, and labour has frequently challenged management's traditional right to make unilateral decisions in these and other matters. So strong is this trend that little credence can be given any longer to the concept of "sacred management prerogatives." The history of labour-management relations makes it clear that yesterday's management prerogatives are circumscribed in today's union contract, and those that management regards as inviolate now may be on the bargaining tables tomorrow.

5. Continuing high levels of economic activity have made labour scarce and expensive. Fringe benefits, transferable pension rights and guaranteed annual wages add up to a substantial management investment in each employee, whether he continues to be productively employed or not. Increasingly complex technology demands skills which cannot be produced entirely through pre-employment education and management is consequently faced with high costs of training after the worker gets on the job. Frequent changes in technology would mean even higher training costs if management did not build on the skilled and experienced staff it already has.

> When a new computer installation is staffed with retrained employees we have found it to have a far greater chance of success than one staffed by new hires. Aside from the obvious morale advantages the reason for this is really quite simple. It is usually easier to train someone in computer techniques than it is to teach a man your business.[1]

It is generally accepted in the private sector that competitive success depends more on the quality of people employed by an organization than on technological innovation. The latter will provide at best a temporary

---

[1]M.J. Rausco, "Training Implications of Automated Personnel Systems," *Office Administration* (October 1967).

advantage which is likely to be overcome by competitors, whereas a more competent work force, in particular a creative and capable management group, will be a continuing source of innovation.

Personnel Management and Personnel Administration
Personnel management is that part of management activity which concentrates on making effective use of people in achieving the organization's objectives. For the above reasons personnel management now requires the application of knowledge and skills which supervisors cannot be expected to acquire in addition to mastering the technical side of their jobs. Many aspects of management have become the concern of specialists—finance, law and public relations—and personnel management is no exception. "Personnel administration" is the term applied to the activities of specialists who assist management in the exercise of its personnel functions. These activities can be subsumed under three headings.

Advice. Personnel administrators counsel management on the development and application of personnel policies, and the resolution of problems. They do this in the light of legal requirements imposed by the community and the knowledge of the way people function at work. In this latter respect, their role is analogous to that of the engineer in the physical sciences—they form the link between research and application.

Service. Certain personnel activities which require specialized knowledge and skill are often carried out by personnel administrators as a service to or on behalf of management. The employment office, for example, conducts selective recruitment and tests candidates for basic qualifications, thereby relieving supervisors of the need to interview all but a few candidates to fill a position. Analysts write job descriptions for use in manpower planning, recruitment and training, and they identify and describe factors of significance in the job which are used in establishing wage and salary levels for individual positions.

Control. There are two kinds of control. One involves telling a person what he can or cannot do, and applying sanctions to enforce compliance. The other has come into prominence as a result of developments in cybernetics, and involves monitoring or feedback. This second form of control is the function by which an organization derives information from its own activities, analyzes it, and determines the need for changes. The personnel administrator has a control function in this sense. He informs management, for example, about the number and kind of grievances or accidents that are occurring, the incidents of illnesses among individuals or groups of people, and the frequency and causes of labour turnover (particularly resignations and dismissals). And he advises management on changes in policy and practices which will bring about improvements.

The proper relationship of personnel administration to management is summed up by describing the personnel officer's work as a staff function. He directs no one but his own subordinates. He advises members of management on policies and practices required for effective personnel management, and he assists them in dealing with specific problems. He may provide services for them, such as the employment office and the central administration of benefit programs. He can and should act as the senior executive's spokesman in dealing with lower levels of management, and as his eyes and ears in ensuring that the approved policies are carried out. This role requires that he be a person of considerable influence. But he must nevertheless respect the right of managers at lower levels to disagree with him and go to the senior executive for a decision. They are not going over his head, for he does not stand between them and the head of the organization. Should he attempt to do so, his influence will be short-lived, for he will have destroyed relationships without which he cannot do his job.

The Influence of the Political Environment
Despite broad and growing similarities, personnel management in the public service is different in many ways from its counterpart in the private sector. One of the principal differences can be identified at the highest level in government organization. In the public service, the concept of management must include the political heads of departments—that is, the ministers of the Crown. It is commonly thought that the deputy minister—the senior appointed official under the minister—is the top management official in the department, but reference to any of the acts of Parliament establishing government departments will dispel this notion. For example, Section 2(2) of the Government Organization Act (1969) reads as follows:

> The Minister of Fisheries and Forestry holds office during pleasure and
> has the management and direction of the Department of Fisheries and
> Forestry.

If the minister is a manager, he is also a politician. Indeed, perhaps first and foremost a politician, for he will not remain a minister for long unless he can get elected to Parliament, be reelected whenever the occasion demands, and exercise considerable political skill in executing his portion of the government's program.

In a commercial enterprise, the product or service must be produced at a profit. In the long run, there must be prospects of a reasonable rate of return on investment to bring the business into being and ensure its continued existence. The profit criterion is at once an important motive underlying plans, policies and decisions, and a yardstick against which their effectiveness can be assessed. Personnel directors in the private sector are in general agreement that one of their chief objectives is to contribute to their firms' profitability.

The pervasive characteristic of the public service is political rather than commercial. The administrator in the public service implements public policies and programs which have been shaped by political forces. His superiors are politicians—leaders of a political party or coalition which obtained, if not a majority, at least the largest number of seats in the House of Commons because it convinced the electorate it had the best program and was best qualified to carry it out. These elected executives will tend to do the things likely to ensure their reelection and to avoid doing things which jeopardize it. The public service is subject to their direction and accountable to them. They in turn are accountable to Parliament for the conduct of the public service and not the least of the senior public servant's concerns is to avoid embarrassing his minister. Thus the political criterion is to the public service what the profit criterion is to industry—the thread which runs through the decision-making process, and the standard against which these decisions must ultimately be weighed. That is not to say that every action must be calculated for the political advantage of the party in power any more than every action in business must be calculated to maximize profit. Short-run disadvantages must sometimes be borne and there are many actions whose political consequences are too remote to affect decisions significantly. But in the long run top management of the public service must on balance redound to the credit of the party in power and in the short run, actions which may produce adverse political consequences must be avoided as much as possible.

If these considerations are true of management generally in the public service, they are equally true of personnel management in particular. In a commercial organization, personnel policies and actions are evaluated by the profit criterion. The political criterion, however, is a nebulous thing at best and less susceptible to objective estimates. It is more likely to be applied by evaluating the sum of immediate consequences arising out of policies and actions. There is a temptation to regard each personnel action as an opportunity to secure a return of political advantage and to avoid those which are politically dangerous. For example, before the reform of the Canadian public service it was generally accepted that the party in power would use its power of appointment to secure or reward political support, and the opponents of reform argued that a government must be able to depend on the loyalty of those who administer its policies.

Whatever may be said in theory for personnel practices based on short- or long-term political advantages, the results were generally unfortunate. Although political appointees were sometimes people of great ability (Mackenzie King got his start in the public service as a patronage appointee), it was generally true that their qualifications for the job in question were a secondary consideration and frequently even minimum standards of ability were disregarded altogether. Security of tenure was uncertain and few political appointees tended to regard the public service as a career. The inevitable result was a low standard of competence and a poor quality of service to the public. At a time when government activity was highly circumscribed by today's standards, this situation could be tolerated. However, as the activities of the government began to expand, it became more and more necessary to employ people with the highest possible level of technical and administrative ability. To achieve this, methods of appointment and conditions of employment had to be changed.

The Merit Principle and Merit Systems

The merit principle which has replaced the patronage system as one of the cornerstones of personnel policy in the public service is an attempt to abandon political considerations altogether in managing the human resources of the public service. The significance of this policy may not be readily appreciated. To take politics out of public personnel management is to run counter to the very nature of the public service as an organization established to pursue political objectives. However necessary such a course may be, it generates stresses which are comparable to the psychological effects of repression. The political character of the public service which is denied outward expression in personnel management is none the less at the root of many of its problems, and accounts for many of its inconsistencies and shortcomings. One of the criteria by which public personnel management must be judged is its ability to cope with this dualism in its own character.

The merit principle is really two interrelated principles:

1. Canadian citizens should have a reasonable opportunity to be considered for employment in the public service.
2. Selections must be based exclusively on merit, or fitness to do the job.

These principles are among the most important goals of policy in public personnel management. The merit system is the mechanism in use at any given time by which these goals are achieved. The merit principle has become, and should remain, a relatively stable part of our public ethic, although like all ethical tenets it may suffer somewhat in practice. A merit system is an administrative device which can and should be adapted to changing circumstances.

18/Merit and the Public Service*

*Special Committee on Personnel Management
and the Merit Principle*

The Public Service Employment Act (PSEA) was passed by Parliament to ensure that public service appointments would be based on merit. While merit is not defined in the act, it has historically meant selection of the most qualified candidates competing for a position, based on their relative knowledge, experience and abilities, without discrimination or favouritism.

The determination of merit is left to the discretion of the Public Service Commission, which implements and enforces the principle through the merit system—the regulations, directives, policies and procedures related to the employment of public servants, and to their development and advancement in the service.

While the merit system may have been appropriate for conditions that prevailed in years past, and though it continues to achieve its purpose of preventing patronage, new and changed priorities necessitate a reinterpretation of merit. From this should flow a redesigned merit system, attuned to the demands that will be placed on it in the eighties. This suggests a frank and open insistence (reflected in legislation) that the interests of employees cannot be maintained in a state that frustrates the efforts of management to achieve reasonable levels of efficiency in staffing the public service.

Merit and Organizational Theory

The design and dynamics of modern organizations must take into account different conditions from those faced in the past. When merit was first adopted in the Canadian public service, the school of scientific management prevailed. The classification of work into discrete positions resulted in selection based on the particular duties of a single position, and none other. This position-based merit system, which exists to this day, is based on traditional bureaucratic principles of specialization of skills, differentiation of work, stable assignment of tasks and hierarchical organization, with progressively greater discretion allowed at higher levels. A selection system based on merit involves, in this context, the determination of individual suitability to perform a fixed set of duties within established limits of discretion. While parts of today's public service reflect some of the above characteristics, we would be hard

*Reprinted and abridged by permission from *Report of the Special Committee on Personnel Management and the Merit Principle* (Ottawa: Supply and Services, 1979), pp. 78-94.

pressed to find this degree of stability in most of our organizations. Yet the merit system continues to reflect these bureaucratic characteristics.

Current organizational theory, which views organizations more in terms of social systems, suggests that individuals should know the results expected of them, and have some influence over the work they perform and over the possible application and development of their own abilities to varying tasks in support of those results. It views healthy organizations as profiting from the interaction among individuals and work groups at all levels of the organization. Merit in such postindustrial organizations involves the determination of an individual's suitability in terms of the skill or potential he or she brings to the organization, including the ability to function in a self-directed environment.

Those who view organizations as systems interacting with larger systems and subject to constant influence from the environment, believe that organizational structures and individuals must be able to adapt readily to outside forces, such as changing societal demands and developing technology. Merit, in their terms, involves the determination of an individual's basic abilities, combined with a sensitivity to environmental forces, and ability to develop new skills as change dictates.

Among the organizations that comprise the public service are found structure, managerial style and systems that reflect the entire range of organizational theory. Yet our merit system is firmly rooted in the school of scientific management and no other. If the public service is to attract the talent it needs, legislation must permit selection on the basis of criteria beyond the individual's ability to meet no more than the requirements of a specific set of duties. There must be provision for recognition of potential to develop the knowledge and skills that will be required to meet projected staff needs.

Collective Bargaining
Even with the advent of collective bargaining, the merit principle has been considered an inappropriate subject for negotiation. There clearly must continue to be legislative commitment to the merit principle to protect the long-term public interest in the competence of the public service. The meaning of merit must not be eroded in the expedient interest of the employer or of the various bargaining agents. However, under this legislation there is room for a great deal of involvement of both management and employee representatives in determining the most appropriate system to give expression to the merit principle.

Political and Administrative Patronage
The likelihood of any return of political patronage is about nil. There are many more forces that work against it today than was the case when government first decided to enact prevailing legislation. In addition,

every government since then has demonstrated its determination to protect the merit principle.

Today we live in an increasingly open society, where the move towards greater freedom of information makes the internal administration of the bureaucracy much more a matter of common knowledge than ever before. Any attempts to make patronage appointments would quickly become known. They would be fiercely resisted by unions and would generate considerable pressure of public opinion against them.

In regard to internal appointments, a number of practices can exist that may create an impression that merit is not fully respected. In the first place, frank administrative patronage is possible in the absence of adequate selection processes. Secondly, there are managers who prefer to promote an employee whose performance they know to be satisfactory over one whose performance may even be superior, but whom they do not know. Finally, an employee who is clearly superior to his peers may win advancement through a process that gives visibly little consideration to others in the field of competition. Yet many employees want the opportunity, often for their own education, to compete for a position, knowing full well that another candidate is better qualified.

Clearly there is a need for a process of full and objective assessment of all candidates and, most important, that it is perceived to be so. It is the quality and nature of the selection process—the system which ensures adherence to merit—and the demonstrated commitment of managers to select according to merit which will inspire confidence in employees that they are being treated fairly and equitably. Legislation should continue to enshrine merit as the basis for selection and advancement.

Merit and Employment

There is no legal protection of tenure in the PSEA, and the experience of very recent years has demolished the perception that the size of the service makes it immune to economic adversity. The public service generally does not treat harshly those promoted beyond their level of competence. Rather, it tends to accept a measure of responsibility for such situations and expends no little effort in finding better job matches for those employees. In this respect, practices in the public sector parallel those of most large private sector employers and continue to frustrate those who search each annual report of the PSC to see how many public servants were fired. This practice, coupled with the fact that some incompetent people do remain on the payroll, has led to the perception that public service employment is secure. Managers must accept the responsibility for initiating remedial action to improve unacceptable levels of performance, to identify more appropriate placement, or ultimately to separate a problem employee.

Career Public Service and Protectionism

One of the advantages of those who enter the public service is the preference accorded to employees over outsiders in competing for higher-level jobs. In staffing terms this means that, generally, a competition cannot be opened to the public if there is anyone within the public service who is minimally qualified.

This preference is the single feature of a career service to be found across the whole of our system. What is more, it is often argued by some that competitions cannot be opened more often to the public because we have a career public service!

It is quite misleading to label the Canadian public service as a career service. A true career service has certain distinctive features which are absent in our service. Most true career services—often based on European practice—determine the relative merit of a candidate for a range of jobs, and accompany rigorous selection at career milestones with conscious strategies to train and develop employees towards future requirements, somewhat as our Administrative Trainee and Career Assignment Programs are designed to do for limited groups of public servants.

Career development programs (Administrative Trainee, Career Assignment Program) have been grafted onto our classification, staffing and training systems only with difficulty, particularly in cases where a person needs to be advanced through several classification levels over the life of a program. The general system is based on the assumption that appointments must be made to a specific position, for which the successful candidate possesses the precise qualifications at the time of appointment. The development programs mentioned, in contrast, are based on the assumption that an individual will develop the qualifications to assume a broad range of responsibilities through performance of a sequence of jobs with coaching to develop the individual's ability even though, at the time the individual assumes each of the jobs, he or she does not possess all of the qualifications.

It would not be realistic, however, to designate the whole of the federal government as a career service, given changing values concerning careers and the work place. Many individuals are increasingly considering management of their careers as their own responsibility, opting in and out of opportunities as they choose. On the other hand, in those occupational groups where a career service is appropriate (for example, the foreign service), development must not be left to chance. Personnel mechanisms, such as rigorous assessment tools and demanding training and development programs are needed.

The question of a career service aside, there is considerable support for the practice of limiting the manager's access to the public to fill positions. There are certain advantages claimed for promotion from within—greater motivation for employees to continue to develop their competence, and better protection of the organization's investment in the employee's knowledge and experience. In recognition of these advantages, some feel that employees should continue to take precedence over outsiders for career opportunities and that, within the limits of practicality, public servants should have as wide an access as possible to compete for those opportunities for which they are qualified.

However, there is a price to be paid for an employee preference. In the absence of clear developmental strategies, the selection practice of taking a snapshot of a candidate's qualifications for a specific job at a specific time, leaving developmental considerations aside, combined with a haphazard approach to training, at the very least compromises the future overall quality of the public service. The tendency to appoint and retain employees who are qualified, but barely, and give them no further training, dilutes the competence of the service.

The interests of service effectiveness strongly suggest that the law should not be seen or interpreted as giving employees virtually unqualified preference in appointment. There is a value in public servants standing the test of competition with those in the outside labour market. The present employee already enjoys the advantage over an outside candidate of an insider's knowledge and experience. In cases where recent competitions or knowledge of the availability of specialized expertise within the public service have established that there is not a reasonable likelihood that a highly qualified public servant is to be found, the search should simultaneously reach public servants and outside candidates.

There is also a value in injecting fresh blood into the public service to ensure that the service is in touch with recent developments in other sectors and generally to improve its sensitivity. There is much to be gained from fresh approaches, new insights and different perspectives. Furthermore, there are times when considerably better-qualified candidates are available from outside than from within. It seems reasonable that some of these more highly qualified "outsiders" should be admissable to the public service. Then too, certain organizations require a work force clearly identified with the full range of interests of the communities they serve. Particularly where impartiality and balance among the interests served are critical, certain staff members need to be recognized for their understanding of the forces at play, normally acquired only by employment in an organization served by the public service. Tribunals which deal with issues in the labour relations arena, where staff must be drawn from management and union sources, are an example. In such circumstances, there is a justification for searching immediately outside the public service. Finally, the extension of open competitions should improve the recruitment of francophones and women.

Merit and Other Principles

Merit has never ruled out related principles of good management, such as efficiency, effectiveness, sensitivity, equity and equality of opportunity. In fact, some argue that these principles are inherent in merit. Practice, however, has demonstrated that merit has been given an interpretation that leaves little room for recognition of these collateral qualities. There is wide agreement within the public service that the additional principles need to be highlighted in legislation to signify Parliament's explicit recognition of these principles.

The discussion below will develop the considerations which should form the basis for any decisions to incorporate additional principles in legislation, along with merit.

Service to the Public

The conclusions of a recent task force on sensitivity to the public merely confirmed the prevalent belief of Canadians that government employees do not generally go out of their way to meet citizens' needs. Providing fast, courteous, well-informed services becomes a way of life in organizations only if this emphasis permeates the organization's value system so far that continued employment and career advancement depend on it. We found examples in both the public and the private sectors, where personnel systems, by design, reinforce the understanding of employees concerning the importance of customer service. In these cases, demonstrated ability to deal effectively with the public was an important factor in the selection process.

Sensitivity to the public must become characteristic of the public service. Proven sensitivity should be an explicit element of merit. Further, sensitivity to particular client groups should be built into standards of selection and evaluation of performance. Training programs should include specific goals relating to the achievement of a sensitive public service. Those who aspire to positions of responsibility in the public service must accept the need to gain an understanding of the geographic, social and economic fibre of Canada.

Special Treatment of Designated Groups

There is a general agreement that merit should offer the assurance of equal opportunity of employment without discrimination on the basis of race, religion, age, sex or marital status. There has been an active debate, however, over a number of years as to whether merit allows special treatment of members of groups that are underrepresented in the public service. Those who have been responsible for progress in the implementation of the bilingualism policy, for example, acknowledge that accommodations to the rigid interpretation of the merit principle have been necessary. Selection gates were loaded by aggressive recruiting of

French-speaking Canadians. Complementary action was deemed necessary to assure English-speaking career public servants access to promotional opportunities. Hence, an exclusion order was passed by the governor-in-council suspending the language ability requirements for selection to bilingual positions until the successful candidate was trained. In sum, progress has been difficult and slow. The fact must be faced—if there is to be more rapid achievement of goals respecting participation, changes will have to be made in how the merit principle is now applied.

Personnel management legislation and systems must be kept in tune with government policy concerning employment in the federal service if they are not to thwart that policy. If the goal is a representative public service, merit will need to be accompanied by explicit recognition of the need for special treatment for designated groups whose members are judged to be in a disadvantaged position with respect to access to public service employment. The PSEA must be constructed to accommodate government policies, or the manager will continue to be faced with a choice between failing to implement government policy or violating the PSEA.

Any action which virtually constitutes inequality of opportunity for those who do not receive special treatment will inevitably cause strains. We believe, however, that it is a lesser hazard to make explicit provision for suspending merit as we have known it than to force managers to flaunt the present rules in order to appoint to the public service those who historically have been barred from the education or experience which would qualify them for work at all levels of responsibility.

It should be emphasized that special measures are an extraordinary response to extraordinary circumstances. A precedent with respect to merit was set by the decision to allow preference to veterans which was appropriate to the postwar circumstances. Today's circumstances are different. Women have not yet achieved proportional representation. However, there are women of proven competence and capacity for further development in the public service or outside. The strategy for attracting and advancing women would differ from the strategy necessary to open public service jobs to indigenous people who may possess skills which are elements of merit for employment in certain jobs, but who need extensive training to prepare them for others.

The point to be made is that merit can and should be temporarily suspended by parallel provision for special treatment of members of designated groups in support of eventual real equality of opportunity. Such explicit recognition is essential to gaining support of public service managers. If they were given the support of systems which did not tie their hands in creating fair employment opportunities in the public service for Canadians from all segments of society, they would willingly devote their energy to the pursuit of this goal. Those now employed in the public service, too, deserve an honest explanation of the special treatment which will be given designated groups, and of its likely effect on their own careers.

Merit and Effective Management

There is a firmly ingrained perception that the merit system ties management's hands in its pursuit of effective personnel management. Although merit does impose constraints, such criticism is properly levelled at the imperfections in the system, rather than at the principle. The application of merit should help to assure the fair treatment of employees. It should also be designed to allow managerial flexibility to deploy staff according to changing program demands and fluctuating workloads without trampling on employee rights. It should be susceptible to interpretation sufficiently broad that it allows planning and action to develop staff to meet future organizational requirements, also without doing violence to the fair treatment of employees.

It is clearly possible to adapt the merit system to management's needs. Indeed, it is imperative to do so. The goal of efficient personnel management in support of effective government services must be recognized as another consideration which must be viewed in conjunction with the merit principle.

Some employees have expressed their conviction that the merit principle is disregarded. One manifestation of this, in their eyes, is that while merit means selecting the best candidate available, departments do not see all candidates who are available—area of competition guidelines may be the villain. Common sense, however, dictates that cost be an important consideration in structuring a competition. To go to the extreme, only by making all competitions Canada-wide would the purist, who insists on absolute merit, be satisfied. It must become accepted that considerations of efficiency and some other principles will have to limit the purist's view of merit.

Merit and the Employee

The PSEA recognizes the value of promotion from within an organization by giving present employees first consideration for public service jobs. This provision has led some employees to believe that they have the right to be considered for any opportunity which offers favourable career prospects. In addition to promotional opportunities, there is an expectation of competition for transfers and training. Employees have a right to appeal appointment decisions. While we share the belief that overprotection of employees' interests must not take precedence over operating requirements, it must be recognized that the above provisions reflect rights conferred by Parliament, not privileges claimed by employees.

Legislation should explicitly highlight the principles which, in conjunction with merit, should continue to provide a basis for personnel management. Such legislation should incorporate sensitivity and responsiveness, equality of opportunity, efficiency, effectiveness and equity as principles which are supplemental to merit.

Protection of the Merit Principle

The powers of public service commissions, as a minimum, normally include the right to review selection or release decisions, either in reply to an appeal from an employee or on the agency's own initiative, with the powers to rescind an action if merit has not been served. In the Canadian system, the PSC also protects merit by defining it and by exercising direct authority over public service appointments. As a result, the PSC has a direct involvement in staffing to and within the public service. Although most internal staffing is done by departments under delegation, it is the PSC which oversees the application of merit by recommending regulations, by establishing policies and procedures, and by auditing departmental performance. The PSC also initiaties corrective action by supporting departmental efforts to improve and by adjusting the terms for renewal of delegation. As long as the public service is to be staffed on the basis of merit, there is a need for such an independent parliamentary agent, charged with protection of merit.

19/Management Development
for Canada's Public Services*
Kenneth Kernaghan

The subject of management development in our government services is not generally perceived as a major public policy issue. It is not a topic that has aroused much controversy in our public forums or private salons. However, the calibre of human resources at the senior echelons of our public services is crucial to the effective and responsible development and implementation of public policies. Discussions of public policy issues are frequently based on the questionable assumption that the appropriate

---

*Reprinted and abridged by permission from Kenneth Kernaghan, "Management Development for Canada's Public Services: Report of the Rapporteur," in *Executive Manpower in the Public Service: Make or Buy*, ed. Kenneth Kernaghan (Toronto: Institute of Public Administration of Canada, 1975), pp. 1-18.

number and quality of government employees will be available to develop solutions and put policy decisions into effect. The federal Cabinet acknowledged the importance of the manpower issue when in 1969 it identified public service personnel management as a matter of high priority. The Cabinet's concern was expressed as follows:

> Without greatly improved executive personnel and public service management, the government will not be able to elaborate policies and implement programs in a speedy, imaginative and progressive manner, much less gain the confidence and participation of the public service and of the public in a modern, efficient and socially sensitive government administration.

Thus the issue of management development intertwines with all major public policy questions. The examination of management development in this essay is divided into the following three sections:

I.   Definitions
II.   The Identification of Needs
III. Make and/or Buy?

I. Definitions

As a basis for discussion, it is important to define such central terms as executive, manager, management development, public sector management and human resource planning.

The word *manager* denotes a clearer and more useful administrative role than the word *executive*. At the municipal level, the word executive is not commonly used to describe senior administrators. At the federal and provincial levels, the term executive designates or connotes a distinct category or group of senior administrators with diverse skills and responsibilities.[1]

Thus the term executive is too broad in one sense and too narrow in another. It includes some individuals whose primary responsibilities are not managerial and it refers to the most senior group of administrators, thereby excluding a large number of officials discharging important management functions at lower levels of government service.

The managerial cadre can usually be separated from the larger executive cadre which is composed of a heterogeneous group of senior

---

[1][Editor's Note]: In July 1980, the federal government announced the creation of a new management category in the public service composed of about 4500 positions. This new category includes an Executive Group (EX) made up primarily of the former senior executive category, and a Senior Management Group (SM) consisting of the top grades of about 55 occupational groups. The major purpose of establishing the management category is, among other things, to improve managerial development and effectiveness by identifying a cadre of senior public servants who will receive appropriate recognition in the way of career development, compensation, conditions of work and accountability for results.

officials, many of whose major responsibilities lie in the sphere of policy advice or policy coordination rather than of management. Admittedly, most executives perform some management functions but there are executives who fulfil primarily management functions and who can appropriately be described as senior managers. Also the management role is performed by officials extending vertically from the first-line supervisor to the executive or senior manager. It is therefore essential to identify and prepare managers at lower levels for ascendancy to senior positions.

Moreover, it is necessary to keep in mind the variety of knowledge and skills required of the senior manager at different levels of government. It is equally important to remember that postsecondary institutions are engaged in the education of persons who enter government service considerably below the executive level.

A second problem of definition arises from various usages of the terms *management development, management training* and *management education*. Governments and community colleges usually describe their efforts to improve the management knowledge, skills and attitudes of public employees as management training and development programs, whereas universities customarily use the term management education. In some government jurisdictions, development is viewed as a part of the general training effort; in others, development refers to efforts to enhance the employee's capacity to take on greater responsibilities, whereas training refers to efforts to improve the employee's skills so that he may perform his existing duties more effectively.

This diverse usage of the same words constitutes a significant obstacle to effective communication among those involved in management training and education. My reading of the literature in this area suggests that it is useful and proper to view management development as a process which aims to improve managerial performance by increasing knowledge, developing skills, moulding values and broadening perspectives. Thus the process of management development subsumes both training and education, and includes on-the-job experience as well.

Although the words training and education are often used interchangeably, an important distinction may be made between them. Management training is practical in its objective and content; it is designed to develop skills which are directly relevant to the employee's existing job; and most of this training is conducted within the government services, although the resources of external education and training institutions may be utilized. Management education is less practical in its orientation; it seeks to prepare individuals, whether they are existing or aspiring public employees, for a future position in the career government service, usually at the middle to senior levels of the services; and most of this education is now provided by the universities but is also provided by governments and by other educational institutions (for example, community colleges and educational consultants).

Thus the key components of the process of management development in the public sector are:

1. Formal classroom training, primarily within the government services.
2. Formal classroom education, primarily within the universities.
3. On-the-job training and experience.

It is important for subsequent discussion to keep in mind that only governments can provide the third component.

The term *public sector management* tends to be used more frequently by practitioners than the term *public administration*. The increasing usage of the former term by university teachers of public administration indicates that they are prepared to admit they are engaged in "management" education. This usage also connotes an approach that is more practical and professional than theoretical and academic. While the terms are often used synonymously, it is clear that public administration is a broader, more inclusive term than public sector management.

The concept of human resource planning is closely related to management development. Human resource planning in the public sector is the process through which a government strives to ensure (1) that it has the appropriate number and quality of human resources to carry out its responsibilities now and in the future, and (2) that opportunities are provided for individual employees to pursue and realize personal career ambitions. Human resource planning requires the integration of a government's need for human resources of a particular quality with individual needs and aspirations. The essential components of a human resource plan are (1) a staffing and recruiting policy; (2) a training and development policy; and (3), in some government jurisdictions, a language policy. The focus in this essay is on the second component, namely training and development policy.

II. The Identification of Needs

There are two major dimensions to needs' identification in relation to management development in the government services. These are:

1. the determination of the knowledge, skills and attributes required to fill present and projected management positions; and
2. the determination of the number of persons with the appropriate qualifications required to fill the gap between the existing supply of and the anticipated demand for human resources.

These two dimensions are examined below under the headings of management profiles and human resource needs.

Management Profiles

A management profile refers here to a descriptive statement of the knowledge, skills, experience and personal characteristics required for management positions at a specific level and location in the administrative hierarchy now and in the foreseeable future. No single management profile can be applied to all management positions. There is need for a number of management profiles which set out the educational, experiential and personal qualifications required of those who now hold or will hold management positions at various levels of the administrative pyramid and at all levels of Canadian government. This is a formidable challenge indeed! The profiles must provide a picture of existing as well as projected management positions and are therefore difficult to formulate in precise terms. Profiles, however, are a valuable tool because they inform manpower planners of the types of people to be recruited, trained and educated to fill particular positions.

Until recently, little effort was made to develop profiles of occupational groups—much less of the large number of government employees who are managers but who are spread throughout a variety of occupational groups. Most of the work completed or under way in this area is a result of federal initiatives.

Public service managers, like managers in any large organization, require a common core of knowledge and skills related to the performance of management functions. They also require special knowledge, skills and values related specifically to government employment. Based on these premises, management training and education for government service should include:

1. a *management* core consisting of such components as organization theory, administrative behaviour, finance, personnel, economic analysis and quantitative methods; and
2. a *public management* core consisting of such components as policy analysis, the political, economic and social environment of public sector management, public law and public service ethics.

Once an existing or prospective public manager has acquired these two sets of core capacities, he may further his public sector management education by specializing in substantive policy areas (for example, urban policy, social policy, intergovernmental relations) or in management areas related specifically to the public sector (for example, planning, budgeting, personnel, industrial relations).

Some public servants contend that management education for public service can be obtained in schools of business as well as in schools of public administration or public management and that individuals educated in management can adapt to the public service environment. Others believe that business schools provide a perspective, philosophy and knowledge base that is not as appropriate to public sector employment as that transmitted in schools of public administration. They assert further that the development of a "public service ethic" which, interpreted broadly, entails dedication to the public's interest, is central to public service management and thus to public service education and training.

There is much debate among teachers and practitioners of public administration whether management is, or can be, a profession and whether a primary purpose of management development is the creation of a group or class of professional managers. Discussion of this issue is complicated by confusion whether the debate is about the profession of management or the profession of public management and by the absence of a consistent definition of the word *profession*.

Views on the possibility and desirability of management as a profession range from missionary zeal to abhorrence. Advocates contend that professional managers already exist, that there is a management role which requires the performance of common functions in all large organizations, and that therefore there is a core of management knowledge and skills which forms the basis of a profession. Opponents raise the spectre of a powerful class of managerial technicians who share the same knowledge and skills base and the same value system and whose management capacity enables them to move from one organization to another regardless of environmental differences. There is some concern that elected officials cannot have sufficient influence on the shape of society if they depend on advice from apolitical—even amoral—technocrats. Some opposition to professional management is also based on the belief that courses offering the common core of management knowledge and skills confer literacy in the field of management, not professional status.

If we adopt the very liberal definition of profession, namely "(1) a reasonably clear-cut occupational field, (2) which ordinarily requires higher education at least through the bachelor's level, and (3) which offers a lifetime career to its members."[2] then a profession of public management already exists and includes a very large number of people. Under this definition, public management would not, however, constitute a profession in the same sense as such fields as medicine and law which meet stricter criteria for professional status. A typical list of such criteria states that a profession:

1. Involves activities essentially intellectual.
2. Commands a body of specialized knowledge.
3. Requires extended professional preparation.

---

[2]Frederick C. Mosher, *Democracy and the Public Service* (New York: Oxford University Press, 1968), p. 106.

4. Demands continuous in-service growth.
5. Affords a life career and permanent membership.
6. Sets up its own standards.
7. Exalts service above personal gain.
8. Has a strong, closely knit professional organization.[3]

Those who support the fact or the potential of public management as a profession are impatient with others who insist that the field meet all or most of these criteria. There is, however, little point in claiming to be a professional if your own colleagues, much less those members of well-established professions, do not acknowledge this status. Neither university teachers nor administrative practitioners recognize a formal set of standard educational requirements for admission to a profession of public management. It is true that there is increasing agreement among university teachers on a body of specialized knowledge and skills which should be acquired for the master's degree in public administration. However, only a small proportion of existing public service managers have acquired these formal educational prerequisites. Most have acquired equivalent qualifications through practical experience and are therefore entitled to an equal opportunity to enter the ranks of professional management. It is no easy task to specify with any precision the necessary qualifications for acceptance as a professional public service manager since managers come to their posts from a variety of directions and with a variety of backgrounds.

Despite these considerations, public servants at the senior levels of their respective governments view the practice of management as a profession and consider themselves to be professionals. Moreover, in the United States, the practice of public administration is commonly referred to as a profession and many—indeed most—university programs in public administration are described as professional programs. Developments in Canada appear to support the view that public management or public administration is moving closer to a profession in that there is substantial agreement on a common body of knowledge essential for public managers; pre-entry and continuing education are more widely available in universities and colleges; opportunities for in-service training and education are expanding; and there is much emphasis on public service as a career. Several central criteria for professional status still remain to be fulfilled, however. Whether these requirements will eventually be met depends largely on the extent to which teachers, scholars and practitioners cooperate in the pursuit of professional public management. A significant indicator of our proximity to this professional status

---

[3]National Education Association, *The Yardstick of a Profession* (Washington, D.C.: National Education Association, 1948), p. 8.

will be the ability of governments and universities to develop senior public service managers with the increasingly sophisticated qualifications specified by management profiles.

Human Resource Needs

The success of the search for the best and the brightest public service managers will be greatly enhanced by the availability of accurate and up-to-date management profiles. It is clearly important to know what kinds of managers are needed at what levels and by what date before it is possible to specify with any precision the requirements for management training and education.

We have seen, however, that the preparation of management profiles is at a very rudimentary stage in most governmental jurisdictions. Thus much staffing and management development is based on impressionistic evidence of human resource needs. Few governments have made a systematic effort to identify their existing and future needs for public service managers and to devise programs to train and educate persons to fill these needs. There are, however, a number of obstacles to designing and implementing a rational, comprehensive approach to management development.

In the first place, many elected representatives and senior government employees are unaware of the dimensions of the problem and of the pressing need for action. It is understandable that elected representatives are not sensitive to the need for management development. Politicians are not anxious to allocate resources to training and education programs for public employees because the benefits are not immediately evident or easily evaluated.

Senior government employees have a long-term interest in the quality of public service management. Yet even among this group there is insufficient recognition of the necessity for management development. It is important that senior appointed officials persuade their political masters to support training and education programs and that these officials provide opportunities for their subordinates to participate in such programs. In some jurisdictions, however, there appears to be little interest in the adequacy of personnel to meet the demands of existing positions and no concern about planning for those managers required in the 1980s and beyond. The "hope and a prayer" method of operation, according to which governments trust that qualified personnel will somehow emerge when needed, is woefully inadequate. Some of the questions which senior officials should ask are these: Are existing managers well enough qualified to perform their duties? Do they need training to update or improve their ability to do their jobs effectively? Will they be qualified to take on greater responsibilities at more senior levels in the future? What opportunities for management development are available?

A second major obstacle to the development of highly skilled and knowledgeable public service managers, even among those governments where the importance of management development is readily acknowledged, is the scarcity of financial resources. Training and education is a costly venture, not only in terms of the infrastructure required to make opportunities available but also in terms of the time lost from substantive work while staff members are taking courses.

Financial support for management development is related also to some aspects of what might be termed "the great training robbery." It is reasonable to ask whether a good case has been made for management training and education. Can it be shown that those who have completed some of the great assortment of available courses are better able to perform their present responsibilities or to take on new and more challenging tasks? Can a sensible program of management development be mounted if reasonably accurate management profiles and estimates of manpower needs are not available? How can we evaluate the numerous programs and courses offered by governments, by postsecondary institutions and by other organizations, including educational consultants?

A third impediment to effective planning for management development is the demands of career planning. Human resource planning would be a much simpler task if governments could treat present and future employees as automatons. Individuals could then be inserted into the appropriate slots in the administrative structure as they completed the prescribed forms of management development. However, career development does not always conform to organizational needs. Individuals have career goals, job preferences and personal idiosyncrasies which often run counter to the government's need for employees with particular qualifications. Individuals may not wish to accept positions for which they have the requisite skills and experience or they may not wish to engage in any management training and education, or in some forms of it.

Finally, the merit principle, as it is implemented through the mechanism of the merit system, conflicts in some respects with effective planning for management development. Under a merit system where staffing must take account not only of merit but also of such factors as the representativeness of candidates, the best managers are not always appointed or promoted. Moreover, since employee unions insist that positions be filled by a process of competition, the selection of persons for special management development and assignments is viewed as discriminatory.

III. Make And/Or Buy?
Governments must not only determine as precisely as possible the number and quality of public service managers required but also whether the gap between the supply and the demand should be filled by making or

buying managers. The making of managers involves the provision of training and education by the governments themselves and on-the-job experience; the buying of managers involves recruiting graduates of management programs from postsecondary institutions, recruiting managers from other governments and nongovernmental organizations, and sending government employees to postsecondary institutions for training and education.

The need for competent managers is so great that governments must make *and* buy the human resources they need. The relevant question then is the balance which each government should strike between developing its own managers and relying on other institutions for this task. The answer will depend largely on the financial and personnel resources available within governments for management training and education and on the capacity of nongovernmental institutions to provide this service at an appropriate cost. Thus governments cannot give a well-considered response to the make or buy issue until their staffing needs have been identified and internal and external resources for management development have been assessed.

In discussing the respective roles of governments and external educational institutions, it is useful to identify the major components of management development, of which some can be provided only by governments and others only by postsecondary institutions. These components are:

1. Graduation from a postsecondary institution.
2. Postgraduate university education.
3. Graduation from a postsecondary institution with specialization in management.
4. Postgraduate university education with specialization in management.
5. Graduation from a postsecondary institution with specialization in *public sector* management (or public administration).
6. Postgraduate university education with specialization in *public sector* management (or public administration).
7. On-the-job experience in government during the course of one's formal, pre-entry education (e.g. internships).
8. On-the-job experience in government as a regular employee.
9. On-the-job experience in nongovernmental organizations.
10. In-service management training.
11. Mid-career training and education in external education institutions, notably in postsecondary institutions.

Existing managers have acquired differing groups of these components during their educational and government experience. Some senior managers have attained their lofty positions solely on the basis of an undergraduate education supplemented by lengthy experience in government; others have postgraduate degrees in public management, on-the-job experience in government or other large-scale organizations, in-service training, and continuing education in postsecondary institutions. The present and future challenge of the management role means that increasingly important components in the preparation and development of a senior manager will be (1) postgraduate education in management, preferably public sector management, and (2) continuing training and education, either in governments or in postsecondary institutions. These two components of formal management education and training, on a pre-entry and continuing basis, will bring the individual closer to what might be termed a "professional manager," as described earlier. The appropriate mix of these components in a manager's development will depend on the level of government at which he works, his position in the hierarchy and his particular responsibilities. This will affect in turn the extent to which governments and universities respectively contribute to his development.

It is evident that individuals can and do enter the process of management development at different points. For example, a university undergraduate who wishes to pursue a career in public management may seek a graduate degree in that field and then move on to other components of management development after he joins government service. In contrast, a professional scientist who aspires to a management position but who has no management training or experience will normally begin with in-service training.

The variety of points of entry to the management development process presents governments and postsecondary institutions with a difficult task. Opportunities for training, education and practical experience should, ideally, be made available in a comprehensive and coordinated fashion. At the same time, these opportunities, in the form of programs, courses, internships, rotations and educational leaves, must meet the needs of persons with widely varying education and experience. The creation and improvement of cooperative and consultative mechanisms by governments and educational institutions could improve significantly the overall quality and effectiveness of management development.

20/Collective Bargaining in the Canadian Federal Public Service

P.K. Kuruvilla

This essay briefly reviews the evolution and present status of collective bargaining in the Canadian federal public service. An account of the development of employer-employee relations in the public service is followed by an analysis of the Public Service Staff Relations Act and problems arising from its implementation.

Canadian civil service associations which emerged in the late nineteenth century and pressed the government for improved conditions of employment did not make significant advances until the mid-1940s. In 1944 the government established the National Joint Council of the Public Service of Canada made up of representatives of the staff associations and senior officials representing the government as employer. The purpose of this body, as outlined by the government, was

> to provide machinery for regular and systematic consultation and discussion between the employer and employee sides of the public service in regard to grievances and conditions of employment, and thereby to promote increased efficiency and better morale in the public service.[1]

The council served as a valuable consultative device between management and staff and as a forerunner to full collective bargaining. Among the many significant benefits it produced for employees were superannuation, medical insurance, travel regulations, the five-day week and the check-off of membership fees. As an alternative to collective bargaining, however, the council had major limitations: it lacked the authority to deal directly with the important issue of civil service salaries, and there was no provision for the settlement of disagreements between the staff and officials of the council. As a result, the postwar decade was one of considerable ferment in public service staff relations.

The statutory right to be consulted on pay determination was extended to employee associations in 1961 by a new Civil Service Act. However, the consultative process was cumbersome because it obliged the associations to make representations to two bodies—the Civil Service Commission and the Treasury Board. Furthermore, the final determination of rates of pay and conditions of employment was still subject to unilateral decision by the Treasury Board. The demand by

---

[1]J.L. Ilsley, Minister of Finance, referring to Order-in-Council P.C. 3676 of May 16, 1944, quoted in C.W. Rump, "Employer-Employee Consultation in the Public Service," *Civil Service Review* 45 (June 1972): 8.

employee organizations for the right to negotiate directly with government without consulting intermediaries continued unabated until the promulgation of the Public Service Staff Relations Act in March 1967.[2]

This act is unique in several respects. It grants public service associations the status of trade unions with the right to collective bargaining, compulsory arbitration, conciliation and even strike action. It also provides machinery through which employees with grievances about the terms and conditions of their employment have access to a formal grievance procedure permitting third party adjudication. Finally, the act not only outlines the legal steps to be observed in the resolution of disputes but also sets up an administrative apparatus to enforce its provisions. The act is administered by the Public Service Staff Relations Board (PSSRB).[3]

Before an employee organization can negotiate with the government for a collective agreement, that organization must be certified as a bargaining agent.[4] The Public Service Alliance of Canada, which represents 170000 employees, is the largest certified union. Other major public service unions include the Canadian Union of Postal Workers (23000), the Professional Institute of the Public Service (17000), the Letter Carriers' Union of Canada (16500) and the Canadian Postmasters' Association (8200). Within a particular bargaining unit, all employees must be in the same occupational group. Each group belongs to an occupational category.[5]

Following the certification of an employee organization as a bargaining agent for a given bargaining unit, the bargaining agent must specify

---

[2]Canada, *Statutes*, 1966-1967, chapter 72.
[3]The board is a politically independent body whose major responsibilities include defining bargaining units, certifying bargaining agents, investigating complaints alleging infringement of the act, deciding on the lawfulness of strikes and making regulations on such matters as complaints, the hearing of questions of law and jurisdiction, the rules of procedure for its own hearings and for those of the arbitration tribunal and adjudication boards.
[4]Some unions act as bargaining agents for more than one bargaining unit with the result that, in 1976, fifteen bargaining agents represented eighty-one bargaining units.
[5]According to the present classification there are six occupational categories in the Canadian public service: Executive; Professional and Scientific; Technical; Administrative and Foreign Service; Administrative Support; and Operational. The Executive category does not come under the collective bargaining provisions of the act. The Public Service Commission has the responsibility of specifying and defining the occupational groups in each of the five occupational categories that come under the collective bargaining provisions of the act. So far, seventy-two occupational groups have been set up. These are: twenty-eight occupational groups in the Professional and Scientific category; thirteen in the Administrative and Foreign Service; thirteen in the Technical category; six in the Administrative Support category; twelve in the Operational category.

the process of dispute resolution it wants to follow in the event that negotiations are unproductive. There are two options: referral of the dispute to a conciliation board while retaining the right to strike, or referral of the dispute to an arbitration tribunal for binding award. Regardless which option is chosen, the act requires that the choice be made before collective bargaining can begin and that it remain in effect until it is altered before another round of bargaining.

When conciliation is chosen, either party in the dispute may request the PSSRB to appoint a conciliator to assist in reaching agreement. The conciliator can only make suggestions; he cannot make binding directives. If the chairman of the PSSRB believes that a conciliator would not help to resolve the dispute, he may refuse to appoint one and proceed directly to appoint a conciliation board. The chairman may also refuse to appoint a board and allow a lawful strike if he believes that a board would not help settle the dispute.

The act stipulates that certain "designated employees" may not participate in a legal strike because their "duties consist in whole or in part of duties the performance of which at any particular time or after any specified period of time is or will be necessary in the interest of the safety or security of the public."[6] Thus a conciliation board will not be established until the parties agree, or the PSSRB determines, which employees or classes of employees in the bargaining unit are essential.

The parties in a dispute are free to accept or reject the report of a conciliation board. If the report is unacceptable, the union has the right to declare a strike seven days after the report is received by the chairman of the PSSRB. The right to strike is clearly not an unconditional one. In addition to the constraints described above, no employee may strike when a collective agreement applying to his bargaining unit is in force, and no employee organization may declare a strike that would cause employees to participate in an unlawful strike. The officers or representatives of the organization are forbidden to counsel or procure the declaration of such a strike.[7]

When arbitration has been specified as the means of dispute settlement, an arbitration tribunal is appointed. The tribunal is composed of an impartial chairman and two members, one from a panel of employer representatives and one from a panel representing the employees. An arbitral award may deal with rates of pay, hours of work, leave entitlements, standards of discipline and other related terms and conditions of employment. However, no award may deal with "the standards, procedures or processes governing the appointment, appraisal, promotion, demotion, transfer, lay-off or release of employees, or with any term or

6Public Service Staff Relations Act, Section 79.
7Ibid., Sections 101-102.

condition of employment of employees that was not a subject of negotiation between the parties during the period before arbitration was requested in respect thereof."[8] Awards made by a tribunal are binding to both parties.

The act also establishes a grievance procedure that permits third party adjudication. This procedure covers all employees, including those in managerial and confidential positions who are not allowed to belong to a bargaining unit. An employee may present a grievance on a wide variety of matters affecting the terms and conditions of his employment.[9]

Most grievances are settled within the employee's department. However, if the employee has exhausted his departmental remedies and is not satisfied with the result, he may refer the matter to adjudication by an adjudicator or an adjudication board. Most cases are heard by adjudication boards. The governor-in-council, on the recommendation of the PSSRB, appoints adjudicators, one of whom is designated the chief adjudicator. An adjudication board is composed of the chief adjudicator plus one member nominated by one party and one member nominated by the other party. The adjudication decision is binding on both the employer and the employee.

Public service employees have voiced several criticisms of the provisions and administration of the act. One important source of dissatisfaction is the restrictions on matters deemed negotiable and arbitrable under the act. Employees cannot negotiate on matters with as profound an impact on terms and conditions of employment as job security, classification and superannuation. The restrictions on arbitrable matters outlined earlier in this essay are even greater. The result is that only some matters subject to bargaining are arbitrable. Even if a matter is arbitrable, if it was overlooked originally as a subject of negotiation, the oversight cannot be rectified by placing the matter before an arbitration tribunal. Moreover, although agreement may have been reached on some nonarbitrable issues before an arbitration tribunal, once the employees choose arbitration as a means of dispute settlement, the employer is free to withdraw from the previous agreement. Employees have argued, therefore, that the scope of negotiable subjects should be expanded to cover all employer-employee problems which conceivably

---

[8]*Ibid.*, Section 70.

[9]Other important types of appeals in the public service are covered by the Public Service Employment Act (Canada, *Statutes*, 1966-1967, Chapter 71) and are administered by the Public Service Commission. These appeals relate to (1) appointment, including promotion; (2) demotion or release because of incompetence or incapability; (3) dismissal for violation of provisions of the Public Service Employment Act dealing with political activity; and (4) revocation of appointment because of fraudulent practices during an examination conducted by the commission.

could lead to an impasse and that the existing distinction between matters subject to bargaining and matters subject to arbitration be erased.

A second major cause of employee dissatisfaction is that several classes of employees are specifically excluded by the act from the collective bargaining process.[10]

A third contentious issue is the act's provisions regarding the establishment of bargaining units and the certification process. The Public Service Commission defines and specifies the occupational groups within each of the five occupational categories, and the establishment of bargaining units must be based on these occupational groups and not on the occupational categories. Employees argue that if bargaining units were based on occupational categories, bargaining could be simplified through negotiation of general contracts covering conditions of employment for each broad occupational category. Similarly, if certification of bargaining units was based on majority membership in an occupational category rather than a group, it would have been easier to enlist the necessary membership in each broad category and obtain bargaining rights on their behalf. Thus employee organizations contend that the existence of over eighty bargaining units imposes an unnecessary burden as well as delays and complicates certification proceedings by causing excessive proliferation of bargaining units, organizational strife and costly legal battles.

Fourthly, employees contend that they have no manoeuvrability in the bargaining process: requirements dictate that they choose either conciliation-strike or arbitration before bargaining begins and that the method chosen must remain in effect until it is changed before the next round of bargaining. The employer, however, can manoeuvre by obliging unions to accept less in nonarbitrable areas to avoid going to arbitration in other areas. The employer can also force trade-offs in regard to nonarbitrable issues because, if nonarbitrable issues are in dispute, the unions have to accept trade-offs demanded by the employer or drop the issues entirely.

The conciliation-strike option also has drawbacks for the unions. This option is denied to such bargaining units as correctional officers, firefighters and hospital workers because all or the majority of their members are "designated employees." Also many of those who legally possess the right to strike may find they cannot exercise the right without risking serious consequences. Unlike the postal employees, many bargaining units find it difficult to mount a successful legal strike because their members are dispersed among various departments and their strike may not bring about immediate, serious and visible disruption of public services. Moreover, some unions and some employees cannot

---

[10]Section 2.

afford the cost and loss of income resulting from even a short strike.

During the late 1960s and early 1970s the trend in dispute settlement was towards negotiation and arbitration rather than conciliation and strike. Between 1967 and 1974, 322 collective agreements were reached without strikes; there were only 10 legal strikes although there were about 50 unlawful work stoppages lasting a day or more. Since then there have been 16 lawful strikes, as of the end of May 1980. For the 1980/81 fiscal year, 46 bargaining units representing 176 000 employees chose the conciliation-strike route, compared to 36 units representing 155 000 employees in 1979/80. Binding arbitration in the event of a breakdown in negotiations was chosen in 1980/81 by 67 bargaining units representing 80 000 employees compared to 73 units with 101 000 members in 1979/80.

Barnes and Kelly suggested in 1975 that this shift towards the conciliation-strike route is a result of the following factors: (1) the replacement of older leaders in public service unions by younger, more militant leaders; (2) the adoption by arbitrators of a narrow, legalistic approach to the scope of arbitration compared to the broader approach exercised under conciliation; (3) the lack of consistent criteria for making arbitral awards; (4) the excessive delays in handing down awards; (5) the suspicion of employees that arbitration has sometimes been subject to government influence; (6) the lack of confidence of employees in the Pay Research Bureau's data on which arbitrators depend.[11]

While employee unions argue that the act has stacked the cards against them, the public has developed

> a growing dissatisfaction with work stoppages in the public sector. . . . That means disaffection with the right to strike. . . . In increasing numbers of cases the withdrawal of services is exercised not against the prevailing or the countervailing power but against the public. . . . When the public interest appears to be victimized, private citizens are much more prone to conclude that they are being prejudiced by cynical manipulation and will urge a change in the system to provide the protection to which they feel they are entitled.[12]

Thus the government has been faced with the competing demands of employee unions for expansion of their collective bargaining rights and the public for uninterrupted public services. To obtain a basis for assessing the provisions and administration of the act, the government, in April 1973, asked Jacob Finkelman, chairman of the PSSRB, to make recommendations on how the act should be revised and improved. In his

---

[11] L.W.C.S. Barnes and L.A. Kelly, *The Arbitration of Interest Disputes in the Federal Public Service of Canada* (Kingston: Industrial Relations Centre, Queen's University, 1975).

[12] A.W.R. Carrothers, quoted in *The Globe and Mail*, October 27, 1972, p. B-4.

report,[13] submitted in March 1974, Finkelman concluded that the act was basically sound and needed no drastic revision. The report, however, contained 231 recommendations for legislative change covering such aspects of employer-employee relations as the scope of collective bargaining; arbitration, conciliation and the right to strike; the grievance process; and the structure and powers of the PSSRB.

Although many proposals were of a technical nature, Mr. Finkelman did recommend some significant changes. For example, he proposed that the scope of arbitration be broadened to include conditions of employment and benefits normally referred to as "the compensation package." Secondly, he proposed that the classification of positions remain under the employer's authority but that provision be made for third party adjudication of classification grievances and for formal consultative machinery on classification standards supplemented by third party mediation in the event of a stalemate. Thirdly, he proposed a new set of procedures for the definition of management and confidential personnel in a bargaining unit. Finally, he proposed that the powers and responsibilities of the PSSRB in settling disputes be expanded. In regard to the right to strike, Finkelman stated that "to outlaw strikes by public servants at this juncture would be counterproductive. We should go to great lengths to make the bargaining process work better."[14]

The majority of the Finkelman proposals were generally acceptable to the unions. They continued to make representations to the government, however, with respect to substantive matters on which Mr. Finkelman did not support them or on which his recommendations did not go far enough. The views of the unions and other interested parties were then heard by a special Joint Committee of the Senate and the House of Commons on Employer-Employee Relations in the Public Service.[15] This committee, which was established to study and make recommendations on the Finkelman Report, reported in February 1976. The committee agreed with Finkelman that the existing act is basically sound and that the rights granted to employees should not be withdrawn merely to overcome inconvenience to the public and the government. Most of the committee's seventy-two recommendations were similar to those of the Finkelman Report. However, in such areas as penalties for illegal strikes, voting procedures in the unions, and managerial and confidential exclusions, the committee's recommendations were contrary to the unions' demands and went far beyond the Finkelman Report.

The committee recommended more severe penalties against em-

---

[13]*Employer-Employee Relations in the Public Service of Canada: Proposals for Legislative Change* (Ottawa: Information Canada, 1974), Part 1, 301 pp. and Part II, 82 pp.

[14]*Ibid.*, Part I, p. 125.

[15]See especially *Report to Parliament*, issue no. 47, February 26, 1976.

ployees, employee representatives and employee organizations for unlawful strike activity. For example, Section 4 of the act now provides a maximum fine of $150 against an employee organization for each day that an illegal strike remains in effect. The committee recommended that this penalty be raised to a maximum fine of $10000 plus $1000 for each day of unlawful strike activity. Where infractions involve designated employees, maximum penalties should be at least twice as high as those imposed on nondesignated employees. (For designated employees the committee recommended a maximum penalty of $25000 plus $5000 per day.)[16]

In regard to union voting procedures, the committee recommended that when a bargaining agent conducts a strike vote or submits a collective agreement to its membership for approval, the vote should be held by secret ballot in accordance with procedures set down by the PSSRB. Every member of the bargaining unit should be entitled to vote, and any act by a union or union official to prevent a member from voting should constitute an offence under the act and be subject to penalty. The committee also recommended that the number of managerial and confidential exclusions from the collective bargaining process be increased and that "health" be added to the criteria for determining essential services.

The employee unions described these recommendations as grossly repressive and anti-union. In their view, the committee gave the government almost everything it wanted and gave the unions very little. In March 1978, two years after the committee submitted its report, the government introduced in Parliament two bills (C-22 and C-28) to amend the PSSRA. The government claimed that a number of the proposed amendments were based on the recommendations made by Mr. Finkelman and the Special Joint Committee of Parliament. The unions, however, levelled strong opposition at the bill, charging that the government conveniently adopted only those recommendations which would enhance the employer's negotiating power and undermine the union's right to bargain collectively and to strike. The principal amendments which were fiercely opposed by the unions included:

First, the creation of a "managerial category" and the removal from the bargaining unit of persons with senior professional and managerial responsibilities as well as those who have an annual rate of pay of $33500 and above;

Second, the establishment of the employer's right to lay off workers temporarily for lack of work because of a strike;

Third, the vesting of the employer with the right to assign duties to employees in addition to the existing right to assign duties to positions; and

---

[16]*Ibid.*, pp. 47: 18-19 and 47: 33-34.

Fourth, the removal of the existing Pay Research Bureau from under the umbrella of the PSSRB and the creation of a new national PRB to compile data on the basis of total compensation comparability between the public and private sectors.

The employee opposition to the proposal to tie public service benefits to those of the private sector on the basis of total compensation seems to have been primarily based on the following arguments.

First, any prearranged, legislatively determined formula for fixing compensation is fundamentally incompatible with the very essence of collective bargaining. Second, under a system based on total compensation, the public service bargaining agents will not be able to alter the "mix" in any way through the process of negotiations as far as a large number of important wage-related conditions and benefits of service (for example, superannuation, leave entitlements, overtime premium pay, supplementary death benefits and disability insurance) are concerned because such items are nonnegotiable under the PSSRA. Third, it would be virtually impossible to determine with accuracy and fairness the actual value of certain hidden elements of private sector compensation such as bonuses, stock options, discount purchase plans, company cars, and so forth for purposes of comparison. Fourth, contrary to the government's claim, the so-called "independent and neutral" Pay Research Bureau will not have the capability necessary to determine levels of compensation for various public service occupational groups, especially because it would comprise persons handpicked by the government who could be manipulated to suit its goal. Fifth, partly because there has always been a lag in producing survey data, benefits and working conditions of public servants traditionally have tended to lag behind their counterparts in the private sector. With the complexity involved in compiling data for use under a total compensation system, there would even be a much greater lag in public service pay and benefits. Finally, using average comparability as a criterion would mean that average compensation outside the public service will be used as a maximum for the public service at all levels.[17] Whether there was merit or not in these much maligned (by employees) amendment proposals and notwithstanding its initial insistence to the contrary, the government ultimately heeded the opposition of public service unions and allowed both bills to die on the order paper.

In the final analysis, there are no simplistic solutions to the embit-

---

[17]For details, see "Wider based bargaining: the complicating factors," the PSAC brief to the Commission of Inquiry on Wider Based Bargaining, *The Civil Service Review* 51, (December 1978): 14-17; "Determination of Wages and Working Conditions," policy paper No. 14, PSAC fifth triennial convention, *The Civil Service Review* (September 1979) 52: 6-10; The Public Service Alliance of Canada, *The Truth About Bill C-22*, December 1978, pp. 1-8.

tered employer-employee relations that exist in the public service at present. Academics and others have advanced numerous proposals for solving them, from banning strikes by legislation to introducing compulsory arbitration. Although none of these proposals promises to be foolproof, there is certainly considerable scope for improving the climate and procedures of collective bargaining in the public service. It must not be forgotten that collective bargaining in the federal public service is still in its infancy. As has been shown above, the PSSRA in its present form provides the employer with far too much leverage and public service employees are left with far more limited collective bargaining rights than their counterparts in the private sector. This is not to suggest that the public service unions are without blemish. The periodic strikes and other confrontations in the public service are perhaps proof of an increasingly militant posture some of them have been adopting over the years. Devising an equitable and equally appealing formula for all the parties concerned—the government, the employees and the public at large—is a seemingly insuperable political problem. Nevertheless, collective bargaining in the public service can be vastly improved if Ottawa proceeds with its long-delayed amendments to the PSSRA and especially if the amendments are based essentially on the recommendations made by Mr. Finkelman and the Special Joint Committee of Parliament. At least, it is worth trying.

Case References
Canadian Cases in Public Administration

The Difficult Supervisor
The Health of Mr. Cole
Friends and Lovers
Robbery or Delusion?
The Auditor's Lament
Public Interest or Collective Interest?
The Minister and the Doctor

Bibliography

Archibald, Kathleen. *Sex and the Public Service*. Ottawa: Queen's Printer, 1970.
Baker, Walter. "Executive Manpower Requirements of the Canadian Public Services in the 1980's." In *Executive Manpower in the Public Service: Make or Buy*, edited by Kenneth Kernaghan, pp. 39-62. Toronto: Institute of Public Administration of Canada, 1975.
Bolduc, Roch. "Le perfectionnement des cadres." *Canadian Public Administration* 17, no. 3 (Fall 1974): 482-94.
Callard, K.R. *Advanced Administrative Training in the Public Service*. Toronto: University of Toronto Press, 1958.
Canada, Civil Service Commission. *Report of the Preparatory Committee on Collective Bargaining*. Ottawa: Queen's Printer, 1965.
Canada. *Royal Commission on Administrative Classification in the Public Service, Report*. Ottawa: King's Printer, 1946.

Connell, J.P. "Collective Bargaining in the Public Service of Canada." In *Collective Bargaining in the Public Service*, pp. 45-55. Toronto: Institute of Public Administration of Canada, 1973.

Corson, John J., and Paul, Shale R. *Men Near the Top: Filling Key Posts in the Federal Service*. Baltimore: John Hopkins Press, 1966.

Crispo, John. "Collective Bargaining in the Public Service." *Canadian Public Administration* 16, no. 1 (Spring 1973): 1-13.

Frankel, S.J. *Staff Relations in the Civil Service: the Canadian Experience*. Montreal: McGill University Press, 1962.

Goldenberg, Shirley B. "Collective Bargaining in the Provincial Public Services." In *Collective Bargaining in the Public Service*. pp. 11-43.

Hodgetts, J.E. et al. *The Biography of an Institution: The Civil Service Commission of Canada, 1908-1967*. Montreal: McGill-Queen's University Press, 1972.

Hodgetts, J.E., and Dwivedi, O.P. *Provincial Governments as Employers*. Montreal: McGill-Queen's University Press, 1974.

Institute of Public Administration of Canada. *Collective Bargaining in the Public Service*. Toronto: Institute of Public Administration of Canada, 1973.

Johnson, A.W. "Education and the Development of Senior Executives." *Canadian Public Administration* 15, no. 4 (Winter 1972): 539-57.

Kernaghan, Kenneth. *Ethical Conduct: Guidelines for Government Employees*. Toronto: Institute of Public Administration of Canada, 1975.

Kernaghan, Kenneth, ed. *Executive Manpower in the Public Service: Make or Buy*. Toronto: Institute of Public Administration of Canada, 1975.

Kernaghan, Kenneth. "Management Development for Canada's Public Services." In *Executive Manpower in the Public Service: Make or Buy*, edited by Kernaghan, pp. 1-18.

Kernaghan, Kenneth. "Perfectionnement des cadres de gestion dans la fonction publique au Canada." In *Executive Manpower in the Public Service: Make or Buy*, pp. 19-38.

Pertuiset, Dorothy. "Méthodes pédagoqiques au sein du gouvernement et de l'université." In *Executive Manpower in the Public Service: Make or Buy*, edited by Kernaghan, pp. 106-21.

Plunkett, T.J. "Municipal Collective Bargaining." In *Collective Bargaining in the Public Service*, pp. 1-10.

Stahl, O. Glenn. *Public Personnel Administration*. 7th ed. New York: Harper & Row, 1976.

Warner, Kenneth O., ed. *Collective Bargaining in the Public Service: Theory and Practice*. Chicago: Public Personnel Association, 1967.

Warner, Kenneth O., and Henessey, Mary L. *Public Management at the Bargaining Table*. Chicago: Public Personnel Association, 1967.

Wilkins, T.J., "Wage and Benefit Determination in the Public Service of Canada." In *Collective Bargaining in the Public Service*, pp. 57-84.

Part VI

POLITICS, POLICY
and PUBLIC SERVANTS

21/Power and Public Servants
in Canada*

Kenneth Kernaghan

The precise nature and extent of bureaucratic power in the contemporary political system are not well documented in Canadian social science literature. It is generally acknowledged, however, that public servants exercise significant power both in policy formation and policy execution. In a 1977 lecture on the threat to parliamentary responsible government, the former leader of the Opposition, Robert Stanfield, stated that "while the House of Commons has been losing control, so also has the Government. The ministers just do not have the time to run such a vast show and make such a vast range of decisions. Consequently, more and more is for all practical purposes being decided by and implemented by the bureaucracy."[1] And in a reminiscence on thirty years as a senior public servant and a minister, Mitchell Sharp observed that "top public servants are powerful persons in the machinery of government at the federal level. They wield great influence. They do because they are, in the main, professionals who have been selected for their proven administrative ability and who devote their full time to government. In many cases, they have a greater influence upon the course of events than have Ministers, particularly the weaker and less competent."[2] The extent of this bureaucratic power clearly varies in accordance with such factors as the government's view of the proper role of public servants in the political process,

---

*Reprinted and substantially abridged by permission from Kenneth Kernaghan, "Changing Concepts of Power and Responsibility in the Canadian Public Service," *Canadian Public Administration* 21 (Fall 1978): 389-406.
[1] The George C. Nowlan Lecture, Acadia University, February 7, 1977. Reprinted in *The Globe and Mail*, February 8, 1977.
[2] Mitchell Sharp, "Reflections of a Former Minister of the Crown." (Address to the Toronto Regional Group of the Institute of Public Administration of Canada, November 29, 1976), pp. 6-7.

the policy or program under consideration, the department or agency involved, and the style and competence of ministers and their officials.

A framework for examining the power of public servants may be devised by utilizing the doctrine of political neutrality which explains the nature of the interaction between public servants and other actors in the political system.[3] It also permits us to focus on the changing nature of bureaucratic power and on the role of public servants in both policy development and implementation. The major elements of the traditional doctrine may be summarized as follows:

(a) politics and policy are separated from administration: thus politicians make policy decisions; public servants execute these decisions;

(b) public servants are appointed and promoted on the basis of merit rather than on the basis of party affiliation or contributions;

(c) public servants do not engage in partisan political activities;

(d) public servants do not express publicly their personal views on government policies or administration;

(e) public servants provide forthright and objective advice to their political masters in private and in confidence; in return, political executives protect the anonymity of public servants by publicly accepting responsibility for departmental decisions; and

(f) public servants execute policy decisions loyally and zealously irrespective of the philosophy and programs of the party in power and regardless of their personal opinions; as a result, public servants enjoy security of tenure during good behaviour and satisfactory performance.[4]

As a basis for explaining the nature of bureaucratic power in the political process, each of these six statements will be examined briefly.

The Policy Role of Public Servants

For the purpose of this essay, the key element of the traditional doctrine of political neutrality is that politics and policy are separated from administration so that ministers formulate policy and public servants administer that policy. This strict dichotomy is a convenient means of differentiating between the responsibilities of politicians and public servants; it is not, however, an accurate portrayal of reality. Public servants are now actively involved in both the formation and the execution of public

---

[3]In this discussion of the role of public servants in the political system, the word political is not used in the narrow sense of partisan activity; rather it is used in the broad sense of involvement in the authoritative allocation of social values. "Political life concerns all those varieties of activity that influence significantly the kind of authoritative policy adopted for a society and the way it is put into practice." David Easton, *The Political System* (New York: Alfred A. Knopf, 1953), p. 128.

[4]This framework is drawn from Kenneth Kernaghan, "Politics, Policy and Public Servants: Political Neutrality Revisited," *Canadian Public Administration* 19 (Fall 1976): 432-56.

policy—and it is often difficult to distinguish between the two activities.

In the sphere of policy formation, the power of public servants was perceived to be so great by the late 1960s that Prime Minister Trudeau endeavoured to place more policy-making power in the hands of politically accountable authorities, especially Cabinet ministers. To this end, the cabinet committee system and the parliamentary committee system were reformed, the coordinating capacity of the Privy Council Office was strengthened and the policy influence of the Prime Minister's Office was expanded. The use of such alternative sources of policy advice as task forces, white papers and advisory councils provided a competing influence to departmental advice. The impact of these changes has been discussed at length elsewhere. However, it is notable that these changes did increase the role of ministers in policy formation. Indeed, Mitchell Sharp has lamented that ministers expended too much effort discussing each other's proposals in cabinet and in committees. He notes that "decisions might have taken less time, we might have had a better perspective on events and more time for politics had we delegated more to our civil service advisors and left more time for reflection."[5] It appears also that the power of the so-called "public service mandarins" has been diffused among a broader range of political actors and among a greater number of senior public servants.

Despite these reforms, certain public servants continue to exercise significant power by virtue of their central positions in the policy process (for example, the deputy minister of finance, the clerk of the Privy Council). Moreover, despite the greater variety of available sources of policy advice, the very technical, complex and time-consuming nature of certain policy issues obliges ministers to continue to rely heavily on the advice of their expert and experienced officials.

In the sphere of policy execution, public servants also exercise substantial power. Many of the day-to-day decisions of public servants involve the straightforward, objective application of general rules to specific cases and require the exercise of little or no judgment. However, many other decisions permit or require public servants to exercise considerable judgment in the administration of policy. In the course of interpreting, clarifying and applying policy, public servants may significantly influence the success of policy decisions taken by ministers and legislators. The accuracy and enthusiasm with which public servants administer policy determines to a large extent the success of that policy. A series of individual, relatively minor decisions in a particular policy area can have a significant cumulative impact on the extent to which the original intent of Cabinet and Parliament is realized. Moreover, such decisions can help to determine the content of subsequent changes in existing policy. In

---

[5]Sharp, "Reflections," p. 15.

wielding such discretionary powers, public servants are of course expected to ensure that their decisions are broadly attuned to the general policy of their minister and their department.

The discretionary powers of public servants in policy execution are especially evident in the making and enforcement of regulations under authority delegated to them by Parliament or subdelegated to them by a minister or by Cabinet. The statutory provisions authorizing the making of regulations are often phrased in general or imprecise language which permits public servants to exercise significant discretion both in the wording of the regulations and in the application of their provisions to particular cases. The delegation by Parliament of power to make regulations is now very common and a large number of regulations has been made. The Special Committee on Statutory Instruments which reported in 1969 found that 420 of 601 statutes perused by the committee provided for delegated legislation and that an annual average of 530 regulations had been passed between 1956 and 1968.[6] Then, in 1977, the Senate-House Committee on Regulations and Other Statutory Instruments, on the basis of its inquiry into "the subordinate law made by delegates of Parliament," provided examples not only of the substantial volume of subordinate law but also of cases where public servants had exceeded the regulation-making authority granted to them by Parliament.[7] The committee recognized the need for subordinate legislation but made a number of recommendations to ensure more effective parliamentary scrutiny of this legislation and more attention to the rights of individuals affected by it.

It is clear that administration has important implications for policy and that politics and policy cannot be easily separated from administration. Contrary to the dichotomy enshrined in the traditional doctrine of political neutrality, public servants are engaged in both policy formation and policy execution. Moreover, this power of public servants in the political process is likely to continue to grow in pace with the scale and complexity of government operations.

Political Appointments

Preservation of the political neutrality of public servants requires that they be appointed and promoted on the basis of competence and performance rather than on the basis of service to a political party. Most political appointments to senior positions in government are made to agencies, boards and commissions rather than to regular departments

---

[6]House of Commons, *Special Committee on Statutory Instruments*, 3rd Report (Ottawa: Queen's Printer, 1969), p. 4.

[7]Senate and House of Commons, *Standing Joint Committee on Regulations and Other Statutory Instruments*, 2nd Report (Ottawa: Queen's Printer, 1977), esp. pp. 2-12.

and central agencies. However, during the Trudeau administration, much publicity has been given to a small number of political appointments to senior departmental and central agency posts and to the staff of the Prime Minister's Office. Criticism of these appointments has been directed more to the commitment of the appointees to the governing party than to their lack of merit.

Political appointments to senior positions usually occupied by career public servants limit the influence of these public servants by blocking their access to some of the highest positions in government. Moreover, long-serving officials are obliged to share their influence in the policy process with newcomers who may have fresh ideas and unorthodox approaches and who may not share the administrative values to which most public servants have become socialized. It is generally acknowledged that the recent growth in the influence of officials in the Privy Council Office and the Prime Minister's Office has diminished to some extent the influence of departmental public servants. This shift in power is primarily the result of changes in policy-making structures, however, rather than of the fact that some positions in these offices are held by appointees aligned with the governing party. Moreover, officials dedicated to service of the state rather than service of a political party continue to hold the great majority of senior positions and to exercise the power associated with those positions.

Partisanship

Between 1918 and 1967 the convention that public servants do not engage in partisan political activities was buttressed by the Civil Service Act of 1918 which specifically prohibited such activities. In 1967 the Public Service Employment Act removed this prohibition. Most public servants who wish to seek political office are now permitted to take a leave of absence to stand for nomination and election. Also, despite continuing restrictions against working on behalf of a candidate, public servants may engage in such activities as making financial contributions to a political party or candidate and attending political meetings. Senior public servants and those holding "sensitive posts" (such as those with personnel or regulatory responsibilities) are still excluded from partisan activities.

This change has not had significant influence on the exercise of administrative power, especially since those officials most actively involved in policy development are excluded from participation. Thus the political sympathies of the most powerful public servants remain generally unknown. Indeed, open identification with the governing party would break with tradition and would not necessarily enhance a public servant's influence with his political superiors or his administrative colleagues. It would certainly jeopardize his administrative career in the event of a change in government.

Moreover, one of the attractions of government employment at the senior levels is the opportunity to exercise influence in relative privacy and anonymity. While there have been some notable examples of public servants being transformed into Cabinet ministers, a Cabinet post is by no means a sure reward for a public servant who is elected to political office. And a senior public servant may well exercise more influence on policy from his departmental office than from a backbench in Parliament.

Public Comment

It follows that unless public servants are involved in approved forms of political partisanship, they should not engage in public and political controversy. By convention, public servants are not permitted to influence public opinion by expressing in public their personal views on government policies or administration. However, this conventional rule does not reflect the complexity of the issue of public comment and the difficulty of defining its permissible limits. Public servants can engage in a variety of forms of public comment which permit, encourage or require the expression of personal views but which do not usually involve criticism of government. It is important to distinguish public comment from public criticism.

In the performance of their duties public servants are often obliged to discuss (a) the meaning and administration of government policies; (b) available remedies to problems with existing policies; and (c) matters on which government policy is undecided. These three categories constitute a zone of discretion within which public servants may move from description and explanation of existing or proposed government policies to the expression of personal views on these policies. Public servants are increasingly involved in situations where opportunities arise for the expression of personal views on public matters. The large scale of government's service and regulatory activities has led to public demand for more information about government programs and intentions and for discussion of policy issues in public. This demand has increasingly been met by public servants, who are required to represent their ministers in public forums, either because of severe demands on the time of ministers or because of the complicated and technical nature of certain policies and programs.

Public servants cannot, however, fulfil their ministers' partisan political role. They strive to retain their impartiality by resisting the temptation to advocate specific policy options or to support or reject the policy suggestions of others. They also try to avoid personal identification with views which may be rejected by their minister or by a subsequent government. The danger of straying over the line between administration and policy is especially great when public servants are discussing matters on which government policy is unclear or undetermined. However, experienced public servants tend to know when they are near the line and few of them have been caught on the wrong side of it.

Public servants are much less circumspect when meeting with various individuals and groups in private and in confidence. In this much less public milieu, public servants engage in such political activities as negotiation and accommodation on behalf of their ministers. It is on these occasions that members of the public may see most clearly the nature and extent of administrative power in the policy process.

Public servants will increasingly be required to appear at public meetings to provide information about the substance and implementation of government policies and programs. As a result, the public will become more aware of the influence which public servants bring to deliberations on public policy matters. It is often difficult for public servants to discuss government policy without indicating, inadvertently or otherwise, some measure of the influence they have—or could have—over the content of the policy.

Anonymity

By engaging more actively in public comment on government policies and programs, public servants have moved more directly into the public spotlight and have thereby lost some of their anonymity. Despite this development, public servants strive to retain as much anonymity as possible. They give frank and impartial advice to their ministers in a private and confidential manner. Ministers, for their part, are expected to shield their officials from public attack by bearing public responsibility for all the actions—good or bad—of their administrative subordinates. This is the essence of the doctrine of ministerial responsibility. Recent experience in Canada demonstrates, however, that ministers occasionally fail to protect their officials from public criticism in cases of real or alleged maladministration.

Although ministers are sometimes unwilling or unable to protect their public servants from being named or blamed by opposition members or by the media, the confidentiality of official advice, whether in oral or written form, is usually preserved. This private advisory function gives public servants enormous influence over the content of public policy. Their advice is persuasive because it is informed and supported by administrative and professional personnel within their departments. This advice is especially influential, however, because it is proffered in confidence where it cannot be openly challenged and debated by other political actors.

Thus the tradition and practice of administrative secrecy which are so ingrained in the Canadian parliamentary system help to maintain the influence of public servants in the policy process. To the extent that knowledge is power public servants are in a position to preserve and expand their power by keeping certain information secret. Public servants are becoming more visible to the public but the confidentiality and influence of their advice to ministers are retained.

The anonymity of public servants has been diminished by their more frequent appearances before parliamentary committees. Their diplomatic skills are often severely taxed as they strive to describe and explain their department's programs fully and frankly while preserving their loyalty to their minister and their reputation for impartiality. On occasion, however, legislators, pressure group members, media representatives and others concerned with the committees' deliberations can discern the actual or potential power of public servants in the political process.

A further incursion on anonymity has resulted from the increasing interest of the news media in the activities of public servants, whether these activities take place in parliamentary committees, in public gatherings or in departmental offices. This media coverage makes public servants and their views better known to the public. Thus it helps to limit the power of public servants by exposing their activities to public questioning and criticism.

Permanence
An important source of administrative power is the permanence in office which public servants enjoy as long as they serve their political masters loyally regardless of the party in power. This security of tenure enables a career public servant not only to establish and wield influence in the policy process but to continue to exercise such influence even if there is a change in the governing party. Long tenure in office enables public servants to acquire knowledge and experience both in specific policy fields and in the political-administrative system within which policy decisions are made.

The permanence in office of public servants increases their power vis-à-vis politicians. Ministers cannot hope to match the expertise of their senior officials, and the frequent rotation of ministers prevents them from accumulating much experience in particular policy areas. The effort of the Trudeau administration to rotate senior public servants more frequently has probably reduced somewhat the attachment of officials to certain policy fields and diminished the knowledge and experience they acquire in any single policy field.

There is some support in Canada for a system of political appointments similar to that in the United States. Under this system, the incumbents of the most senior public service positions would be replaced whenever a change in government occurred. Some senior appointments would thus be held on a temporary rather than a permanent basis. The power of career public servants would be reduced because they would not normally be appointed to the highest administrative posts in government. However, assuming regular changes in the governing party, the tenure in office of senior political appointees would be too brief to enable them to exercise as much power based on experience and expertise as career public servants do.

At present, there is little possibility of a shift to a system of political appointments. Such a shift would be more likely if the political neutrality of public servants declined much more than it has. Thus, to preserve their permanency in office, senior public servants must maintain their impartiality by avoiding partisan activity and inappropriate public comment and, so far as possible, preserving their anonymity. Despite the tenure in office which public servants in general enjoy, it is likely that a few political appointments to senior departmental and central agency posts will continue to be made.

On the basis of this examination of the major elements of the doctrine of political neutrality, two major conclusions may be drawn:

(a) public servants are more active participants in the political process than the traditional doctrine of political neutrality suggests;

(b) this participation accounts in large part for the nature and extent of the power which public servants exercise in contemporary Canadian government.

22/The Cabinet and the Canadian Bureaucracy
William A. Matheson

There are two theories regarding the relationship between the Cabinet and the civil service. One theory states that policy making is the sole prerogative of the Cabinet, and it is the responsibility of the civil service to administer policy once it has been determined. This theory is derived to a large extent from government practice in Great Britain. According to one scholar, "The traditional view of British Government was that all decisions on matters of policy were taken by the Cabinet or by individual ministers so that the civil service merely carried out instructions."[1] The second, and possibly more popular, theory is that our society has become increasingly subject to administrative control, and the real initiative in

---

[1]John P. MacKintosh, *The British Cabinet* (London: Stevens and Sons, 1962), p. 453.

policy formation has tended to pass from the hands of politicians to those of the civil servants.

It appears that each theory has an element of truth in it. The senior civil servant, in addition to his administrative duties, is involved in policy making, and the more senior his position the more time he spends on policy matters. ". . . In fact the deputy (minister) spends as much of his time on policy advising and devising as he does on implementation."[2] It is, therefore, incorrect to assume that the business of government is conducted on two distinct planes, policy and administration, with the Cabinet or individual minister being responsible for the former and the civil service for the latter. It is equally erroneous to assume that the civil service dominates the policy-making process in Canadian government.

It should be noted, however, that while the senior civil servant is involved in both administrative and policy matters, the converse is not quite true of members of the Cabinet since there has been a very strong tendency in Canada for the Cabinet to leave responsibility for adminis-tration almost exclusively to civil servants. Lord Bridges has noted that in Great Britain, since ". . . no minister can do everything, he will rightly concentrate his main endeavours on policy and will leave its execution to others as far as he can. . . ."[3] In Canada this tendency is reinforced by the pattern of recruitment of Cabinet ministers; administrative ability seems to be one of the least looked for qualities in a potential minister.

> In the formation of a Cabinet an incoming Prime Minister is subject to very distinct limitations and restrictions. He is not free to choose ministers at his personal wish or will. Considerations of geography, of the size and total population of the provinces, as well as economic, racial and religious considerations, of total and party membership in the House of Commons and the special qualifications called for in the filling of certain portfolios are all among the factors of which full account should be taken.[4]

Since administrative capacity of the potential minister is clearly a minor consideration in Cabinet formation, concern for policy implemen-tation has usually been left to the ministers' administrative subordinates, that is, the civil service. Indeed, Mr. King once remarked in the House of Commons that: ". . . Different qualities are required for effective work as a Cabinet minister from those required in an administrative or executive post."[5]

---

[2]A.W. Johnson, "The Role of the Deputy Minister," *Canadian Public Administration* 4, no. 4 (December 1961): 303. Reprinted on p. 256.
[3]Rt. Hon. Lord Bridges, "The Relationship between Ministers and the Permanent Departmental Head," *Canadian Public Administration* 7, no. 3 (Sept. 1964): 271.
[4]Mackenzie King to P.L. Hatfield, quoted in H. Blair Neatby, *William Lyon Mackenzie King, A Political Biography* (Toronto: University of Toronto Press, 1958), p. 172.
[5]*Debates.* Commons, July 8, 1940, p. 1400.

The principle of having representatives in the Cabinet from various areas and groups within the country has become a rigid Canadian convention, and has been an important means of helping to maintain the unity of the country. It has also had considerable impact on the relationship between the Cabinet and the civil service.

The fact that the Cabinet is the significant federal body in Canada has made it necessary for it to function much more as a collegial body than Cabinets in other countries. A large number of matters have come up for discussion and decision at Cabinet level which could have been settled more efficiently at a lower level by individual ministers and their senior advisers. "Almost every decision of a Minister, even of the most trivial importance, is thus, at least in theory, brought before his colleagues for the purpose of obtaining their collective approval, which is necessary for its validity."[6] As a result, while civil servants have had considerable influence on policy formulation at the department level, that is, influence over their ministers individually, their influence has been sharply reduced at full Cabinet level. At this point their advice and recommendations have been subjected to the scrutiny of a large number of ministers. Sectional and group interests make it ". . . politically dangerous to give Ministers untrammelled authority over the policy of their departments. Each Minister tends to have a sort of veto of executive actions affecting the part of the country which he is known to represent in the Cabinet. . . ."[7] This understanding was explicitly affirmed in an order-in-council, dated June 14, 1904, which stated that "In the case of members of the Cabinet, while all have an equal degree of responsibility in a constitutional sense, yet in the practical working out of responsible government in a country of such vast extent as Canada, it is found necessary to attach a special responsibility to each minister for the public affairs of the province or district with which he has close political connections. . . ."[8] This rule, which is similar to that of senatorial courtesy in the American Senate, has tended to limit the policy influence of Canadian civil servants.

Another effect of the representation principle in the Canadian Cabinet is that the immersion of the Cabinet in policy matters has tended to allow the civil service considerable autonomy in administrative matters. Time that a minister might otherwise spend on administration has been spent on other matters in Cabinet, attendance in the House or on his political obligations. Moreover, the minister's constitutional responsibility to Parliament and the public for everything done in his department has been somewhat vitiated by the Canadian tendency to resort to orders-in-council rather than to ministerial directives for

---

[6]Sir George Murray, *Report on the Public Service of Canada*, 1912, Sections 5, 6, 8.
[7]J.R. Mallory, "Cabinets and Councils in Canada," *Public Law* (Autumn 1957): 236.
[8]Canada, Sessional Papers, 1905, no. 13, p. 2.

executive action. Since "Almost every ministerial act is covered by the authority of a Cabinet minute or order,"[9] it is often difficult to hold a particular minister responsible in cases of alleged maladministration. Consequently, it is even more difficult for members of Parliament to single out administrative officials for criticism. Ministers greatly appreciate this custom; as Mr. Winters remarked ". . . it is a comfortable position for any minister to be in to be able to refer matters to the Governor-in-Council."[10]

A concomitant feature of Canadian government, at least in its first fifty years, was the tendency to have a larger number of departments than the business of government actually required in order to provide adequate representation for the various interests competing for Cabinet appointments. When the responsibilities of government grew, however, the creation of new departments would have made the Cabinet too large and cumbersome. An enlarged Cabinet would also have created problems in preserving sectional and group balance. Consequently, certain tasks were assigned to various departments more for expedient than functional reasons. Thus ". . . some departments have come to embrace a variety of ill-assorted functions simply as a means of housing what otherwise might become administrative orphans. The consequent problems of coordination through the Cabinet and other centralized agencies have been acute."[11] Again, this development has helped to increase the immunity of Cabinet members and the civil service from effective criticism. An exasperated member of Parliament complained that:

> We now have four ministers dealing with problems in respect of the wheat board. . . . The Minister of Industry, Trade and Commerce is still involved with problems of wheat sales. The new Minister without portfolio is charged with responsibility for the Wheat Board. We also have the . . . Minister of Transport . . . who is interested in moving grain. The Minister of Agriculture would naturally be interested in the welfare of the agriculture industry.[12]

The principle of representation tends to enhance greatly the role of the prime minister. The prime minister of Canada ". . . enjoys a preeminence other parliamentary systems seldom provide."[13] The prime minister is the *only* member of the Cabinet with a national constituency; all other members tend to be delegates from particular groups or areas. Thus, to a large extent, his considerably greater prestige and power

---

9Mallory, *op. cit.*, p. 236.
10*Debates*, Commons, June 18, 1956, p. 5126.
11J.E. Hodgetts, "Challenge and Response: A Retrospective View of the Public Service of Canada," *Canadian Public Administration* 7, no. 4 (Dec. 1964): 414.
12*Debates*, Commons, October 29, 1969, p. 254.
13James Eayrs, *The Art of the Possible* (Toronto: University of Toronto Press, 1961), p. 3.

". . . are most obviously accounted for by the lesser lustre of his colleagues in Cabinet."[14] Ministers ". . . are dependent for leadership on the Prime Minister. They tend to recognize his paramount position and accept his leadership because their political survival in the Cabinet and in the House of Commons depends on him."[15] Since both Cabinet ministers and deputy ministers are appointed by the prime minister, it is likely that his will prevails in cases of conflict over issues of policy formation or execution. The deputy minister's position as the appointee of the prime minister (and prime ministers have jealously guarded this prerogative) provides him with a measure of security in disagreements with his minister. In the event of conflict a deputy minister is not obliged to yield as a matter of course. If the prime minister must adjudicate such a conflict, the deputy minister can present his case from a position of relative strength. However, if a prime minister is determined to dismiss a deputy minister, he can do so without question, even if the deputy is supported by his minister. Mr. Clark demonstrated this well in 1979 with his dismissal of the then deputy minister of finance.

It is important to note also that the nature of the prime minister's position demands that he possess, among other talents, a very specific capacity for reconciling the diverse interests and groups in Canada. "It was not by chance that the three Prime Ministers who had the greatest proclivity for holding on to office in Canada's history, Macdonald, Laurier and MacKenzie King, had the ability to keep divergent interests together."[16] It is likely that in searching for deputy ministers a prime minister looks for individuals with the same ability. Consequently, there is less likelihood of conflict between ministers and their deputies.

It is true that prior to World War II, ministers were actively involved in both policy and administration. The limited functions of government and the consequent small size of the civil service made it possible for ministers to supervise closely the work of their departments and still determine policy. Moreover, the inordinate number of ministers in the Cabinet resulting from the representation principle assured that no particular minister (with the possible exception of the prime minister) was overworked. The Cabinet was able to decide policy, defend it in Parliament, and in a general sense, oversee its implementation.

"Until 1939 the major and minor details of government policy were capable of being understood and actively considered by ministers and

---

[14]*Ibid.*
[15]R. Barry Farrell, *The Making of Canadian Foreign Policy* (Scarborough, Ont.: Prentice-Hall, 1969), p. 13.
[16]Sister Teresa Burke, "The Canadian Cabinet 1867-1869—An Analysis of the Federal Convention," (Ph.D. thesis, Columbia University, 1958), p. 297.

dealt with by the Cabinet."[17] The advent of World War II, however, completely changed the Cabinet's method of operation and affected its relationship with the civil service. The enormous number of decisions which had to be taken necessitated much more independence for the civil service. The volume of business conducted is illustrated by the fact that in the period 1939-1945 over 60000 orders-in-council and over 60000 Treasury minutes had been passed.[18] This average of over 10000 per year can be compared with the number for 1968, 2248 and 1234 respectively.[19]

While the influence of Parliament over policy making had never been supreme, the emergency conditions of wartime hastened a shift of power into the hands of the executive—both Cabinet and civil service. "The public began to look to the Prime Minister and the members of the Cabinet. They and they alone came to be regarded as responsible for everything concerned with the war. This increased the prestige of the Cabinet and Government enormously and correspondingly decreased that of Parliament."[20] During this period Cabinet ministers could not possibly supervise everything carefully and much power was, of necessity, delegated to civil servants. "Operating collectively in large affairs the Cabinet's chief advisors became almost a second Cabinet, at times more potent than the first. A managerial revolution was under way and could never be repealed."[21] Thus, during this period, many policy decisions were determined largely by members of the civil service.

At the conclusion of the war, the deep involvement of civil servants in policy making continued for a variety of reasons. The problems of postwar reconstruction and the continuing evolution of the welfare state imposed a heavy burden on the Cabinet and prevented a complete return to prewar practices. Moreover, much of the planning for the postwar period was done, on the instructions of the government, by civil servants who thus acquired a great store of technical knowledge. This knowledge was indispensable to the Cabinet and it came to rely more and more on the civil service.

A second factor tending to enhance the power of the civil service was the long tenure in power of the Liberal party. A very close relationship grew up between ministers and senior civil servants. This was natural since: "The careers of many of these top public servants were administra-

---

[17]J.R. Mallory, "Delegated Legislation in Canada," *Canadian Journal of Economics and Political Science* 19, no. 4 (Nov. 1953): 462.

[18]*Debates*, Commons, October 31, 1945, p. 1681.

[19]*Debates*, Commons, November 19, 1969, p. 985.

[20]C.G. Power, "Career Politicians: The Changing Role of the M.P." *Queen's Quarterly* 63, no. 4 (Winter 1956): 488-9.

[21]Bruce Hutchison, *The Incredible Canadian* (Toronto: Longmans Green & Co., 1953), p. 266.

tively linked with long-serving cabinet members, not in a political way but as individuals working professionally on the same problems of government."[22] Cabinet members and senior civil servants came to share the same outlook and, as a consequence, civil servants became increasingly involved in matters formerly left to the politicians. One observer after looking over the 1957 Liberal platform commented: "A generation of Liberal politicians and a generation of presumably neutral senior permanent officials have worked hand in hand to create what is now described as a Liberal program."[23]

It is possible that this development had an adverse effect on the Liberal party. The lengthy term in office of the Liberal party brought about a situation where group and sectional influence was to a large extent neutralized. "A party long in power ... apparently comes more and more to think exclusively in national terms particularly if most of the speculation and planning is done not by the party as such but by Ottawa based and Ottawa minded ministers assisted by Ottawa based and Ottawa minded civil servants."[24] Policy making was left more and more to the civil servants, reaching its zenith under Mr. St. Laurent. "Most of the best ideas emanating from Ottawa during the latter part of the St. Laurent administration originated not with cabinet members but with senior civil servants. In fact, the functions of the two groups almost seemed to merge."[25] Thus it could be said about Mr. St. Laurent's regime that "even on important matters of policy, the cabinet appeared to take little initiative. . . ."[26] It may be that the *national* type of thinking mentioned above contributed to the downfall of the Liberals in 1957.

Under Mr. Diefenbaker, who tended to distrust the civil service, the pendulum began to swing back the other way. There seemed to be little need for this distrust, however, as the civil service proved itself to be flexible and cooperative. Shortly after the Conservatives took office, Mr. Green remarked that "we have had the finest assistance from the members of the Canadian civil service."[27] In this period the Cabinet did assume more control over the policy-making process and the influence of the civil service was reduced.

The return of the Liberals to office under Mr. Pearson did not

[22]Farrell, *op. cit.*, p. 27.

[23]J.E. Hodgetts, "The Liberals and the Bureaucrats," *Queen's Quarterly* 62, no. 2 (Summer 1955): 176.

[24]John Meisel, "The Formulation of Liberal and Conservative Programmes in the 1957 General Election," *Canadian Journal of Economics and Political Science* 26, no. 4 (Nov. 1960): 573.

[25]Peter Newman, "Backstage in Ottawa," *Maclean's Magazine* 70, no. 11 (June 1, 1963): 3.

[26]Dale Thomson, *Louis St. Laurent, Canadian* (Toronto: Macmillan, 1967), p. 385.

[27]*Debates*, Commons, November 15, 1957, p. 1211.

restore the civil service to its earlier preeminence. While the Pearson government contained several ministers who had been civil servants at one time, such as Mr. Sharp and Mr. Drury, the minority government situation under which the Liberals had to operate tended to prevent a return to the type of situation existing under Mr. St. Laurent. Thus the influence of the politician over policy continued. The Cabinet no longer was in control of the House of Commons and was continually in danger of defeat. The House was aware of this and members tended to display considerable determination with respect to influencing policy. ". . . With the minority situation and the length of sessions, ministers have never been more exposed to the influence of their own backbenchers. . . . In certain cases it is not an exaggeration to say that they meet private members more often than their own officials."[28] A major problem during the Pearson era was coordinating the implementation of Cabinet decisions by the various departments. There was no clear system of priorities and no mechanism to ensure coordination among the various departments.

Under the Trudeau government there has been another change in the relationship between the Cabinet and the civil service. The seeds of this change were sown during World War II when Mr. A.D.P. Heeney was appointed both clerk of the Privy Council and secretary to the Cabinet. Gradually a secretariat grew up which prepared an agenda for Cabinet meetings and followed up decisions taken at such meetings. A small staff was established in the Privy Council Office which was responsible directly to the prime minister and provided this service for the Cabinet and its committees.

Until the time of the Trudeau government all matters discussed in Cabinet committees were sent on to the full Cabinet for further discussion, that is, the existence of a committee system, even a highly structured one as under Mr. Pearson, did not in any way detract from the collegial nature of the Cabinet's decision-making process. Under Mr. Trudeau, however, there has been ". . . a restructuring of the cabinet committee system which enables the cabinet to function more effectively."[29] Now, all matters which formerly came before the full Cabinet are sent first to a Cabinet committee, which is in effect a Cabinet in its own right with power to make its own decisions. At these Cabinet committee meetings (which departmental and other officials may attend on invitation) either a decision is reached or a recommendation is made to Cabinet. Those ministers not on the committee are immediately informed

---

[28]M. Lamontagne, "The Influence of the Politician," *Canadian Public Administration* 11, no. 3 (Autumn 1968): 268.

[29]*Debates*, Commons, February 27, 1968, p. 6015.

of any decision taken. If a minister disagrees with a committee decision, he may, after advising the prime minister, raise the matter before the full Cabinet; otherwise the decision stands. The recommendations of Cabinet committees are discussed by the full Cabinet. The Cabinet secretariat, by providing secretarial service and research assistance for the committees and in following up decisions made by both the Cabinet and its committees, ensures a measure of coordination lacking in previous administrations.

Each committee has its own secretary who ranks as an assistant secretary of the Cabinet. The duties of the assistant secretary for the Cabinet Committee on Priorities and Planning were outlined in the House of Commons as follows: "He is ... responsible for the preparation, appropriateness and form of Cabinet materials concerning priorities and planning. His specific duties include developing the schedule of work for one of the Cabinet committees, preparing minutes of committee meetings and records of decisions."[30]

If a *department* wishes to submit a policy proposal, it is forwarded to the Cabinet secretariat in the form of a memorandum signed by the responsible minister. The Privy Council Office examines the proposal in the light of government objectives and then refers the proposal to the appropriate committee(s) for consideration or returns it to the department. It can be argued that the ability to make this decision has provided the officials in the Privy Council Office with considerable power. Given, however, the very senior position and role of the Cabinet Committee on Priorities and Planning (composed of the prime minister and senior ministers), it would appear that quite firm guidelines are provided, and that discretion regarding departmental proposals is limited. Nevertheless, the Privy Council Office is responsible directly to the prime minister, and its officials have access to information and suggestions coming from such sources as task forces and royal commissions, which also report to the prime minister. This type of information enables the Privy Council Office to provide advice independent of departmental influence and is an alternative and possibly a competing source of information to that of civil servants. The role of the department official will now, to a large extent, be restricted to:

(a) assisting in the preparation and development of policy proposals,
(b) advising ministers in Cabinet committee meetings (thereby eliminating many interdepartmental committees utilized since 1939),
(c) implementing Cabinet or Cabinet committee decisions.

It can be seen that this role more closely approximates the traditional role of the civil service.

---

[30]*Ibid.* June 11, 1969, p. 9984.

In addition, there are now deputy minister committees ". . . which provide a forum for testing the adequacy and timeliness of proposals and a mechanism for encouraging the resolution of issues not requiring referral to the Cabinet Committees."[31] There is also a Coordinating Committee of Deputy Ministers chaired by the secretary to the Cabinet which mirrors the Cabinet Committee on Priorities and Planning and concerns itself with interdepartmental issues. "It is not the purpose of these Committees to determine the content or timing of proposals to Cabinet Committees; that is the responsibility of Ministers. . . ."[32] Rather, their purpose is to provide information and coordination services for the various Cabinet committees. It appears that however rational this Committee system may seem, it substantially increases the workload of both ministers and deputy ministers.

One innovation of the Trudeau government which has caused concern is the establishment of a major policy and executive centre in the Prime Minister's Office (distinct from the Privy Council Office). By March 3, 1975, the size of the staff in the Prime Minister's Office had increased from 39 persons under Mr. Pearson to 98, and according to a return tabled in the House of Commons, 24 of these individuals were appointed from outside the civil service. This means that most of the prime minister's staff are not civil servants in the conventional sense of that term but are political appointees. There is a great deal of evidence that these staff people are exercising considerable influence on policy, influence of a type formerly restricted to civil servants. This seems to confirm the contention that ". . . the decision-making system at the federal level is changing, with policy innovation now shifting back to the Cabinet and particularly to a strengthened Office of the Prime Minister."[33] It is alleged that the decision to reduce Canada's commitment to NATO and the decision to phase out the Department of Indian Affairs were taken counter to the recommendations made by the departments concerned. An outstanding example of a shift in influence was the decision to send Professor Ivan Head, one of Mr. Trudeau's personal assistants, rather than an official of the Department of External Affairs, to negotiate with the Nigerian government regarding relief flights into Biafra. There has also been a proliferation of royal commissions and task forces designed to bring more persons outside the government into the policy-making process. Thus in future the civil service must expect to share the responsibility for policy advice with other groups, a responsi-

[31]Government of Canada, Privy Council Office, *The Policy and Expenditure Management System*, Ottawa, 1981, p. 7.

[32]*Ibid.*

[33]Fred Schindeler and C.M. Lanphier, "Social Science Research and Participatory Democracy in Canada," *Canadian Public Administration* 12, no. 4 (Winter 1969): 490.

bility which until recently has been almost exclusively that of the civil service. This is the major change in the relationship between the Cabinet and the civil service brought about by the Trudeau government.

The chief reason for concern is the possibility that the experience and expertise of the departmental civil service may be overlooked or inadequately utilized in the policy-making process. To some extent this concern appears to be exaggerated in that Cabinet ministers will still have to rely heavily on the advice of their civil service advisers. The difference is that their advice will now be acceptable only on its own merits, rather than qua civil service advice. As a result, the situation will no longer exist that ". . . when the Establishment (i.e. the civil service) mind was united behind or against a certain policy its advice was accepted by the Cabinet. . . ."[34]

The 1970s was a time of rapid expansion in both new and existing policy areas, in government expenditures (from 13.5 to 54.8 billion between 1969/70 and 1979/80) and in the number of civil servants employed by the federal government. While the changes introduced by Mr. Trudeau seemed to have maintained political control over the policy-making process during this period, the traditional practice of giving a relatively free hand to the bureaucracy in administering policy led to charges that the government had got out of control and that as a result the Cabinet and Parliament had lost control over the bureaucracy. The auditor general, for example, claimed in March 1976 "that Parliament—and indeed the Government—has lost, or is close to losing effective control of the public purse."

What appears to have happened is that in the 1970s "by and large, responsive government became synonymous with growth and expansion. In the process, institutional and internal accountability systems were often challenged by external influences that demanded responsiveness without strict responsibility and accountability of government for its actions."[35] Because of preoccupation with policy, the Cabinet and senior members of the bureaucracy had neglected to develop mechanisms which ensured political control over the civil service. "As ministers' responsibilities have increased, deputy ministers have assumed greater responsibility for policy and administration in their departments."[36] Their increased responsibility for administration was not accompanied by the establishment of internal management systems which would check and balance (and hence control) administrative action.

Partly in response to these criticisms, the Royal Commission on

[34]Lamontagne, *op. cit.*, p. 265.
[35]A.D. Doerr, *The Machinery of Government in Canada* (Toronto: Methuen, 1981), p. 191.
[36]*Ibid.*, p. 194.

Financial Management and Accountability (the Lambert Commission)[37] was established in 1976 and its report was highly critical of excessive emphasis on policy development at the expense of administration and management.

> Good administration is, in fact, essential to policy development because it provides the foundation for the allocation and efficient use of the resources required to implement policy. Careful planning and administration become even more necessary to the success of policy initiatives when these resources are in short supply. . . . The present quality of management in government falls short of acceptable standards.[38]

It should be noted that while the tone of the commission's report was critical, it was not critical of the civil service per se but rather of the lack of adequate planning which in turn had had an adverse effect on the performance of the bureaucracy in general. The commission has recommended extensive reforms throughout the bureaucracy and in Parliament in order to strengthen accountability and control systems and, in effect, to bring about increased political control over the administration of policy.

It is clear, then, that since Confederation the Cabinet and the civil service of Canada have worked well together. The Cabinet has relied heavily on the civil service for advice and information on policy matters but has, in the main, made the final decisions itself. The special circumstances of World War II resulted in greater responsibilities for the civil service and set a pattern which was difficult to dissolve in the postwar period. If it can be concluded that during this latter period the civil service exerted undue influence, the Cabinet, rather than the civil service, was responsible for this situation. Although in recent years there has been a reduction in the influence of the civil service on policy making, this change has not resulted from the provision of poor advice or undesirable policies by the civil service; rather it has resulted from the government's desire to admit other groups to the decision-making process and to return the prime role in policy making to the political executive. Some of the language used to describe recent changes in the government apparatus can be interpreted as questioning the quality of advice provided in the past by the civil service. There is no evidence to support this view, and Lord Morrison's remarks about the British civil service can be applied to Canada equally well. "What the reader can be sure of is that the British Civil Service is loyal to the government of the day. The worst that can be said of them is that sometimes they are not quick enough in

---

[37]For an excellent discussion of the recommendations of the Lambert Commission see Doerr, *op. cit.* and *Canadian Public Administration* 22, no. 4 (Winter 1979).
[38]Royal Commission on Financial Management and Accountability, *Report* (Ottawa: Supply and Services), p. 178.

accustoming themselves to new ideas. . . ."[39] The civil service of Canada must now deal with new ideas regarding its role in the governing of Canada, especially in the areas of policy implementation and of accountability to its political masters. In the past it has proved adaptable and flexible. It is being challenged to continue this tradition in the future.

23/Power, Parliament and Public Servants: Ministerial Responsibility Reexamined*

Kenneth Kernaghan

Neither the evolution nor the contemporary state of interaction between Parliament and the public service has received much attention in the literature of Canadian political science and public administration. Yet relations between Parliament and the public service affect significantly the exercise of power in the Canadian political system, especially by Cabinet ministers, parliamentarians and public servants.

The conventional wisdom among students of Canadian government and politics is that during the last century there has been a decline in the power of Parliament and a rise in the power of the public service. The growth in the power of the public service, especially since the beginning of the Second World War, is generally acknowledged. Whether the overall power of Parliament has actually declined has recently been shown to be a debatable and complex issue.[1] Nevertheless, it is widely recognized that at present Parliament does not exercise effective power, in the sense of control and influence, over the executive in general and the public service in particular.

---

[39]Lord Morrison of Lambeth, *Government and Parliament* (Oxford: Oxford University Press, 1954), p. 335.

---

*Reprinted and abridged by permission from Kenneth Kernaghan, "Power, Parliament and Public Servants in Canada: Ministerial Responsibility Reexamined," *Canadian Public Policy* 3 (Summer 1979): 383-96.
[1]See Allan Kornberg and William Mishler, *Influence in Parliament: Canada* (Durham, N.C.: Duke University Press, 1976), pp. 52-7; Robert J. Jackson and Michael M. Atkinson, *The Canadian Legislative System* (Toronto: Macmillan, 1974), pp. 1-9; and John B. Stewart, *The Canadian House of Commons: Procedure and Reform* (Montreal: McGill-Queen's University Press, 1977), pp. 22-30.

The power of Parliament over the public service is wielded primarily in an indirect fashion through questioning and criticism of ministers responsible to Parliament for the administration of their departments. Since ministers are the formal constitutional intermediaries between parliamentarians and public servants, Parliament's ability to affect the recommendations and decisions of public servants rests heavily on the interpretation and application of the constitutional convention of ministerial responsibility. Ministerial responsibility is in turn tightly bound up with the conventions of political neutrality and public service anonymity. These three constitutional conventions (or doctrines) are central to the achievement of administrative responsibility in that their definition and usage shape to a large extent the pattern of interaction between public servants on the one hand and parliamentarians and ministers on the other.

The primary purpose of this paper is to examine the meaning and interrelationships of these conventions and their implications for Parliament's power over the public service. The convention of public service anonymity, which is closely tied to that of political neutrality, is subsumed for analytical purposes under the broad heading of political neutrality.

Ministerial Responsibility and Political Neutrality

The convention of ministerial responsibility has achieved much more academic and popular attention than that of political neutrality. Indeed, the meaning and relevance of ministerial responsibility have been the subject of continuing controversy in Canada in recent years. A major source of confusion and debate has been the inconsistent manner in which members of Parliament on both sides of the House have interpreted ministerial responsibility during parliamentary battles for partisan advantage. Opposition members have accused individual ministers and the Cabinet as a whole of utilizing varying interpretations of the convention for the purposes of administrative convenience and of evading responsibility for maladministration. For example, the government has cited ministerial responsibility as an obstacle to enacting freedom of information legislation which confers final authority in the review process on anyone other than a minister. Yet ministers have refused to accept responsibility for illegal activities by members of the RCMP and a few ministers have even named and blamed departmental officials publicly.

On the basis of such events and of an historical review of the application of ministerial responsibility, many politicians, journalists and academic scholars in Canada have concluded that the convention is a myth or that it is dead.

An examination of scholarly writings and popular debates on

ministerial responsibility shows that conflicting views on its vitality and utility are sometimes the result of disagreement over its meaning. It is important, therefore, to clarify the present meaning of ministerial responsibility and its relation to political neutrality so as to provide a foundation for informed discussion of its effects on the exercise of parliamentary and bureaucratic power.

Collective and individual ministerial responsibility are separate but interrelated conventions. In its application to the government as a whole, *collective* responsibility prescribes that the prime minister and the Cabinet must resign or ask the governor general for a dissolution of Parliament if the House of Commons passes a vote of no confidence in the government. In its application to individual ministers, collective responsibility prescribes that a minister must support government decisions in public or at least suppress any public criticism of them. If a minister finds a particular decision unacceptable, he must either stifle his objections or submit his resignation.

This paper is concerned primarily with the convention of *individual* rather than collective responsibility. In the academic literature, several meanings and implications are attributed to individual ministerial responsibility, but there is widespread agreement that it has two major components.[2] The first is that the minister is answerable to Parliament for all the administrative errors of his departmental subordinates in the sense that he must resign in the event of a serious error by his department. This component of ministerial responsibility is often described as a myth. The second component of the convention is that the minister is answerable to Parliament in that he must explain and defend the actions of his department before Parliament. The importance of this component is ignored or minimized by some Canadian commentators on ministerial responsibility.

The convention of political neutrality, like that of ministerial responsibility, merits analysis in terms of the extent to which it reflects contemporary political and administrative practice.[3] Interpreted broadly and incorporating the convention of public service anonymity, the traditional doctrine of political neutrality entails the separation of administration from politics and policy; the selection and promotion of public

---

[2]See, for example, S.E. Finer, "The Individual Responsibility of Ministers," *Public Administration* 34 (1956): 379; A.H. Birch, *Representative and Responsible Government* (London: George Allen and Unwin, 1964), pp. 139-140; R.M. Punnett, *British Government and Politics* (New York: Norton, 1968), p. 182; Jeffrey Stanyer and Brian Smith, *Administering Britain* (Glasgow: Fontana/Collins, 1976), pp. 180-181; Geoffrey Marshall and Graeme C. Moodie, *Some Problems of the Constitution*, 4th revised edition (London: Hutchinson, 1967), pp. 67-74.

[3]For an analysis of the evolution and present status of the convention of political neutrality, see Kenneth Kernaghan, "Policy, Politics and Public Servants: Political Neutrality Revisited," *Canadian Public Administration* 19 (1976): 432-456.

servants on the basis of merit rather than partisanship; the avoidance by public servants of partisan political activity and of the public expression of personal views on government actions; the provision by public servants of confidential advice to their ministers; ministerial protection of public service anonymity; and the loyal implementation of government decisions by public servants regardless of their personal views.

The Resignation of Ministers

The first component of the convention of ministerial responsibility requires that a minister must resign if a serious administrative error committed by his department is exposed. Despite frequent calls by Opposition parties for ministerial resignations on the grounds of actual or alleged departmental mismanagement, in practice ministers in Canada do not resign as penance for administrative bungling in their department. It is now almost universally accepted that it is unreasonable to hold a minister personally responsible in the form of resignation for the administrative failings of his subordinates. A minister cannot hope to have personal knowledge of more than a small percentage of the administrative actions taken by his officials. Moreover, he must restrict his attention to those administrative matters which are especially important or politically sensitive. Even a single department conducts a very broad range of complex and technical activities.

These factors of size and complexity, together with the burden of the minister's political obligations, compel him to rely on his senior officials for advice on the administrative, technical and political implications of policy proposals and decisions. The power of public servants to make discretionary decisions in the implementation of policies further enhances their policy role in that the implementation process has a substantial impact on the success of policy decisions and on the content of future policies. Thus public servants are actively involved in politics in the sense of determining or influencing the allocation of public resources among competing forces. It is clear that the first element of the doctrine of political neutrality outlined earlier, namely that administration is separated from politics and policy, is a fiction. In a formal sense, ministers do make decisions and public servants execute those decisions but public servants exercise enormous influence on both policy development and implementation. It is, therefore, unrealistic to expect a minister to accept personal responsibility for all the acts of his departmental officials. Why should a minister "carry the can" when he has little or no knowledge of its contents?

Thus the vicarious responsibility of a minister for his department's actions is limited and is tied to the particular circumstances of the case at hand. This view has been supported recently by a committee of senior public servants who asserted that

. . . a Minister is subject to various degrees of responsibility. He must certainly accept full responsibility for matters done properly under his instructions or in accordance with his policy. However, in the case of a problem not affecting an important question of policy, he is generally thought to have met his responsibility if he takes the matter in hand. Where the matter is essentially between a complainant and a particular official, the Minister can hardly be expected to have had prior knowledge of the case or to have had an opportunity to influence it personally. He cannot be acquainted with, or personally criticized for, every detail of administration in his department.[4]

This statement implicitly raises the often ignored issue of distinguishing the minister's personal mistakes from those of his officials. It is usually a formidable task for Parliament and the public to discover whether specific administrative acts were "done properly under his (the minister's) instructions or in accordance with his policy." A minister is understandably reluctant even to admit that an administrative error has been made by his department. And when confronted with proof of error, he will usually deny personal knowledge of or involvement in the events in question. On this basis, he then contends that he should not be obliged to accept full responsibility in the form of resignation or indeed to assume any personal blame. If departmental failures are admitted or apparent, ministers are inclined to blame their officials rather than to accept personal or vicarious responsibility. The usual practice is that the minister informs Parliament that the fault lies with his officials and he promises that the offenders will be disciplined and their mistakes corrected.

Cases do arise where the personal culpability of a minister is evident or where the magnitude of the error causes the government considerable embarrassment. Even if the minister "accepts full responsibility" in such situations, the practical effects on his career depend largely on personal, partisan and situational factors. If the minister under attack is unpopular among his Cabinet colleagues, if the electorate is unusually outraged or if the government is in a minority position in Parliament, the prime minister might be tempted to seek or accept the minister's resignation. The longstanding practice in Canada, however, is to enfold the offending minister in the Cabinet's protective cloak so that a matter of individual ministerial responsibility becomes one of collective responsibility. Nevertheless, the minister's reputation suffers from the unfavourable publicity accompanying demands for his resignation so that after the next Cabinet shuffle or the next election, he may be heading a less prestigious department or sitting on a government backbench.

---

[4]Government of Canada, *Report of the Committee on the Concept of the Ombudsman*, Ottawa, July 1977, p. 16.

Two other aspects of ministerial resignation deserve brief mention. First, a number of recent cases in Canada show that a minister will almost invariably be compelled to resign if personal misconduct in the form of unethical, immoral or illegal activities is revealed. Secondly, an incumbent minister cannot be held responsible, especially by way of resignation, for administrative sins committed during the tenure of his predecessors.

We can conclude that in practice ministers do not resign to atone for either serious mismanagement by their officials or personal administrative mistakes. Indeed, if ministerial protestations of innocence are accepted at face value, ministers rarely make mistakes. Thus the demand for ministerial resignations on the grounds of maladministration may appear to be a feeble weapon in the parliamentary arsenal of Opposition parties. Yet this component of ministerial responsibility has important consequences for both ministers and public servants. Parliamentary and public calls for one's resignation, like the probability of being hanged the next morning, effectively concentrate one's attention. The minister's efforts to refute or defuse the allegations are vigorously supported by their senior officials whose duty it is to keep their minister out of trouble. The reputation and career prospects of public servants tend to prosper or suffer along with those of their minister.

In the event of maladministration by departmental officials, the conventions of both ministerial responsibility and political neutrality require that ministers protect the anonymity of the wrongdoers by declining to identify them publicly. Since public servants are expected to serve their minister loyally by supporting departmental policy in public even if they oppose it vigorously within the confines of the department, ministers are expected to shield them from public criticism. However, in recent years there have been some notable departures from conventional practice by ministers who have named and blamed officials in public.

Although the instances in which ministers have publicly criticized their officials are exceptional, it is clear that officials cannot invariably rely on their ministers to protect their anonymity. Moreover, in return for ministerial protection, public servants must not abandon the shelter of ministerial responsibility by engaging in unapproved forms of partisan political activity or in public criticism of government policies. Despite the loosening in 1967 of restraints on the political activities of public servants, officials in senior and sensitive positions are still excluded from such activities. Public servants are actively involved in various forms of public comment in the normal course of their duties but public criticism of government—no matter how constructively motivated—may incur severe ministerial displeasure. Also public servants must moderate their public praise of government actions and avoid public identification with specific policies, decisions or views, so that they may retain their office in the event of a change in the governing party. All these considerations point to the strong links between political neutrality and ministerial responsibility.

The Answerability of Ministers

The second component of the convention of ministerial responsibility corresponds closely to its current practice. Ministers do explain and defend their department's policies and administration before Parliament, especially during question period. Opposition members and, on occasion, government backbenchers utilize a variety of other opportunities (for example, motions, Opposition days) to seek information and explanations from ministers. But an inordinate amount of parliamentary, media and public attention centres on the daily oral question period. It is notable that ministers almost always respond to parliamentary questions in their sphere of responsibility despite the fact that they can neither be obliged to answer nor to give reasons for refusing to answer.[5] A strong impetus to answer to Parliament is that a minister may suffer adverse political consequences for declining to answer. The Speaker of the House has observed that he "is not in a position to compel an answer—it is public opinion which compels an answer."[6] Certainly, a minister who refuses to answer questions on an important issue, especially if he does not provide a reasonable explanation for his position, receives severe criticism from Opposition members and the news media. There is, therefore, both constitutional and political pressure on ministers to justify their department's actions to Parliament.

The willingness of ministers to answer questions in the House does not ensure that all their replies are informative, plausible or even comprehensible. Experienced ministers tend to be artful dodgers who often bob and weave to avoid direct hits from Opposition inquiries and allegations. Chapman admits that ministerial responsibility "may be a useful tag for harrying ministers in Parliament" but he notes that "even then it smacks rather of a verbal game of cowboys and Indians."[7] Nevertheless, on the premise that ministerial evasion and circumlocution on a serious matter may be motivated by a desire to conceal politically embarrassing information, not only Opposition members but also journalists may be prompted to investigate the matter more vigorously.

The fact that a single identifiable minister is answerable for the activities of a specific department assists backbench members of Parliament in their handling of constituents' inquiries or complaints about government administration. A question in the House is sometimes the

---

[5]Arthur Beauchesne, *Rules and Forms of the House of Commons of Canada*, 4th ed. (Toronto: Carswell, 1958), sec. 181(3), p. 153.

[6]House of Commons, *Debates*, February 6, 1978, p. 567.

[7]Brian Chapman, *British Government Observed* (London: George Allen and Unwin, 1963), p. 38.

last recourse of a member who has been unable to obtain a satisfactory answer through private correspondence with a minister.

Although, as noted earlier, a minister is not expected to resign for departmental errors made during the term of office of his predecessors, the rule is firmly established that he must answer to Parliament for those errors. This rule ensures a focus of continuing responsibility for government administration despite changes in the political heads of departments or in the governing party itself. Parliament's capacity to control and influence public servants is enhanced because one minister is required to answer for their actions no matter when these actions took place. The incumbent minister will usually be obliged to rely heavily on his departmental officials for knowledge of what occurred during the tenure of his predecessors. In such situations, the ability of a minister to answer to Parliament for his department rests largely on the continuity of administration provided by his permanent public servants. Thus the operation of ministerial responsibility is closely tied to the permanency in office of public servants. Permanency in turn depends on the preservation of several of the other elements of the convention of political neutrality described earlier.

An important corollary of the answerability of ministers for the administration of their departments is that public servants do not answer directly to Parliament for their decisions and recommendations. In the words of S.E. Finer, "the minister alone speaks for his Civil Servants to the House and to his Civil Servants for the House."[8] The application of this principle protects the anonymity of public servants since it provides that the minister and only the minister is answerable to Parliament. The willingness of a few ministers occasionally to name and blame their officials has had no significant effect on the status of official anonymity. The impact of allegations made against public servants by members of Parliament in general has also been minimal.

Yet a combination of factors related to the growth of bureaucratic power is bringing about a gradual decline in public service anonymity. The increasing extent to which officials are required to explain government policies in public forums has heightened their visibility. Also, journalists who are knowledgeable about the nature and magnitude of the influence of officials in private government offices have expanded their coverage of the activities and identities of specific officials.

Another reason for the decline in official anonymity is that public servants now appear more frequently before parliamentary committees to give testimony, especially on departmental estimates.

The burden of defending and debating policies remains with the

---

[8]Finer, "The Individual Responsibility of Ministers," p. 394.

minister. However, the difficulty of separating policy from administration and the explanation of policy from its defence enables committee members to discern the important contribution of public servants to policy development. This in turn reinforces Parliament's concern that public servants be held accountable for the exercise of this power.

The reform of the committee system has shifted to the committees much of Parliament's capacity to scrutinize the administration of government departments. Thus public servants have become more directly answerable to Parliament through their appearances before parliamentary committees. If ministers become less willing or able to answer to Parliament for the administration of their departments, efforts to enhance the direct answerability of public servants to parliamentarians, especially in committees, are likely to grow.

The traditional interpretation of ministerial responsibility not only precludes public servants from answering directly to Parliament; it also prevents them from responding publicly to parliamentary criticism of their administrative actions. The minister replies to charges against his officials. In the face of allegations of serious administrative error, however, public servants, with the permission of their minister, have appeared before parliamentary committees to explain and defend their actions, (such as the committee hearings on the foot and mouth disease epidemic and on the Bonaventure refit). The practice of official reticence and ministerial defence which normally prevails extends to attacks on public servants by persons outside Parliament, notably journalists. As a result, responsibility for departmental administration is focused on the minister, and public servants help to preserve official anonymity by avoiding involvement in public or political controversy.

Conclusions

On the basis of the preceding analysis, the resignation component of the convention of ministerial responsibility may be restated as follows: The minister is not answerable to Parliament for all the administrative errors of his department in the sense that he must resign in the event of a serious error by his department. The second component of the convention, namely that the minister is answerable to Parliament in that he must explain and defend the actions of his department before Parliament, is unchanged.

Reports of the death of individual ministerial responsibility are greatly exaggerated. If the life of the convention depended on ministerial resignations for the misdeeds of departmental subordinates, it would be mortally wounded. But because of the vitality of its answerability component, ministerial responsibility remains a central, operative convention of the Canadian constitution. Indeed parliamentary debate on ministerial responsibility has centred on its interpretation and application, not on its existence. The concept of ministerial responsibility helps to define and determine how power is and should be exercised in the Canadian political system and who is or should be held responsible for the exercise of that power. It provides a major frame of reference for the allocation of power and responsibility among ministers, legislators and public servants. The fact that the practice of ministerial responsibility does not correspond in full to its theory does not justify denial of the existence or importance of the convention—especially in the absence of a viable alternative.

24/The Role of the
Deputy Minister*
A.W. Johnson

The role of the deputy minister is to create the conditions which make it possible for the minister and the Cabinet to provide the best government of which they are capable—even better if either of them happens to be weak.

It might seem more exact to say that the deputy minister is responsible for implementing government policies. This is true, but to say only this might be to imply a certain differentiation between policy formulation and policy execution, with the deputy minister responsible only for the latter. In fact the deputy spends as much of his time on policy advising and devising as he does on implementation.

What is more, despite the nice precision of saying what the deputy minister is responsible for, the plain fact is that he is not really responsible for anything. No matter how much he may feel responsible for what he does and what his department does, and no matter how much his minister may hold him responsible for departmental behaviour, in constitutional fact only his minister is responsible.

I would argue, indeed, that it is incorrect to use entirely active verbs in describing the deputy minister's role. "Making something possible" is certainly less active than "doing" or "being responsible for." But this lack of precision is necessary. For the deputy minister must display a curiously two-sided nature in dealing with his ministers—sometimes active and sometimes passive, depending upon how firmly resolved they are to

*Reprinted and slightly abridged by permission from A.W. Johnson, "The Role of the Deputy Minister," *Canadian Public Administration* 4, no. 4 (December 1961): 363-69.

follow a certain course of action, or how actively involved they wish to be in doing so.

While it might be useful in describing the role of the deputy to employ the familiar administrative schema of policy formulation and policy execution, it would be misleading to do so unless one first were to describe the "uniqueness" that is characteristic of a deputy minister's job. It is true, of course, that the deputy minister is a sort of general manager. But it is equally true that his job has characteristics which are not likely to be found in most general managers' jobs.

Between the Partial Politician and the Impartial Public Servant

The key to this uniqueness is to be found in his position in the organization—sandwiched as he is between the "neutral" civil service on the one hand, and his "political" minister on the other. This is a relationship which is clothed with constitutional or organizational conventions—conventions which are supposed to clarify the relationship, but which sometimes seem to obscure it. And it is a relationship that is full of paradoxes.

First, the deputy minister is supposed to be impartial or politically neutral serving a political master. In fact it is extraordinarily difficult to be wholly neutral when it is one's profession to deal in public affairs. What is more, the deputy is exposed constantly to most of the pressures of public life—to members of Parliament, to irate citizens, to interest groups—each of them arguing for some change in public policy. They do so with the expectation that the deputy has or will develop a point of view concerning the policy in which they are interested. And in fact he will. For one of his prime tasks is to try to develop an appreciation of long-run social and economic trends as they affect or will affect the policies of his department. And then he evaluates these policies in that context.

Despite this convention of impartiality most people would be quite surprised if any deputy turned out not to have a point of view concerning the policies of his department. Indeed, the public often seems implicitly to hold him responsible for his minister's policies. As for the minister, he would be more than surprised if his deputy seemed not to have a loyalty to his policies, or for that matter a taste for the "political facts of life."

The second convention is even more obvious than the first: the deputy minister, like all civil servants, must remain anonymous in everything he does. This is particularly so, of course, with respect to the advice he gives his minister. There is no paradox in this convention, but there are real difficulties. Frequently the senior public servant has occasion, with the approval of his minister, to discuss potential policies with people outside the civil service. In doing so he may unwittingly express a point of view in such a fashion as to make it clear when the ministerial decision is reached that he was not in accord with it. Participation in the policy-formulating process makes difficult the achievement of this goal of anonymity where policy formulation involves more than civil servants, but the essence remains the same: the deputy minister must renounce any desire for public recognition of his efforts or for a personal identification with the government programs in which he has an interest.

The third convention concerns the so-called division between "policy" and "administration." The minister is responsible for framing policies and the deputy is responsible for implementing them. Now it is true that to most deputy ministers this convention is a useful one when they are put on the spot by an irate taxpayer. But I do not think any of us has any illusions about the existence of these two compartments or about the exclusive occupancy of one by the minister and the other by the deputy. In fact the convention is really useful only when one is trying to define the prime interests and concerns of a minister, or when trying to explain the primacy of the Cabinet and of the elected representatives.

But even if there were two such compartments, administration is not uniquely characterized by impartiality nor policy formulation necessarily by partisanship. One cannot administer a program without developing some keen loyalties to it. Nor is it likely that ministers will evolve policies without an objective appraisal of their goals and implications—no matter how keen their sense for the political winds.

The final convention I want to mention concerns the loyalties of the deputy minister. Most people consider the deputy to have but a single loyalty—that to his minister. He is to express no disagreement with his minister's policies; in fact, if he fails to defend them in public, he may expect whispers of a "rift" between him and the government.

Again, this is an oversimplification. The deputy minister has many loyalties. His first is to his minister, of course. But he also has a loyalty to the institution of Parliament, and he feels a responsibility to assist members of Parliament, on whichever side of the House they sit, when they seek his aid. He has a loyalty to the programs he administers, a loyalty which Opposition members sometimes construe to be a political loyalty. He has a loyalty to his own profession and to his own conscience, a loyalty which causes him to speak out against certain policies, or remain silent about them, depending on whose company he is in. And both the talk and the silences are easily misunderstood.

This is the context within which one must evaluate the role of the deputy minister—indeed in some ways the context has already defined the role.

Policy Execution
But let me return to the schema of public administration and give you some of my personal impressions of the deputy minister's role, first in the

field of policy execution, and secondly in that of policy formulation.

You will quickly discover that what I have to say is not particularly original and that it does not even apply exclusively to deputy ministers. A great many of the characteristics of a deputy's job are common to any senior civil service post. In many ways there is nothing unique about the deputy minister's role in implementing policy. He is like any other senior executive: he must create an appropriate organization and staff it well, then seek to employ all the arts of administration in directing and coordinating and controlling it. But there are some features about this part of the deputy's job which are unusual.

First, the deputy faces a special difficulty in creating that "climate of freedom" which characterizes really effective and dynamic organizations. Of course he must seek to achieve this, and by the usual administrative devices—notably the maximum delegation of responsibility. But in doing so he must face the fact that his is not the final decision as to how much shall be delegated. Ideally, public servants in the field should be given wide discretion in interpreting policy, and in applying it to circumstances as they find them. But they are not the architects of public policy—Parliament is, and woe betide the civil servant who strays too far from what Parliament intended.

What is more, what was delegated today may be withdrawn tomorrow—not by the deputy, but by the minister. And then it may be withdrawn only by implication. Policy may have been interpreted a certain way for five years, but if that interpretation is called into question by a citizen or an interest group, the minister is bound to review it. This inevitably creates uncertainty on the part of civil servants as to what lies within their competence, and as to when policy interpretations should be referred "up the line." What the minister and deputy may wish to leave to the man in the field may be different from what the taxpayer thinks should be left to him. And the line keeps shifting.

So it is the deputy's job somehow to maintain the desirable "climate of freedom" in the face of what harassed civil servants describe as "interference." In essence he is an "interpreter": he must try to interpret to his staff the rationale for ministerial forays into the day-to-day work of the civil service. Putting it another way, the deputy must seek to reconcile the political process with the administrative process.

He has the same sort of role when his staff encounters the impediments to freedom of action which are imposed—apparently capriciously—by central agencies of government. Of course, it is true that many of these Treasury controls, Public Service Commission controls, Purchasing Agency controls are unwarranted, and we who have some responsibility for central agencies should root them out. But the best-run government will still have some such controls—if it has a Parliament—and it is the deputy's job to interpret them to an impatient staff.

The Public Service Commission may be slow and meticulous in the recruitment of staff, but this is because Parliament rightly insists upon every citizen having an equal right to try for a job. Appropriation and allotment controls may impose on field workers certain delays, but parliamentary control over expenditures is much more important than these minor inconveniences. The same applies to controls over individual expenditures: these must be reported in the Public Accounts in order that Parliament might review them, and a good deal of "book work" is justified in making this possible.

What I am trying to say is that there are some special problems in trying to create a climate of freedom in a department of government. The political process and the existence of Parliament *do* impose impediments and these must be accepted by the civil service. The deputy's role, in common with that of all senior civil servants, is to try to communicate to his staff the dual loyalty which is necessary in the public service—one to the program and the other to the very processes of government which produce these frustrations.

My second comment about the role of the deputy in program administration concerns the development of what I might call a "pride of public service." No matter how idealistic one is about the public service, he must recognize that there are areas of work which are boring, unrewarding and repetitive. And the supervisors in these areas have no "profit motive" to move them to introduce work simplification, performance standards and the rest. But what there is in the civil service instead of the profit motive is a certain pride in effective public service. And this is the attitude which must prevail among departmental supervisors if optimum efficiency is to be achieved in these routine procedural operations. Again the role of the deputy and of the senior public servant is unique: he must not only engender a certain enthusiasm for efficiency, but he must seek and communicate a rationale for that enthusiasm.

There is a final impression about this part of the deputy's role upon which I would like to comment. It concerns the relationship of his department to the public.

It is true that in many ways the deputy minister is like an executive in any enterprise: he has a responsibility for maintaining good public relations. But in government this phrase has a very special meaning. The public is at one and the same time the involuntary recipient of the services the civil servants render, and their master. If the public does not have to buy your services you will likely develop a certain solicitude for their feelings: if it does, you may not. It is the job of the deputy and his senior people somehow to instil in the department a sense of public service, an understanding of public reaction to the impersonal and powerful forces of government and, above all, a profound respect for what is paramount in every program: the rights of the citizen. Again it is a matter of diluting program enthusiasm with a second loyalty: that to the political process and the rights of the individual.

Beyond this is the other relationship between the public and the public service: what I might call the master-servant relationship. Obviously this is not a matter of obsequiousness on the part of the civil servant. Rather it is a matter of searching out the public reaction to the programs he is administering in order that a more mature evaluation might be made of their effectiveness.

Undoubtedly this is an everyday event in the lives of most civil servants, but to the deputy minister it is a matter of ensuring that he hears about the public reactions which his staff routinely receives. Similarly he must organize so as to solicit and receive from interest groups their views on the programs for which he is responsible to his minister. One might almost go so far as to say that he has a responsibility to seek out public advice on his area of government.

I hope I am not making the deputy minister sound like a "permanent politician." This, by the way, is how one political scientist describes senior civil servants.[1] In fact, I do not think any civil servant has the right to compete with the minister in his role of testing, sensing, reacting to public opinion. If he does he will find what an art it is, and what an amateur he is! But he must surely recognize that the public cannot react to elected representatives on every detail of program administration; consequently he should seek to "represent" to his minister the public view of the policies for which he is responsible. This is the sense in which I would agree with those who argue that the civil service should become a representative bureaucracy.[2]

Policy Formulation

This discussion leads very naturally to an examination of the second major area of the deputy minister's job, that of advising his minister on policy. For it is as difficult to write separately about policy formulation and policy execution as it is to differentiate between them in one's day-to-day work.

Here the unique thing about the deputy minister's role and that of senior civil servants generally is that they *are* expected to advise their ministers on policy—that they are expected to do so despite the conven-

---

[1]"Their functional position is best described, perhaps, as that of permanent politician." J. Donald Kingsley, *Representative Bureaucracy* (Yellow Springs: The Antioch Press, 1944), p. 269.

[2]This point of view is most effectively expressed by C.J. Friedrich of Harvard University. See his *Constitutional Government and Democracy* (Boston: Ginn and Company, 1946).

[3]For a discussion of different kinds of authority see C.J. Friedrich, ed., *Authority* (Cambridge, Mass.: Harvard University Press, 1958).

tion about the minister's policy role and the civil servant's administrative role.

One wonders, however, what the basis is for the wide acceptance of this policy role. Certainly the deputy has no "right" to advise his minister: he does so only at his minister's pleasure. And I hope that none of us takes himself so seriously that he agrees with this misleading but fairly prevalent view: "The real focus for the development of new policies is not the political process, but the civil service." Indeed the facts speak otherwise. It seems to me that the rationale for the deputy minister's policy role is to be found in the fact that a truly successful deputy minister—if there is such a thing—should possess three kinds of "authority." (I use this word in the sense in which it is employed in political theory.)[3]

First, he enjoys the authority which derives from his post, not his person: the minister, the members of Parliament and the public expect him to subject proposed new policies to critical scrutiny. His is the job of evaluating the ideas that emerge from the political process—considering their implications, examining the premises upon which they are based, evolving alternatives for achieving the same goals; in short, of ensuring an objective examination of every aspect of a proposal.

Secondly, the deputy is clothed—I do not say always rightly—with the authority of his profession. If his academic training and his experience in public affairs mean anything at all, they should mean that he possesses the ability to anticipate social and economic problems and find a solution to them. This is as much a part of the senior civil servant's job as simply evaluating the proposals put forward by others. For he is supposed to study these trends, he is supposed to identify emerging problems, he is expected to have some insight as to how these might be solved. A British political scientist puts it this way:

> Even though he must of course accept the minister's decision, he should always be thinking ahead of it, and he should always be ready to express his own views and to provide the information upon which they are based. For he is primarily concerned with the making of policy, and policy should not wait upon events.[4]

The third reason for this advisory role is the special relationship the deputy has with his minister. Each of them comes to know the other: his strengths and weaknesses, his interests and his blind spots, his insights and his obtuseness. So in the process of formulating policy each comes to look to the other to contribute those particular capacities and talents which he knows him to possess.

If there is some legitimacy to this role of policy adviser, what does it entail? Essentially it involves the initiation of policy suggestions without

---

[4]H.R.G. Greaves, *The Civil Service in the Changing State* (London: Harrap, 1947), p. 48.

seeking to appropriate the initiative from the minister and the government; it involves inaugurating policy studies without usurping the minister's role. The cynics may suggest that this is power without responsibility: I suggest it is more akin to responsibility without power.

The principal task the deputy minister faces is trying to develop in himself and his organization that knowledge and perspective which makes possible an effective evaluation of social and economic trends, and their effect on the area of government in which he works. To do this he must make room for contemplation and study, when all the pressures of events would rule these out. As Sir Edward Bridges, former permanent secretary to the British Treasury, puts it: "He must be a practical person, yet have some of the qualities of the academic theorist; his work encourages the longest views and yet his responsibilities are limited."[5]

The long view is particularly important in government. This is so not just by reason of the nature of government programs, and because of their impact on social and economic development, but also because the political view tends to be short. One might almost say that it tends to move in four- or five-year cycles. So the deputy always must try to find the longer view and introduce it, and to achieve a certain coexistence between it and the shorter view.

Secondly, the deputy minister must place a special emphasis on the development and maintenance of a dynamic department. This means that he must employ all of the arts he has developed—and they are never enough—for appropriate staffing, encouragement of ideas, rewarding the unusual, and so on. This is particularly difficult in government.

I say this not because civil servants are lazy, or because they lack enthusiasm for the public service. Quite the opposite is true, in my experience. But the civil servant is exposed to certain frustrations which are peculiar to work in government. When he enters the public service, he may be an unqualified enthusiast for his program—be it highway building or social welfare. But sooner or later he will meet with one or both of the frustrations which are typical of government.

First, he may find that despite the logic of his recommendations concerning his program, there are political factors to which his political masters give greater emphasis than they do to his logic. Alternatively, they may accept the validity of his proposals but decide in making their budgetary choices that some other program is more important. This will seem inconceivable to the program enthusiast, but there it is.

How do you maintain enthusiasm in the face of these rejections? In business, if your idea will save money or increase sales you have a sporting chance of success. But in government the choices do not involve a

---

[5]Sir Edward Bridges, *Portrait of a Profession* (Cambridge: University Press, 1950), p. 28.

single value system—more or less profit; they involve hierarchies of social values, all of which are subjective. And it is the elected representatives' value systems which are important, not those of the public servant. So it is up to the deputy to try to interpret to his staff the government's goals and its program emphasis, in order somehow to maintain their enthusiasm and dynamic.

Thirdly, the deputy minister must try to develop a certain talent for seeking out advice, without becoming the captive of those who give it. (If this is a problem for the deputy, by the way, how much more so it is for his minister. As a matter of fact, I think this is part of the basis for mutual understanding between minister and deputy: in a sense they are in the same boat.)

The deputy and his minister need advice both from program specialists and from the interested public (or publics). In fact, one of the deputy's major jobs is to organize so as to ensure getting good advice of both kinds. Within the department he must organize so as to create foci of policy thinking and advice, tempered by the experience his people gain in policy execution. This means a certain kind of organization and an appropriate combination of "thinkers" and "doers." It means too that he must cultivate channels of communication which will facilitate a "feedback" or public reaction. Outside the department, the deputy will seek to develop the formal and informal consultations with the interested public that I have talked about earlier.

In all of this he must come to develop a sense of participation in policy formulation, without inducing a sense of paternity for ideas. After all, he is not himself formulating policies. This is a delicate position. For his staff will expect him to display a fighting loyalty to their ideas, if they are good ones, and will be disappointed if he seems not to go to bat for them with the minister. Interest groups, in turn, will seek to win him over to their point of view, or to cultivate in him a certain sympathy for their problems.

So the deputy minister finds himself in the curious position of being exposed to the political process, without at the same time being part of it. He must not permit himself the luxury of becoming too attached to ideas or positions. Somehow he must find a way of maintaining a cordial relationship with those who assist and advise him without ever losing sight of the fact that his first loyalty is to his minister. His first loyalty can never be to his staff or to the public affected by his minister's policies. To quote Sir Edward Bridges again:

> A civil servant has to combine the capacity for taking a somewhat coldly judicial attitude with the warmer qualities essential to managing large numbers of staff. Detached, at times almost aloof, he must be if he is to

maintain a proper impartiality between the many claims and interests that will be urged upon him.[6]

Finally, the deputy minister must make a determined effort not to succumb to the ever present temptation of merely anticipating ministerial will or political necessity, when framing policy recommendations. After all, the minister and his colleagues are subject to enough pressures to take the short-run view, without the deputy seeking to play in the same political league.

This is not to suggest that the deputy should evolve ideal systems which are clearly impractical in a given political situation. But it is one thing to evolve the ideal policy, then amend it, or have it amended on the basis of political necessity, and quite another merely to evolve courses of action which are based upon a civil servant's appraisal of what his minister wants.

Let the minister play his role, and the deputy his. It seems to me, in fact, that there are few enough areas in the political process where the broader span of time and events can be brought to bear in influencing policy, without the deputy minister abdicating his role in this regard. What is more, I think I can make a case for this view: given the broadest perspectives in decision making, the minister will make less "political" decisions, in the narrow sense of that word, than will a civil servant who is trying to "play politician."

This it seems to me is the role of the deputy minister in advising his minister on policy. He must seek out and then try to integrate what is suggested by social and economic trends, what is proposed by the academic theorists, what is propounded by the program specialists, and what is advocated by interest groups and the public. Having done this, he must then make an effort to adapt the ideal solutions to the practical difficulties his minister faces.

---

[6]*Ibid.*, p. 28.

25/Bureaucratic Politics in Canadian Government*

Kim Richard Nossal

In 1968, Graham T. Allison, synthesizing the work of organizational theorists and analysts of United States politics and foreign policy, developed a paradigm for the study of foreign policy which he termed the "governmental politics," or more commonly, the bureaucratic politics model.[1] Allison took issue with the dominant mode of accounting for foreign policy: that by determining the motives of a government choosing from among a set of alternatives a course of action best serving the national interest, the analyst will successfully account for foreign policy decisions and actions. The bureaucratic politics paradigm was offered as a more accurate method of examining foreign policy outcomes. It posited a number of axioms. Governments are not unitary actors, but comprise sets of players holding policy-making positions. Diverse sets of players within government have diverse interests they wish pursued and translated into policy, and thus have different, and often divergent, policy preferences on the same issue. Motives can be ascribed not to governments, but to individual players, whose interests will be shaped by their own conceptions of the public good or the national interest, by their organizational affiliation and by their own career ambitions. Players interact with each other along regularized circuits of the policy process ("action channels" in Allison's terms) attempting to ensure that their proposal receives authoritative approval. The process of interaction among these sets of players determines outcomes.

The purpose of this essay is to determine whether the bureaucratic politics model represents a useful heuristic device for the study of policy decision making in Canada in particular and in parliamentary systems in general. I will argue that six features of the Canadian policy-making system make the suitability of the model likely, although it is recognized that bureaucratic politics in a parliamentary system will demonstrate differences in tone, and in effect on outcomes.

The bureaucratic politics model has not been widely used in the

*Reprinted and abridged by permission from Kim Richard Nossal, "Allison through the (Ottawa) Looking Glass: Bureaucratic Politics and Foreign Policy in a Parliamentary System," *Canadian Public Administration* 22 (Winter 1979): 610-26.
[1]Graham T. Allison, "Conceptual Models and the Cuban Missile Crisis," *American Political Science Review* 58 (1969); *Essence of Decision* (Boston: Little, Brown, 1971); Allison and Morton H. Halperin, "Bureaucratic Politics: A Paradigm and Some Policy Implications," in *Theory and Policy in International Relations*, ed. Raymond Tanter and R.H. Ullman (Princeton: Princeton University Press, 1972); Morton H. Halperin, *Bureaucratic Politics and Foreign Policy* (Washington: Brookings Institution, 1974). For a useful overview, see B. Guy Peters, "The Problem of Bureaucratic Government," *Journal of Politics* 43 (February 1981).

study of Canadian public policy and administration. It has, however, been applied to the study of intergovernmental relations[2] and its utility for the study of Canadian foreign policy has been discussed in scholarly writings. Throughout this essay, illustrations will be drawn primarily from the literature on Canadian foreign policy.

There appears to be a consensus that the structure of the policy-making system of a parliamentary government such as Canada's vitiates the effects of bureaucratic politics on policy outcomes. Stairs, for example, has argued that bureaucratic politics in Canada is considerably "muted" because (i) there is a conscious effort to coordinate policy; (ii) this coordination is made easier by the "casual processes of intra-bureaucratic consultation and exchange;" and (iii) Cabinet is able, where necessary, to settle serious conflicts among departments with divergent interests and preferences.[3] Purver has concluded that on the question of Canadian negotiations on the Seabed Treaty, bureaucratic politics played a minimal role because differences of opinion between government agencies were mitigated by a number of factors, including efforts to coordinate. "External Affairs' Disarmament Division," Purver writes, "successfully melded the various potentially competing interests, and the cabinet was presented with nothing other than unanimously-agreed recommendations."[4] Similarly, Winham has argued that in negotiations with the United States, the Canadian positions are well coordinated, in sharp contrast to the American positions.[5]

On the other hand, much of the literature recognizes that conflict is not entirely absent within the policy process in Canada. Both Matthews and Langdon, in their examinations of policy toward Africa, discovered considerable differences in views between officials in the Canadian International Development Agency (CIDA), the Department of Industry,

---

[2]Richard J. Schultz, "Prime Ministerial Government, Central Agencies, and Operating Departments: Towards a More Realistic Analysis," in *Apex of Power*, ed. Thomas A. Hockin, 2nd ed. (Scarborough: Prentice-Hall, 1977) and *Federalism, Bureaucracy and Public Policy* (Montreal: McGill-Queen's, 1980), esp. chaps. 1 and 8; Simon McInnes, "Crisis Management and Bureaucratic Politics in Canada" (Paper delivered to the Southwestern Ontario Inter-university Conference on Comparative Politics, London, Ontario, March 1979).

[3]Denis Stairs, "The Foreign Policy of Canada," in *World Politics: An Introduction*, ed. James N. Rosenau, Kenneth W. Thompson and Gavin Boyd (New York: Free Press, 1976), pp. 185-86.

[4]Ronald G. Purver, "Canadian Foreign Policy and the Military Uses of the Seabed," in *Canadian Foreign Policy and the Law of the Sea*, ed. Barbara Johnson and Mark W. Zacher (Vancouver: University of British Columbia Press, 1977), p. 241.

[5]Gilbert R. Winham, "Choice and Strategy in Continental Relations," in *Continental Community? Independence and Integration in North America*, ed. Andrew Axline et al. (Toronto: McClelland and Stewart, 1974), pp. 230-31; for similar findings in Canadian-American environmental interaction, see Kim Richard Nossal, "The Unmaking of Garrison: United States Politics and the Management of Canadian-American Boundary Waters," *Behind the Headlines*, 37 (December, 1978).

Trade and Commerce (IT&C), and the Department of External Affairs (DEA).[6] On international development assistance policy, Lyon has noted the incidence of "fierce interdepartmental conflict"; Sanger claims that at meetings of the Aid Board[7] and its subcommittees, representatives from IT&C and the Department of Finance "generally act as the heavy elder brother" against CIDA.[8] At a more general level, the empirical research of Byers, Leyton-Brown and Lyon has shown that policy makers have sharp differences of opinion depending on where they are situated within government.[9] Similarly, many historical analyses recognize the importance of disputes between, and within, departments.[10]

Despite indications in the literature that differences of opinion and divergent views and interests exist within the government, there is little explicit recognition that process has a continual and dominant impact on policy outcomes, and that decisions and actions cannot be accounted for without reference to how policy is made. For example, most analysis of Canadian foreign policy focuses on choices made by Cabinet as the source of foreign policy behaviour. To formal decisions of Cabinet are attributed motives which purport to explain either a particular policy or decision.[11] Thus, while the existence of conflict at the bureaucratic level

[6]Robert O. Matthews, "Canada and Anglophone Africa," in *Canada and the Third World*, ed. Peyton V. Lyon and Tareq Ismael (Toronto: Macmillan, 1976); Steven Langdon, "Canada's Role in Africa," in *Foremost Nation: Canadian Foreign Policy and a Changing World*, ed. Norman Hillmer and Garth Stevenson (Toronto: McClelland and Stewart, 1977).

[7]The Canadian International Development Board is the formal governing body of CIDA. Jorgensen notes that this panel of deputy ministers from affected departments chaired by the CIDA president is usually bypassed in the procedures for project and program approval. See Jan J. Jorgensen, "The Canadian Response to Third World Needs" (Paper presented to the Conference on Government, Society and the Public Purpose, Montreal, March 1979), p. 18.

[8]Lyon and Ismael, *Canada and the Third World*, p. xxxi; Sanger, "Canada and Development in the Third World," in Lyon and Ismael, p. 302.

[9]R.B. Byers and David Leyton-Brown, "Canadian Elite Images of the International System," and Peyton V. Lyon and David Leyton-Brown, "Image and Policy Preference: Canadian Elite Views on Relations with the United States," both in *International Journal*, 32 (1977); Leyton-Brown, Byers and Lyon, "Images of the Future: Consensus and Dissensus in the Canadian Foreign Policy Elite," in *Canada's Foreign Policy: Analysis and Trends*, ed. B. Tomlin (Toronto: Methuen, 1978); Lyon, Byers and Leyton-Brown, "How 'Official' Ottawa Views the Third World," *International Perspectives* (January-February). 1979.

[10]Don Munton and Don Page, "Planning in the East Block: The Post-Hostilities Problems Committees in Canada, 1943-1945," *International Journal*, 32 (1977); O. Mary Hill, *Canada's Salesman to the World: The Department of Trade and Commerce, 1892-1939* (Montreal: McGill-Queen's, 1977), pp. 337-43; James Eayrs, *In Defence of Canada*, vol. 3: Peacemaking and Deterrence (Toronto: University of Toronto Press, 1972), pp. 172-94.

[11]Most notable is the work of John W. Holmes: see, for example, his *The Better Part of Valour* (Toronto: McClelland and Stewart, 1970); *Canada: A Middle-Aged Power* (Toronto: McClelland and Stewart, 1976); *The Shaping of Peace: Canada and the Search for World Order, 1943-1957*, vol. 1 (Toronto: University of Toronto Press, 1979).

is recognized, Cabinet choice is seen as a factor mitigating the impact of such conflict on policy outcomes.[12]

One of the major problems is that partial use of the paradigm obscures the bureaucratic politics model's basic premise: that policy is the result of *interchange* between *players*. First, it is too often assumed that this interaction must be marked by conflict, and that only when conflict exists will there be outcomes shaped by bureaucratic politics, and the bargaining and "pulling and hauling" associated with the model. The basic premise of the model is that when any two players look at an issue, their views as to the "best" outcome, or how best to achieve goals, will differ. The magnitude of this difference may be great or small, and may or may not produce conflict. However, the bureaucratic politics approach is ultimately concerned with how the resolution of that difference affects the flow of policy. Thus, if the resolution of differences results in a compromise position being forwarded to, and ultimately endorsed by, Cabinet, that is as much an indication of an outcome shaped by bureaucratic politics as a full-blown battle between competing bureaucracies with deeply entrenched interests that requires mediation by the political leadership. Second, bureaucratic politics is not only concerned with bureaucrats.[13] Securing a minister's approval for a policy action; securing Cabinet agreement; or securing the implementation of a Cabinet directive are all outcomes of "politics." Ministers as well as bureaucrats are the focus of the bureaucratic politics approach, however inappropriate the nomenclature.

Thus it could be argued that a partial application of the paradigm— an application that seeks only indications of conflict in the policy process, or looks only at interchange between bureaucrats—ignores the essence of the paradigm; that bureaucratic politics *is* interchange in the policy process, and that the nature of that interchange (coercion/conflict/bargaining/compromise/persuasion/acquiescence/agreement) is of secondary, but by no means incidental, significance; and that interchange occurs at both the bureaucratic and ministerial levels.

The literature on Canadian public administration and Canadian public policy reflects this perspective. Even a brief glimpse would suggest a confirmation of the view that policy outcomes are determined not by rational choice of policy alternatives to which motives and intentions of a unitary actor ("Cabinet") can be attached, but by a process of bargaining and compromise at both the bureaucratic and ministerial levels. Campbell and Szablowski's examination of Canada's central agencies points to a

---

[12]Stairs, "Foreign Policy of Canada," p. 185.
[13]Allison termed it a "governmental (bureaucratic) politics" paradigm; the parenthetical term was adopted although the model is used to analyse the policy process at the political leadership level.

continuous tension between program department officials and central agents, and pointedly demonstrates that the constraining and coordinating power of central agencies can often reshape policy proposals emanating from program or line departments.[14] The perspectives provided by Hartle (a former deputy secretary to the Treasury Board) and Johnson (a former deputy minister of welfare) carry much the same message: that, as Hilsman would have it, "policy making is politics."[15] Both McInnes and Schultz have adopted the Allison model; both contend that outcomes of policy making at the intergovernmental level in Canada can usefully be examined by employing a bureaucratic politics approach.[16]

Of the many changes in the structure and process of policy making introduced by the Trudeau government in 1968, four would suggest that the Allison paradigm would be a useful tool to account for public policy in the 1970s. These four changes are:

- The central agencies of the government (the Prime Minister's Office [PMO], the Privy Council Office [PCO], the Treasury Board Secretariat and the Department of Finance[17]) acquired a more active and, by some accounts, a more powerful role in the policy process, reducing somewhat the impact of program departments.[18]

- More and more policy issues are discussed by a proliferation of standing or ad hoc interdepartmental committees.[19]

- At the ministerial level, the committees of Cabinet were restructured and a reform of procedure introduced to provide for a more rational

---

[14]Colin Campbell and G.J. Szablowski, *The Superbureaucrats: Structure and Behaviour in Central Agencies* (Toronto: Macmillan, 1979), p. 98: the quotation from a Treasury Board Secretariat official provides an indication.

[15]Roger Hilsman, "Policy Making is Politics," in *International Politics and Foreign Policy*, ed. James N. Rosenau (New York: Free Press, 1969); D.G. Hartle, *A Theory of the Budgetary Expenditure Process* (Toronto: Ontario Economic Council, 1976), pp. 67-91; A.W. Johnson, "Public Policy: Creativity and Bureaucracy," *Canadian Public Administration*, 21 (1978). A fictional, but instructive, perspective is offered in Hartle's "'The Draft Memorandum to Cabinet' Case Program" in *Canadian Public Administration* (1976), #104C.

[16]See McInnes, "Crisis Management," and Schultz, "Prime Ministerial Government" and *Federalism, Bureaucracy and Public Policy*.

[17]The most recent analysis of central agencies during the Trudeau period is Campbell and Szablowski, *Superbureaucrats*, esp. chap. 2.

[18]For one analysis, see D.G. Hartle, *The Expenditure Budget Process in the Government of Canada* (Toronto: Canadian Tax Foundation, 1978), chap. 1.

[19]Kirton, "Foreign Policy Decision-Making"; also W.M. Dobell, "Interdepartmental Management in External Affairs," *Canadian Public Administration* 21 (1978); A.S. McGill, "A Study of the Role of the Department of External Affairs in the Government of Canada," mimeo. (Ottawa: Department of External Affairs, 1976).

flow of policy, and greater ministerial involvement in policy development and decision making.[20]

- At the intersection of the bureaucratic and ministerial levels—the interaction of deputy ministers and ministers—the Trudeau government introduced the practice of having senior civil servants participate in Cabinet committee deliberations.[21]

These changes would indicate that many more governmental participants were engaged in more interchange over more diverse issues than in the previous three decades. Following from this, it is argued that six features of the policy-making system in Canada make the bureaucratic politics approach both useful and applicable in the Canadian context.

Functional overlap: In many policy fields the mandates of program departments overlap. There is sufficient evidence to show that players in the Canadian bureaucracy, as in any bureaucracy, have parochial perceptions, priorities and interests that tend to be fashioned by their position, and by the exigencies of organizational health. When officials of different departments intersect on an issue, so will their parochially determined preferences, leading to a jockeying for resources, status and influence. The practice of assigning a department (or a division within a department) the "lead"—the task of steering an issue through the bureaucracy—will not eliminate differing preferences, but will merely provide a forum for their resolution. The growing tendency in Ottawa to assign the formulation of policy to standing or ad hoc interdepartmental committees would confirm the applicability of the paradigm because the interchange of bureaucrats with divergent preferences has been institutionalized.[22]

The coordinative function: A premium is placed on coordination of policy in Ottawa, an outgrowth of the structural changes introduced by Trudeau in the first two years of his tenure as prime minister. But the outcomes of a policy process that is marked by both structure and conscious effort to coordinate are highly sensitive to bureaucratic politics. The very word suggests, in a policy context, the rearrangement of some priorities to achieve harmony with others. Similarly, trade-offs are an integral part of coordination. Whose priorities are being rearranged, who is doing the rearranging, what trade-offs are to be made and by whom are important questions which the bureaucratic politics approach attempts to address.

---

[20]Laurent Dobuzinskis, "Rational Policy-Making: Policy, Politics and Political Science," in *Apex of Power*, ed. Hockin.

[21]Campbell and Szablowski, *Superbureaucrats*, p. 157.

[22]The penchant for interdepartmental coordination as a tool for achieving foreign policy goals is evident in Franklyn Griffiths' imaginative *A Northern Foreign Policy* (Wellesley Papers 7, 1979), pp. 77-80.

For two or more sets of players of roughly equal status and influence, coordination can become synonymous with compromise over the long haul: like players in a prisoner's dilemma game played many times over, players of roughly equal power in the policy game will tend to opt for the minimax or satisficing position.[23] There is, as Halperin suggests, an implicit recognition that overt conflict can prove counter-productive.[24] For sets of players of unequal status or influence, coordination can often mean the rearranging of the priorities of the weaker to fit those of the stronger. In the long run, this may result in a continuous application of the "rule of anticipated reaction": the conscious suppression of policy preferences by weaker players in the expectation that a fight, if fought, will be lost.

Thus it is suggested that the strong coordinative tendencies structured into the policy process do not eliminate the play of the bureaucratic politics paradigm, but rather, as Stairs has suggested, mute the struggle. Coordination also changes the face of policy outcomes: it is unlikely that policy decisions that have been through the coordinative mill will reflect the kind of "victories"[25] attainable in Washington, but compromise—a satisficing position in which no one set of players wins (or loses) absolutely.

The power of central agents: The Canadian policy-making system is marked by strong central agencies which dominate access to the political leadership and also to the public purse. Their power and influence vis-à-vis program departments is a matter of some contention. Schultz, for example, cautions against "exaggerated claims" about the power of central agents.[26] The findings of the Lambert Commission demonstrate that deputy ministers do not attribute considerable influence over policy to central agents.[27] Campbell and Szablowski, on the other hand, characterize central agents as superbureaucrats to underscore their super-ordinate position in the policy hierarchy, and the authors back their contentions with impressive interview data. They argue that positional authority and superior status enable central agents to monitor and control expenditures, determine personnel levels for program departments, evaluate and coordinate program and policy proposals. Central

---

[23]See Herbert A. Simon, "A Behavioural Model of Rational Choice," in Simon, *Models of Man* (London: John Wiley, 1957), esp. pp. 250-52; Thomas C. Schelling, *Micromotives and Macrobehaviour* (New York: W.W. Norton, 1978), pp. 216-18, for a description of prisoner's dilemma.

[24]Halperin, *Bureaucratic Politics*, p. 110.

[25]Allison, *Essence of Decision*, p. 173.

[26]Schultz, "Prime Ministerial Government," p. 234.

[27]Canada, Royal Commission on Financial Management and Accountability, *Final Report* (Ottawa: Supply and Services, 1979), pp. 486-87.

agencies are also in a strong position to mediate or arbitrate disputes between program departments.

It could be argued, from Campbell and Szablowski's analysis at least, that outcomes of interaction between central agents and program department officials, and indeed between central agents themselves, will be marked by compromise that is the result of persuasion, negotiation or mediation. While clearly interaction at the bureaucratic level involving central agents is not a zero-sum game, central agents are likelier to register more wins than losses if only because of the poor bargaining position of program departments. Their dependence on central agents for their organizational health is one important factor; their lack of retaliatory resources is another.[28] This relatively asymmetrical power balance at the bureaucratic level would suggest that particularly on issues involving central agents, the bureaucratic politics approach would be useful to account for outcomes.

Cohesiveness of the senior civil service: It has been noted that the senior echelons of the civil service in Canada are officials with "some cohesiveness as a group and an orientation to intellectual values. . . ."[29] There are three reasons for this cohesiveness beside the similarity in socioeconomic backgrounds cited by Porter. The first is that the nature of Cabinet government precludes organizational independence. Collective responsibility for policy requires that a certain centrality of control be maintained: the constraints on autonomy at the senior bureaucratic level are therefore necessarily considerable. Second, size has an impact on the development of cohesiveness. Whereas in the United States there are over six thousand "supergrade" (that is, senior bureaucratic) positions, in Canada the total number of senior appointments (central agents and program department officials at or above the rank of assistant deputy minister) is about three hundred. The third is the degree to which the bureaucratic structure is staffed by career civil servants. In 1975/76, of the 6251 positions in the senior echelons of the United States federal bureaucracy, 2023 were filled by presidential appointments and non-career executive assignments (NEA's); the remaining 4228 were staffed by careerists.[30] In Canada, the federal bureaucracy (with the exception of the PMO) is staffed exclusively by civil servants.

The cohesiveness of the senior bureaucracy will have an important

---

[28]See, however, Schultz, "Prime Ministerial Government," pp. 232-33, who argues the program departments have not inconsiderable resources available to them in their relations with central agents.

[29]John Porter, *The Vertical Mosaic: An Analysis of Social Class and Power in Canada* (Toronto: University of Toronto Press, 1965), p. 448.

[30]Hugh Heclo, *A Government of Strangers: Executive Politics in Washington* (Washington: Brookings Institution, 1977), p. 38.

impact on the tone and outcome of bureaucratic politics. While senior officials will try to secure acceptance of their policy preferences, will try to enhance organizational interests, and will try to exercise personal influence, it is unlikely that one will see the kind of overt conflict evident in Washington. Similarly, cohesiveness has an impact on outcomes: compromise is more willingly sought as an acceptable solution to inter-departmental conflict.

The nexus of decision: During the Trudeau years, the nexus of formal decision making shifted from plenary Cabinet to committees of Cabinet, largely as a result of the 1968 Cabinet reforms. Unlike practice in Britain, senior officials in Canada participated in Cabinet committee meetings during this period, and this, as Campbell and Szablowski forcefully show,[31] can have an impact on policy outcomes. The participation of senior officials at this level means that there was institutionalized inter-change between ministers and mandarins. There is little doubt that it was never interchange between equals: both ministers and their bureaucratic deputies recognize the hierarchy implicit in their respective positions. But it is likely that mandarins brought into Cabinet committees parochial perceptions and priorities which could be brought to bear (albeit subtly) on deliberations at this level.[32]

Cabinet: Collective leadership collectively responsible to Parliament does not eliminate the play of bureaucratic politics, but only masks it from public view. The collectivity should be regarded not as a unitary actor, but as thirty men and women who bring into the Cabinet Room their own parochial perceptions and priorities, shaped by their portfolios, the demands of their electoral and regional constituencies, the imperatives of their relations with their department officials, and their own ambitions within Cabinet. Nor are the thirty members equal in influence or posi-tional authority: there will be a hierarchy of influence and effectiveness, with the prime minister usually at the apex. The effectiveness of each minister will be determined by his portfolio, his closeness to the prime minister and his relations with his colleagues. Unless a minister is able to convince his confrères to allow him latitude over an issue area, even though they may not be convinced of a proposal or its consequences, it is likely that outcomes of cabinet deliberations will be marked by the "pulling and hauling" associated with Allison's paradigm.

From these six features of the Canadian policy-making system can be

---

[31]Campbell and Szablowski, *Superbureaucrats*, pp. 156-57, provide an account of a senior official's performance in Cabinet committee.
[32]Cf. McInnes, "Crisis Management," p. 9, who argued that bureaucratic politics between Cabinet and the bureaucracy will be unlikely because "Cabinet is clearly in a commanding, and agencies in an obeying position."

drawn five generalizations about the applicability of the bureaucratic politics approach in Canada in particular and parliamentary systems in general:

—The more jurisdictions (departmental or intergovernmental) overlap, the more likely will outcomes (decisions and actions) be the result of bargaining and compromise among players.

—The greater the effort to coordinate (at the bureaucratic level, by central agencies, at the intergovernmental level, or by cabinet or its committees) the more will outcomes reflect compromise and a melding of divergent interests.

—The greater the power, influence or authority of central agencies, the more will outcomes be the result of bargaining, arbitration or mediation, often at the expense of the program departments.

—The more cohesive the upper level of the bureaucratic structure, the more likely will compromise be actively pursued by actors at that level.

—Outcomes of deliberations in plenary cabinet or its committees will not be the result of collective choice rationally arrived at, but will be a "resultant" determined by the effectiveness of ministers in attempting to secure acceptance and approval of their preferences.

However, those features of the parliamentary system in Canada which make the model useful also change the basic characteristics of the game. Solidarity in Cabinet, strong political control of the bureaucracy, powerful central agencies with coordinative and integrative functions, cohesiveness of the senior bureaucracy, and a highly institutionalized system of interdepartmental consultation on policy issues which overlap jurisdictions would suggest that the dominant characteristic of the game is, as Hartle has claimed, friendly competition,[33] and not conflict—despite indications of conflict in the policy process in Ottawa. Similarly, the dominant outcome of the game in parliamentary systems will tend to be compromise between differing and contending preferences of the players in the system, at both the ministerial and bureaucratic levels.

---

[33]Hartle, *A Theory*, pp. 67-85, esp. p. 73.

26/Pressure Groups and the
Canadian Bureaucracy
J.E. Anderson

"When I see members of Parliament being lobbied, it's a sure sign to me that the lobby lost its fight in the civil service and the Cabinet." "It's the deputy minister, not ministers, who are courted by most lobbyists, which suggests where the real power in Ottawa lies." "The actual rate of fiscal protection (tariffs) has become, in effect, a matter of departmental rather than parliamentary politics. . . . Thus, emphasis has tended to shift to influencing the policies and activities of government boards, commissions and departmental officials. . . ."

These views of pressure group activity in Canada span a period of more than thirty years and carry the authority of an Ottawa lobbyist, a journalist for one of Canada's leading newspapers and a distinguished Canadian sociologist.[1] The significance of interaction between civil servants and pressure groups is widely, although many times only implicitly, recognized in studies of Canadian pressure groups. With very few notable exceptions, these studies allude almost incidentally to civil service-pressure group relations through description of the organization or general activities of pressure groups.[2] The topic of this essay, then, like many other subjects touching Canadian public administration, remains in that rough and preliminary stage of study that requires reliance on scattered references in scholarly writings, the rare statements of various actors in the political process and informed speculation based on the literature of comparative politics.

More detailed study has been difficult and rare, simply because the activities of pressure groups and civil servants occur so close to the core of government and politics. Much information is kept secret or is unavailable because consultation between civil servants and pressure group officials is often informal rather than formal or institutionalized. Moreover, the interaction process may be very complex. Any one civil servant or pressure group official moves in a web of relationships

---

[1]Respectively, an anonymous lobbyist cited in F.C. Englemann and M.A. Schwartz, *Political Parties and the Canadian Social Structure* (Scarborough: Prentice-Hall, 1967), p. 105; Hugh Winsor, "A Primer for Innocents on the Art of Lobbying," *The Globe Magazine*, Toronto, February 27, 1971, p. 7; and S.D. Clarke, "The Canadian Manufacturers' Association: A Political Pressure Group," *The Canadian Journal of Economics and Political Science* 4 (1938): 251.
[2]Most of the published literature on Canadian pressure groups is identified in the bibliographies in F.C. Englemann and M.A. Schwartz, *op. cit.*, and W.D.K. Kernaghan, *Bureaucracy in Canadian Government* (Toronto: Methuen, 1973).

between people, parties, pressure groups, political leaders and civil servants. The individual is probably aware to some extent of these inter-relationships and acts in part at least in anticipation of the reaction of others; in part, too, he may have very private and even idiosyncratic motives. We may assume, however, that the extent, variety and content of the interaction between administrators and pressure groups depend largely on the government leaders' perception of the proper role of civil servants. The range of civil service activities considered appropriate may include the initiation and evaluation of policy proposals, the administration and adaptation of existing policies, advice on the likely public acceptability of policies, the explanation or defence of policies before the public, and the education of public opinion for the acceptance of new policies. Civil servants may in turn consult with pressure group representatives on one or all of these aspects of the policy process.

The increasingly complex and demanding nature of modern society has obliged governments to utilize available sources of special knowledge and experience outside the public service. This need for expertise explains the development of bureaucratically organized pressure groups which accompanied the growth of public bureaucracies in this century. It also predetermined the close relations now existing between civil servants and informed pressure groups. The importance which civil servants attach to the expertise of certain pressure groups depends of course on the extent to which they must take account of alternative political resources possessed by other pressure groups, for example, votes and money. The care and frequency with which civil servants must make such calculations rests largely on political and constitutional factors. Civil servants become more politicized in a governmental system in which they have more than one constitutionally determined political master and in which political leaders compete for bureaucratic support. In these circumstances, civil servants tend to seek the independent political support of pressure groups, legislators and political executives. This situation creates a favourable milieu for the operations of organized special interest groups. Governments which are experiencing or have experienced this politicization of civil servants include the United States, because of its separation of governmental powers, and contemporary Italy, Third and Fourth Republic France and Weimar Germany because of their combination of powerful, stable legislative committees and unstable executives.

By way of contrast, under a Cabinet system with a reliable legislative majority, and particularly in the case of one-party dominance, the civil servants best promote their own interests by serving and defending their ministers and the government. Nevertheless, to a lesser extent than in the United States and the European regimes noted above, civil servants will calculate the effect on voting behaviour of widely beneficial social and economic policies on the one hand and the impact of campaign contributions from disadvantaged interest groups on the other. These considerations constitute at least part of what is meant by "political" advice to the government. It is difficult to appraise the political costs and benefits of pursuing widely beneficial policies, since governments can fail by cumulatively disaffecting small minorities. A Canadian Cabinet minister, perhaps conscious of the difficulty of assessing the relative effects of choosing between general and particular interests, and perhaps hoping to escape the dilemma, has suggested to pressure groups that "the strategy area where the interests of the politician, or bureaucrat, and the lobbyist effectively overlap is that which concerns itself with the sensitivity to the common good."[3] In Canada, it appears probable that the long dominance of the Liberal party and its peculiar independence of specific economic interests because of the reliability of its support from Quebec has encouraged civil servants to emphasize "the public interest." They have, therefore, recommended generally beneficial policies even when these policies affect specific pressure groups adversely. These conditions also suggest that in Canada the relations between civil servants and pressure groups are usually dominated by civil servants.

Recognition of Pressure Groups

Allen Potter defines recognition as a prescriptive right to receive "a response which is more than an acknowledgement," one which is an agreement, an argument or a request for additional information. He notes also that "governmental [and other] requests for information from an organized group are a measure of its standing."[4] Where a pressure group already exists, recognition is manifested by the extensiveness of civil service replies or the frequency of their requests for information. In reference to the Canadian Better Business Bureaus' attempt to assume a leading role in consumer education, the bureaus' president recognized that first

> the bureaus must achieve rapport with the government agencies working in the area of consumer protection and, more particularly, with the Consumer Affairs Department. . . . Recently, however, it [Consumer Affairs] has asked the BBB to distribute a circular dealing with misleading ads for hearing aids and department officials have been requesting information from the bureaus increasingly often ("I don't know if Mr. Basford knows how often") and it is possible that, as Mr.

---

[3]Honourable Donald S. Macdonald, "Notes for Remarks to the Twenty-Third Session of the Canadian Institute for Organization Management," President of the Privy Council Press Release, June 19, 1969.
[4]Allen Potter, *Organized Groups in British National Politics* (London: Faber and Faber, 1961), pp. 203, 190.

Dollard says, they will "come to depend on each other for exchange of information."[5]

It appears that civil servants grant recognition to interest groups primarily because these groups possess valuable knowledge and experience. One of the consequences of this emphasis on expertise is that civil servants will interact most frequently with those interests which must themselves be most diligent in producing and acquiring information in the ordinary pursuit of their own affairs, that is, with management more than with labour, with trading companies more than with farmers or consumers, and with self-governing doctors more than with salaried teachers. This bias in favour of relations with particular kinds of pressure groups may be corrected by the recognition of less expert groups. The purpose of this recognition may be a self-conscious pursuit of the public interest, an acknowledgment of the voting power of these groups or simply the creation of an illusion of countervailing powers. Whatever the purpose for their recognition, however, these less expert groups tend to remain of low status, to be prestige conscious and to be fearful of manipulation by government and civil servants. The recognition of pressure groups, then, is based most securely on expertise and the communication of this expertise to civil servants.

In granting recognition to a pressure group, public officials support it politically or, in some cases, maintain its sheer viability. Using a rational self-interest theory analogous to that of economics, Mancur Olsen has explained why many vocational and other economically concerned pressure groups need direct government aid or governmentally determined status to ensure membership loyalty and thus survival.[6] This is one aspect of pressure group politics which has been relatively well studied in Canada. Accounts of the Canadian Federation of Agriculture and the Canadian Labour Congress emphasize the importance these groups attach to their annual presentation to Cabinet and to other formal relations with the government. It is probable that these presentations are most directly related to the need for status.[7] The Consumers' Association

---

[5]Glenn Somerville, "Better Business Bureaus' president questions government techniques in handling consumer complaints," *The Globe and Mail*, Toronto, October 13, 1970, p. B3. (The article is from the *Globe's* "Man in the News" series, a particularly good newspaper source of current material on pressure group activities.)

[6]Mancur Olsen, *The Logic of Collective Action* (Cambridge, Mass.: Harvard University Press, 1965), esp. chaps. 1 and 2. See also Ronald Manzer "Selective Inducements and the Development of Pressure Groups: the Case of Canadian Teacher Associations," *Canadian Journal of Political Science* 2 (1969): 103-117.

[7]See Helen Jones Dawson, "Relations between Farm Organizations and the Civil Service in Canada and Great Britain," *Canadian Public Administration* 10 (1967): 565-573; David Kwavnick, "Pressure Group Demands and the Struggle for Organizational Status: The Case of Organized Labour in Canada," *Canadian Journal of Political Science* 3 (1970): 56-72. For recognition of the same phenomenon in the United States see David Truman, *The Governmental Process* (New York: Alfred A. Knopf, 1951), esp. pp. 459-60.

of Canada actually needs a direct governmental financial subsidy to survive.[8] These are examples of the *government's* decision to grant essential political support to pressure groups.

Much of this kind of political support, however, is channelled through *civil servants* who may go so far as to encourage the formation of pressure groups from unorganized but potentially useful interests. Long before the dramatic confrontation with a Cabinet minister which led to the Canadian Federation of Agriculture's regular annual presentation, a civil servant appears to have been helpful in establishing the organization. H.H. Hannam, its first president, has related how the late Clifford Clark, then deputy minister of finance, informally suggested the establishment of a national farm organization and how Hannam used Clark's prestige to enlist support for the organization of the federation.[9] The viability of the Canadian Manufacturers' Association in its early days was very much aided by the decision of the Department of Railways and Canals to solicit the association's views on rail rate changes.[10] Doubtless, many more instances of such bureaucratic initiative are unrecorded and civil servants rather than politicians made the supportive decision. Indeed, it may be inevitable that the public administrator be the agent most involved in the government's political support of pressure groups since that support is in large part just the obverse of the consultative, administrative relationship.

The importance of a pressure group's status with government also enables civil servants to exert counterpressure on a group. By looking elsewhere for information or for administrative assistance, civil servants can threaten pressure group officials and so achieve more compliance than the groups may otherwise be inclined to grant. Moreover, by means of a cool response or a disinclination to communicate with a particular group representative, civil servants may sow discontent and discord among the group's leadership or even encourage part of the leadership to act as a more compliant influence within the group. If a group resists such pressure, civil servants may try to dilute its public influence. The Canadian Drug Manufacturers' Association was organized upon the suggestion of a civil servant and acted as a rival to the long-established Pharmaceutical Manufacturers Association of Canada.[11]

---

[8]Helen Jones Dawson, "Consumers' Association of Canada," *Canadian Public Administration* 2 (1969): 103-117.

[9]H.H. Hannam, "The Interest Group and Its Activities," Institute of Public Administration of Canada, *Proceedings of the Fifth Annual Conference*, 1953, pp. 172-173.

[10]S.D. Clarke, *The Canadian Manufacturers' Association* (Toronto: University of Toronto, 1939), pp. 48-49.

[11]An interview conducted by the author.

Policy Making

Pressure groups gain recognition more easily and more rapidly if they are frequently invited to provide expertise to civil servants. The provision of this special knowledge also gives pressure groups an opportunity to participate in policy formulation. By supplying information used in the creation of policy, a pressure group contributes to policy making in a "passive" sense. The government may ask a pressure group for comments on the potential effects of a proposed policy in such areas as future investment, employment, costs and prices. The government may also make a general request for suggestions as to how it might assist a group to contribute to economic development or the general welfare. Evidence that government invites groups to participate in policy making as a matter of course and that the main arena of such participation is civil service pressure group interaction is provided by this statement of a Canadian Cabinet minister:

> In the process of preparing legislation and also in considering general policy changes, the government requires as much information as possible about the areas to be affected and the possible implications of any proposed changes. In addition to all the other reasons why associations or organizations should be in continuous contact with government, this particular need for information and consultation to influence government policy is probably the most important. . . .
>
> What is of the greatest value is for the minister to be apprised of the impact of the legislation from the particular viewpoint of the group concerned. Legislation must of necessity speak generally, but there may be special cases which persons in a particular industry or group might recognize more easily than can someone in government, surveying industry or the community generally.
>
> Equally, it is of greater value to have positive alternative suggestions with respect to carrying out the general purpose of the statute rather than negative dissent only. . . .
>
> . . . . if there has not been . . . general public discussion preceding legislation, it is important that the particular interest be brought to the attention of departmental officials so that it may be taken into account in policy formulation and it will be useful for the minister also to have these viewpoints so that he may raise them with officials.[12]

The minister's comments relate to policy advice on legislation. Pressure groups are also asked for advice on policy making which occurs in the drafting and amendment of regulations. Frequent illustrations of this type of policy making may be gleaned from the pages of a daily newspaper. For example, it was recently reported that:

---

[12]The Honourable Donald S. Macdonald, *loc. cit.*

> Mr. Ross [president of the Independent Petroleum Association of Canada] expects the federal government will invite industry inspection of new regulations and tax changes, as promised, before making its new policies public and binding.[13]

The participation of the Canadian Medical Association and the Canadian Federation of Agriculture in policy making at various levels has already been recounted.[14]

The relationships between the Pharmaceutical Manufacturers Association of Canada (PMAC) and the Food and Drug Directorate (FDD) of the Department of National Health and Welfare are typical of the relationships between interest groups and civil servants. In an address to the 5th Annual General Meeting of the PMAC in 1964, Judy LaMarsh, then minister of national health and welfare, stated that:

> Dr. Morrell (director, Food and Drug Directorate), who is well known to all of you, would I am sure be the first to acknowledge that while he has in his Directorate able and qualified scientists, his task would be immeasurably more difficult if he did not have access to the combined knowledge of the industry and receive its support. . . .
> The role of a responsible trade association, in my view, is the advice and assistance it can offer to government in carrying out its responsibility to the Canadian people. . . . In Canada, in the many associations with which we deal, we have learned to look to them, not only for the benefit of experience and knowledge, but also for support in carrying out the task for government. Your Association is no exception to this and we have received from you in the past valuable help and assistance in the development and administration of our drug regulations which are so essential.
> Many of you will recall that in the formulation of our present Act, committees of your Association met with officers of the Department and worked out matters which are now reflected in the provisions of the law itself. . . . [The minister went on to discuss three different sets of regulations, the problems involved in them, and the views of the government and of the PMAC]. I appreciate that these regulations do not go as far as some of the members of the Association would have wished. . . .
> . . . having paid deserved tribute to your Association . . ., I am sure that Dr. Morrell does not think for a moment that his problems will automatically disappear and life in his Directorate will henceforth be Utopian . . . it is in the recognition that there may be different points of

---

[13]Thomas Kennedy, "IPAC president praises know-how, Arctic effort, despite handicaps," *The Globe and Mail*, Toronto, March 25, 1971, p. B12.

[14]Malcolm Taylor, "The Role of the Medical Profession in the Formulation and Execution of Public Policy," *The Canadian Journal of Economics and Political Science* 26 (1960): 108-127, and Helen Jones Dawson, "Relations between Farm Organizations and the Civil Service in Canada and Great Britain," *op. cit.*

view and a willingness to reconcile those differences in the public
interest that the success of peaceful coexistence in this area lies. . . .
. . . I think it is well acknowledged that any aspect of our control which is
unnecessary or unreasonable would be open to review. . . . I mention
this as an indication of the willingness of government to take account
of the views of a trade association and, to the extent that public interest
makes it possible, to reflect those views in its administration.[15]

The minister's speech clearly indicates that civil servants and
pressure group officials are "well known" to each other, that the PMAC
influences policy making at various levels of the policy process and that
formal arrangements for participation have been established. It is
important to note that the government retains the right to invite or to
refuse to engage in policy consultations with pressure groups. When the
FDD was changing regulations on the distribution of drug samples to
physicians, it did not seek advice or give forewarning since it expected
great difficulty in reaching agreement with the industry. When the FDD
does want advice on a regulation, it simply publishes an intention of
amendment or a proposed amendment in the Trade Information Letter
which it regularly circulates to the pharmaceutical companies and the
PMAC. The PMAC reaches a decision based on consultation with the
companies in the industry and conveys that decision to the FDD. If, for
scientific, administrative or economic reasons, the PMAC deems an
amendment unworkable, it requests a meeting with the FDD to present
its case. Depending on the nature of the problem, if agreement cannot be
reached, the FDD will either proceed without agreement or yield to the
industry's argument. Decisions to yield, however, may be accompanied
by a clear warning that there will be additional work on the problem and
further attempts to reach a solution satisfactory to the FDD. Most communication occurs in such irregular meetings or in ad hoc study
committees.

Conflicts between government and pressure groups may range from
major disputes over general policy to disagreements over the day-to-day
administration of a regulation. If the conflict centres on a detail of a
regulation or on some other minor point that can be settled in private, the
administrator must carry the major part of the burden of argument,
persuasion and cajolery. When a conflict arises over general policy,
however, the political role of the administrator again comes into play.

If the decline of civil service anonymity—inferred above by Miss
LaMarsh—continues, civil servants will in the future carry a larger part
of the political defence of government policy. Civil servants are already
expected to be helpful to members of the public and to provide information as a matter of course or on request to news reporters, pressure

---

[15]Text of address. Permission to quote given by Miss LaMarsh.

group officials and members of Parliament. The decline of civil service anonymity, accentuated by the smallness and intimacy of the political community in Ottawa, will expose the civil servant to a growing number of such requests. He must constantly make judgments on the propriety of a response since the guidelines setting limitations on his discretion are so general. In supplying this information, the civil servant acts as a de facto source of political support for the government. This activity may be characterized as a "passive" political role because it occurs only in response to specific requests.

Civil servants play a more "active" and deliberately political role when they are allowed or even required by their ministers to act as publicists or propagandists to prepare public opinion for a policy change. Under these conditions, civil servants must take the initiative in providing information, especially the "right" information, to the public. This task can be accomplished primarily through civil service testimony in open hearings of royal commissions, government task forces and parliamentary committees. It may also be necessary, however, to take some initiatives to achieve the desired interpretation of this material even by those who are predisposed to support the government. To perform this information service effectively, civil servants are obliged to adopt techniques commonly used by professional public relations agencies. For example, in the case of drug prices, the likely policy was opposed by an established, competent pressure group before the government publicly and fully committed itself to a proposal.[16] Civil servants and pressure group officials then acted as the major protagonists and used similar methods to win public support. While the drug prices problem was being investigated by a special committee of the House of Commons, both civil servants and PMAC officials sought out members of Parliament to provide them with selected information and refutations of their opponents' arguments. Moreover, both civil servants and pressure group officials gave special briefings to selected journalists who then assisted by presenting one side of the argument and criticizing the other. This was an especially important technique not only because of the readership enjoyed by reporters who wrote the original stories, but also because of the tendency of the press to reuse information and interpretations ad infinitum. In addition, both civil servants and PMAC officials sought out potential allies, encouraged them to testify before a Commons' Special Committee and provided them with the necessary information and arguments for their briefs. Indeed, it is likely that of those persons and groups

---

[16]The following account is based on a variety of documentary sources and on interviews conducted by the author with reporters, members of Parliament, civil servants in several departments and officials of several pressure groups. Each assertion here could be supported by a number of independent sources.

not directly representing the pharmaceutical industry, only a very few who testified did so on their own initiative. It is only an example of rare candour that the Canadian Medical Association referred in its brief to information provided by the PMAC.[17]

Such "cooperative lobbying" is well recognized among students of pressure groups.[18] What is more instructive to note is that the civil servants also constructed an effective cooperative lobby to testify before the Special Committee. The lengthy brief presented on behalf of the Province of Alberta was prepared after an especially thorough and extensive briefing of its author by civil servants. The Canadian Drug Manufacturers' Association, the creation of which had been suggested by a civil servant, did not give as effective testimony as some civil servants had anticipated. The Consumers' Association of Canada brief presented two quite separate arguments. The first, on drug safety, differed from the civil servants' assumptions, while the second, on drug prices, was largely similar to that of the civil servants. This second argument was added to the association's brief only after civil servants had examined the proposed brief and, through informal channels, had contacted one of the vice-presidents of the association to show him the arguments upon which civil servants had based their decisions. The attempts of civil servants to build a larger cooperative lobby with the aid of the Canadian Labour Congress and the Canadian Federation of Agriculture may be inferred from their frequently expressed regrets that these groups did not choose to present briefs on drug prices.

This discussion of the recognition of pressure groups and their interaction with civil servants in the policy process describes only part of the whole relationship. One important area, not explored at length here, is the delegation of administrative responsibilities by bureaucrats to pressure group organizations. When a group establishes standards for membership or rules for the self-regulation of its trade or profession, when it answers questions from its membership about the applicability of the law to a particular case, or when it publishes explanations of government policy in its trade or professional journal, it is performing a task that otherwise might be required of civil servants.[19] Yet another significant aspect of the bureaucracy group system is the etiquette or "rules of the game" accepted by both parties. These "rules of the game" include agreement on when confidential materials may be exchanged and

---

[17]House of Commons, *Special Committee on Drug Costs and Prices, Minutes of Proceedings and Evidence*, no. 6, June 28, 1966, p. 413.
[18]Donald R. Hall, *Cooperative Lobbying—the Power of Pressure* (Tucson: University of Arizona Press, 1969); and Malcolm Taylor, *op. cit.*, p. 118.
[19]The delegation of administration to a pressure group is described in more detail in Malcolm Taylor, *op. cit.*

under what conditions the parties may agree to disagree. In every discussion of such rules of the game the emphasis is on privacy and confidentiality—in short, on secrecy.[20] While such secrecy is convenient to the pressure groups, the civil servants and the government, it is probably the government which most demands and enforces it. Civil servants may lose their anonymity but the government insists on retaining its secrets.[21] As suggested earlier, the interaction of civil servants and pressure groups occurs in a context of other relationships; not least among these is the relationship between the government and its civil servants. It is that relationship which probably most effectively governs the interaction of the public and group bureaucracies.

Case References
Canadian Cases in Public Administration
>   Public Interest or Collective Interest?
>   The Kroeker Case
>   A Sensitive Position
>   The Foot and Mouth Disease Epidemic, 1952

Bibliography

Altshuler, Alan A., ed. *The Politics of the Federal Bureaucracy.* 2d ed. New York: Harper & Row, 1977.

Appleby, Paul H. *Policy and Administration.* University, Ala.: University of Alabama Press, 1949.

Aucoin, Peter. "Pressure Groups and Recent Changes in the Policy-Making Process." In *Pressure Group Behaviour in Canadian Politics,* edited by A. Paul Pross. Toronto: McGraw-Hill Ryerson, 1975.

Aucoin, Peter. "Public Policy Theory and Analysis." In *Public Policy in Canada,* edited by G. Bruce Doern and Peter Aucoin, pp. 1-26. Toronto: Macmillan, 1979.

Balls, Herbert R. "Decision-Making: the Role of the Deputy Minister." *Canadian Public Administration* 19, no. 3 (Fall 1976): 417-31.

Bellamy, David J. "Policy-Making in the 1970's." *Canadian Public Administration* 15, no. 3 (Fall 1972): 490-95.

Bryden, Kenneth. *Old Age Pensions and Policy Making in Canada.* Montreal: McGill-Queen's University Press, 1974.

Cameron, David R. "Power and Responsibility in the Public Service: Summary of Discussions." *Canadian Public Administration* 21, no. 3 (Fall 1978): 358-72.

---

[20]F.C. Englemann and M.A. Schwartz, *op. cit.,* pp. 103-104. See also Allen Potter, *op. cit.,* pp. 230-236 and the complaint against secrecy in S.E. Finer, *Anonymous Empire,* 2nd ed. (London: Pall Mall Press, 1966), pp. 136-145.

[21]For example, after describing her unhappiness about the tactics of the insurance industry lobby against the Canada Pension Plan, Miss LaMarsh suggested to Cabinet that she "would hereafter hear all representations but only when the press was present. Pearson and all my colleagues were appalled." Judy LaMarsh, *Memoirs of a Bird in a Gilded Cage* (Toronto: McClelland and Stewart, 1969), p. 88.

D'Aquino, Thomas. "The Prime Minister's Office: Catalyst or Cabal?" *Canadian Public Administration* 17, no. 1 (Spring 1974): 55-79.

Dawson, Helen Jones. "Consumers Association of Canada." *Canadian Public Administration* 6, no. 1 (March 1963): 92-118.

Dawson, Helen Jones. "Interest Group: The Canadian Federation of Agriculture." *Canadian Public Administration* 3, no. 2 (June 1960): 134-49.

Dawson, Helen Jones. "National Pressure Groups and the Federal Government." In *Pressure Group Behaviour in Canadian Politics*, edited by A. Paul Pross.

Dawson, Helen Jones. "Relations between Farm Organizations and the Civil Service in Canada and Great Britain." *Canadian Public Administration* 10, no. 4 (December 1967): 450-70.

Doern, G. Bruce. "Recent Changes in the Philosophy of Policy-Making in Canada." *Canadian Journal of Political Science* 4, no. 2 (June 1971): 243-64.

Doern, G. Bruce. "The Development of Policy Organizations in the Executive Arena." In *Structures of Policy-Making in Canada*, edited by G. Bruce Doern and Peter Aucoin, pp. 29-78. Toronto: Macmillan, 1971.

Dror, Yehezkel. "Muddling Through—Science or Inertia." *Public Administration Review* 24 (September 1964): 154-57.

Dror, Yehezkel. *Public Policy-Making Re-Examined*. San Francisco: Chandler Publishing Company, 1969.

Dvorin, Eugene P., and Simmons, Robert H. *From Amoral to Humane Bureaucracy*. San Francisco: Canfield Press, 1972.

Dye, Thomas R. *Understanding Public Policy*. 2d ed. Englewood Cliffs, N.J.: Prentice-Hall, 1975.

Etzioni, Amitai. "Mixed Scanning: A Third Approach to Decision-Making." *Public Administration Review* 27, no. 4 (December 1967): 385-92.

Forget, Claude E. "L'administration publique: sujet ou objet du pouvoir politique." *Canadian Public Administration* 21, no. 2 (Summer 1978): 234-42.

French, Richard D. *How Ottawa Decides*. Toronto: James Lorimer, 1980.

French, Richard D. "The Privy Council Office: Support for Cabinet Decision Making." In *The Canadian Political Process*, 3rd ed.; edited by Richard Schultz et al., pp. 363-94. Toronto: Holt, Rinehart and Winston, 1979.

Gélinas, André. *Les parlementaires et l'administration au Québec*. Québec: Les Presses de l'Université Laval, 1969.

Hartle, Douglas. *Public Policy Decision Making and Regulation*. Montreal: Institute for Research on Public Policy, 1979.

Hawkins, Freda. *Canada and Immigration: Public Policy and Public Concern*. Montreal: McGill-Queen's University Press, 1972.

Hodgetts, J.E. "The Civil Service and Policy Formation." *Canadian Journal of Economics and Political Science* 23, no. 4 (November 1957): 467-79.

Hodgson, J.S. "The Impact of Minority Government on the Senior Civil Servant." *Canadian Public Administration* 19, no. 2 (Summer 1976): 227-37.

Hoffman, David. "Liaison Officers and Ombudsmen: Canadian MP's and their Relations with the Federal Bureaucracy and Executive." In *Apex of Power*, edited by Thomas A. Hockin, pp. 146-62. Toronto: Prentice-Hall, 1971.

Hughes, S.H.S. "The Public Official—Parliament, Public and the Press." *Canadian Public Administration* 3, no. 4 (December 1960): 289-98.

Jenkins, W.I. *Policy Analysis: A Political and Organizational Perspective*. London: Martin Robertson, 1978.

Johnson, A.W. "Management Theory and Cabinet Government." *Canadian Public Administration* 14, no. 1 (Spring 1971): 73-81.

Johnson, A.W. "Public Policy: Creativity and Bureaucracy." *Canadian Public Administration* 21, no. 1 (Spring 1978): 1-15.

Kernaghan, Kenneth. "Changing Concepts of Power and Responsibility in the Canadian Public Service." *Canadian Public Administration* 21, no. 3 (Fall 1978): 389-406.

Kernaghan, Kenneth. "Politics, Policy and Public Servants: Political Neutrality Revisited." *Canadian Public Administration* 19, no. 3 (Fall 1976): 432-456.

Kernaghan, W.D. Kenneth. "The Political Rights and Activities of Canadian Public Servants." In *Public Administration in Canada*, 2d ed., edited by W.D.K. Kernaghan and A.M. Willms, pp. 382-90. Toronto: Methuen, 1971.

Kirby, M.J.L.; Kroeker, H.V.; and Teschke, W.R. "The Impact of Public Policy-Making Structures and Processes in Canada." *Canadian Public Administration* 21, no. 3 (Fall 1978): 407-417.

Lalonde, Marc. "The Changing Role of the Prime Minister's Office." *Canadian Public Administration* 14, no. 4 (Winter 1971): 538-55.

Lindblom, Charles E. *The Policy-Making Process.* Englewood Cliffs, N.J.: Prentice-Hall, 1968.

Lowi, Theodore J. "Four Systems of Policy, Politics and Choice." *Public Administration Review* 32, no. 4 (July-August 1972): 298-310.

Mainzer, Lewis C. *Political Bureaucracy.* Glenview, Illinois: Scott, Foresman, 1973.

Mallory, J.R. "The Lambert Report: Central Roles and Responsibilities." *Canadian Public Administration* 22, no. 4 (Winter 1979): 517-29.

Mallory, J.R. "The Minister's Office Staff: an Unreformed Part of the Public Service." *Canadian Public Administration* 10, no. 1 (March 1967): 25-34.

Mallory, J.R., and Smith, B.A. "The Legislative Role of Parliamentary Committees in Canada: the Case of the Joint Committee on the Public Service Bills." *Canadian Public Administration* 15, no. 1 (Spring 1972): 1-23.

Meier, Kenneth J. *Politics and the Bureaucracy.* Belmont, Calif.: Duxbury Press, 1979.

Nakamura, Robert T., and Smallwood, Frank. *The Politics of Policy Implementation.* New York: St. Martin's Press, 1980.

Nossal, Kim Richard. "Allison through the (Ottawa) Looking Glass: Bureaucratic Politics and Foreign Policy in a Parliamentary System." *Canadian Public Administration* 22, no. 4 (Winter 1979): 610-26.

Phidd, Richard, and Doern, G. Bruce. *The Politics and Management of Canadian Economic Policy.* Toronto: Macmillan, 1978.

Pickersgill, J.W. "Bureaucrats and Politicians." *Canadian Public Administration* 15, no. 3 (Fall 1972): 418-27.

Pitfield, Michael. "The Shape of Government in the 1980's: Techniques and Instruments for Policy Formulation at the Federal Level." *Canadian Public Administration* 19, no. 1 (Spring 1976): 8-20.

Porter, J. "Higher Public Servants and the Bureaucratic Elite in Canada." *Canadian Journal of Economics and Political Science* 24, no. 4 (November 1958): 483-501.

Pressman, Jeffrey L., and Wildavsky, Aaron. *Implementation.* Berkeley: University of California Press, 1965.

Pross, A. Paul. "Input Versus Withinput: Pressure Group Demands and Administrative Survival." In *Pressure Group Behaviour in Canadian Politics,* edited by Pross.

Pross, A. Paul, ed. *Pressure Group Behaviour in Canadian Politics.*

Robertson, Gordon. "The Changing Role of the Privy Council Office." *Canadian Public Administration* 14, no. 4 (Winter 1971): 487-508.

Rourke, Francis E., ed. *Bureaucratic Power in National Politics.* 2d ed. Boston: Little, Brown, 1972.

Rowan, Malcolm. "A Conceptual Framework for Government Policy-Making." *Canadian Public Administration* 13, no. 3 (Fall 1970): 277-96.

Santos, C.R. "Public Administration as Politics." *Canadian Public Administration* 12, no. 2 (Summer 1969): 213-23.

Sharp, Mitchell. "Decision-Making in the Federal Cabinet." *Canadian Public Administration* 19, no. 1 (Spring 1976): 1-7.

Sharp, Mitchell. "The Bureaucratic Elite and Policy Formation." In *Bureaucracy in Government,* edited by W.D.K. Kernaghan, pp. 82-87. Toronto: Methuen, 1969.

Swainson, Neil A. *Conflict Over the Columbia.* Montreal: McGill-Queen's University Press, 1979.

Taylor, Malcolm G. *Health Insurance and Canadian Public Policy.* Montreal: McGill-Queen's University Press, 1978.

Tullock, Gordon. *The Politics of Bureaucracy.* Washington, D.C.: Public Affairs Press, 1965.

Vickers, Sir Geoffrey. *The Art of Judgment: A Study of Policy Making.* London: Chapman and Hall, 1965.

Williams, Blair. "The Para-political Bureaucracy in Ottawa." In *Parliament, Policy and Representation,* edited by Harold D. Clarke et al., pp. 215-29. Toronto: Methuen, 1980.

Part VII

ADMINISTRATIVE RESPONSIBILITY

27/Responsible Public Bureaucracy*

Kenneth Kernaghan

Public concern about responsibility in government has been stimulated in recent years by events ranging from political espionage and scandal to conflicts of interest and disclosures of secret information. Discussion of these incidents has revealed that both the general public and students of government are in disagreement as to what constitutes irresponsible conduct, who should assume blame in particular cases, and what penalty should be paid.

The scope and complexity of government activities have become so great that it is often difficult to determine the actual—as opposed to the legal or constitutional—locus of responsibility for specific decisions. Political executives are held responsible for personal wrongdoing. They are not, however, expected to assume *personal* responsibility by way of resignation for the acts of administrative subordinates about which they could not reasonably be expected to have knowledge. Yet it is frequently impossible to assign individual responsibility to public servants for administrative transgressions because so many officials have contributed to the decision-making process. The allocation of responsibility in government has been complicated even further by the interposition of political appointees or temporary officials between political executives and permanent public servants.

While the involvement of political executives and their appointees in dramatic and well-publicized events has drawn much attention to the issue of *political* responsibility, the status of *administrative* responsibility has also become a matter of increasing concern. Although elected officials make the final decision on public policy questions, administrative officials have accumulated vast powers to influence policy decisions and to affect the individual and collective rights of the citizenry. As a consequence, the long-standing interest of scholars and practitioners in the

---

*Reprinted and substantially abridged by permission from Kenneth Kernaghan, "Responsible Public Bureaucracy: A Rationale and a Framework for Analysis," *Canadian Public Administration* 16, no. 4 (Winter 1973): 572-603.

preservation of administrative responsibility has become more acute. This concern is shared in varying degrees by all major actors in the political system—whether legislators, political executives, judges, interest group and mass media representatives, or members of the general public. In an effort by all these individuals to promote what they perceive to be responsible administrative conduct, the decisions of public servants are subject to an almost bewildering assortment of controls and influences.

The primary purpose of this essay is to examine the meaning and nature of administrative responsibility in contemporary democratic society. First, the conventional theory of administrative responsibility and challenges to this theory are described. Then, a distinction between objective and subjective responsibility provides a focus on the *sources* of administrative responsibility and on the *values* of public servants. These two elements are examined separately by means of an institutional and a value framework for administrative decision-making and the theoretical links between the two frameworks are demonstrated with reference to the concept of administrative responsibility.

Meanings and Interpretations

The Conventional Theory

The traditional concepts of administrative responsibility may be explained by reference to the celebrated debate between Carl Friedrich and Herman Finer during the period 1935-1941.[1] Both Friedrich and Finer correctly identified the source of burgeoning administrative power as the rapid expansion of government's service and regulatory functions. They disagreed severely, however, on the most effective means of guarding against abuse of administrative discretion so as to maintain and promote responsible administrative conduct. Their disagreement was in large part an outgrowth of their differing conceptions of the adaptive capacity of political systems and the proper role of public officials. In the defence of administrative responsibility, Finer placed primary faith in controls and sanctions exercised over officials by the legislature, the judiciary and the administrative hierarchy. In his insistence on the predominant impor-tance of political responsibility, he claimed that "the political and administrative history of all ages" had shown that "sooner or later there

---

[1]Carl J. Friedrich, "Responsible Government Service under the American Constitution," in *Problems of the American Public Service* (New York: McGraw-Hill, 1935), pp. 3-74 and "Public Policy and the Nature of Administrative Responsibility," in *Public Policy*, ed. Carl J. Friedrich and Edward S. Mason (Cambridge: Harvard University Press, 1940), pp. 3-24. Herman Finer, "Better Government Personnel," *Political Science Quarterly* (1936): 569 ff. and "Administrative Responsibility in Democratic Government," *Public Administration Review* 1, no. 4 (1941): 335-50. The most comprehensive statements of the opposing positions are found in the 1940/41 exchange of articles.

is an abuse of power when external punitive controls are lacking."[2] Friedrich relied more heavily on the propensity of public officials to be self-directing and self-regulating in their responsiveness to the dual standard of technical knowledge and popular sentiment. While he admitted the continuing need for political responsibility, he argued that a policy was irresponsible if it was adopted

> without proper regard to the existing sum of human knowledge concerning the technical issues involved—[or] without proper regard for existing preferences in the community, and more particularly its prevailing majority. Consequently, the responsible administrator is one who is responsive to these two dominant factors: technical knowledge and popular sentiment.[3]

Friedrich contended also that "parliamentary responsibility is largely inoperative and certainly ineffectual"[4] and that "the task of clear and consistent policy formation has passed—into the hands of administrators and is bound to continue to do so."[5]

Finer admitted the difficulty, but stressed the necessity, of remedying the several deficiencies of political control over administrative officials. He believed that the means and modes of legislative control should be improved.[6] He argued further that officials should not determine their own course of action. Rather, the elected representatives of the people should "determine the course of action of public servants to the most minute degree that is technically feasible."[7] Finer described the sum of Friedrich's arguments as *moral* responsibility as opposed to Finer's own emphasis on *political* responsibility.

An understanding of the Friedrich-Finer debate is an essential foundation on which to construct subsequent discussion in that it raises several of the major issues of administrative responsibility still being debated by contemporary scholars, albeit in a vastly different social and political environment. These issues are of enduring concern and continue to challenge the capacity of scholars to appreciate their dimensions and the ingenuity of practitioners to adopt institutional and procedural innovations to meet their demands.

The strength of Finer's approach lay in his recognition of the continuing need for political controls over the bureaucracy. Its primary weakness lay in his failure to anticipate the inadequacy of these controls to ensure administrative responsibility in a period of ever accelerating

---

[2]Finer, "Administrative Responsibility in Democratic Government," p. 337.
[3]Friedrich, "Public Policy and the Nature of Administrative Responsibility," p. 232.
[4]*Ibid.*, p. 10.
[5]*Ibid.*, p. 5.
[6]Finer, pp. 339-40.
[7]*Ibid.*, p. 336.

political and social change. The strength of Friedrich's argument rested on his awareness of the deficiency of solely political controls. Its major weakness lay in the difficulty of reconciling conflicts between the two criteria of technical knowledge and popular sentiment.

Assault on Conventional Theory

During the past three decades, the Friedrich and Finer approaches have been subject to a number of critiques, and alternative interpretations have been formulated.[8] Their approaches have remained the dominant contending ones, however, and most writers on administrative responsibility have referred to their debate with a view to supporting, attacking or updating one or both sides of the argument. Until recently, scholarly debate has been carried on within the context of these two conventional interpretations. In the past few years, however, these traditional notions of administrative responsibility have come under severe attack.

Michael Harmon, for example, has argued that both Finer and Friedrich, despite their differences, take a negative view of the nature of man and of administrative man in particular because they agree that "without the checks provided by either the law or the processes of professional socialization, the resultant behaviour of administrators would be both selfish and capricious."[9] Harmon looks to the existentialist's notion of self-development and self-actualization as a basis for a new theory of administrative responsibility. Officials are expected to become much more actively engaged in the initiation and promotion of policy. Harmon fails, however, to reconcile this increased participation with the conventional idea that administrators' decisions should be guided by the values and goals of elected politicians within the constraints of the law and the administrative hierarchy.[10]

Theodore Lowi's approach to administrative responsibility[11] is antithetical to Harmon's redefinition. Among what Lowi describes as "proposals for radical reform" in the United States are suggestions which are reminiscent of the position articulated by Finer in the early 1940s. Lowi recommends that the Supreme Court declare "invalid and unconstitutional any delegation of power to an administrative agency that is not

---

[8]See, for example, the excellent summary and critique of five major interpretations in Arch Dotson, "Approaches to Administrative Responsibility," *Western Political Quarterly*, vol. 10 (September 1957), pp. 701-27.

[9]Michael M. Harmon, "Normative Theory and Public Administration: Some Suggestions for a Redefinition of Administrative Responsibility," in *Toward a New Public Administration: The Minnowbrook Perspective*, ed. Frank Martini (Scranton, Pa.: Chandler, 1971), p. 173.

[10]See John Paynter, "Comment: On a Redefinition of Administrative Responsibility," *ibid.*, p. 187.

[11]Theodore J. Lowi, *The End of Liberalism* (New York: Norton, 1969).

accompanied by clear standards of implementation."[12] This call to the legislature to specify the course of action of public servants in more precise terms is complemented by a plea for "early and frequent *administrative rule making*."[13] Rather than relying primarily on case-by-case adjudication under a statute delegating broad powers in vague language, bureaucrats should formulate rules which provide standards for the adjudication of cases under that statute.

The views and proposals of Lowi and Harmon offer a different but related version of the Finer-Friedrich debate.

Accompanying such recent redefinitions of administrative responsibility is the argument that the traditional focus on devising and altering ways to promote responsible administrative behaviour has left us in a perilous position. We lack imaginative and innovative proposals to cope with the issue of administrative responsibility in an era of uncertainty and unprecedented rapid change. The complex and technological society to which we have so long alluded in a vaguely apprehensive and fearful manner is upon us with a vengeance.[14] The present and the anticipated effects of technical change on the structures and procedures of democratic government require that public administrative institutions keep the way open for rapid and perhaps radical reform.

Objective and Subjective Responsibility

In the face of recent attacks and new perspectives on conventional notions and practices of administrative responsibility, it is appropriate to seek a broader, more inclusive classification than the Friedrich-Finer categories. The two meanings of administrative responsibility set forth by Frederick Mosher meet this requirement admirably.[15] He asserts that *objective* responsibility "connotes the responsibility of a person or an organization *to* someone else, outside of self, *for* some thing or some kind of performance. It is closely akin to *accountability* or *answerability*. If one fails to carry out legitimate directives, he is judged *irresponsible*, and may be subjected to penalties."[16] *Subjective* or *psychological* responsibility, by

---

[12]*Ibid.*, p. 298.

[13]*Ibid.*, p. 299.

[14]See the following articles in *Public Administration in a Time of Turbulence*, ed. Dwight Waldo (Scranton, Pa.: Chandler, 1971)—Edward I. Friedland, "Turbulence and Technology: Public Administration and the Role of Information-Processing Technology," pp. 134-50; Orion White, Jr., "Organization and Administration for New Technological and Social Imperatives," pp. 151-68; and Allen Schick, "Toward the Cybernetic State," pp. 214-33. See also Hubert Marshall, "Administrative Responsibility and the New Science of Management Decision," in *Toward Century 21: Technology, Society and Human Values*, ed. C.S. Wallia (New York: Basic Books, 1970), pp. 257-68.

[15]Frederick C. Mosher, *Democracy and the Public Service* (New York: Oxford University Press, 1968), pp. 7-10.

[16]*Ibid.*, p. 7.

way of contrast, focuses "not upon to whom and for what one *is* responsible (according to law and the organization chart) but to whom and for what one *feels* responsible and *behaves* responsibly. This meaning is more nearly synonymous with identification, loyalty and conscience than it is with accountability and answerability."[17]

In addition to postulating a valuable theoretical distinction between the broad concepts of objective responsibility and subjective responsibility, Mosher's classification serves two other important purposes. First, it draws attention to the *sources* from which one derives one's sense of responsibility, that is, the individuals to whom one *is* or *feels* responsible. The sources of administrative responsibility on which there is a substantial measure of agreement in scholarly writings include political executives, legislators, judges, administrative superiors, members of the general public and interest group and mass media representatives. Secondly, by distinguishing between such values as accountability and answerability on the one hand and identification, loyalty and conscience on the other, Mosher points to the significance for administrative responsibility of the official's value system.

Subsequent discussion will focus on these two central and related elements of administrative responsibility: (1) the institutional framework within which interaction between bureaucrats and other policy actors takes place; and (2) the value framework within which administrative decisions are made. Then the inextricable links between these two frameworks will be explained with particular reference to the issue of administrative responsibility.

The Institutional Framework of Administrative Decision Making

The sources of administrative responsibility referred to above constitute the major policy actors who may exercise *power* over bureaucrats with a view to affecting the nature and content of administrative decisions. *Power* is defined here as "the capacity to secure the dominance of one's values or goals."[18] In the analysis to follow, power is viewed as having two major forms, namely *control* and *influence*. *Control* refers to that form of power in which A has authority to direct or command B to do something. *Influence* is a more general and pervasive form of power than control. According to Carl Friedrich, influence "usually exists when the behaviour of B is molded by and conforms to the behaviour of A, but

---

[17]*Ibid.*, p. 8.

[18]John M. Pfiffner and Frank P. Sherwood, *Administrative Organization* (Englewood Cliffs, N.J.: Prentice-Hall, 1960), p. 77. I acknowledge the existence of many definitions of power which differ both from one another and from the definition used in this essay.

without the issuance of a command."[19] Thus, when A orders or directs B to behave in a certain fashion, A exercises control over B. When B conforms to A's desires on the grounds of suggestion, persuasion, emulation or anticipation, A exercises influence over B.

To exercise control, A must possess *authority* in the sense of having access to the inducements, rewards and sanctions necessary to back up his commands. The possession of authority also gives A formal, legal or hierarchical status that enables A to exercise influence as well as control. The phenomenon which accounts in large part for this situation is "the rule of anticipated reactions."[20] Application of this general rule to the public bureaucracy is manifest in the innumerable instances in which an administrative official "anticipates the reactions" of those who have power to reward or constrain him. The official thus tends to act in a fashion that would be applauded—or at least approved—by those whose favour he seeks. Aside from the influence of anticipated reactions, those individuals or institutions with formally designated power may exercise that power not in the way of direction or supervision but by suggestion, insinuation or intimation—that is, as an influence rather than a control.[21] It is important to keep in mind, therefore, that those individuals ordinarily perceived as exercising control (for example, political executives) can also exercise influence by affecting a bureaucrat's decisions in an informal, unofficial—even in an unintentional—way. What distinguishes individuals with the capacity to exercise either control or influence from those possessing only influence is that the former have at their disposal sanctions and inducements *formalized by law and the organization chart.*

Influence then can be used to shape an official's conduct by those who do not have legally or formally sanctioned power to command and supervise. For example, interest group or mass media representatives may seek official favours by offering inducements, such as gifts, or imposing penalties, perhaps ostracism, but they have no legal or formal capacity to compel compliance to their wishes. This does not mean, however, that such influence may not be as effective as control or, in some instances, even more effective. An official may well grant special favours to interest group or mass media representatives despite formal directions to the contrary from his administrative superior. Thus influence may be exercised by those without authority through a variety of means including persuasion, friendship, knowledge and experience.

---

[19]Carl J. Friedrich, *Man and His Government*, New York, McGraw-Hill, 1963, p. 200.
[20]The best single treatment of this concept may be found in Friedrich, *Man and His Government*, chap. 11.
[21]Some organization theorists distinguish between "formal" and "informal" controls. In the context of our definition of control and influence and throughout this essay, all controls are of a *formal* nature; informal controls are subsumed under the broad definition of influences.

Clearly, the bureaucrat is subject to an enormous variety of controls and influences both from within and from outside the public service. It is important to note, however, that power relations between bureaucrats and other policy participants flow in two directions. Bureaucrats are not defenceless against pressures brought to bear on them. An examination of the real or potential impact of controls and influences over the bureaucracy must take account of the potent resources which bureaucrats may use to resist pressure and to exert power over others. Among the resources which bureaucrats possess to control and/or influence other policy actors are expertise, experience, budgetary allocations, confidential information and discretionary powers to develop and implement policies and programs. Such resources may be utilized in various ways. For example, bureaucrats may prevail over political superiors by virtue of special knowledge of a policy area; they may feed selected bits of information to mass media representatives to enhance support for a certain program; or they may disarm external critics by organizing them into advisory bodies.

There is clearly an enormous array of variables involved in interaction among bureaucrats and between bureaucrats and other participants in the political-administrative system. Yet even a comprehensive identification of controls and influences would be insufficient to explain the decisional behaviour of *the individual* bureaucrat. The various policy participants, whether they exercise power from within or from outside the public service, are forces *external to the individual*. The controls and influences by which a single bureaucrat is affected and the resources he employs to counter these forces depend to a very large extent on his *values*. Therefore, we now turn our attention from the multitude of controls and influences affecting administrative decision making in general to the means by which the value system of the individual official is moulded.

The Value Framework of Administrative Decision Making

A value is defined here as "an enduring belief that a particular mode of conduct or that a particular end-state of existence is personally and socially preferable to alternative modes of conduct or end-states of existence."[22] Values "are organized into value systems, which are hierarchical rank orderings of importance."[23] An *administrative* value, then, is an enduring belief that, in administrative decision making, a particular mode of conduct or a particular end-state of existence is per-

---

[22]Milton Rokeach, "The Role of Values in Public Opinion Research," *Public Opinion Quarterly* 32 (Winter 1968): 550.
[23]*Ibid.*, p. 551.

sonally or socially preferable to alternative modes of conduct or end-states of existence. The bureaucrat develops a value framework or value system in which various administrative values are ranked, admittedly very roughly, even unconsciously, in order of importance.

The bureaucrat seeking guidance as to the appropriate content of his administrative value system will find much advice, but little solace, in scholarly writings. Various authors single out different values for the "ideal" or the "responsible" administrator. There is substantial overlapping in the emphasis of different writers, however. Charles Gilbert, in his analysis of administrative responsibility in the United States, has distilled from the scholarly literature the values most frequently associated with the responsible administrator.[24] These administrative values are responsiveness, flexibility, consistency, stability, leadership, probity, candour, competence, efficacy, prudence, due process and accountability.

Situational Considerations

Since the list of values isolated by Gilbert is extrapolated largely from American literature, it is culture-bound in its application. The primary values affecting an official's decision tend to differ from one cultural setting and political system to another. The dominant administrative values of a society, which will be reflected in administrative performance, depend on the complex of political, economic and social conditions extant in that society. Moreover, the relative importance of these values alters with changes in these conditions. For example, the administrative values of responsiveness and flexibility may become predominant during a period when the general public or the government feels that the interests of certain disadvantaged minority groups must be better represented and their needs and demands better understood and satisfied. During such a period, considerations of consistency and stability may be relegated to a secondary order of importance.

Factual Considerations

If an administrative issue is significant enough to require the formal or conscious preparation of alternative solutions and the evaluation of their possible consequences, each alternative will be an amalgam of what Herbert Simon refers to as the value and factual elements in any decision.[25] The mix of fact and value will, of course, vary greatly from one decision-making circumstance to another. Many decisions of a very

---

[24]Charles Gilbert, "The Framework of Administrative Responsibility," *The Journal of Politics* 21 (August 1959): 373-407.
[25]Herbert A. Simon, *Administrative Behavior*, 2d ed. (New York: The Free Press, 1957), pp. 45-60.

routine and repetitive nature (programmed decisions) require little, if any, conscious value selection. Other decisions of a unique or novel nature (nonprogrammed decisions) may contain a substantial mix of value and factual elements. As Herbert Simon contends:

> Decisions are something more than factual propositions. To be sure, they are descriptive of a future state of affairs, and this description can be true or false in a strictly empirical sense; but they possess, in addition, an imperative quality—they select one future state of affairs in preference to another and direct behaviour toward the chosen alternative. In short, they have an *ethical* as well as a factual content.[26]

The Power of the Bureaucrat

Power was defined earlier as "the capacity to secure the dominance of one's values or goals." In this sense, administrative officials possess vast power by virtue of their role in policy development and execution. If the machinery of government could be so arranged that bureaucrats simply implemented laws spelled out in very specific terms by the legislature, enforced judicial decisions interpreting these laws, and administered policies and programs under the close supervision of political executives and their senior administrative officials, few value problems would exist for most bureaucrats. The realm of policy and political considerations would belong to elected representatives and would be sharply delineated from the administrative sphere. The value issues in any situation would be worked out by others so that the bureaucrat's primary concern would be responsiveness to values emerging from the legislative, judicial and senior executive levels of government.

The historical record shows that an era of such bureaucratic innocence has never existed in modern democratic states. There is in reality a considerable area of discretion where the official's value preferences determine the nature of the decision made. Given the complexity of contemporary government and the interweaving of political, policy and administrative issues, it is unrealistic to assume that any combination of controls and influences could so diminish the scope of administrative judgment that no room would remain for the injection of personal values into public policy formation and implementation.

Writers on bureaucratic power have long recognized the enormous influence of bureaucrats in the initiation and development of new policies. Senior officials in particular make significant discretionary decisions as to the policy alternatives to be set before their political masters. Moreover, in the formulation and presentation of policy proposals, these officials are expected to be attuned to the *political* as well as the administrative and technical implications of their recommendations.

---

[26]*Ibid.*, p. 46.

Discussions of the policy role of the bureaucracy must also take account of the impressive discretionary powers which officials wield in the implementation of both new and ongoing policies and programs.

Sources of the Bureaucrat's Values

A focus on the bureaucrat's values is especially important in that decisional behaviour may be explained or interpreted in terms of the interplay (1) among the individual bureaucrat's values, and (2) between the bureaucrat's values and the values of those with whom he interacts. Before an individual joins the public service, his general value system, as well as his particular attitudes and orientations toward the public service, are moulded by powerful and enduring forces. This is accomplished through the process of socialization, that is, "an individual's learning from others in his environment the social patterns and values of his culture."[27] The socializing "agencies" involved in this process include family, peer groups, schools, prior employment and adult organizations. As a result of this socialization experience, an individual does not take up government employment with a *tabula rasa* so far as values relevant to bureaucratic decision making are concerned. In varying degrees, the several socializing agencies continue to affect the bureaucrat's values during his public service career.

The focus of our analysis is the sources of values impinging on the individual as a consequence of his employment as a bureaucrat and of his occupancy of a particular bureaucratic position. The individual's personal values and his perceptions of the public service are altered by a process of *organizational socialization* which begins the very day he is recruited for a public service position. *Organizational socialization* refers to the process (a) through which the individual learns the expectations attached to the position he occupies in the organization, and (b) through which he selectively internalizes as values certain of the expectations of those with whom he interacts.

The bureaucrat is located at the focal position or core of a network of counterpositions occupied by such other policy actors as political executives, legislators and administrative superiors. Each policy actor manifests certain expectations as to how the bureaucrat should behave in his official position. These expectations, in the form of commands, directions, guidelines, standards and suggestions, express the values of the policy actor, and the bureaucrat is expected to reflect these values in his decisions.

The Crucial Link

It is precisely at this juncture that the theoretical link between the value framework of administrative decision making and the institutional

---

[27]Kenneth P. Langton, *Political Socialization* (New York: Oxford University Press, 1969), p. 3.

framework described earlier may be demonstrated. The bureaucrat is expected to be responsive to the values of the various policy participants as these values are expressed through the exercise of specific controls and influences.

Since various policy participants pursue different, and sometimes mutually exclusive, ends in their relations with bureaucrats, the official occupying a certain position will be the object of conflicting expectations and pressures as to his behaviour. The purpose of each participant's interaction with the bureaucrat will usually be the dominance of the participant's particular values and goals over those of both the bureaucrat and other participants. The problem for the bureaucrat is clearly posed—how can he be responsive to the multiplicity of values expressed?

The linkages between the institutional and the value frameworks help to explain the means by which the number and assortment of variables impinging on the bureaucrat may be reduced to more manageable proportions.

Over a considerable period of time and in a variety of bureaucratic positions, an official might conceivably interact with virtually the whole range of policy participants and be subjected to a wide variety of controls and influences. As the incumbent of a specific position over a shorter period, he will, however, only interact with and be subjected to the power resources of a limited number of actors. The range of these actors will be confined to those with a stake in the activities of the occupant of a particular position or in the issue at hand. For example, a deputy minister of consumer and corporate affairs is the object of much greater pressure from outside the public service (for example, interest group and mass media representatives) than a deputy minister of supply and services. More important, during the process of organizational socialization, the bureaucrat learns what kinds of decisional behaviour will bring reward or punishment from various policy actors and what values they are seeking to realize. The bureaucrat's value system is usually most directly moulded by the values of those hierarchical associates on whom he relies most heavily for approval and reward, that is, his political and administrative superiors and his peers and subordinates. He is also expected, of course, to be responsive to the values of such other policy actors as legislators, interest group representatives and the general public. Faced with complementary, conflicting and contradictory expectations issuing from various sources, the bureaucrat inculcates certain of the values manifested by those with whom he interacts.

Value Conflict
Despite all efforts to minimize the number of variables involved in any given decision-making situation, a condition of value conflict is a frequent one, especially for senior bureaucrats. Herbert Simon contends that

at the lower levels of the hierarchy, the frame of reference within which decision is to take place is largely given. The factors to be evaluated have already been enumerated, and all that remains is to determine their values under the given circumstances. At the higher levels of the hierarchy, the task is an artistic and inventive one. New values must be sought out and weighed; the possibilities of new administrative structures evaluated. The very framework of reference within which decision is to take place must be constructed.[28]

The major categories of value conflicts which the bureaucrat encounters are those: (1) between personal values and administrative values; (2) between and among administrative values; and (3) between administrative values and the values of other policy participants. The resolution of value conflicts involving personal and administrative values (for example, ambition versus accountability or avarice versus integrity) depends on the personality and character of the particular bureaucrat. There is no escape from the reality that "most officials are significantly motivated by self-interest when their social function is to serve the public interest."[29] From among Anthony Downs's typology of "purely self-interested officials" (that is, climbers and conservers) and of "mixed-motive officials" (that is, zealots, advocates and statesmen), we may for analytical purposes utilize the "statesmen" type. Statesmen are "motivated by loyalty to society as a whole and a desire to obtain the power necessary to have a significant influence upon national policies and actions. They are altruistic to a high degree because their loyalty is to the 'general welfare' as they see it."[30]

Although the statesman—the least self-seeking and most public-oriented of bureaucrats—has comparatively little difficulty in reconciling personal and administrative values, he is occasionally obliged to choose between and among administrative values he holds equally dear, (for example, accountability versus integrity or accountability and consistency versus responsiveness and efficacy). Similarly, the bureaucrat's values come into conflict with the values expressed by those with whom he interacts (for example, accountability versus responsiveness to an interest group's request or accountability versus competence expected by a professional colleague).

Depending on the factual and contextual elements of any decision-making situation and on the character of the bureaucrat, it is evident that he may conceivably pass through one, two or all three stages of value conflict. In practice, of course, these stages are not chronological; rather, they overlap and interact with one another. Thus a choice between the

---

[28]Simon, *Administrative Behavior*, p. 217.
[29]Anthony Downs, *Inside Bureaucracy* (Boston: Little, Brown, 1967), p. 87.
[30]*Ibid.*, p. 88.

administrative values of accountability and responsiveness is likely to be made in conjunction with and to be affected by controls and influences reflecting the values of other policy actors.

Value Conflict Resolution

The following analysis is based on the premise that the weight of evidence supports the existence of a concept of *the public interest* which has both theoretical and practical utility. The numerous, often brilliant, debates on the issue will not be reviewed here.[31] It is clear, however, that no interpretation of the public interest has won universal acclaim as relevant and appropriate in all contexts. One interpretation of the public interest—as the best possible accommodation of conflicting particular interests—provides an essential element of specificity. This interpretation requires some refinement, but offers a promising base for the formulation of a definition of the public interest.

The adjustment of the claims of special and private interests connotes a power struggle among competing groups, each possessing approximately equal access to the decision maker and devoting roughly equivalent resources to the struggle. In reality, both access and resources in money, organization, supporters and research capacity are uneven among various groups. Moreover, the interests of some sectors of the population may not be represented because these sectors are underprivileged, uneducated, uninformed, inarticulate, unorganized or simply uninterested. Even if the whole range of relevant special interests is taken into account, our definition is still incomplete. Public interest theorists commonly assert that the public interest is not the mere sum of special interests, no matter how evenly and equitably these interests are represented.

The critical contribution to the determination of the public interest comes from the decision maker. But the avenue to some decisions runs through a myriad of conflicting and complementary values. Among the obstacles along the road is the temptation to succumb to personal or particularistic interests when a decision in the broader interest of the general public or of substantial sectors of the general public is required. The fact that the bureaucrat, whether consciously or unconsciously, follows a multi-stage route of value conflict resolution does not guaran-

---

[31]See especially Pendleton Herring, *Public Administration and the Public Interest* (New York: McGraw-Hill, 1936); Frank Sorauf, "The Public Interest Reconsidered," *Journal of Politics* 19 (November 1957): 616-39; Glendon Schubert, *The Public Interest: A Critique of a Political Concept* (Glencoe: The Free Press, 1960); Carl J. Friedrich (ed.), *Nomos V: The Public Interest* (New York: Atherton Press, 1962); Herbert J. Storing, "The Crucial Link: Public Administration, Responsibility and the Public Interest," *Public Administration Review* 24 (March 1964): 39-46; and Richard E. Flathman, *The Public Interest* (New York: Wiley, 1966).

tee the "best" decision at the end of his journey. Nor does it ensure that the occasional public servant, like other human beings, will not stray from the well-trodden path into the mire of self-interest.

Except in situations where the bureaucrat has been given complete discretionary authority, he may be able to shift the burden of choice among contending values to his hierarchical superior. *Hierarchy* in administration is a prime safeguard to administrative responsibility in that it forces "important decisions to higher levels of determination or at least higher levels of review where perspectives are necessarily broader, less technical and expert, more political."[32] At the highest policy-making levels of government, it may be argued that in the final analysis the determination of the public interest is the task of the elected representative. Constitutional and political imperatives do not, however, permit the official to escape the responsibility of providing his political master with the best possible advice. Moreover, if only in the cause of personal survival, the official cannot evade the responsibility of pointing out the political, economic and social costs and benefits of selecting one course of action over another.

The voluminous writings on the public interest demonstrate the difficulty of establishing specific and immutable criteria for its determination in any given situation. The public interest may fruitfully be viewed as a dynamic concept. Its content changes from one situation to another and depends in large part on the values of both the decision maker and the interests whose claims are considered.

No one expects the bureaucrat to proceed through a detailed checklist of the great variety of pressures in his decision-making environment. Few will deny, however, the necessity for the official to step back on occasion to examine the value premises on which he has been acting. "In general," the public interest "is a spur to conscience and to deliberation."[33]

An important distinction may be made between a *passive* as opposed to an *active* pursuit of the public interest. The official who considers the claims only of *organized* special interests and whose range of values is narrow and inflexible is passive in the search for the public interest. By way of contrast, the official who seeks the views of *all relevant interests* and whose value framework is comparatively broad and flexible is in active pursuit of the public interest. No judgment is made here as to the desirability of one orientation over the other. Each has its virtues and drawbacks at various levels of the organizational pyramid.

---

[32]Mosher, *Democracy and the Public Service*, p. 212.
[33]J. Roland Pennock, "The One and the Many: A Note on the Concept of the Public Interest," in *Nomos V: The Public Interest*, ed. Friedrich, p. 182.

Administrative Responsibility
and the Public Interest

The passive and active orientations toward the public interest may be linked with our earlier distinction between objective and subjective (psychological) responsibility. In a brief and admittedly oversimplified fashion the main characteristics of two hypothetically extreme types of bureaucrat—the objectively responsible and the subjectively responsible official—are suggested here.

The objectively responsible bureaucrat feels responsible primarily to the legal or formal locus of authority and takes a passive approach to the determination of the public interest. His most prominent characteristic and value is accountability to those who have the power to promote, displace or replace him. The controls and influences which he internalizes in the form of administrative values are those expressed by his hierarchical superiors. In making and recommending decisions, he anticipates and reflects the desires of his superiors. It is they who have legitimate authority and who may most easily threaten or impose penalties to ensure compliance. This type of bureaucrat does not actively seek the views of policy actors other than those of his superiors unless he is required or directed to do so. For example, he consults certain interests about impending regulations affecting their activities only if such consultation is required by law or expected by his superiors. His foremost administrative values include answerability and efficiency. He does not take initiatives or risks which may get him or his superiors into trouble. He prefers, if possible, that others, notably his political and administrative superiors, resolve any value dilemmas and determine the content of the public interest for him.

The objectively responsible bureaucrat is ultimately responsible to the general public through the administrative hierarchy, the political executive and the legislature. His behaviour is based on the possibility and the desirability of separating policy and administration—even at the senior levels of the public service. In Finer's terminology, he is therefore, "politically" responsible.

The subjectively responsible bureaucrat is a striking contrast. He feels responsible to a broad range of policy participants and is active in the pursuit of the public interest. His most outstanding characteristic and value is commitment to what he perceives to be the goals of his department or program. Since he views the expectations of a variety of policy actors as legitimate, the sources of his administrative values are numerous and diverse. Tension and conflict between the subjectively responsible official and his superiors are frequent, but he is minimally concerned by the threat of negative sanctions. He seeks the views of interests affected by his decisions and recommendations in the absence of, and even in violation of, any legal or formal obligation to do so. His primary administrative values include responsiveness, effectiveness and flexibility. He is innovative, takes risks, and bends the rules to achieve his objectives. He urges his superiors to follow certain courses of action and is prepared to resolve by himself the value dilemmas he encounters in his search for the public interest.

The subjectively responsible bureaucrat rejects the possibility and desirability of separating policy and administration—especially at the senior echelons of the bureaucracy. To use Finer's language again, this type of official is "morally" responsible in that he looks to his own conscience rather than to "external punitive controls" for guidance.

Neither the purely objective nor the purely subjective type is appropriate as a model of the responsible bureaucrat. Some characteristics of both types produce conduct which scholars and public officials generally view as undesirable. Undue emphasis on certain elements of objective responsibility may lead to behaviour which is inflexible, unimaginative, unresponsive or ineffective. At the other extreme, too great emphasis on particular aspects of subjective responsibility may bring equally undesirable results in the way of behaviour which is unaccountable, inconsistent or unpredictable.

If the public service "writ large" is composed predominantly of either objectively or subjectively responsible officials, it will tend to manifest the same objectionable features. The "ideal" situation, then, is a public service in which each official strikes that balance between the objective and subjective elements of responsibility which is appropriate to his level in the hierarchy and to the requirements of his particular position. The determination of the "appropriate" balance for all positions would, however, be a Herculean and impracticable task. In every instance, the determination would involve a personal judgment as to the optimum blend of objective and subjective values and orientations.

Conclusions

The issue of administrative responsibility cannot be separated from that of administrative power. Indeed, the essence of the debates between Friedrich and Finer and between their intellectual descendants is the most effective means of constraining administrative power in democratic states. The literature abounds with proposals for new and improved institutional and procedural means (for example, an ombudsman, strengthened legislative committees) by which administrative power and administrative responsibility may be reconciled. The aim of such proposals is to attain a larger measure of objective responsibility by holding bureaucrats more accountable for their decisions.

On the basis of the preceding analysis, however, it may be argued that policy actors should devote more attention to bringing about an environment in which subjective responsibility may be fostered. Since external policy actors will continue to rely on institutional and procedural devices to control and influence administrative conduct, the task of encouraging subjective responsibility falls on senior officials within the public service itself. Senior administrators have traditionally endeavoured to instil in their subordinates a commitment to organizational and program goals through their personal influence and example. The scale and complexity of the public service are now so great, however, that other means to the same end must be utilized. Evidence now available in Canada, for example, suggests that to stimulate administrative responsibility—indeed, to avoid disruptive dissent—senior officials must break through the hard rock strata of the administrative pyramid. They must permit and encourage participation in the policy process by those highly educated, articulate and restless officials in the middle to upper ranks of the hierarchy.

Despite the multitude of external controls and influences over the bureaucracy, the preservation and encouragement of responsible administrative conduct requires vigorous and sustained effort by the public servants themselves. At a time when the pace of administrative reform is already hectic and unsettling,[34] some officials may reasonably be expected to resist further change—even if it is justified on grounds of administrative responsibility. Nevertheless, there is cause for optimism both in present reform efforts in the public service and in J.E. Hodgett's contention that "among our major political institutions the public service has given more attention to and shown the greatest willingness to experiment with adaptations in form and procedure."[35]

Changes not only in structures and procedures, however, but also in values and modes of thought are required. By striving to meet the challenge, the public service can ensure that the power of the bureaucrat will be more evenly matched by his sense of responsibility—to his superiors, to the public and to his own conscience.

---

[34]H.L. Laframboise, "Administrative Reform in the Federal Public Service: Signs of a Saturation Psychosis," *Canadian Public Administration* 14, no. 3 (Fall 1971): 303-25 and Walter Baker, "Administrative Reform in the Federal Public Service: The First Faltering Steps," *Canadian Public Administration* 16, no. 3 (Fall 1973): 381-98.

[35]J.E. Hodgetts, *The Canadian Public Service: A Physiology of Government, 1867-1970* (Toronto: University of Toronto Press, 1973), p. 353.

28/Growth of Discretions—
Decline of Accountability*
Eric Hehner

The functions of the public service have changed in a fundamental way which requires reappraisal of the positions of Parliament and of the courts of law. This change has happened so quietly that its extent, its basic nature and its significance to our system of government have not yet been widely recognized. The administrator has gained vastly wider powers and the legislature is losing both knowledge of, and effective control over, the way in which the powers it has conferred are exercised. This has created a new relationship between the individual and the state, and over a period of many years has progressively contributed to the sterilization of Parliament.

Parliament, the public service and the courts of law were designed for limited functions of government. The ideal of legislation was to be definitive and precise, and to leave little to the imagination or to opinion. Our forefathers undoubtedly fell far short of this ideal, but the ideal was there. The public service performed administrative and service functions. The courts were adjudicators of facts and defenders of injured individuals from other individuals or from the state. Judicial decisions were made under a rule of law with the rules fixed beforehand and equally applicable to all.

Government today is expected to offer direction and to execute policies of a positive nature—to be an active participant in economic and social affairs, not just a writer of rules and an umpire. Had our economic and social structures and the technology on which they in part rest been relatively static, a rule of law as known in the past might have provided an adequate mechanism to enable government to play an increased role. However, the expansion of the scale of economic processes has been great enough to produce differences of nature, not just of size. It has made necessary the use of discretions by governmental authority, which cannot be exercised by Parliament itself.

The activities of government have changed to meet the needs of the times, but our political and legal structure has failed to keep pace. There has been increasing delegation of authority by Parliament to the Cabinet, to departments and boards and to nameless public servants. Since the government is playing a more active and positive role at a time of rapidly changing technology, changing patterns of domestic and international

*The editor extends appreciation to Mr. Hehner for his work in updating this selection. Mr. Hehner is Chairman of the Board, Corporation House Limited, Ottawa.

trade and changing social viewpoints, it cannot spell out in statutes all the provisions and exemptions needed to look after the innumerable variations of modern requirements. Our need for greater flexibility in administration has been growing, and the location of responsibility for executive, legislative and judicial functions has become somewhat vague. The activities of departments of government are no longer separable into neat, mutually exclusive areas of interest. As the functions and direct participation of government have extended, the machinery of administration has become more complicated and has ceased to be merely administrative.

We have changed the activities of government to an extent that makes even more discretionary powers inevitable. We have provided for many such powers, and at an accelerating pace. However, instead of entering wholeheartedly into the creation of discretions with our eyes open to its implications and needs and simultaneously providing machinery to prevent the abuse of discretionary powers, we tried to pretend that there had been no basic change. We left discretions to be exercised as much in the shadows of secrecy as possible. It has become more difficult to tell where lawmaking stops and administration starts. It has become harder to place responsibility for actions (or lack of them) among the multiplicity of government agencies now involved. Even greater use of discretionary powers may be essential but these powers carry with them potential for abuse unless there are surrounding safeguards.

It became the norm for a statute to delegate authority to make regulations to achieve objectives which have been expressed in very general terms. If regulations extend only to details of mechanical procedures, no real discretionary powers are delegated. However, where the statutory provisions are only a skeleton and it is left to regulations to say "what, where, when, why, how and who," then we have created meaningful discretionary powers and should examine the mechanisms available to review the exercise of these powers. When regulations are issued by the governor-in-council, or even by a minister of the Crown, there is at least a degree of accountability for this first step. Where the power is conferred upon a board or commission, review of its exercise becomes more difficult and remote. However, if the discretions have been consciously delegated to a named body directly responsible to the legislature, there is at least a placing of responsibility. If persons or bodies possessed of delegated powers redelegate them, we come to a state that may be described as "dispersed discretions." When discretionary judgments are not the result of a conscious act which has placed the responsibility upon a named person or body, but are the results of pretending that matters of opinion are matters of fact, we are farther into an area of trouble.

The courts have been the traditional safeguard for the rights of one individual against another or against the state, but the courts were designed to adjudicate matters which at least purport to be issues of fact in relation to pre-established law. Courts lack both the powers and in most cases the capacity to substitute their judgment for opinions which others have been empowered to express. In essence, the traditional courts are incapable of playing a constructive part in the newly developing functions of government, where exercise of discretions is required. For this reason positive action was frequently taken by legislatures to exclude the exercise of delegated discretions from the jurisdiction of the courts, if it was found or suspected that the courts might be in a position to intervene.

The magnitude of the developments described has been generally unrecognized. Most people still think that Parliament makes the laws except for small details; that public servants just administer; and that those exercising delegated discretions are accountable for their actions in fact as well as in theory to the elected representatives of the people. In fact, the rule of law as we knew it until World War II has just about gone and effective accountability to Parliament has been lost over a wide area of governmental activity.

These are not just impressionistic statements. Let us look at some specific examples of this continuing process of growth of discretions. It would not matter what year's legislation we look at. The pattern has been the same session after session. The following examples are taken from the acts of the third session of the 28th Parliament (October 8, 1970-January 12, 1972) which continued the process of legislating in generalities, leaving the substance to be prescribed by regulations to be administered beyond the control of Parliament. There were sixty-five public bills introduced in that session which subsequently became law. Many of these were of a mechanical nature such as redefining electoral boundaries and repealing the Leprosy Act, or formalisms such as proclaiming "Pollution Awareness Week," and similar measures of limited interest and content. Of the bills which affected the public at large, the majority conferred new discretionary authority.

Subsequent legislation has merely continued the pattern set during the 1970-1972 session. However, to give one current example, a draft Special Import Measures Act is at the time of writing under study by the Subcommittee on Import Policy, Standing Committee on Finance, Trade and Economic Affairs, House of Commons. Of thirty-five operative sections in the draft act, fifteen provide for the substance to be "prescribed" by order-in-council, to be whatever "the Minister specifies," or to be determined by "the opinion of the Deputy Minister." It should also be noted in connection with discretionary powers conferred on the deputy minister, that *deputy minister* is defined as including "any person authorized by him to perform his functions and duties under this Act."

Under the Consumer Packaging and Labelling Act (Bill C-180), full power to exempt goods from the application of the act is delegated to the governor-in-council. The labelling requirements that are to apply to goods are to be prescribed by regulations. Thus, in passing the act, Parliament prohibited the sale or import of goods not packaged in compliance with regulations that had not yet been made and were therefore unknown to Parliament. Similarly, the act delegates the power of entry without warrant and the seizure of goods at the sole discretion of inspectors in order to enforce regulations made under the act and therefore unknown to Parliament when the act was passed.

It should not go unnoticed that the Statutory Instruments Act (Bill C-182),[1] "to provide for the examination, publication and scrutiny of regulations and other statutory instruments," itself created new discretionary powers by authorizing the governor-in-council to prescribe by regulation that regulations or classes of regulations need not be examined, published or scrutinized. This the governor-in-council subsequently did, in the Statutory Instruments Regulations.[2]

Another example is the Clean Air Act (Bill C-224). "Air quality objectives" are left to be "prescribed by the Governor-in-Council." What are to be regarded as "air contaminants" are left to be prescribed by regulation. Those types of operations to be subject to regulation are left to be "specified by the governor-in-council." Powers to decide who should be required to conform to standards, who should be exempted, and what the standards should be are also delegated to the minister. Discretionary enforcement powers are delegated to "inspectors," to be exercised according to what the inspectors "may reasonably believe" to be the facts, or as an inspector "deems necessary."

The act to amend the Canada Labour (Standards) Code (Bill C-228) had twenty-four sections. Thirteen of these delegate discretions by reference to "as prescribed by regulations" or the use of similar phrases.

The Unemployment Insurance Act, 1971 (Bill C-229) is an outstanding example. The definition of "insurable earnings" was left to be "prescribed by regulation." What are "excepted employment" and "insurable employment" were left to be defined by regulations which might be general, or restricted to areas in the country, groups of persons, or even applicable only to individual persons. Unemployed persons can be disentitled to benefits by regulation. Wide powers to make regulations are given to the minister, and the minister is given power to authorize others to exercise his powers. The Unemployment Insurance Commission is not only given wide powers to issue regulations, but is empowered in turn to delegate its powers to any employees it desires. There are close

---

[1]Canada, *Statutes* (1971).
[2]SOR/71-592, P.C. 1971-2485, November 9, 1971.

to seventy-five references in the act to the power to make regulations or requirements to comply with regulations. Without the regulations the act is hollow.

In addition to legislative acts of this nature, there is the whole area of "Rules, orders, regulations, by-laws or proclamations which are made by regulation-making authorities in the exercise of a legislative power"— commonly known as Statutory Orders and Regulations. In any year these are numbered in the thousands, and not only delegate authority but frequently redelegate it.

For example, the powers to make regulations provided by the Unemployment Insurance Act, 1971, were promptly and frequently exercised. Authority to exercise judgments and make determinations was extended through the use of such phrases as "in the opinion of the Commission," "approved by the Commission," "in the manner set out in the instructions from the Commission," "may be determined by the Commission." Regulations redefine significant words and phrases from meanings given to them in the statute. There is redelegation of powers, through such phrases as "Where it is established to the satisfaction of an officer of the Department of National Revenue, Taxation. . . ." The Unemployment Insurance Act, 1971, came into effect on various dates starting in June 1971. In the following twelve months the Unemployment Insurance Regulations were amended twelve times, and the revisions took up about ninety pages of small type in the *Canada Gazette*. One can appreciate a comment of Mr. Stanley Knowles, M.P., when this series of amendments had barely started:

> It is our experience in Parliament time and time again to think we knew what we passed when we gave final approval to a piece of legislation, only to find months later that things were being done or restrictions were being imposed of a kind we did not believe appeared in the bill at all. When we try to find out what happened, we discover that we had given authority to the Governor-in-Council to make regulations for the carrying out of the purposes of the act and that under this authority restrictive regulations were passed, or restrictive definitions introduced of such a nature as to produce quite a different result from the result we thought had been intended. I could give a number of examples . . . let me give just one, not in order to be contentious, but merely to make my point. Take the new Unemployment Insurance Act. Because we gave the Governor-in-Council the power to define "earnings" we found that things were happening which we did not expect and that in many cases benefits were greatly reduced.[3]

The statutes and regulations used as examples have the merit of being published documents. In addition, there is a large area of unpublished orders-in-council and ministerial prescriptions. There is also the

---

[3]*Debates* (Commons), October 4, 1971, p. 8681.

broad field of so-called administrative decisions (or lack of decisions) which are equally exercises of discretion. These are by nature difficult to deal with in public, because they frequently involve decisions relating to private and confidential affairs of individual persons or companies. One can only learn of the details through a confidential relationship to those affected. However, these unpublished orders-in-council, ministerial prescriptions or administrative decisions are frequently of general application and remain unknown to many persons affected by them because they are not published.

The report of a Special Committee on Statutory Instruments, presented October 22, 1969, reiterated the importance of the area of delegated legislation, using such phrases as:

> . . . public knowledge of governmental activities is the basis of all control of delegated legislation. For parliamentary democracy is a system of government which requires that the executive be responsible to the legislature and that both be accountable to the people, and there can be neither responsibility nor accountability where there is no knowledge of what has been done. . . .
>
> Your Committee can agree with the view of Dr. D.C. Rowat that the general tradition of administrative secrecy is based on an earlier system of royal rule in Britain that is unsuited to a modern democracy in which the people must be fully informed about the activities of their government. . . .
>
> Your Committee's contention is, therefore, that there should be, as a general rule, public knowledge of the processes of delegated legislation, before, during, and after the making of regulations, and that any derogation by government from this rule requires justification.[4]

The Committee made extensive recommendations (twenty-three in number). Some were subsequently accepted by the government, others were not. In June 1970 the president of the Privy Council stated government policy and intentions as follows:

> Due to the nature of the committee's recommendations it is not practical, nor is it reasonably possible, to proceed with their implementation by any one means. Rather, implementation of the committee's recommendations will require action of three different kinds: first, legislative action by Parliament to replace the existing Regulations Act by a new statutory instruments act; second, a number of cabinet directives to implement several of the recommendations which cannot be dealt with by general legislation and, third, amendment of the Standing Orders for the purpose of establishing a scrutiny committee to review regulations.
>
> The government accepts fully the principle that both Parliament and

---

[4]Canada, *Third Report of the Special Committee of the House of Commons on Statutory Instruments,* October 22, 1969.

the public are entitled to be fully informed of, and to have convenient access to, regulations and other instruments made under the authority of Acts of Parliament. The legislation and other measures that will be proposed by the government will be guided by this paramount principle, and only demonstrably necessary and carefully defined exceptions to the general requirements of the law relating to the examination, registration and publication of such instruments will be permitted.[5]

There had already been a positive step in a related area through the introduction in March 1970 of a bill to establish the Federal Court of Canada, to replace with extended powers the Exchequer Court. This measure, which was proclaimed effective June 1, 1971, repealed provisions in many statutes which had specifically prohibited appeals to the courts against procedures, or from findings, of a number of semi-judicial boards and tribunals. This measure now affords protection against arbitrary action and the failure of such boards or tribunals to proceed in a judicial manner. However, it does not, of course, empower the court to substitute its judgment for that of the bodies empowered to exercise discretions.

In November 1970, Bill C-182, "to provide for the examination, publication and scrutiny of regulations and other statutory instruments" was introduced. The Honourable John Turner, then minister of justice, restated government intentions as being:

1. To issue Cabinet directives "to deal with departmental directives and guidelines and the conferring by legislation of regulation-making powers."
2. To replace the existing provisions for scrutiny and publication of regulations by a new and broader Statutory Instruments Act.
3. To provide a parliamentary committee to review statutory instruments.

The Cabinet directives are said to have been issued, but what they said cannot be reported. When a question on this matter was addressed to the Privy Council Office, access to them was denied. The official reply was that they are confidential, "They are not in the public domain."

The Statutory Instruments Act came into force January 1, 1972, together with regulations made thereunder. Adequate commentary on the Statutory Instruments Act and the regulations thereunder is not possible within the scope of this article. However, a few major points should be noted. It would be an error to think that the requirements of the act extend to all of the many orders-in-council, rules, orders, regulations, by-laws, proclamations, prescriptions—call them what you will—that affect the rights and responsibilities of individuals. The statute

---

[5]*Debates* (Commons), June 16, 1970.

applies only to certain "regulations" and "statutory instruments" as defined in the act. The definitions are both restrictive and obscure in their wording. They make broad provision for exemptions from requirements of inspection before issuance, registration, publication or public access—even access by Parliament. A large area of the exercises of administrative discretions has been left outside the scope of the act.

The act also applies only to those regulations and statutory instruments (as defined, and not then excluded) made subsequent to its passage. It leaves untouched the thousands of preexisting "regulations" and "statutory instruments," as well as the mass of other provisions considered to lie outside these narrowly defined phrases. The provisions of the Statutory Instruments Act did not, and do not, carry out stated government policy, namely that ". . . both Parliament and the public are entitled to be fully informed of and to have convenient access to regulations and other instruments" and that ". . . only demonstrably necessary and carefully defined exceptions to the general requirements of the law relating to the examination, registration and publication of such instruments will be permitted." In fact, the provisions are a mockery of these statements of principle.

With respect to the "scrutiny committee" the act did provide that certain types of statutory instruments (as narrowly defined) after the coming into force of the act

> . . . shall stand permanently referred to any Committee of the House of Commons, or the Senate or of both Houses of Parliament that may be established for the purpose of reviewing and scrutinizing statutory instruments.

In 1974 a Joint Committee of the Senate and the House of Commons started work. In 1977 it published a report highly critical of a large proportion of the regulations and other statutory instruments which it had reviewed, but even more critical of the lack of cooperation of the administrative departments in government, and in particular of the Department of Justice, in withholding information.

More recently, the Fourth Report of the Joint Committee (submitted in July 1980) repeated and enlarged on these complaints. Two of its comments were:

> There are also traditions in the Public Service, most notably in the drafting of both statutes and subordinate legislation, which are more in keeping with administrative ease than accountability to Parliament and observance of the law. The absence of a clearly articulated philosophy of respect for liberty and of propriety in the activities of the executive government of Canada is a most serious problem.

> Your Committee specifically condemns certain practices and devices commonly employed in the drafting of subordinate laws:
> (i) the use of subjective instead of objective tests in granting power to

determine whether a regulation applies to a particular set of circumstances. The bare opinion of an official should not be a criterion for action. The only purpose of the use of phrases such as "in the opinion of" or "where the Minister is satisfied" is to impede judicial review. . . .

A recurring theme is the narrow interpretation accorded the words "statutory instruments" and "regulations" for purposes of the Statutory Instruments Act and denial that documents which purport to be regulations are subject to review by the Joint Committee. Another recurring theme is that even where the Joint Committee is considered to have jurisdiction, and reports that statutory instruments and regulations are poorly drafted, unjust, indeed may be ultra vires, its reports are then merely ignored. To quote again from the Fourth Report:

Your Committee's effectiveness will be severely hampered if its criteria relating to impropriety continue to be ignored.

Perhaps what has happened has been inevitable; it may even be desirable—but not as long as we pretend that nothing has really happened to change the old order. If we permit the proliferation of powers—dispersed discretions—without setting up an effective mechanism to supervise the exercise of these powers, a free community will not long survive. Unless we find some way of bringing Parliament back into the picture, its individual members, legislating only in generalities and without effective means of seeing how their servants are acting, are reduced to comparative impotence.

Delegated legislation is sufficiently significant to deserve a special mechanism for review of its exercise. Unless members of Parliament fulfil this function, Parliament as we have known it will become relatively impotent. Some public servants have questioned whether members of Parliament can be expected to approach review of the exercise of discretions in a nonpartisan manner. They seem to feel that politicians will refuse to distinguish between the essentially political acts of determining policy and voting for legislative programs, and the essentially nonpartisan function of studying how powers delegated by legislation are being exercised. Perhaps the question might be phrased, "Can members forget party politics long enough to be objective in protecting the rights of the individual to the end that there is equal justice for all, and efficient, nondiscriminatory application of the law?" This is a function which the courts cannot fulfil in relation to the exercise of delegated discretions. If members of Parliament cannot, or will not, do this job through committees established for this purpose, then we should at least abandon the pretence that they are able to do so now, even with the Statutory Instruments Act.

29/Parliament and Administrative Responsibility*

Kenneth Kernaghan

An essential condition for a complete and comprehensible system of responsibility in government is that elected or appointed officials, or both, bear responsibility for all government actions. In a parliamentary democracy, if officials waste public funds, break the law or violate citizens' rights, the public expects that someone will be held accountable for these misdeeds. If ministers do not accept responsibility for departmental transgressions, the focus of blame shifts to public servants. But the conventions of ministerial responsibility and political neutrality still protect the anonymity of public servants and restrict their answerability to Parliament. As a result, some commentators claim that these conventions, even as restated, permit public servants to exercise power without publicity or responsibility.[1] On those exceptional occasions when blame is publicly attributed to specific officials, disciplinary action is handled as an internal administrative matter with the result that the public rarely learns what penalties, if any, are imposed (for example, in the cases of the foot and mouth disease epidemic, the Bonaventure refit, the RCMP security activities). Moreover, successive auditors general have documented the "horrible stories" of a widespread and continuing absence of economy, efficiency and effectiveness in the government's expenditure of public funds. Consequently, it appears to the public that on some occasions a gap exists between ministerial and administrative responsibility because neither ministers nor public servants seem to be held accountable for maladministration.

It is generally recognized that Parliament could play a more effective role in promoting responsibility in government. Advocates of parliamentary reform have proposed a variety of measures to enhance Parliament's control and influence over ministers and public servants. Improvements in Parliament's ability to hold ministers to account would affect public servants indirectly through their responsibility to their minister. But the ministers' political burdens together with the large scale and complexity

---

*Reprinted as a short excerpt by permission from Kenneth Kernaghan, "Power, Parliament and Public Servants in Canada: Ministerial Responsibility Reexamined," *Canadian Public Policy* 3 (Summer 1979): 383-96.
[1]See, for example, J.R. Mallory, "Responsive and Responsible Government," Presidential Address, section II, *Transactions of the Royal Society of Canada*, series IV, 12 (1974), p. 221; and Claude E. Forget, "L'administration publique: sujet ou objet du pouvoir politique?" *Canadian Public Administration* 21 (1978): 234-242.

of their departments' operations present substantial barriers to a significant increase in ministerial answerability to Parliament.

Some proponents of reform contend that responsibility in government should be borne by those who actually exercise the power and that our constitutional conventions should be altered to reflect political and administrative reality. They suggest that the accountability of ministers to Parliament should be supplemented by the accountability of public servants. It is desirable, therefore, to consider whether proposals designed to increase administrative accountability to Parliament can be comfortably accommodated within our existing constitutional arrangements.

Among the most common proposals for parliamentary reform are measures which will enhance the effectiveness of committees in evaluating the policies and scrutinizing the administrative actions of the executive. Proposed changes include a more vigorous investigative role for committees, policy field specialization by committee members and improved support facilities in the form of research staff and funds. The feasibility of such proposals depends to some extent on the objectives of parliamentary committees in their relations with ministers and officials but it depends primarily on whether the government will permit changes in the nature of these relations.

The functions of parliamentary committees may for analytical purposes be divided into policy development (involving primarily evaluation of the purpose and content of proposed legislation), review of existing policies and scrutiny of departmental administration (especially through examination of the estimates). In practice these functions often overlap and committee members vary in the emphasis they place on each function. Kornberg and Mishler[2] estimate that standing committees as a whole "spend about 50% of their time considering the estimates of the departments and divide the remainder of their time between scrutinizing current legislation and conducting investigations, collecting information on particular problems and preparing reports for the consideration of the House."

Public servants already answer to parliamentary committees by explaining the administrative and technical implications of existing and proposed policies. An increase in the investigative work, specialization and expertise of committee members would enable them to engage in better-informed and more penetrating questioning of officials. This would encourage public servants to perform their administrative tasks more economically, efficiently and effectively, especially if committee members focused their attention on the scrutiny of departmental

---

[2]Allan Kornberg and William Mishler, *Influence in Parliament: Canada* (Durham, N.C.: Duke University Press, 1976), p. 33.

administration. If members devoted a substantial portion of their efforts to policy development and policy review, officials would continue to refer to their minister those inquiries involving policy matters. But the enhanced competence of committee members combined with the difficulty of separating policy and administrative considerations would cause public servants to reveal more frequently and clearly their influence on policy formation. The effect on ministerial responsibility would be negligible because ministers would continue to deal with questions on the substance and direction of government policy.

The reinforcement and extension of the activities and expertise of parliamentary committees would improve Parliament's capacity to hold public servants accountable for the administration—but not for the content—of government policies. Thus these reforms would not satisfy those who contend that the responsibility of public servants should be commensurate with their power in the political process. They claim that for Parliament to play a significantly greater role in promoting administrative responsibility, there must be some shift in answerability for policy from ministers to public servants. Advocates of this reform have not examined rigorously the implications of their proposal for our parliamentary institutions and practices. Moreover, it is unlikely that the government would allow such a fundamental change in our present constitutional arrangements. The advent of direct answerability by public servants for their policy recommendations would have very important consequences for the responsibility of ministers and the political neutrality of public servants.

Relations between ministers and public servants would be complicated by the difficulty of distinguishing their respective contributions to the development of specific policies. The answerability of public servants to Parliament would compete with their accountability and loyalty to their minister. The remaining healthy component of ministerial responsibility—the answerability of ministers—would be severely weakened. Even the convenient fiction of a separation between policy and administration would be extremely difficult to maintain. There would be a dramatic decline in public service anonymity and the senior echelons of the service would be politicized. Public servants would be compelled to defend their policy recommendations before parliamentary committees and the public. Officials would become personally associated with particular policies and would, therefore, become involved in political controversy. Security of tenure for senior officials would be replaced by a system of political appointments and a consequent turnover of public servants with a change in government.

This hypothetical pattern of relations among politicians and public servants indicates that public servants cannot be held answerable to Parliament for policy matters without major modifications in the present practice of ministerial responsibility and political neutrality. It also demonstrates the comparatively small extent to which the conventions have evolved towards this pattern of behaviour from their traditional interpretation. Current trends suggest that the conventions will continue to evolve or will be altered in the direction of greater administrative answerability to Parliament but that ministers will retain formal responsibility for the defence of government policy. Thus Parliament has the potential to effect a modest increase in its power over the public service, especially in the sphere of overseeing administration, without breaching those constitutional conventions affecting most directly the conduct of the public service.

Whether Parliament will realize its potential depends on political and personal considerations by ministers and parliamentarians that can only be mentioned here. The power of Parliament over the public service rests largely on its ability and inclination to control and influence the executive as a whole. But Parliament's success in checking the executive hinges on such factors as the devotion of committee members to their work, the creation of a nonpartisan atmosphere in committee deliberations, the government's willingness to take committee reports seriously and improved access to much government information now treated as confidential. This last factor merits brief elaboration.

Parliament's efforts to exercise power over the public service have been impeded by the tradition and practice of secrecy which surrounds much executive action in Canada. Not only members of Parliament but also journalists, academics and other segments of the public have been denied access to government information which they deem essential to the evaluation and surveillance of the recommendations and decisions of public servants. In parliamentary governments of the Westminster type, the reconciliation of freedom of information with the conventions of ministerial responsibility and political neutrality is a complicated and contentious matter. Many advocates of public access legislation in Canada claim that the importance of these conventions as barriers to the enactment of such legislation has been overstated. They contend further that ministerial and public service resistance to freedom of information legislation is motivated not by concern over constitutional proprieties but by fear of political or personal embarrassment and of administrative inconvenience. It is notable also that the conventions have evolved in a direction which will facilitate the adoption of a freedom of information act acceptable to Parliament and the public and compatible with our constitutional traditions.[3]

---

[3]See Kenneth Kernaghan, *Freedom of Information and Ministerial Responsibility*, Research Publication No. 2 (Toronto: Ontario Commission on Freedom of Information and Individual Privacy, 1978).

The present workload of ministers precludes any significant increase in their answerability to Parliament and the conventions of ministerial responsibility, political neutrality and anonymity restrict public servants from answering to Parliament on policy matters. However, reforms in the structures and processes of Parliament would help to augment Parliament's power over both ministers and public servants. In particular, several measures could be adopted to increase the answerability of public servants for departmental administration. The Royal Commission on Financial Management and Accountability (the Lambert Commission)[4] made several useful recommendations for reforms to enhance the accountability of both ministers and senior bureaucrats to Parliament.

According to the commissioners, the doctrine of ministerial responsibility is "a cornerstone" of the Canadian constitution; ". . . it identifies who has the final responsibility for decisions taken—the minister, and provides a forum in which he is publicly accountable—Parliament."[5] They contend, however, that the doctrine "must not become an obstacle to holding to account those who carry out tasks on the basis of delegated authority—the officials of departments and agencies."[6]

The commission's recommendations involve a much more active role for parliamentary committees. The commissioners suggest that a Standing Committee on Government Finance and the Economy be established to examine, among other matters, a five-year fiscal plan which the government would submit to Parliament each autumn. The deputy minister would be designated the chief administrative officer of the department and would be held directly accountable to Parliament through the Public Accounts Committee for specified administrative duties. Ministers would remain accountable for policy objectives and decisions. The number and size of standing committees in the House of Commons would be reduced and these committees would be allowed to recommend the partial reduction of proposed government expenditures and to submit substantive reports on the estimates to the House. Also, each committee would have a chairman elected for the life of a Parliament and a budget to engage staff assistance.

The commissioners are satisfied that their proposed reforms will not erode the doctrine of ministerial responsibility. Indeed, they contend that "the concept of direct accountability of officials before Parliament through one of its committees would reinforce the minister's and the Cabinet's ability to be responsible for the conduct of the affairs of government."[7] In the light of the analysis presented in this paper, the

---

[4]*Final Report* (Ottawa: Minister of Supply and Services, March 1979).
[5]*Ibid.*, p. 371.
[6]*Ibid.*
[7]*Ibid.*, p. 375.

commissioners' aspirations for Parliament seem unduly optimistic. But they do acknowledge that the success of efforts to increase government's accountability to Parliament on administrative matters depends largely on the determination of ministers and parliamentarians to achieve this end.

Students of the Canadian Parliament tend to be pessimistic that the changes in the machinery and attitudes of government needed to increase significantly Parliament's power over the public service will be made. In any event, Parliament is a potentially important but far from a sufficient instrument to ensure a responsible public bureaucracy. In the search for an appropriate balance between administrative power and administrative responsibility, the role of Parliament must be supplemented by a broad range of controls and influences exercised by other actors in the political system.

30/Representative Bureaucracy*
Kenneth Kernaghan

The representativeness of the Canadian federal public service is an important matter because of the relation of francophone representation[1] to the central issue of national unity and because of recent demands for the increased representation of women and native peoples. This essay reviews the arguments for and against representative bureaucracy, with particular reference to the Canadian situation.

Representative bureaucracy is a tricky concept and it has been inter-

*Reprinted and substantially abridged by permission from Kenneth Kernaghan, "Representative Bureaucracy: the Canadian Perspective," *Canadian Public Administration* 21 (Winter 1978): 489-512.
[1]See also Kenneth Kernaghan, "Bilingualism in the Public Service of Canada," in this volume at p. 94.

preted in a variety of ways.[2] A strict interpretation of representative bureaucracy would require that the public service be a microcosm of the total society in terms of a wide range of variables, including race, religion, education, social class and region of origin. However, there is disagreement in academic writings as to what representative bureaucracy means, what purposes it serves, what degree of representativeness is desirable and what variables should be included. There is general agreement among contemporary scholars that the importance of representative bureaucracy for the study of politics and public administration lies in its links with the concept and practice of administrative responsibility. Proponents of representative bureaucracy recommend its adoption on the following grounds:

1. Public servants exercise significant power in the political process.
2. External controls over public servants by the political executive, the legislature and the courts are inadequate to check administrative power and so to ensure administrative responsibility.
3. A public service which is representative of the total population will be responsive to the needs and interests of the general public and will therefore be more responsible. This central proposition of the theory of representative bureaucracy is based on several subpropositions:
    (a) If the values of the public service as a whole are similar to those of the total population, then the public service will tend to make the kind of decisions which the public would make if it were involved in the decision making.
    (b) The values of public servants are moulded by the pattern of socialization they experience before they enter the public service, that is, by such socializing forces as education, social class, occupational background, race, family and group associations.
    (c) These values will be reflected in the behaviour of public servants and therefore in their recommendations and decisions.
    (d) Thus the various groups in the population should be repre-

---

[2]For an examination of the theory of representative bureaucracy and of its inadequacies see V. Subramaniam, "Representative Bureaucracy: A Reassessment," *American Political Science Review* 61 (December 1967): 1010-19; Arthur D. Larson, "Representative Bureaucracy and Administrative Responsibility: A Reassessment," *Midwest Review of Public Administration* 7 (April 1973): 78-89; Kenneth John Meier, "Representative Bureaucracy: An Empirical Analysis," *American Political Science Review* 69 (June 1965): 526-42; Kenneth John Meier and Lloyd C. Nigro, "Representative Bureaucracy and Policy Preferences: A Study in the Attitudes of Federal Executives," *Public Administration Review* 36 (July-August 1976): 458-69; and V. Seymour Wilson and Willard A. Mullins, "Representative Bureaucracy: Linguistic/Ethnic Aspects in Canadian Public Policy," *Canadian Public Administration* 21 (Winter 1978): 513-38.

sented in the public service in approximate demographic proportion so that public servants will be responsive to their interests both in policy development and program delivery.

Critics of representative bureaucracy acknowledge the extensive power of public servants and the consequent need to provide controls to preserve and promote administrative responsibility. They contend, however, that the assertion that external controls are inadequate to ensure responsible administrative conduct requires more investigation. These critics also point to the logical and empirical failings of the theory of representative bureaucracy as it is outlined above.

They contend first of all that in a representative public service the values of the public service *as a whole* will not be similar to those of the general population; rather, the values of *individual* public servants *may* be similar to the values of those groups in the population they are supposed to represent. Moreover, the public service as a whole does not make decisions; rather, decisions are made by individual public servants who, by acting on behalf of groups whom they represent, would serve the interests of particular segments of the public rather than the total population. Also it is not sufficient for the public service as a whole to be broadly representative of the general population; for all interests to be represented in the decision-making process, each major administrative unit must be representative of the total population, especially at its senior levels where the most important recommendations and decisions are made.

Opponents of representative bureaucracy observe further that a public servant with certain social and educational origins will not necessarily share the values of persons outside the public service who have similar origins. The lifelong process of socialization continues after entry to the public service in the form of resocialization to the values of the service as a whole or of particular administrative units. Moreover, representatives of a specific group in the population, especially if they achieve high office in the public service, are likely to be upwardly mobile and may well share the socioeconomic and other values of those with whom they work rather than of the group from which they came. In this regard, Peta Sheriff regrets the lack of research on the strength of pre-occupational and post-occupational experience and concludes that although "the very cornerstone of the representative bureaucracy thesis has no direct evidence to support it ... the suspicion that pre-occupational socialization must have *some* influence is sufficient to maintain the thesis."[3] More recently, on the basis of an empirical analysis of the United States public service, Meier and Nigro assert that "apparently, agency socialization

---

[3]Peta E. Sheriff, "Unrepresentative Bureaucracy," *Sociology* 8 (1974): 449.

tends to overcome any tendency for the supergrades to hold attitudes rooted in social origins."[4] Even if we assume that public servants continue to share the values of certain groups despite organizational socialization, these values may not be significantly reflected in the public servants' behaviour.

Thus, public servants will not necessarily be more responsive to groups in society which are represented in rough demographic proportion in the public service. It is logically possible to have a representative public service which is not responsive and to have a responsive public service which is not representative. Indeed, Meier and Nigro state that the most senior levels in the United States public service "are an unrepresentative demographic group holding quite representative attitudes."[5]

The Canadian Literature

Scholarly discussion of the virtues and limitations of representative bureaucracy has been rare in Canada. However, a valuable exchange of views by John Porter and Donald Rowat centres on the utility and implications of representative bureaucracy in the Canadian context.[6] Rowat contends that Porter, in his analysis of the Canadian bureaucratic elite based on Weber's "ideal type" of bureaucracy, emphasizes the efficiency and neutrality of the public service to the detriment of representativeness.

Porter states that groups will be represented in the public service in about the same proportion as in the total population if government recruitment and promotion policies do not discriminate against particular groups, if educational facilities to qualify persons for public service appointments are equal as between these groups, and if these groups are equally motivated to join the public service. He notes that "in the theoretically ideal bureaucracy the candidate for office neither gains nor loses as a result of ethnic, religious or regional origins."[7] Rowat claims that the assumptions of Porter's ideal type do not hold for the Canadian situation and that representativeness must be actively sought— even at the expense of technical efficiency and neutrality. But he argues that this cost need not be incurred. Intelligent persons with the potential to rise to higher levels in the service could be recruited and provided with

---

[4]Meier and Nigro, p. 467.
[5]Meier and Nigro, p. 467.
[6]John Porter, "Higher Public Servants and the Bureaucratic Elite in Canada," *Canadian Journal of Economics and Political Science* 24 (November 1958): 483-501; Donald C. Rowat, "On John Porter's Bureaucratic Elite in Canada," *ibid.*, 25 (May 1959): 204-207; and John Porter, "The Bureaucratic Elite: A Reply to Professor Rowat," *ibid.*, 25 (May 1959): 207-209.
[7]Porter, "Higher Public Servants," pp. 490-91.

the necessary in-service education and training. Also competent members of underrepresented groups could be brought into the public service from outside. Porter opposes the recruitment of outsiders on the grounds that this practice threatens the neutrality of the service and the concept of the bureaucratic career. He states that

> Modern bureaucracies ideally require social eunuchs who have been neutralized as persons within their own societies and who have divested themselves of interests in social groups and institutions involved in the struggle for power. Since the bases of power associations are frequently ethnic, regional, or religious, the idea that these groups should be represented in the bureaucracy contradicts the notion of the official as the servant of the state.[8]

Rowat does not agree with Porter that the appointment of "bureaucratic outsiders" would endanger political neutrality and he argues that a public service which complemented career public servants with outsiders would be more responsive since a career bureaucracy tends to "lose contact with and lack understanding of the changing feelings, needs and desires of the great variety of people and groups found in our dynamic, pluralistic society."[9]

Rowat does not suggest that underrepresented groups should be represented in precise proportion to their presence in the total population and he rejects the use of quotas for recruitment and promotion as unworkable. He does suggest, however, that the Public Service Commission should be guided in its policies by the principle of representation.

Porter raises objections to Rowat's plea for representativeness which are similar to some of those raised by American critics of the theory of representative bureaucracy. He first poses the fundamental question as to which of the many and varied groups in society should be represented in the public service. He then contends that Rowat's proposals for recruiting members of underrepresented groups and providing them with in-service training serve the principle of equal opportunity rather than representativeness. He states also that "in a society of classes, the upwardly mobile are seldom representative of the social interests from which they originated."[10] Finally, he notes the assumption in the theory of representative bureaucracy that political institutions are inadequate to cope with modern demands and questions the view that "ways can be found for governmental bureaucracy to make up for the deficiencies in our representative political institutions."[11]

A recent contribution to the debate on representative bureaucracy in

---

[8]*Ibid.*, p. 490.
[9]Rowat, p. 207.
[10]Porter, "The Bureaucratic Elite," p. 208.
[11]*Ibid.*, p. 209.

Canada, by Wilson and Mullins, focuses on francophone representation within the framework of an examination of the theoretical and practical arguments for and against representative bureaucracy. The authors conclude that the pursuit of representative bureaucracy in the belief "that it would be politically representative in any meaningful sense is not only bogus, but also dangerous. . . ."[12] They contend, however, that despite the inadequacies of the concept of representative bureaucracy it

> actually illuminates and extends the principle of merit in its widest and most socially advantageous sense. . . . With respect to Canada, in particular, there is evidence that the merit system has been too narrowly conceived, and that it has therefore failed to recruit a broad range of talents that could revitalize and strengthen the public service.[13]

Representation in the Canadian Public Service

Very little information is available on the composition of the Canadian public service in relation to the total population. From the data that are available, however, it is clear that the public service is not a microcosm of Canadian society. A number of important groups are underrepresented in the service and the senior echelons are especially unrepresentative of the general population. On the basis of published research findings,[14] we may conclude that the middle levels of the public service are more representative than the senior levels along all major dimensions and are proportionately representative in relation to birthplace and geographic origins.[15] The middle levels of the service are not a mirror of Canadian society but "the federal administration is a relatively open and talent-hungry organization at the middle level. It draws amply from native stock and newcomers to Canada, from all geographic regions except Quebec, a variety of ethnic-religious strains, urban and rural areas, and with some favouring of the top levels, the several social classes in the country."[16]

As indicated earlier, the representativeness of the senior public service is an especially important matter because of the power of senior officials in the policy process. Available data show that in Canada the

---

[12]Wilson and Mullins, p. 534.

[13]*Ibid.*

[14]John Porter, *The Vertical Mosaic* (Toronto: University of Toronto Press, 1965); P.J. Chartrand and K.L. Pond, *A Study of Executive Career Paths in the Public Service of Canada* (Chicago: Public Personnel Association, 1969); Christopher Beattie, *Minority Men in a Majority Setting* (Toronto: McClelland and Stewart, 1975); Dennis Olsen, "The State Elites," in *The Canadian State: Political Economy and Political Power*, ed. Leo Panitch (Toronto: University of Toronto Press, 1977), pp. 208-17; and Dennis Olsen, *The State Elite* (Toronto: McClelland and Stewart, 1980), pp. 65-83.

[15]Beattie, p. 11-17.

[16]*Ibid.*, p. 50.

senior echelons of the service overrepresent persons who are anglophone, male, members of the United and Anglican Churches, from
Ontario, highly educated, and from the middle and upper classes of
society. Thus the senior levels of the service are unrepresentative of the
general population and are less representative than the middle levels.
However, Dennis Olsen, on the basis of his 1973 study of the social background, career and education of 224 federal bureaucrats, concluded that
"the federal elite is less homogeneous than it was when [John] Porter
studied it in 1953. The elite is now characterized by a greater spread in
class and ethnic origins, which are signs that it is less exclusive. There
seems to be a greater diversity appearing in the elite in universities
attended and in types of discipline learned."[17]

The government's policy is to provide all Canadians with an equal
opportunity for employment, training and career progression in the
public service. The role of the Public Service Commission, which is the
administrative body primarily responsible for implementing this policy,
is "to work with departments and agencies to remove institutional and
attitudinal barriers to effective equality of opportunity and to continue
special efforts among underrepresented groups to ensure that they are
aware of and can compete for positions in the Public Service."[18]

It is not government policy to establish in the public service a microcosm of the Canadian mosaic by pursuing exact demographic representation of all groups in society; rather, the government's aim is to achieve a
more proportionate representation of a limited number of politically
significant but underrepresented groups. In this regard, the Public
Service Commission has stated that the underrepresentation of francophones, women, native peoples and the handicapped "may have the effect
of reducing the sensitivity of the Public Service to the needs of particular
elements of the population."[19] Thus a prime motivation underlying
present efforts to represent these groups more adequately is to make the
public service more responsive both in the provision of policy advice and
the delivery of services. We have already seen that this assumption that
representativeness will promote responsiveness is central to the theory
of representative bureaucracy.

The attainment of a representative public service depends largely on
the extent to which equality of opportunity actually exists for various
groups in society. Members of these groups must be knowledgeable
about government employment opportunities, they must be free from
discrimination in government, and they must have equal access to educa-

---

[17]Olsen, *The State Elite*, p. 82.
[18]Public Service Commission, *Annual Report 1976* (Ottawa: Minister of Supply and Services,
1977), p. 15.
[19]*Ibid.*

tion and training relevant to public service positions. The underrepresentation of important segments of the Canadian population can be explained by the existence of barriers to equal opportunity both in the government and in the community. The government has formally acknowledged "the need for special measures to prevent, eliminate or redress any disadvantages which specific groups of employees or citizens have experienced. . . ."[20]

Francophones, women and native peoples have encountered many institutional and attitudinal obstacles to equal opportunity and therefore to adequate representation in the public service. To overcome these barriers and to attract more members of underrepresented groups to the service, especially to the higher ranks, the government has gradually developed a common pattern of remedial strategies. The three components of this pattern are new or modified administrative structures and practices designed to reduce obstacles to entry to and promotion in the service, active recruitment efforts, and education and training to prepare group members for public service appointments and advancement.

Conclusions

The Canadian public service, especially at its senior levels, is not representative of the total population in terms of such important variables as ethnicity and sex and certain politically significant groups are underrepresented at all levels of the service. Government measures to improve the representation of particular groups are based on the reasonable expectation that the diversity of views resulting from balanced representation in the public service of the major groups in society will make the service more responsive. Moreover, the government's presumption is that members of underrepresented groups who join the public service will maintain sensitivity to the needs and claims of these groups. In view of the deficiencies of the theory of representative bureaucracy outlined earlier, the benefits of representation in terms of increased responsiveness are likely to be less than anticipated. However, we know very little about the extent to which the expanded representation of francophones, women and native peoples has had a policy impact by advancing the substantive interests of these groups.

It is notable that increased representation has effects which are not covered by the theory of representative bureaucracy. Representation has a symbolic impact which explains in part its appeal to government officials and which helps to promote quiescence and stability in the Canadian political system. The statutes, regulations and administrative units designed to increase the representation of francophones, women

---

[20]Treasury Board, *Increased Indian, Métis and Non-Status Indian, and Inuit Participation in the Public Service of Canada,* June 21, 1977, p. 3.

and native people evoke symbols of equality of opportunity and upward mobility for members of these groups. In the name of equal opportunity, the government has instituted programs to recruit and train group members who have not enjoyed equal access to the public service. Also, recruitment to senior posts from outside the service and post-entry training geared to promotion to the higher ranks of the service demonstrate the opportunities for group members to attain senior policy-making posts.

These measures serve a partisan political purpose in that they help to sustain or increase electoral support for the governing party. Evidence of partisan motivation can be seen in the fact that, except for handicapped persons, the groups for whom increased representation has been sought in recent years have mobilized for political action and are highly visible and vocal in their demands for greater participation in the political and administrative systems. Moreover, the timing of the government's concern for increasing the representation of these groups can be tied directly to their growing influence in the political system. The government's efforts on behalf of francophones, women and native people have brought about a more representative public service. It is not practicable, however, to attempt to represent proportionately the myriad groups which make up the Canadian mosaic. Experience to date suggests that future government measures toward a more representative public service will be directed primarily to underrepresented groups which become politically influential. It is likely also that the government will continue to meet legitimate claims for increased representation by using the pattern of remedial steps outlined earlier in this essay.

31/The Ombudsman*

Committee on the Concept of the Ombudsman

The genesis of the ombudsman concept is to be found in Sweden, where over two and a half centuries ago, in 1713, a chancellor of justice was appointed by the king to keep a watchful eye on his officials and thus protect citizens from injustice. In 1809, as part of a constitutional revision, a *justitieombudsman* was appointed as an officer of the legislature charged with ensuring that the laws were adhered to by the administrative authorities and by the courts.

Since then the growth of government has been accompanied by an increasing concern about the need to protect individual rights, particularly as it has become clear that the efficient and fair-minded operation of vast administrative structures is not easily achieved. Mistakes, whether caused by managerial shortcomings, inadequate information, faulty interpretation of known facts or lack of sensitivity to personal circumstances, can and do happen. And even a mistake that appears in the setting of a large-scale organization to be trivial can have serious consequences for an individual. The concept of the ombudsman, although originally invented in an era very different from our own, has come increasingly to be regarded as a potentially useful instrument to help the citizen secure fair treatment from the modern state. As a consequence, the concept has found application in many jurisdictions, especially since the end of World War II.

What is an Ombudsman?

Ombudsmen speak for that elusive entity, the average citizen. They do not deal with broad affairs of state or policy. Rather, they deal with a host of administrative complaints and injustices, many of which seem comparatively unimportant—except to the affected individual.

Because their concern is with complaints about administrative actions or inactions, ombudsmen are typically excluded from certain areas, notably those covering actions of the head of state and the legislature and the deliberations of ministers on policy matters. In addition, they are usually given no capacity to consider the activities of courts of law and commercial state corporations. The rest of government, however—and this embraces a vast array of departments and agencies—falls within their mandate.

Ombudsmen possess influence rather than control. They cannot

---

*Reprinted and abridged by permission from Government of Canada, *Report of the Committee on the Concept of the Ombudsman* (Ottawa: Government of Canada, 1977).

alter administrative decisions. But they are well placed to cause those who have this power to review and change decisions which, after careful examination, appear to be unreasonable, oppressive or simply wrong in the circumstances. This influence, like that of auditors general, derives from their authority to investigate matters in depth and, as a last resort, to report their findings publicly to the legislature.

In carrying out their duties, most ombudsmen find it advantageous to take a conciliatory rather than an adversarial stance. They deal with hundreds of complaints each year, most of which bring them into close contact with government officials. Were an ombudsman consistently to adopt an aggressive and tendentious attitude he would almost certainly find himself frustrated by officials unwilling to expose themselves to personal attack or unpleasant publicity. Most ombudsmen, in fact, report that the great majority of government officials are anxious to rectify an identified wrong.

An ombudsman deals with a case by first determining whether the organization which is the subject of the complaint falls within his jurisdiction. Assuming the matter is within his jurisdiction, he then determines in a preliminary way if the complaint warrants further investigation. For example, he determines whether the complaint is frivolous, whether the complainant has taken all reasonable steps to have the problem resolved by other means, and whether there is some possibility of achieving rectification. If he concludes that the matter deserves to be pursued, he advises the competent authority of the complaint and makes preliminary inquiries. Often this simple indication of interest by the ombudsman is enough to cause a departmental review leading to a satisfactory solution without any significant involvement by the ombudsman or his staff.

In some instances, however, it may be necessary to initiate a detailed investigation. Although ombudsmen are subject to some restrictions about what they can investigate or disclose, these are generally not extensive. Indeed, if they were, it would be impossible for the institution to function effectively. The ombudsman or members of his staff may thus obtain files, call witnesses, and take such other steps as are necessary to investigate the complaint thoroughly. Except in very unusual circumstances, the investigation is carried out in private.

In a significant proportion of investigated cases, the ombudsman finds that the departmental action has been reasonable in the circumstances and that the complaint is unjustified. In such cases, the complainant is notified of the conclusion reached and is normally given a careful explanation of the rationale underlying the action that gave rise to the complaint. There is reason to believe that, even in these circumstances, a good explanation, coming from an independent source, can provide much satisfaction.

If after investigation the ombudsman continues to have doubts about the administrative action in question, he makes representations to the appropriate officials, who then frequently take remedial action. Most remaining cases are resolved in this manner.

From time to time circumstances do arise in which, following contact with officials, the ombudsman considers it necessary to consult the minister concerned. If no meeting of minds can be reached at this level, the ombudsman is empowered to draw public attention to the issue by reporting it to the legislature. This is a comparatively rare occurrence. Most ombudsmen prefer to see a satisfactory solution reached without public controversy, and both ministers and senior officials are similarly motivated.

Since virtually all ombudsmen function in approximately the manner just described, it is not surprising to find a very considerable degree of similarity among the offices in different jurisdictions. Although there are many special features of the office as it finds expression in different constitutional settings, there are also a few key characteristics which recur, and which, in effect, define the essential attributes of the ombudsman concept.

(a) Ombudsmen are nonpartisan, impartial and independent of the executive arm of government.
(b) Their central duty is to take up specific complaints from members of the public against injustice arising from the administrative actions or omissions of government.
(c) They possess the power to investigate, to comment and to criticize, and to make their findings known to the legislature and the public—but they have no power to alter or reverse decisions.

Existing Processes for Handling Complaints

Currently, there are four channels through which redress of a complaint may be sought if a person is aggrieved by an administrative act of government. He may complain directly to the organization responsible for the act in question. Alternatively, he may seek redress through a member of Parliament. Finally, he may lodge an appeal with an appeal tribunal if one is available or he may take action in the courts if the matter is actionable. Each of these channels is discussed in the following paragraphs.

Complaining directly to the responsible organization is a channel that is always available to the citizen seeking redress. No formality surrounds it. All a complainant need do is make known the nature of his complaint to those who occasioned it, either in writing or orally. But this process suffers the weakness that it contains no element of independent review by a third party. Without benefit of a referee, the process may simply perpetuate an adversarial situation between the parties concerned.

A complainant may, of course, lodge a complaint with a superior of the official whose action or inaction gave rise to the grievance, and in that sense seek third-party intervention. But even if this process of escalation is carried right to the top where the deputy head or the minister can be drawn into the matter, the essential weakness remains, for inevitably the investigation will be conducted by officials of the organization concerned. Senior officials may be somewhat blinkered by virtue of their association with the organization, or they may not personally have time to investigate the matter in depth. Their judgment may be affected by the way evidence is placed before them. In short, approaching the organization responsible for a grievance cannot guarantee an impartial review. Many people, cynical about the responsiveness of big institutions, probably do not even bother to approach the source of their complaint.

As an alternative to dealing directly with the government organization concerned, or subsequent to the failure of a move in this direction, a complainant may enlist the aid of a member of Parliament. Normally the member proceeds by asking the relevant minister or, in some cases, an official of the organization involved, for an explanation. He also has the right to raise questions in the House of Commons. Thus the member of Parliament is viewed by many individuals as their problem solver in Ottawa. Although this means of obtaining redress is often very effective, it too has limitations.

To begin with, members of Parliament have neither the staff nor the facilities to conduct extensive investigations into a multitude of complaints. Given their many other responsibilities, they may also not always have the time to give every complaint the degree of attention that a complainant might wish. Furthermore, some members may choose to give complaints a higher priority in their affairs than others, leading to considerable variation in the ways in which essentially similar complaints may be handled and possibly even to different results in terms of the resolution of the issues in question. Whether the member is on the government side or not may inject an element of variability into both his motivation to press the minister and the attitude of the latter toward the response he supplies. Finally, a member does not have the statutory powers that may be required to investigate the details of a case. He cannot, as can an ombudsman, compel the production of documents or the attendance of witnesses, nor can he exercise the right of entry into premises. Such powers would be inconsistent with the concept of parliamentary government. However, there would be no reason why a member could not enlist the assistance of an ombudsman in dealing with a complaint he has received. Indeed, in such circumstances the role of an ombudsman and that of a member of Parliament would be quite complementary.

A minister, of course, has powers of access denied to a member of Parliament and, in principle, he can exercise these in response to a query from a member. However, in practice, the investigation of even a minor administrative complaint can occupy much time, and ministers are not always able to devote enough of their own resources to such inquiries. Thus the burden of preparing the response to an inquiry by a member tends to fall back on the official whose action or inaction gave rise to the complaint in the first place. If the minister finds the official's explanation adequate, there is little the member or the complainant can do. In contrast, an ombudsman has his own resources to conduct a comprehensive "outside" investigation.

In addition to the two channels already discussed, the public may also turn to a number of appellate bodies, such as the Tariff Board and the Tax Review Board, and of course to the courts. Many complaints regarding administrative actions cannot be appealed to these bodies either because the complaint is outside their jurisdiction or because lodging an appeal would be too expensive and time-consuming. For many people, particularly those who are not at ease with complex institutions and the formality that often accompanies them, these bodies can be frightening. Even well-educated members of society often know little about the law and can be apprehensive about dealing with a process they do not understand. Appellate bodies are somewhat less forbidding, but the range of subjects they deal with is more limited than those which may be brought before the courts. Finally, neither courts nor appellate bodies are centrally concerned with the main preoccupation of ombudsmen, that is, complaints about administrative actions which normally involve allegations not of illegality but of "unfairness." In the latter realm, the ombudsman can sometimes be very effective whereas the courts and the various appeal bodies generally cannot.

Ministerial Responsibility

Recent constitutional experience suggests that it is unrealistic to hold a minister personally accountable for every aspect of administration. A minister is subject to various degrees of responsibility. He must certainly accept full responsibility for matters done properly under his instructions or in accordance with his policy. However, in the case of a problem not affecting an important question of policy, he is generally thought to have met his responsibility if he takes the matter in hand. Where the issue is essentially between a complainant and a particular official, the minister can hardly be expected to have had prior knowledge of the case or to have had an opportunity to influence it personally. He cannot be acquainted with, or personally criticized for, every detail of administration in his department. However, he is expected to be responsive to individual cases and to see that individual wrongs are righted.

Thus, the degree of ministerial responsibility seems to diminish—or, perhaps more precisely, the *nature* of ministerial responsibility seems to change—as one moves out of the realm of broad policy and into the domain of administrative action that occurs in a specific and limited context. Conversely, the mandate of an ombudsman starts at the opposite end of the spectrum, with matters of a particular and limited character, and should properly stop short of issues of policy. The result is that, in their application, the two concepts dovetail remarkably well.

Moreover, it must be remembered that the powers of ombudsmen are restricted to reporting. They cannot change matters themselves. Given this absence of executive authority in an ombudsman, the committee found it difficult to identify any basic conflict between the doctrine of ministerial responsibility and the concept of the ombudsman.[1]

An Ombudsman for Canada?

Ombudsmen function smoothly and well in several jurisdictions, including most of the Canadian provinces. Clearly, given sound judgment and good will, the concept can be made to work and work well, providing members of the public with a good deal of assistance in matters of direct and personal importance to them. Experience elsewhere demonstrates that the success of the office hinges above all on the wisdom and judgment of the incumbent. Carefully drafted legislation and due regard for constitutional principles and practices are clearly important. But, in the final analysis, no amount of drafting and attention to detail can substitute for the qualities of the incumbent.

If a suitable incumbent is selected, an ombudsman would do much to promote improvements in the handling of individual administrative complaints, and would do so without creating the need for complicated new structures or procedures within the public service. His mere presence would increase the awareness of ministers and officials of the need to deal promptly and equitably with individuals who perceive that they are victims of an administrative injustice. His independent position

---

[1]The eminent British constitutional expert, Professor H.W.R. Wade, has expressed this view well: ". . . the ombudsman operates in exactly the area where the doctrine of ministerial responsibility failed to work efficiently . . . so far from weakening ministerial responsibility, therefore, the ombudsman has supplemented it and helped it to work better by being able to investigate and report so that Members of Parliament can if necessary call the minister to account." "The British Ombudsman: A Lawyer's View," *Administrative Law Review* (1972).

should also provide an excellent platform from which to explain the problems and concerns of the private citizen to the bureaucracy and vice versa.

Thus an ombudsman would be a desirable adjunct to the existing system of complaint handling in the departments and agencies of the federal government.*

32/Freedom of Information
in Canada*
Kenneth Kernaghan

The government of Canada has traditionally operated on the principle that all government information is secret unless the government decides to release it. Many proponents of freedom of information legislation contend that this principle should be reversed so that all government information will be released unless the government can make a good case for keeping it secret. Under this latter approach, the burden on the public of justifying requests for the disclosure of information would be lifted; the burden of justifying nondisclosure of information would be imposed on the government, specifically on ministers and public servants.

This essay will examine efforts to achieve freedom of information legislation at the federal level of Canadian government; the impact of the doctrine of ministerial responsibility on these efforts; and the Liberal government's Access to Information Bill, with particular reference to its provisions on exemptions and the review process.

---

*[Editor's Note]: In April 1978, the Liberal government introduced Bill C-43, entitled the *Ombudsman Act*. For a critical analysis of the bill, see K.A. Friedmann and A.G. Milne,"The Federal Ombudsman Legislation: A Critique of Bill C-43," *Canadian Public Policy*, vol. 6 (Winter 1980), pp. 63-67.

---

*Based in part by permission on Kenneth Kernaghan, *Freedom of Information and Ministerial Responsibility*, Ontario Commission on Freedom of Information and Individual Privacy, Research Publication no. 2 (Toronto, 1978).

Background

In Canada, a series of significant developments beginning in 1965 has brought the federal government close to the enactment of freedom of information legislation. During 1965, Professor D.C. Rowat published his landmark paper attacking the principle of administrative secrecy in Canada,[1] and Barry Mather, a New Democratic Party member of Parliament, introduced a private member's bill on government administrative disclosure.[2] The Reports of the Royal Commission on Security (Abridged)[3] and the Task Force on Government Information Services,[4] both of which were published in 1969, devoted small sections to the matter of administrative secrecy. However, neither report had much impact in the way of improving public access to classified information.

Then, on March 15, 1973, the Liberal government tabled in the House of Commons a Cabinet directive which required all departments and agencies to provide information to members of Parliament except where the information fell within the scope of sixteen enumerated exemptions.[5] These guidelines, which are generally viewed by Opposition members and the media as too vague, too broad and too restrictive, are also used by the government to decide what information should be made available to the public. The guidelines were referred to the Standing Joint Committee of the House and Senate on Regulations and Other Statutory Instruments. In June of the same year, another Cabinet directive[6] confirmed the "thirty-year rule" in effect since May 1, 1969[7] which directed departments to release most public records after thirty years. Departments were also instructed to transfer to the Public Archives records less than thirty years old and to make these records available with the permission of the appropriate ministers.

In late 1974, a private member's bill on freedom of information which had been introduced each year since 1969 by Gerald Baldwin, a Conservative member of Parliament, was also referred to the Committee on Regulations. On February 12, 1976, Parliament adopted unanimously the committee's report of December 16, 1975, stating that it approved in principle the concept of freedom of information legislation. Parliament

---

[1]D.C. Rowat, "How Much Administrative Secrecy?" *Canadian Journal of Economics and Political Science* 31 (November 1965): 479-98.

[2]Mr. Mather introduced this bill as a private member's bill each year from 1965 to 1970.

[3]Canada, *Report of the Royal Commission on Security (Abridged)* (Ottawa: Queen's Printer, 1969).

[4]Canada, *To Know and Be Known—Report of the Task Force on Government Information Services* (Ottawa: Queen's Printer, 1969).

[5]Cabinet Directive No. 45, "Notices of Motion for the Production of Papers."

[6]Cabinet Directive No. 46, "Transfer of Public Records to the Public Archives and Access to Public Records Held by the Public Archives and by Departments."

[7]See statement by Prime Minister Trudeau on "Release to Archives of Records in Existence for Thirty Years," *Debates* (Commons), May 1, 1969, pp. 8199-8200.

then referred the matter back to the committee. And on July 14, 1977, Parliament passed *The Canadian Human Rights Act*,[8] first introduced in July 1975. This act, among other things, grants Canadian citizens a right of access to personal records held by the government and permits them to correct inaccurate or obsolete information.

An important development in the movement towards more openness in Canadian government was the publication in June 1977 of the Liberal government's Green Paper entitled *Legislation on Public Access to Government Documents*.[9] This Green Paper contains a brief but quite comprehensive examination of the possible consequences for government of freedom of information legislation. The paper was referred to the Committee on Regulations which submitted its recommendations on the paper to Parliament in June 1978.[10] On October 24, 1979, the newly elected Progressive Conservative Government introduced Bill C-15— the Freedom of Information Act. Then, on July 17, 1980, the reelected Liberal government introduced Bill C-43—the Access to Information Act. We shall return to discussion of these two bills.

Ministerial Responsibility

Much discussion of freedom of information legislation in Canada has centred on the issue of whether such legislation would encroach unduly on ministerial responsibility. Somewhat less concern focused on the possible reduction in the political neutrality and anonymity of public servants.

It is easy to understand why ministers and senior public servants do not share the enthusiasm of persons outside government for freedom of information legislation in general and for access to material on the decision-making process in particular. The release of information revealing ministerial and public service contributions to and debates over policy has important implications for both ministerial responsibility and political neutrality. Documents which disclose disagreement among ministers or between ministers and public servants could be exploited by the government's opponents to the political disadvantage of the ministers. It is natural that ministers should not want to answer to the legislature and the public for the content of documents which are likely to be controversial and which could be kept secret. Ministers do not deliberately seek trouble.

Similarly, senior public servants generally resist the expansion of public access to official documents which lay bare their personal views

---

[8]Canada, *Statutes*, 1976-1977, c. 33.
[9]Honourable John Roberts, secretary of state, *Legislation on Public Access to Government Documents* (Ottawa: Supply and Services, 1977).
[10]Committee on Regulations Respecting Green Paper, Issue no. 34, June 27, 1978.

and values on policy issues. If public servants are drawn into public debate over their contributions to policy development, their anonymity will decline. Moreover, to the extent that their written advice is at odds with their minister's decision, both ministers and public servants may be publicly embarrassed. Ministers may strive to avoid such situations by surrounding themselves with political appointees or with yes-men. This will threaten both the frankness and the completeness of departmental advice and also undermine the security of tenure associated with a career in the public service.

The impact of more open government on the doctrines of ministerial responsibility and political neutrality should not, however, be exaggerated. The gradual evolution of these doctrines that has already occurred has been explained elsewhere.[11] The implementation of freedom of information legislation would require further evolution of these doctrines; it would not require their drastic alteration or abandonment. The importance of the doctrine of ministerial responsibility in particular will be evident in the next two sections of this paper on exemptions and the review process.

Exemptions

The subjects of exemptions and review mechanisms are closely related. Judgments on the number and nature of exemptions considered desirable depend to a large extent on the method adopted to review complaints about nondisclosure. If ministers make the final decision whether a particular document falls into an exempted category, they may approve legislation providing for a small number of specific exemptions. If a person or body independent of ministers makes the final decision on exemptions, ministers may only support legislation which contains a large number of specific exemptions or a smaller number of very broad exemptions. Thus decisions on the exemptions to be included in the legislation should be taken in relation to the review mechanism that will be adopted.

There is much agreement from one governmental jurisdiction to another that certain types of information should be kept secret, such as documents relating to national defence and security, personal information on individual citizens, trade secrets and financial or commercial information of a confidential nature and records on criminal investigations. There is, however, considerable variation among governments in the comprehensiveness of the exclusions within the different classes of information.

In Canada, the exemptions set out in Bill C-43 are quite similar to

---

[11]See Kenneth Kernaghan, "Power, Parliament and Public Servants: Ministerial Responsibility Reexamined," in this volume at p. 227.

those in Bill C-15—and are quite substantial. Bill C-43 provides, subject to a number of exemptions, that a Canadian citizen, a permanent resident or a Canadian corporation "has a right to and shall, on request (in writing), be given access to any record under the control of a government institution" (S.4). However, records containing information obtained in confidence from a foreign government, an international organization or a provincial, municipal or regional government in Canada are exempted from disclosure unless the government or the organization in question agrees to release or permit the release of the records (S.13).

Bill C-43 contains a much broader exemption than Bill C-15 with respect to intergovernmental matters. Records will not be disclosed "which could reasonably be expected to be injurious to the conduct . . . of federal-provincial affairs, including . . . (a) information on federal-provincial consultations or deliberations; and (b) information on strategy or tactics" of the Canadian government bearing on the conduct of federal-provincial *affairs*[12] (S.14). Very broad exemption is provided also for nine categories of information which, if disclosed, "could reasonably be expected to be injurious to the conduct of international affairs, the defence of Canada or any state allied or associated with Canada or the detection, prevention or suppression of subversive or hostile activities. . . ." (S.15).

In addition, records are exempted from disclosure if they contain information relating to law enforcement and investigation (S.16) or if their release might threaten the safety of individuals (S.17) or affect adversely the financial interests of Canada (S.18). Records are also exempted if they contain personal information (S.19) or if they contain trade secrets, financial, commercial, scientific or technical information which if disclosed could harm a third party (that is, firms and corporations) (S.20).

Exemptions relating to the operations of government reflect the concern of ministers and public servants about the preservation of ministerial responsibility and public service anonymity. The following Cabinet documents are exempted from disclosure: Cabinet memoranda; Cabinet agendas or records of Cabinet deliberations or decisions; records relating to consultation among ministers in respect of government decisions and policies; and records used to brief ministers on these decisions and policies. Cabinet discussion papers are exempted only before decisions are made and draft legislation is exempted only before it is introduced in Parliament (S.21).

Finally, records will not be disclosed if their confidentiality is required under any other statute (S.25) and the nonexempt portion of an exempted document may be severed and released (S.26).

---

[12]Emphasis added. Bill C-15 used the narrower term *negotiations*.

The length and breadth of this list of exemptions have been severely criticized by many segments of the Canadian population[13] and the government has agreed to amend some of the exemption provisions in the bill. Thus the review mechanism established to make the final decision on the interpretation of the exemptions is a critically important component of freedom of information legislation.

The Review Process

Initially, the task of applying the exemption provisions to requests for access to government documents is performed by public servants. However, instances will arise where citizens wish to appeal to a higher authority against a public servant's decision to deny access to all or part of certain documents. Thus freedom of information legislation must provide a review process which specifies the person or persons with authority to review the decisions of public servants.

Ministers and public servants tend to favour a review process in which ministers have ultimate authority to decide whether a particular document will be released. However, many individuals and groups in Canada prefer a review mechanism which allows ministerial decisions on access to be overruled. The Green Paper noted that the ideal review process would be characterized not only by speed, efficiency and minimal cost but also by public credibility and consistency with ministerial responsibility.[14] The difficulty facing the drafters of public access legislation is that the latter two attributes may be mutually incompatible. The challenge is to devise a review mechanism which will satisfy the public but which will not infringe unduly on ministerial responsibility. The major choice is between two categories of review mechanism:

1. those which confer final authority on a minister; and
2. those which bestow final authority on a person, body or institution other than a minister.

Among the review mechanisms that have been proposed in the Canadian context are Parliament, an information auditor, an ombudsman, an information commissioner with advisory powers, an information commissioner with powers to order disclosure, and judicial review. The latter three mechanisms have received the most serious consideration and will, therefore, be discussed in this essay. Proposals have also been made for a review process which combines two of these three mechanisms.

An *information commissioner* with advisory powers could be appointed to inquire into complaints about nondisclosure, to scrutinize the documents in question and to make a prompt report to the com-

---

[13]See, for example, Minutes of Proceedings and Evidence of the Standing Committee on Justice and Legal Affairs regarding Bill C-43, beginning with Issue no. 15, March 3, 1981.
[14]*Legislation on Public Access to Government Documents*, p. 16.

plainant which the government would not be obliged to accept. The strength of this proposal lies in the fact that the news media and Opposition parties could put pressure on the minister to reverse his decision by publicizing those reports where the commissioner disagrees with the minister's decision. The weakness of the proposal lies in the fact that the minister still has the final word on disclosure and on most occasions is likely to "tough it out" by sticking to his original decision to deny access.

The appointment of an *information commissioner with powers to order release* would confer that authority on a person independent of the minister. This arrangement would receive strong public support because the commissioner could reverse ministerial decisions to deny access. Ministers would have no guarantee that the commissioner would interpret the exemption provisions of freedom of information legislation so as to withhold documents which might be politically embarrassing. In the federal Green Paper, the government opposed this mechanism on the grounds that it would infringe on the doctrine of ministerial responsibility. In any event, most persons who are willing to have ministerial decisions reversed by an independent review mechanism favour judicial review.

The preference for *judicial review* can be explained in part by the experience of Sweden and the United States with review by the courts. An equally important consideration is a widespread lack of confidence in the willingness of ministers to permit adequate access to official information. For example, the brief of the Canadian Association of University Teachers to the federal Committee on Regulations states that

> It has been demonstrated time and time again that governments will resort to all types of subterfuge in order to avoid having to release anything which may be damaging to their political image. The current procedure which allows a minister absolute discretion on the release of a document contravenes one of the basic tenets of the rule of law—that no one should be a judge in his own case—and its entrenchment in a Freedom of Information Act would merely lead to public scepticism and disaffection.[15]

It is evident also that a freedom of information act which permits citizens to appeal to the courts would inspire a high measure of public confidence in the act.

The proposal for a two-tier review mechanism involving an information commissioner and judicial review has received widespread support. Both Bill C-15 and Bill C-43 have adopted this mechanism. Under Bill C-43, an information commissioner is authorized to receive and investi-

---

[15]Committee on Regulations Respecting Green Paper, Issue no. 16, March 14, 1978, p. 16A:47.

gate complaints when access to a record is refused; when unreasonable fees are imposed for searching for or producing a record; where a public official unreasonably extends the time limit for producing a record; when a record is not provided in the official language requested; and "in respect of any other matter relating to requesting or obtaining access to records" under the act. The commissioner may also *initiate* a complaint on "reasonable grounds." After investigating a complaint, the commissioner recommends whether or not a record should be released; he cannot require that a record be disclosed.

Following the commissioner's investigation, the complainant, or the commissioner with the complainant's consent, may apply to the federal court for review of any refusal to disclose a record. The court may then order the head of a government institution to disclose—or not to disclose—all or part of a record. However, where the head of a government institution refuses to disclose a record on the basis of the exemptions for federal-provincial affairs, international affairs and defence, law enforcement or management of the economy, the court may order disclosure only if it decides that the head of the institution did not have *reasonable grounds* for refusal.

This latter provision, which is a departure from Bill C-15, has been defended by the secretary of state on the grounds of ministerial responsibility. He described Bill C-15 (the Progressive Conservative bill) as "a negation of ministerial responsibility"[16] because it left the ultimate decision on the disclosure of certain records in the hands of the judges. He argued that Bill C-43 "is consistent with judicial review because the judges have access to the documents and the minister has to prove to the judge's satisfaction that he had reasonable grounds in refusing access to the documents. . . ."[17] He claimed further that it "is consistent with the principle of ministerial responsibility that areas such as federal-provincial relations, international affairs and national defence should be in the hands of the elected representatives of the people and not in the hands of the judiciary."[18]

Bill C-43 also aims to protect the anonymity of public servants and to ensure that they give candid advice to their political superiors. Thus records will be kept confidential if they contain "advice or recommendations developed by or for a government institution or a minister," an account of deliberations involving public servants or ministers, "positions or plans developed for the purpose of negotiations" carried on by the Canadian government and "plans relating to the management of personnel or the administration of a government institution that have

---

[16]Committee on Justice and Legal Affairs, March 3, 1981, p. 15:35.
[17]*Ibid.*, p. 15:36.
[18]*Ibid.*

not yet been put into operation." However, these exemptions do not apply to records relating to the exercise of a discretionary power or an adjudicative function or to reports prepared by consultants or advisers who were not at the time public servants.

Conclusions

There is a widespread tendency among both advocates and critics of freedom of information legislation to oversimplify what is a very complicated matter. To supporters of such legislation, progress often appears to have been painfully and unduly slow. But in view of the long tradition and practice of administrative secrecy in Canada, it is important to recognize that considerable progress has been made. Moreover, with continued vigilance and public pressure, further progress is highly likely.

A widely held view among proponents of freedom of information legislation is that this legislation will gradually bring about a change in the attitude of ministers and public servants towards public access to official information. It is suggested that government officials will become more supportive of open government when they realize that it has more benefits and fewer disadvantages than they anticipated. Experience in Sweden and, more recently, in the United States suggests that this attitudinal change is likely to occur in other jurisdictions, including Canada. It is essential that a freedom of information act make provision for continuing review of its operation so that it may be amended to take account of changing attitudes and conditions.

33/Codes of Ethics and Administrative Responsibility*

Kenneth Kernaghan

Revelations and allegations of unethical conduct involving government officials quickly arouse public concern and, usually, public displeasure. Indeed, members of the general public seem to find a special fascination in incidents of real or apparent wrongdoing in government. This interest is often initiated, stimulated and sustained by representatives of the news

---

*Reprinted and abridged by permission from Kenneth Kernaghan, "Codes of Ethics and Administrative Responsibility," *Canadian Public Administration* 17, no. 4 (Winter 1974): 527-41.

media who perceive the discovery and exposure of official misconduct as one of their prime duties. Moreover, the government's opponents understandably tend to revel in the political advantage they can gain from fanning the flames of public outrage over unethical conduct.

During the past few years, there has been unusually strong public demand in Canada that the federal, provincial and municipal governments devise means to ensure the ethical conduct of public officials. This concern has arisen in large part from disclosures and charges that ethical offences have been committed by government officials not only in Canada but also in several other western democratic states.

In Canada, the most widely publicized and politically damaging incidents have been conflict-of-interest situations and "leaks" of confidential government documents in which both elected and appointed officials have allegedly been involved. There has been much debate also over the extent to which government employees should engage in partisan political activity or express publicly their personal views on government policy and administration. These issues have, in varying degrees, plagued all levels of government in Canada. Elected officials as well as employees of regular government departments and of agencies, boards and commissions have become entangled in ethical problems.

Recent Canadian Experience

During the period since World War II there has been a recurring pattern in the exposure and disposal of cases of unethical conduct in Canadian governments. An accusation or allegation of unethical conduct has been made; public indignation has been expressed; political advantage has been taken; demands for legislative remedies have been heard; blame has occasionally been laid; and a penalty has occasionally been imposed. Then there has been a rapid decline in public interest as the rush of new events has blocked out yesterday's news from public consciousness. These cycles of rise and decline in public concern have been accompanied by demands for laws and regulations to help ensure that similar incidents do not occur in the future and that appropriate sanctions are available to punish abuses. As public concern has subsided, however, so has the sentiment for formal action to guard against future offences. Although most of the publicity on ethical conduct has surrounded the activities of politicians, there were until very recently few statutes, regulations or guidelines relating to the ethical conduct of elected officials.[1] The extent to which appointed officials have been subject to constraints and direc-

---

[1]For a discussion of the ethical conduct of members of Parliament in the sphere of conflict of interest, see *Members of Parliament and Conflict of Interest*, Sessional Paper No. 291-4/61, 1st Session, 29th Parliament. July 1973.

tions in this area has varied greatly from one department or agency and from one level of government to another.

In the past few years there has been a dramatic break with this traditional pattern. Several governments have responded to the public's outcry against unethical behaviour by drafting and promulgating laws, regulations and guidelines on various aspects of ethical conduct, especially on conflicts of interest. There has been a "chain reaction" as one government has followed another in issuing formal statements on ethical conduct. There has also been a "spillover effect" as anxiety about the proper conduct of elected officials has spread to apprehension about the ethical standards of all public officials, including government employees. Moreover, this concern has been extended not only to employees of regular government departments but also to employees of agencies, boards and commissions.

The recent departure from the conventional ebb and flow of public concern about ethical conduct may be explained in large part by three factors, namely, the activities of the mass media of communication, events in other countries, and changing public expectations about the level of morality in government.

The news media have become increasingly vigilant in seeking out and exposing actual or potential cases of misconduct in government. Investigative reporting and continuing coverage by the news media reveal ethical problems that might not otherwise come to light and help to discourage government employees from yielding to temptation. The current public concern about ethics in government may have arisen less from the commission of new sins than from the greater publicity being given to the old ones. The news media have contributed substantially to the public attitude towards ethics in government by reporting instances of official misconduct in other countries. For example, "Watergate" has become a collective term embracing a variety of illegal, unethical and questionable activities on the part of elected and appointed officials in the United States. Thus international coverage has helped create a widespread climate of opinion in several countries, including Canada, against unethical conduct in government.

During the postwar years there has been a gradual but substantial modification in the public's view of what standards of conduct are appropriate for government officials. The pace of this change has accelerated in recent years and has been an important factor in disrupting the traditional pattern of response to instances of unethical behaviour. Certain kinds of official conduct that used to be tolerated or mildly disapproved are now considered unacceptable and punishable, especially in the area of conflicts of interest. The seriousness of even a *potential* conflict of interest was recognized in a decision made under the federal Public Service Staff

Relations Act.[2] The adjudicator upheld the suspension of a federal employee who established a company offering services that could lead to a conflict of interest with his official duties. The board found that the appearance of conflict was enough to establish a conflict of interest. According to the adjudicator, "it is not sufficient for the public servant or his associates to be convinced of their own innocence and integrity. Nor is it necessary to prove that they have been disloyal to the employer. Even in the absence of evidence of wilful wrongdoing, a conflict of interest or the appearance thereof can be easily recognized by an intelligent citizen as contrary to public policy."[3]

Value of Codes of Ethics
Scholars and practitioners are by no means unanimous in their support for codes of ethics. Opinions on the value of codes range from the view that they are virtually worthless, or at best unnecessary, to the view that they serve as effective controls over administrative action. It is certainly unrealistic to portray codes of ethics as a cure-all for violations of the public trust. It is suggested here, however, that codes may provide preventive medicine against the malady of unethical conduct and a distasteful dose of medicine for an employee who contracts the disease. The extent to which a code of ethics has value depends on whether the code is written or unwritten, on its acceptance by the public and by government employees, and on its form, content and administration.

Written Versus Unwritten Codes
The weight of evidence points to the desirability of a code of ethics as a formally written document rather than an "unwritten" code composed of traditions, practices and understandings. Some public employees assert that a code of ethics is unnecessary because they know what standards of conduct are expected of them. They contend further that they share allegiance to an "unwritten" code of conduct based on customary practices and informal understandings. Opposition to a written code is also based on the fact that the standards of a code are sometimes difficult to apply to specific cases, especially in the conflict-of-interest area. Advocates of a written code, however, do not claim that it provides easy solutions to the great variety of ethical problems that may arise; rather, they seek clarity through written guidelines and recognize the need for flexibility and judgment in the interpretation of these guidelines. Critics of a written code appear to offer no alternatives to the status quo,

---

[2]"Public Service Staff Relations Act Decision, Between Maurice Dudley Atkins, Grievor, and Treasury Board (Minister of Transport), Employer," 21 March 1974, File 166-2-889.
[3]*Ibid.*, p. 30.

namely, reliance on unwritten understandings and practices. It is important to note also that employees may develop informal, unwritten agreements on unethical as well as on ethical practices.

Unwritten codes have distinct disadvantages when compared with formal, written codes. In the first place, the activities and comments of public employees at all levels of government have demonstrated that they do not agree on what kinds of behaviour are permissible or prohibited. Moreover, conduct perceived as generally acceptable by one individual, group or department is often quite different from that acceptable to others. Employees require a common set of standards—in written form—applicable to the administrative unit within which they are working.

Secondly, the extent to which a public employee will adhere to an unwritten code will depend on his personal judgment or the opinion of his colleagues. Heavy reliance must be placed on the conscience of the individual employee. However, an employee's conscience, unencumbered by a statement of written guidelines, may in some situations be his best accomplice. This is not to suggest that appeals to conscience based on traditional practices may not be effective in preserving a high level of ethical conduct but to argue that an employee is less likely to violate written standards than he is to depart from unwritten understandings and practices subject to debate not only on their interpretation but on their very existence. A related disadvantage of an unwritten code is that it is difficult to enforce because penalties cannot easily be attached to unwritten ethical guidelines.

Finally, dependence on an unwritten code of ethics made more sense when the scope of government responsibilities was smaller, when government operations were less complex and technical, and when government employees were less numerous. Certainly there is still an enormous range in the size and activities of administrative units—from huge federal departments at one extreme to a few clerks in tiny rural municipalities at the other. In large cities, in provincial governments and in the federal government, however, expanding discretionary powers are exercised by a larger number of more highly educated employees dealing with increasingly complex and technical matters. Administrative control over one's subordinates used to be more direct and more personal—and based on more adequate understanding of the subject matter at hand. It has become a difficult task for political and administrative superiors to be aware personally of the vast number of decisions taken by their subordinates, much less to know whether some subordinates have made private gain from certain of these decisions.

A written code of ethics also serves a number of important purposes both for the general public and for government employees.

Codes of Ethics and the Public

The public demands that government employees maintain high standards of ethical conduct. They insist that there not be situations where public office can actually or potentially be used for private, personal, political or pecuniary gain—or for any combination of these benefits. The public seems to expect a higher level of morality among government employees than among their counterparts in private business and to be in general agreement also that the level of ethical conduct in government is in fact higher than that found in the private sector of society. There is an apparent tendency for some citizens to expect a public official to adhere to a loftier set of standards than that to which they themselves aspire in their personal lives. The "public" element of public administration gives taxpaying citizens some motivation to be vigilant and indignant about violations of the public trust. The public's vigilance sometimes also seems prompted by envy of officials who are in a position to use their government office for personal gain.

High standards of ethical conduct in government bring more tangible benefits to the public than mere satisfaction that public office is not being misused. High ethical standards may help to promote a greater measure of efficiency in the implementation of government programs. For example, when an official awards a contract to a firm from which he has received a gift, the work may be of lower quality (and higher cost) than if another firm had been awarded the contract on the sole basis of competitive bidding. High standards of ethical conduct will also help to ensure that citizens receive uniform and consistent treatment from impartial and objective government officials. Members of the public do not expect to receive less generous service because others have developed a special, secret, mutually beneficial relationship with government employees. The exposure of abuses committed by a few officials can have an impact out of all proportion to their number and gravity. An undiscriminating public tends to tar all officials with the same brush. Thus any significant number of reported or alleged abuses of the public trust may lead to severe criticism and pessimism about the quality of all public officials and undermine faith in political and administrative institutions generally.

The reaction of the public to instances of official misconduct shows that citizens are confused and disagree among themselves about what kind of behaviour is unethical and what penalties should be imposed for offences. A written code informs the public of the level of ethical conduct expected from government employees. It thereby provides citizens with a set of standards by which they may assess the conduct of public employees and helps to sustain their confidence in the integrity of government and in particular of appointed officials.

Codes of Ethics and Public Employees

The ethical standards of public employees are in large part a reflection of the standards prevailing in society generally. Since government employees are members of the general public when they are not acting in their official capacity, it is not surprising that they are influenced by the level of ethical standards of their fellow citizens. Nor is it surprising that government employees, like their fellow citizens, have differing perceptions of what constitutes unethical conduct.

A code of ethics, then, provides government employees with criteria by which they may evaluate their own behaviour as well as the behaviour of their administrative colleagues—whether their peers, superiors or subordinates. A code is especially valuable in the education of new recruits. It furnishes a guide to which all officials may refer when in doubt about the propriety of their own actions or the actions of others. They have a document that states, with varying degrees of clarity and specificity, that certain kinds of behaviour are not only inappropriate for public employees but are forbidden on the pain of disciplinary action.

With the passage of time, some, if not all, provisions of a code tend to become internalized by many employees as a means of self-discipline—a kind of automatic regulating device. For example, an experienced employee will in the normal course of events, without conscious thought and deliberation, avoid conflict-of-interest situations and maintain the confidentiality of government documents. The role of senior officials is especially important in this process. They must not only keep employees well informed about ethical standards but also by exemplary behaviour provide a model to be emulated by other officials. The senior official should strive to become a personification of the code he has the responsibility of enforcing. Another very important pressure encouraging employees to maintain high ethical standards is the expectations of their peers. A climate is created wherein all those in a work group or section of a department or agency come to share a common view as to what constitutes proper behaviour. This is more likely to occur and the standard of ethical behaviour is likely to be higher if there is a written code serving as a criterion for performance.

There are employees, of course, who are influenced only slightly or not at all by the exhortations of codes of ethics and by the high ethical standards of their superiors and peers. For these employees a code of ethics may serve as an instrument of administrative control. Senior officials may utilize the code as a means of judging whether an employee has acted properly in a given situation and as a basis for disciplining an employee who has acted improperly. With a written code of ethics in their possession, supervisors will no longer be obliged to admonish employees by making reference to vague and uncertain conventions and understandings. Moreover, the means of preventing and punishing unethical conduct will be set out for the direction of all employees. If a code is to have value as a basis for administrative control, it is helpful, although not essential, to spell out the penalties for unethical behaviour in the code itself.

It is not necessary for all employees to "get religion" in the sense of being converted to strong adherence to the tenets of the code. What is especially important is that those in formal positions of authority or in informal positions of influence accept the code as one standard by which an employee's conduct is assessed in connection with promotion and other rewards. The employee will be expected to achieve certain ethical standards as well as technical standards. If the employee does not "get religion," he may at least "get the message" that occupational success and congenial relations with fellow employees depend in part on his demonstrating appropriate ethical standards. Thus a code may be used both as an instrument of control and a means of influence over administrative action.

Ethical Conduct and Administrative Responsibility

Ethical conduct has traditionally been a central component of the larger concept of administrative responsibility. For scholars and practitioners concerned with the preservation of responsible administrative behaviour, the importance of the subject of ethical conduct has been enhanced by the current high level of public and governmental interest in the ethical standards of government employees. Students of government have tended to concentrate on the design and adaptation of institutional and procedural means to check bureaucratic abuse of power and so to promote administrative responsibility. This emphasis has been to the detriment of thought and writing about the ethical climate within which public employees work. It is suggested here that ethics in government will be a continuing and increasingly important concern in the foreseeable future. Whether or not the public's interest in the matter enters its customary decline, it seems appropriate for government employees, academic scholars and mass media representatives to retain their interest in stimulating an ethical sense of responsibility in government.

The development of codes of ethics is one potentially effective means of achieving this end. The relationship of codes of ethics to administrative responsibility may be demonstrated by reference to two major interpretations of administrative responsibility, namely, objective and subjective (psychological) responsibility. Objective responsibility connotes the responsibility of a person or organization to someone else, outside of self, for some thing or some kind of performance. It is closely akin to accountability or answerability. If one fails to carry out legitimate directives, he is judged irresponsible and may be subjected to penalties. "Subjective or psychological responsibility centres not upon to whom and for what one *is* responsible . . . but to whom one *feels* responsible and *behaves* responsibly. This meaning is more nearly synonymous with identification, loyalty and conscience than it is with accountability or answerability."[4]

A written code of ethics may be used to promote both types of administrative responsibility. To help achieve objective responsibility in the sense of accountability, a code should be much more than a brief list of platitudes. To serve as an instrument of control over administrative action, a code should be as specific as possible while allowing for flexibility in its interpretation; provision should also be made for its effective enforcement.

However, in view of the difficulty of holding public employees responsible solely through the threat or imposition of penalties, it is desirable to have a code of ethics become as self-enforcing as possible. A written code provides a common set of standards. If it is accepted by an employee's superiors, peers and subordinates as a model for behaviour, adherence to its provisions will gradually be internalized in the value system of many employees. Through this process, a code may serve as a means by which government employees may influence rather than control the ethical conduct of their colleagues. The forces at work will be conscience and organizational loyalty rather than fear of punishment. In this fashion, a significant measure of subjective or psychological responsibility may be elicited and, thereby, a fuller measure of responsible administrative conduct achieved.

Case References
Canadian Cases in Public Administration

> Reality or Appearance?
> The Renfrew Group
> The Minister and the Doctor
> A "Miner" Problem
> The Resigning Engineer
> The Foot and Mouth Disease Epidemic, 1952

Bibliography

Appleby, Paul H. *Big Democracy*. New York: Alfred A. Knopf, 1945.
Appleby, Paul H. *Morality and Administration in Democratic Government*. Baton Rouge: Louisiana State University Press, 1952.

---

[4]Frederick C. Mosher, *Democracy and the Public Service* (New York: Oxford University Press, 1968), pp. 7-8. See also Kenneth Kernaghan, "Responsible Public Bureaucracy: A Rationale and a Framework for Analysis," *Canadian Public Administration* 16, no. 4 (Winter, 1973): 572-603.

Courtney, John C. "In Defence of Royal Commissions." *Canadian Public Administration* 12, no. 2 (Summer 1969): 198-212.

Denton, T.M. "Ministerial Responsibility: A Contemporary Perspective." In *The Canadian Political Process*, edited by R. Schultz et al., pp. 344-62. 3rd ed. Toronto: Holt, Rinehart and Winston, 1979.

De Smith, S.A. *Judicial Review of Administrative Action*. London: Stevens & Sons, 1959.

Doerr, Audrey. "Parliamentary Accountability and Legislative Potential." In *Parliament, Policy and Representation*, edited by Harold D. Clarke et al., pp. 144-59. Toronto: Methuen, 1980.

Douglas, Paul H. *Ethics in Government*. Cambridge, Mass.: Harvard University Press, 1952.

Dussault, René. *Le contrôle judiciare de l'administration au Québec*. Québec: Les Presses de l'Université Laval, 1969.

Dussault, René. "L'équilibre entre les pouvoirs judiciaire, législatif et exécutif: rupture ou évolution?" *Canadian Public Administration* 22, no. 2 (Summer 1979): 196-207.

Dussault, René. "Relationship between the Nature of the Acts of the Administration and Judicial Review: Quebec and Canada." *Canadian Public Administration* 10, no. 3 (September 1967): 298-322.

Dussault, René. "Vers un code de déontologie adapté aux diverses fonctions de l'administrateur public." *Canadian Public Administration* 22, no. 4 (Winter 1979): 627-38.

Fera, Norman. "Review of Administrative Decisions Under the Federal Court Act." *Canadian Public Administration* 14, no. 4 (Winter 1971): 580-94.

Finer, Herman. "Administrative Responsibility in Democratic Government." *Public Administration Review* 1, no. 4 (Summer 1941): 335-50.

Fox, David. *Public Participation in the Administrative Process*. Study Paper for the Law Reform Commission of Canada. Ottawa: Supply and Services, 1979.

Garant, Patrice et al. "Le contrôle politique des organismes autonomes à fonctions regulatrices et quasi-judiciaires." *Canadian Public Administration* 20, no. 3 (Fall 1977): 444-69.

Great Britain. *Committee on Administrative Tribunals and Enquiries, Report*. London: Her Majesty's Stationery Office, 1957.

Great Britain. *Committee on Ministers' Powers, Report*. London: His Majesty's Stationery Office, 1932.

Harris, Joseph P. *Congressional Control of Administration*. Washington, D.C.: The Brookings Institution, 1964.

Herring, Pendleton. *Public Administration and the Public Interest*. 1936. Reprint. New York: Russell, 1967.

Hewart, G.H. *The New Despotism*. London: Ernest Benn, 1929.

Hodgetts, J.E. "Government Responsiveness to the Public Interest: Has Progress Been Made?" *Canadian Public Administration* 24, no. 2 (Summer 1981): 216-31.

Kane, T. Gregory. *Consumers and the Regulated*. Montreal: Institute for Research on Public Policy, 1980.

Kernaghan, Kenneth. "Codes of Ethics and Administrative Responsibility." *Canadian Public Administration* 17, no. 4 (Winter 1974): 527-41.

Kernaghan, Kenneth. "Codes of Ethics and Public Administration: Progress, Problems and Prospects." *Public Administration* 58 (Summer 1980): 207-24.

Kernaghan, Kenneth. "Power, Parliament and Public Servants: Ministerial Responsibility Reexamined." *Canadian Public Policy* 3 (Summer 1979): 383-96.

Kernaghan, Kenneth. "Representative Bureaucracy: the Canadian Perspective." *Canadian Public Administration* 21, no. 4 (Winter 1978): 489-512.

Kernaghan, Kenneth. "Responsible Public Bureaucracy: A Rationale and a Framework for Analysis." *Canadian Public Administration* 16, no. 4 (Winter 1973): 572-603.

Kersell, J.E. *Parliamentary Supervision of Delegated Legislation: the United Kingdom, Australia, New Zealand and Canada*. London: Stevens & Sons, 1960.

Kersell, J.E. "Statutory and Judicial Control of Administrative Behaviour." *Canadian Public Administration* 19, no. 2 (Summer 1976): 295-307.

Knight, K.W. "Administrative Secrecy and Ministerial Responsibility." *Canadian Journal of Economics and Political Science* 32, no. 1 (February 1966): 77-84.

Krislov, Samuel. *Representative Bureaucracy*. Englewood Cliffs, N.J.: Prentice-Hall, 1974.

Law Reform Commission of Canada. *Independent Administrative Agencies*. Working Paper 25. Ottawa: Supply and Services, 1980.

Law Reform Commission of Canada. *Judicial Review and the Federal Court*. Report no. 14, Ottawa: Supply and Services, 1980.

Levy, Gary. "Delegated Legislation and the Standing Joint Committee on Regulations and Other Statutory Instruments." *Canadian Public Administration* 22, no. 3 (Fall 1979): 349-65.

Mosher, Frederick C. *Democracy and the Public Service*. New York: Oxford University Press, 1968.

Redford, Emmette S. *Democracy in the Administrative State*. New York: Oxford University Press, 1969, chap. 6.

Rohr, John A. *Ethics for Bureaucrats*. New York: Marcel Dekker, 1978.

Rourke, Francis E. *Secrecy and Publicity*. Baltimore: Johns Hopkins Press, 1961.

Rowat, Donald C. "Administrative Secrecy and Ministerial Responsibility: a Reply." *Canadian Journal of Economics and Political Science* 32, no. 1 (February 1966): 84-7.

Rowat, Donald C. "How Much Administrative Secrecy?" *Canadian Journal of Economics and Political Science* 31, no. 4 (November 1965): 479-98.

Rowat, Donald C. *The Ombudsman*, 2d ed. Toronto: University of Toronto Press, 1968.

Rowat, Donald C. *The Ombudsman Plan*. Toronto: McClelland & Stewart, 1973.

Rowat, Donald C. "An Ombudsman Scheme for Canada." *Canadian Journal of Economics and Political Science* 28, no. 4 (November 1962): 543-56.

Vandervort, Lucinda. *Political Control of Independent Administrative Agencies*. Study Paper for the Law Reform Commission of Canada. Ottawa: Supply and Services, 1979.

Wilson, V. Seymour, and Mullins, Willard A. "Representative Bureaucracy: Linguistic/Ethnic Aspects in Canadian Public Policy." *Canadian Public Administration* 21, no. 4 (Winter 1978): 513-38.